D1728085

Wolfgang Michalski

**Capitalising on Change
in a Globalising World**

*A View from Hamburg*

Author and publisher thank the following companies, institutions
and persons for their generous support without which the publication
of this book would not have been possible:

Airbus Operations GmbH
Alfred Toepfer Stiftung F.V.S.
Aug. Bolten Wm. Miller's Nachfolger
Baringa Partners LLP, London, Hamburg, Düsseldorf
Berenberg Bank
Blohm + Voss Shipyards GmbH
Company-Partners CMP GmbH
DAKOSY Datenkommunikationssystem AG
Eugen Block Holding GmbH & Co. KG
F. Laeisz G.m.b.H.
Hamburg Airport
Hamburg@work Association
Hamburger Hafen und Logistik AG
Hamburg Messe und Congress GmbH
Hamburg Tourismus GmbH
Handelskammer Hamburg
Hermann Reemtsma Stiftung
HWF Hamburgische Gesellschaft für Wirtschaftsförderung mbH
Ian K. Karan, Former Senator of Economic and Labour Affairs, Hamburg
NORDMETALL Stiftung
plantours & Partner GmbH, Bremen
PricewaterhouseCoopers
Rolf Bohnhof, Hamburg-Ambassador, Rio de Janeiro, Brasilien
Studio Hamburg GmbH
ThyssenKrupp Marine Systems
Valio Ltd., Helsinki, Finland
Verein Hamburger Rheder (r.V.)
Verein Hamburger Spediteure e.V.
ZEIT-Stiftung Ebelin und Gerd Bucerius

WOLFGANG MICHALSKI

# Capitalising on Change in a Globalising World

## *A View from Hamburg*

MURMANN

This book was printed carbon-neutrally:

*Translated by Ashley Slapp*

Die Deutsche Bibliothek – CIP data applied for.
A CIP block for this publication
is available from the Deutsche Bibliothek.

ISBN 978-3-86774-138-5

1st German Edition, February 2010
Copyright © 2010 by Murmann Verlag GmbH, Hamburg
1st English Edition, December 2011
Copyright © 2011 by Murmann Verlag GmbH, Hamburg

Translation Editors: Steve Elford and David Hill
Cover Design: Rothfos & Gabler, Hamburg
Design and production: Eberhard Delius, Berlin
Typesetting and lithography: Reihs Satzstudio, Lohmar
Typesetted in Minion
Printed and bound by:
Freiburger Graphische Betriebe, Freiburg
Printed in Germany

Visit us on the Internet: www.murmann-verlag.de

We would be interested to hear your opinion of this book!
Please address mails to info@murmann-verlag.de

You can order the Murmann-Verlag Newsletter at
newsletter@murmann-verlag.de

Contents

# I

## From the Beginnings of Globalisation to the Middle Ages: The Geographical and Systemic Expansion of the Political, Economic, Social and Cultural Radius of Action

*Phoenicians, Greeks, Romans, Vikings, and the Hanseatic League*

*Hamburg's Road to Becoming a Major Hanseatic City*

# II

## Globalisation in the Early Colonial Era: Increasing Exploitation of the Periphery by the Centre

*From Portuguese Naval Supremacy to Dutch Dominance of the Global Economy*

*Hamburg: Germany's Largest City and Most Important Port*

# III

## Globalisation on a Global Scale: Industrial Revolution, Free Trade Imperialism, and the Increasing Importance of Overseas Markets

*Continental European Rivalries and the Relentless Rise of Great Britain*

*Hamburg: The European Continent's Leading Port and Trading Hub*

*Hamburg's city centre with Outer Alster and Inner Alster in 1882.*

# Introduction

The term globalisation, according to the *Economist* "the most abused word of the 21st century", may be some 30 or 40 years old. Despite its omnipresence in the political, public and academic debate, there is neither a widely agreed upon definition, nor any consensus on the appreciation of its consequences. For some people globalisation is one of the most powerful forces for economic and social progress — a phenomenon which has tremendously increased the welfare of people world-wide. For others, it is the synonym for societal injustice because, in their view, globalisation exaggerates economic and social differences between countries, regions and people, elevating the rich and impoverishing the poor.

The most common notions in the globalisation discourse are related to the increasing internationalisation of economic relations through trade, foreign direct investment, technology transfer and financial flows. In much of the vast literature reference is also made to social, cultural and even military and terrorist cross-border interactions. A further important dimension is that all this happens between geographically distant economies and societies, going beyond the sphere of a common language and culture.

Both by the narrow economic and by the broader, more comprehensive definition, early signs of globalisation can be traced back over several thousand years. Engraved stone plates discovered in central Anatolian archives dating from some 4,000 years ago, show clearly that caravan traders from Assyria already operated within a widespread and well-established business network which extended over more than 1,000 km into many regions with a great variety of different languages and cultures.

Globalisation processes are the result of a range of different causes or motivations. In a historical perspective, the following four are the most prominent: *First*, campaigns of conquest, based on the quest for political, economic or cultural hegemony; *second*, the effort to become rich, be it through economic exchanges, through migration, through exploitation or even through robbery; *third*, missionary activities aiming at proselytisation through the propaganda of one's own religion, beliefs or ideology; and *fourth*, curiosity and a thirst for adventure without which many discoveries even in modern times would never have been made. There are many illustrations of all these four variants and in many cases the driving forces were either intertwined from the outset or have changed from one to the other over time.

However, not every form of military conquest or occupation of a foreign country or territory should be viewed as an integral part of a process towards globalisation. The same is true for most cases of mass migration, missionary expansion, successful expeditions of discovery or pillage. Even the existence of trans-border trade relations, foreign direct investment or international technology transfer and financial transactions may only be a necessary condition. They are not sufficient to describe a globalisation process which goes beyond economic interactions and includes political, societal and cultural aspects as well. In this wider interpretation, the concept of globalisation becomes more complex, but also much closer to what can be observed in the real world.

For policy analysis and debate, going beyond the mere description of historical developments, it is also necessary to shed light on the significance of certain systemic dimensions which are among the most decisive factors for the direction and dynamism of the globalisation process as well as for the allocation of associated benefits and costs. The crucial element of the globalisation process in this regard appears to be the actual existence and interactive relevance of an overarching framework of rules and/or power structures. This can be based on the influence of a dominant, hegemonic power, on an internationally accepted multilateral system or on both at the same time.

The most recurrent signs of dominance are military, economic and often also technological superiority. On this basis, the more powerful attempt to impose their own commercial practices, legal rules, technical norms and currency, also their language and even their societal norms on the rest of the world. From a policy perspective the explicit inclusion of these aspects makes the definition of globalisation a much more forceful instrument for the analysis of the underlying dynamics and the consequences of the process. It will also contribute to explaining why certain countries, regions or cities succeeded in becoming and remaining long term winners of the globalisation process and why others either became losers or never had a successful take-off.

Applying the above broad definition to the relevant world economy at any time results in the possible distinction of at least six different phases of globalisation over the past two to three thousand years: *First*, an early period which — in a Eurocentric view — covers the whole time span from the golden age of Athens, under the leadership of Pericles, to the end of the Roman Empire. *Second*, the period of the heyday of Venice in the Mediterranean region as well as of the Hanseatic League in North and North-Western Europe. *Third*, the early colonial age starting with the voyages of discovery of Portuguese and Spanish seafarers and ending with the maritime dominance of the Dutch. *Fourth*, globalisation on a world-wide scale with intense intra-European rivalries and the incessant geopolitical, economic and military rise of England. *Fifth*, the first half of the 20th century with the globalisation of war and, between the two World Wars, an illusory boom in the 1920s as well as the Great Depression in the early 1930s. And *sixth and finally*, the period at the end of which we may possibly find ourselves now, namely globalisation as an American-led offensive towards economic growth and prosperity, at least for those regions of the world which became for whatever reasons an integral part of it.

Dividing the process of globalisation into six distinctive, but more or less consecutive phases could be seen by some as highly problematic. And, of course, it would be misleading to interpret historical developments in terms of time, space or cross-border interaction as a one-dimensional course of events. Nevertheless there are a number of convincing arguments which may justify this approach in the present context. On the one hand, each of these six phases of the globalisation process is characterised by a considerable widening and deepening of international exchanges, an increase in international economic and other interdependencies and a growing breadth, intensity and complexity regarding political, economic and social feedback effects. On the other hand, all these six phases, although with repeated changes in the main driving forces over time, have seen distinct relocations of the economic and financial centres of the world economy.

In the ancient world it was Athens and then Rome which held the dominant position in the world economy of their time. Both these cities represented the centre of political, economic and military power. Both, although by quite different means, succeeded in imposing their legal system, their currency, their measurement units, their social norms and their language on all other participants of the then relevant world economy. And their way of life became at least in other important cities a role model for society. Greek temples in the coastal areas of the Eastern Mediterranean Sea and, to the West, on Sicily as well as in South Italy still provide concrete evidence of the significance of the systemic dimension already present in the very early globalisation phase. The same holds true for the many Roman

14

theatres and public baths as well as finds of Roman coins not only in the south of Europe, but even far north of the Alps. And although the fall of the Roman Empire dates back to about 400 AD, still today Roman law is a fundamental basis of the legal system of many continental European countries.

About 700 years later, a time span which at least for Europe can be classified as a period of economic and technological stagnation, the heydays of the North Italian city-republics began. Once Venice had asserted itself against Genoa in 1380, the lagoon city was the economic centre of the Mediterranean area. Venice had the monopoly on the trade in luxurious textiles and expensive spices between the Orient and Northern Europe, and at the same time the city was the dominant maritime power. Being too small to militarily and administratively control the whole Mediterranean region — as Rome had once done — Venice adopted a strategy of colonisation through the establishment of maritime and commercial bases. This allowed the city, wherever it was useful for its foreign economic interests, to gain privileges for its merchants and make its commercial practises, its currency and its measurement units internationally accepted. At the peak of its power Venice was by far the richest city in the then relevant world.

In Northern Europe, a regional globalisation process began to emerge in the middle of the 12th century. In contrast to the hegemonistic model of the South, the developments around the Baltic and the North Sea evolved towards a multipolar power configuration of which the core group included no less than sixty cities. Decisions on important issues were taken unanimously at the so-called Hanseatic Days. This was the over-riding institutional framework, and its mission included the codification of internationally agreed rules for trade, the right of establishment and the law of the sea as well as the formation of a currency union aimed at guaranteeing the stability of money-based international exchanges. In principle, all partner cities had an equal voice. But the vote of the dominant cities such as Lübeck in particular had more weight than that of the majority of the others. Nevertheless, it was most important in this context that the dominant cities also adhered strictly to the rules to make them binding for all — an attitude which was not always shown in a hegemonic configuration including in the recent past.

The successful exploration activities of the Portuguese and the Spaniards in the 15th and 16th century not only resulted in expanding the reach of European influence and trade to the Americas and Asia, but also in shifting the geographic gravity of international economic relations from the Mediterranean and the Baltic Seas to the Atlantic. Although Seville and, until the unification of Spain and Portugal, Lisbon became the new geopolitical power centres and the leaders of the globalisation process in military and missionary terms, the centre of the world economy now moved to Antwerp. This was in particular due to the strong influence of the rich Upper German trading houses such as the Fugger family which had been exploited by Venice over the centuries and had for that reason for many years made major financial contributions in support of the search for a seaway to the so-called Spice Islands. Thus from about 1500 world market prices for most of the internationally traded goods were determined in Antwerp. And this city remained the economic and financial hotspot of the world economy until, after some sixty years, it was replaced in this role by Genoa.

The return of the world economic centre to the Mediterranean region was, however, only of a very short duration. Genoese businessmen had increasingly turned away from trade. The main focus of their activities had become financial services, in particular for the Spanish court. As a result, whenever there was a financial crisis in Spain, and there were at least six between 1557 and 1664, Genoa became the epicentre of the turbulences in Italian and international financial markets. In addition, the Genoese had growing difficulties in defending their traditionally strong position in shipping. On the one hand, after 1630 the English had excluded the Genoese ships from the transport of silver from the Iberian Peninsula to the North. And on the other, after having successfully combated the Portuguese, including in the Indian Ocean, the Dutch had become the world's dominant maritime power. Compared to the Mediterranean ships of the time, their vessels were more seaworthy, faster and, with smaller crews, more cost efficient.

As a consequence, the Dutch were now by far the most competitive supplier of sea transport and logistics. Historians estimate their market share in world merchandise shipping at about 80 % — and this not only on the Atlantic and Indian Ocean routes, but even in the Mediterranean Sea. Hence, from the middle of the 17th century the new hotspot of the world economy — both in economic and financial terms — was Amsterdam. In terms of economic relations to the rest of the world and in particular as regards benefits and costs, the entire third period of globalisation could be described as the exploitation of the periphery by the centre.

If the 17th century could be called the Dutch century, the 19th century became that of England. Not only had Amsterdam suffered from three severe financial crises between 1762 and 1784. England succeeded in breaking the Dutch predominance on the sea. It also became the most important colonial power. And, in addition, it emerged as the springboard of the Industrial Revolution. The maritime superiority, the industrial and technological leadership and the huge possessions overseas made England the first superpower of the modern world. Combined with protectionist trade policies in continental Europe, these three elements gave a new direction and new dynamics to the globalisation process.

Of course, there was always some export of European products overseas. To the extent that the Europeans did not just steal what they wanted, they needed something to exchange. But the new situation was different. From now on the so-called overseas countries, territories and colonies not only served as suppliers of raw materials, tropical products and spices, but also increasingly as markets for European manufactures and industrial products. London became the new economic and financial centre of the world economy, with the British Pound the leading currency for international transactions. And again beyond the narrow economic implications, British imperial measures, the English legal system and other rules were adopted in many countries overseas; the English language became the lingua franca and the British way-of-life spread over much of the relevant world.

In the period between the two World Wars economic globalisation in terms of international trade, foreign direct investment, technology transfer and international financial flows came to a standstill for most of the time. As the United Kingdom had increasingly lost its earlier hegemonic position and the United States was extremely protectionist and principally inward-looking, there was, at least at the beginning of the 1930s no longer anyone who felt responsible for the world economy as a whole, even on the usually forceful basis of self-interest. Internationally uncoordinated pro-cyclical macro-economic policies, increasing protectionism most vigorously pursued by the United States and competitive currency devaluations strengthened the dynamics of a negative spiral leading to the second real world economic crisis after the first which hit the world economy in 1857. But in the early 1930s the forces of globalisation were also still at work. In the economic realm they resulted in the Great Depression and in geopolitical terms they led the world into another global war.

Already during the First World War and even more so during the Second, a further re-location of the economic and financial centre of the world economy began and in the end it was New York which took over from London. The United States had ascended in the meanwhile not only to the global financial leadership position but also in economic terms more generally, including in the industrial sector. As a consequence, this formerly highly protectionist country now felt strong enough to push for a new world economic order, based on free multilateral trade and an international monetary system anchored on the US dollar as the reference currency.

After a short period of reconstruction in Europe and Japan, world economic development embarked on an incredibly dynamic up-swing which with certain, only temporary, slowing-downs could be sustained over several decades. World GDP grew at an unprecedented rate of 3.6 % between 1960 and 2007. And for many years, as was the case before the First World War, international trade and foreign direct investment grew at even higher rates. World capital markets were liberalised somewhat later, and after this it was cross-border capital transactions which outgrew everything else in international economic relations. But there a number of major trend breaks also occurred during this period. These included: Two oil shocks; the arrival of several new players on the world economic scene; the fall of the Soviet Union and the end of the Cold War; and with the collapse of the Bretton Woods System the beginning of the unravelling of the post-WWII world economic order.

In a historical perspective, uneven participation in and uneven distribution of benefits and costs of the globalisation process is nothing new. Looking at all six periods of globalisation as described above, the same patterns always distinguish the winners and the losers. The winners are normally characterised by stable governmental and administrative structures, a reliable legal and regulatory framework, high economic and social dynamics, a well educated and disciplined work force, a more or less stable currency, and in the case of a hegemonic country by political and military power. In addition to these general patterns, depending on the particular conditions of the country, region or city concerned, there is always a set of specific economic and social policies which enhance economic growth and wealth creation.

As regards the losers, apart from war and tribal disputes the most frequent reasons for either decline or remaining behind are: A corrupt government; a societal attitude which perceives change as a threat and not as a positive challenge; economic and societal rigidities which prevent adaptation to changing political, economic, social and technological conditions; domestic policies which do not take sufficient account of international economic interdependencies; the attempt to pursue policies which have been successful in the past but are no longer adequate for the present and even less so for the future; inadequate physical and social infrastructure; low educational and health standards and last but not least, a major financial crisis and/or severe social unrest.

Athens never recovered from the Peloponnesian Wars. Rome fell because of inadequate governance, wide-spread corruption and social unrest. Venice, even before it suffered from war, declined economically due to over-regulation of both the spice trade and textile production and by ignoring international economic interdependencies. Lübeck and Antwerp lost out because they did not adapt to changing economic and technological circumstances. Genoa and Amsterdam illustrate the disastrous impact of a sequence of several severe financial crises. London was weakened after two World Wars and the loss of geopolitical and military weight together with the end of the British Empire. And finally, as regards New York, the question is whether after the most recent economic and financial crisis, the third after 1857 and 1930 with world-wide impact which originated there, Wall Street will still dominate the world economy and in particular international financial markets over the longer term.

Even if the rise and fall of economic and financial centres in the globalised world is a recurrent pattern of development, there are no compelling reasons for regions or cities not to benefit from globalisation in the very long run. Although London is no longer, as in the 19th century, the single dominant economic and financial centre of the world economy, it still ranks together with places like New York, Paris and Tokyo as one of the leading global cities. Most importantly, London is one of the very few still pre-eminent cities in the world which has taken advantage of the globalisation process for around one thousand years and is still doing so. Another good example of a long term winner in the globalising world is Hamburg, which was already a flourishing Hanseatic city when Amsterdam had just been founded and New York and Tokyo did not even exist.

From its beginnings, at least since the end of the first millennium and even more so after the rise of Lübeck, Hamburg served as a trading place at the crossroads between the North Sea and the Baltic Sea region. Around 1320 it became the centre of European beer production, and its exports went to Russia, Holland, England and even Portugal. Thereafter the city dominated European textile trade and became more generally the western gateway to Central and Eastern Europe. In the 17th century it emerged as the hotspot of the European sugar industry. And at the end of the 19th century the city was the pre-eminent trade and financial centre of the European continent and, after London and New York, the third biggest sea port world-wide. Between the two World Wars and again until the early 1980s Hamburg was the location of some of the world's most renowned shipyards and the centre of the German oil industry. But today all this is gone.

Nevertheless, at the beginning of the 21st century, Hamburg is still the most important city in the European Union and the wider European Economic Zone which is not a capital. As in the past, Hamburg is one of the richest cities world-wide. It is the number one industrial city and trading centre in Northern Europe, including all Germany. In terms of economic activity, it is the world's third most important location for the production and maintenance of civil aircraft. Alongside Rotterdam and Antwerp it operates one of the three leading European container ports. It is the home of Europe's biggest copper smelter and one of the most important places in Germany and Europe for new energy technologies. And despite all the industrial activities, which also include steel and aluminium, Hamburg has remained a pleasant place to live and represents an increasingly attractive destination for tourists from all over the world.

That dynamic economic development and concern for a healthy and sustainable environment do not necessarily exclude each other, but may even be mutually supportive, is clearly underlined by the fact that Hamburg has been awarded the official title of "European Green Capital" for the year 2011. In competition against 33 other cities from 17 different European countries Hamburg was in particular praised for its consistent record of achieving high environmental standards and for its serious commitment to a number of ambitious goals, for instance a further reduction of $CO_2$ emissions by 40 % towards 2020 and 80 % by 2050. Perhaps surprisingly for Germany's largest sea port and industrial city, nearly 10 % of its total area is public green space and 89 % of the population lives at a maximum distance of 300 m from a park.

In the context of the globalisation debate the significance of the specific example of Hamburg is threefold: On the one hand, it shows that even a secondary place with no geopolitical and military power can be a major beneficiary of the globalisation process. On the other, it demonstrates that remaining on the winning side of globalisation implies permanent change in economic structures. And finally, there is the clear message that lasting success in the globalised world requires a set of policies which — apart from providing a general economic and social climate that is conducive to entrepreneurship and risk-taking — embrace international openness and competition and thereby enhance creative and dynamic investment.

Looking at the success story of Hamburg from this policy point of view, the following five concrete orientations stand out: *First*, wherever possible, do not actively participate in war and avoid social conflict; *second*, pursue policies of openness not only with regard to trade and investment, but also with respect to migration: *third*, allow economic and social structures to adjust flexibly to changing market conditions: *fourth* adopt a forward-looking approach towards the development of economic and social infrastructure: and *fifth and finally*, be wary about inflation and volatile exchange rates, which all undermine money-based international business

As long as Hamburg was not a part of the German Empire and able to pursue its own foreign policy, it always refrained from becoming involved in the numerous European military conflicts and tried to remain neutral. That avoiding social conflict in the guise of social unrest and worker protest is also a decisive determinant of international competitiveness was something the Hamburg business community had to learn the hard way. Perhaps the most important lesson in this respect was a strike of the dockers in 1896/7 which saw 17,000 dockers stop work for about 11 weeks. Even though this strike ended de facto with a defeat for those who revolted, the political fall-out was such that the Senate of Hamburg clearly recognised from that point that the common good of society had to include the interests of the working class.

Over and over again liberal immigration and settlement policies helped the city to achieve economic growth and rising prosperity. By 1376 Hamburg was not only home to 84 Dutch merchants; another 40 tradesmen had arrived from Lübeck and 35 from Great Britain. In 1564, Hamburg accepted the British Merchant Adventurers, thereby infringing — much to Lübeck's disgust — on the Hanseatic rules governing the right of establishment. As a result, Hamburg gained its leading position in the European clothing and textile business. In the face of bitter resistance from its own Evangelical Lutheran church, the Hamburg Senate also permitted the immigration of Dutch Protestants as well as Spanish and Portuguese Jews by the end of the 16th century.

The positive effects of this immigration for Hamburg were not limited to the fact that the new inhabitants brought with them their commercial and technical skills, their capital and international trade relations. Another key factor was that they were not usually organised in traditional guilds, allowing them to embrace change and break up the rigid traditional economic and social structures. This allowed Hamburg not only to respond to new market opportunities, but also provided the city's economy repeatedly with considerable new dynamics from the inside.

Hamburg was first and foremost a city of trade and its merchants knew that business performance has its ups and downs and that they had to adapt flexibly to unpredictable and ever changing market conditions. This might be one of the reasons why up until the First World War the Senate and the Parliament always refused to provide subsidies in support of which were industries and companies no longer competitive. This applied to the decline of the brewing industry as well as the textile business and sugar industry.

The only, but significant exception to this rule before the First World War was the financial assistance provided to the large trading houses during the first global financial and economic crisis of 1857. In this case, too, the subsidy requests were initially rejected. The option of state support was only approved after it became clear that even the largest companies were on the brink of bankruptcy and that this situation would lead to the collapse of the city's entire economy. In fact, the city was faced with an extremely dangerous systemic crisis — very similar to the situation experienced with the American and European banking sector during the recent financial melt-down in 2008.

On a par with the negative attitude towards state aid was the fundamental rejection of the Senate and the merchants of any kind of protectionist policy. This was clearly demonstrated when Hamburg, just like Bremen and Lübeck, refused to join the German Customs Union, established in 1834. It was primarily due to increased pressure from the Imperial Government that Hamburg became part of the German domestic customs territory in 1888. This step was, however, only implemented after Berlin had accepted that a major part of the port could be a free port. Hamburg's interests as a major trading and logistics centre were and still are anchored in free international trade. It comes as no surprise, therefore, that Hamburg still views certain protectionist tendencies as well as the subsidising of a number of non-competitive industries within the European Union with considerable scepticism.

As early as 1299, when Hamburg prided itself on its first paved road, an in the long-run much more important decision was taken, namely to erect a tower at the mouth of the river Elbe which first served as a simple day-time navigational aid and rescue station, but from 1648 onwards also as a lighthouse. Another project for the improvement of the shipping and transport infrastructure, realised as early as in the 15th century, included the identification of the river fairway with buoys and beacons. Since then and until today the adaptation of the breath and the depth of the Elbe fairway to the growing size of ocean-going ships is a permanent concern. Together with the harbour infrastructure itself and the transport links to the hinterland this determines the competitiveness of Hamburg as an important European sea port and logistics centre.

Hamburg introduced compulsory school attendance as early as 1870. It saw the inauguration of the first mass transport system in 1879 and the first electric circle line in 1895. By 1881 a telephone network with more than 200 participants existed. The airport dates back to 1911. To the extent that infrastructure investments served more or less directly the economic interests of the city, there is hardly any doubt that these policies were farsighted. The opposite was initially the case with those parts of the infrastructure which would have served of the majority of the population. It took several severe cholera epidemics before a sound water supply, efficient and environmentally adequate sewage and waste disposal and effective health care systems were developed. Today both economic and social infrastructures are praiseworthy and exemplary in many areas and contribute considerably to Hamburg's competitiveness as a location.

Hamburg's merchants recognised at a very early stage that international trade is fostered by a stable currency. Already by 1255, Hamburg and Lübeck had agreed upon the establishment of an early monetary union. The silver content of the coins was binding and subject to permanent control. This meant, on the one hand, greatly facilitated trade relations and, therefore, a reduction of transaction costs and, on the other, the guarantee of monetary stability in an otherwise highly inflationary environment. This bilateral currency was, for a long time, the most used currency unit in Northern Germany.

More than 100 years later, it became the model for the Wendish Monetary Union, which existed from 1379 to 1566 and included many other cities besides Hamburg and Lübeck. The fact that Hamburg welcomed the foundation of the European Monetary Union while at the same time voicing its concerns about the stability of the new currency confirms, to a certain extent, a centuries-old tradition — a concern which was, incidentally, also raised when Hamburg had to give up its own strong currency in favour of the Reichsmark in 1875, four years after joining the German Empire.

Foreign policy, immigration policy, subsidy policy, trade policy, monetary policy — all these areas are no longer under the jurisdiction of Hamburg. Even the German Federal Government no longer has a direct say in trade and monetary policies and can no longer act independently without adhering to the rules and regulations of the European Union in many other political areas, such as immigration, competition and state aid. The question arises, therefore, about which lessons derived from the successful development and policies of Hamburg in the past are still relevant today.

Over the centuries, globalisation has always been a process of far-reaching and often unexpected change. Only the countries, regions and cities which did not resist the forces of change were able to be permanently successful in this environment. More than ever before in the history of globalisation, today's geopolitical, economic and social environment is characterised by increasingly fast and deep transformations, boundless interconnectedness and pervasive interdependencies, both at domestic and international level. The consequences are a complexity of higher than ever scale, growing uncertainty and sometimes even doubts regarding the future. The only real constant which still seems to exist in our incessantly moving and globalised world is permanent change. These are powerful times. Most importantly, however, they not only provide for new risks and threats but also promise — as did the process of globalisation in the past — a wide range of new opportunities and chances.

For those who wish to become and remain winners and not losers in this relentlessly transforming world, there is hardly any other option than to accept the challenges of change, to try to co-shape the process of change and, whenever this is not possible, to innovatively and flexibly adapt to the new conditions. This applies to individuals, companies, unions and political parties as well as to governments and society as a whole. From a policy perspective this means enhancing the resilience of the economy and society in face of the unpredictable. In more concrete terms this includes establishing a general economic and social climate that supports a positive attitude towards change, assigns a positive value to the acceptance of risks and rewards creativity — and the latter not just only with money, but also with social prestige.

Even with macro-economic stabilisation for most countries largely outside the control of national policy makers, promoting economic growth, employment and quality of life still remain the basic objectives of economic policy. Alongside providing an adequate social net, structural adjustment as well as regional and location policies are therefore among the most pertinent areas in which governments even in the globalised world can and must act on their own. A first and basic requirement in this realm is to establish an economic and socio-political framework which makes market processes compatible with overriding political goals without permanently affecting the functioning of markets and entrepreneurial initiatives. A reliable legal and administrative environment which provides a sound reference framework for investment and other business decisions is the second imperative.

In addition, even in today's interdependent and globalised world there are a number of specific policy fields, in which it is still possible and, in view of the international locational competition, actually very important to make one's own way. This includes in particular all measures which optimise the economic infrastructure, promote science, research and development, foster education and vocational training, and ensure that the location is an attractive place to live for the most innovative and creative people as well as for a highly qualified workforce.

Sufficiently high economic growth and a low rate of unemployment without a doubt also increase a location's quality of life. This must be supported, however, by adequate housing, a high level of healthcare, good schools, excellent shopping facilities, a diverse and vibrant cultural life as well as a wide range of offers for recreation and entertainment, to name just a few. However, all of this is not very specific. It is additionally important to identify, cultivate and accentuate all the key attributes which distinguish a city, town and region from others. These attributes are not particularly precise. In the case of Hamburg, they include the city by the water, the vibrant port, contemporary urban modernisation in the form of the HafenCity or the city with more bridges than Venice or Amsterdam. Another element is all about atmosphere which can be experienced or felt, but hardly described.

In principle, there is nothing new in this approach. Successful regions and cities have always — although more or less consciously — operated along these lines. What may be new in the foreseeable future, at least compared to the most recent globalisation phase, is once again a major transformation in the geopolitical and broader economic environment. Despite the two oil shocks, the graduation of a number of newly industrialised countries, several financial crises, the increasing importance of a few big emerging economies, the fall of the Soviet Union, some regional wars and the rise of international terrorism the sixty-year period between 1945 and 2005, which encompasses the latest and still prevalent sixth phase of the globalisation process, has been by and large a period of broad and continuous progression. There have been quite a few unexpected discontinuities in the evolution, but no really fundamental trend-breaks.

This may not necessarily represent the most likely development pattern in the future. There are, in fact, several indications that the first half of the 21st century may see the world economy take a new and completely different trajectory. A first such sign is that the number and complexity of global issues such as climate change, longer term food and water security, international migration and their interconnectedness are reaching new heights both in quantitative and qualitative terms. A second pointer is the expected shift from a resource-wasting and fossil fuel-intensive economy towards a green economy. A third marker is the on-going developments in the Arab world, both the regional hegemonic ambitions of Iran and the revolutionary revolt in Egypt, Tunisia and Libya. All these trends may have the potential to prompt dramatic change in the world geopolitical and economic environment.

Last but not least and perhaps most importantly, there is the increasing unravelling of the post-WWII world economic order under the leadership of the United States and the rise of China together with some other major emerging countries such as India, Brazil and Russia. This development will in all probability lead to a new world economic order which might not only be characterised by a multi-polar power structure, but also by a systemic incompatibility between the economies and societies of some of the major players. Even if the United States remain for quite some time the most powerful, one of the richest and the technologically most advanced country in the world, China and most other emerging economies will not — as Europe and Japan have done since 1945 — easily accept US supremacy in world geopolitical and economic affairs. As a consequence, the transition process towards a new global governance architecture is full of uncertainties.

Among the many options three stand out as possible prototypes: The best possible outcome would be a progressive move towards a new, jointly managed global governance framework where both efficiency and legitimacy are assured through an in-depth reform of the relevant international institutions. The opposite scenario could be an erratic and volatile evolution where the new rules are established by political power play based primarily on national interest with little responsibility on the part of the main actors for the world economy as a whole. A third possible option — and perhaps the most probable in the medium term — could be "muddling through", resulting in a global governance system characterised by slow and insufficient institutional reform, adhocracy when a crisis looms and power play whenever international negotiations fail.

These are powerful times. Fundamental change is around the corner but the concrete manifestations are unpredictable. Past trends will less than ever be a reliable orientation for desirable action. Adopting the familiar game plans, reinforcing standard procedures and implementing strategies which were successful in the good old days of the second half of the 20th century are no longer a guarantee for an adequate solution. And even if they apparently alleviate a problem in the short term, they may lay the roots for failure in the longer term.

What is needed in such a situation is the enhancement of resilience to be able to absorb the unexpected and the unforeseeable, strengthening the capacity to innovatively and flexibly adjust to rapidly changing political, economic, social and technological circumstances, and in the political realm stretching what interest groups and people believe is socially acceptable and therefore politically feasible.

This is the lesson from the 2,000 year history of globalisation and the story of a city, Hamburg, which has for 1,000 years successfully remained on the winning side in the globalisation process.

# PART I

From the Beginnings
of Globalisation
to the Middle Ages:
The Geographical
and Systemic Expansion
of the Political, Economic,
Social and Cultural
Radius of Action

*Phoenician ships. The Greek historian Herodotus (circa 485 to 424 BC) report-ed that the Phoenicians had circumnavigated the African continent around 600 BC. He himself had doubts, but from today's point of view it seems quite possible.*

# CHAPTER 1

# Phoenicians, Greeks, Romans, Vikings, and the Hanseatic League

Within the wider European context, the Phoenicians were, with their colonisations and establishment of towns back in the period between the 9th and 6th century BC, probably the first to have given impetus to a centuries-long process of globalisation. One can, at least, take this view if globalisation is understood not only as the existence or expansion of trade relations, but also as the evolution of increasingly interwoven political, economic, social and cultural relationships and interdependencies between geographically distant regions. Greek dominance under the leadership of Athens and, in particular, the later Roman Empire, from approximately 30 BC to 300 AD, marked the climax of this early globalisation phase. This period was followed by several centuries of stagnation and uncertainty until, with the rise of the Italian cities in the Mediterranean, the voyages of the Vikings and the development of the Hanseatic cities also in Northern Europe, a new wave of globalisation was triggered.

## Phoenician Trading Activities, Colonies, and the Establishment of Towns: Forerunners of Globalisation in the Mediterranean

Having set sail from Sidon, Tyre, Byblos and other cities, the Phoenicians not only travelled the Mediterranean but also the European Atlantic coastline. They sailed both south and north of the Straits of Gibraltar, and most probably also circumnavigated Africa on behalf of Pharaoh Necho II. As merchants, they also spread the knowledge and myths of the Assyrians and Babylonians. They took the alphabet they had developed to Greece. By passing on their knowledge of the rapidly rotating potter's wheel and refined methods of metal processing in the Mediterranean region, they actively contributed to the process of technology transfer. Even the political organisational model of the city state, the polis, was spread through the vehicle of Phoenician expansion.

The Phoenicians did not — like the Greeks who came after them — form large colonies and settle extensive territories, but established city-like settlements — initially in Cyprus and the Aegean, and subsequently also in Italy, North Africa, Spain and Portugal. Some of these trading posts still exist as cities to this day, among them for example Palermo, Tripoli, Algiers, Malaga, Cadiz and Mogador — to name but the most important. Yet the most significant city of the Ancient world established by the Phoenicians, said to have been founded in 814 BC, was Carthage, which was quite literally razed to the ground by the Romans during the Third Punic War in 146 BC.

As the narrow hinterland of Phoenician towns, stretching only 10 to 15 kilometres to the mountains, did not permit any large-scale agricultural production, it was only natural that the Phoenicians specialised, from a very early period, in the production of commercial products, in particular of textiles, ceramics, wrought-iron work, the processing of gold and silver, ivory carvings, as well as glass manufacture and shipbuilding. In return, they imported foodstuffs, primarily grain from Sicily and North Africa, as well as metals — in addition to copper and lead, most notably silver — from Sardinia and Spain. Phoenician products could be found throughout the Mediterranean. In later years, however, the products came not only from the cities of the Levant but also from their settlements in the colonies.

In similar fashion to the Dutch in the 17th century, the Phoenicians became the leading sea transporters of their day. In fact, for a period of almost four centuries, they had no other competitors as the Greeks, following the demise of the Mycenaean civilization, had engaged in only little maritime activity. For a period of almost four centuries. Problems began for the Phoenicians in the middle of the 7th century BC when they were, on the one hand, increasingly exposed to attacks by the Assyrians and, on the other, Greek towns, such as Corinth, Megara, Miletus and Phocaea, started to found their own colonies in the Mediterranean.

Nonetheless, by the time the homeland of the Phoenicians, in what is now Lebanon and parts of Syria, was conquered first by the Assyrians, then the Babylonians and finally, in around 540 BC, the Persians, their radius of action spanned the length and breadth of the economically relevant world at that time. The principal long-distance Northern trade route of the Phoenicians led from Cyprus, Rhodes or Crete, and from there on to Greece, to the Aegean and the Black Sea in the one direction, and to the Straits of Messina and Italy in the other. Another southern route ran along the African coastline via Carthage to Morocco, Spain and Portugal. Yet there was also a shorter, more dangerous open sea route, from Crete to the Iberian Peninsula via Malta, Sicily, Sardinia and the Balearic Islands.

Interaction in the form of trade and competition with the Greeks, but also with the Etruscans, who controlled the Tyrrhenian Sea, were most intense along the northern route. Only after Alexander the Great succeeded in conquering Tyre, too, in 333 BC, did relations between the homeland and the original Phoenician colonies begin to fade away. Foreign relations, most notably trade with Carthage, were subsequently limited to the colonies in the western Mediterranean and along the Atlantic coast, including the west coast of Africa in the south and possibly, via Portugal, to the British Isles in the north. Relations no longer encompassed the entire world economy of that time.

Nevertheless, the question arises as to the degree to which this early development was driven simply by the individual initiative of the merchants and voyagers or whether there actually was already some sort of a multilaterally accepted regulatory control system of political power respectively an overarching political power behind it all. That the Phoenicians spread their common language, religion and culture throughout the Mediterranean region is beyond dispute. It is also certain that they did not just establish trading posts but founded new towns in which they not only established industries and shipbuilding but also exercised political influence. Yet it also appears to have been widely proven that the Phoenician towns taken together never — except in the context of bilateral and temporary cooperation — saw themselves as a defined political entity and power centre of whatever kind.

The term Phoenician quite unmistakably derives from the Greeks. The so-called Phoenician merchants and seafarers, however, considered themselves to be people from Sidon, Tyre, Byblos, or even Carthage. Comparable systemic elements, like those which characterised the Hanseatic towns and cities 1,500 years later, really do not seem to have existed. There is strong evidence in favour of the assumption that the Phoenicians, like the first Greek colonists who initiated the Hellenisation of the Mediterranean even while the Phoenicians still retained trade and maritime supremacy, should most probably be seen more as the forerunners of the first phase of globalisation and not as those who actually implemented this process.

# Hellenisation of the World
## and the First Phase of Globalisation

Imbalances between demographic development and agricultural resources, together with political and social causes, triggered a sustained period of emigration pressure in Greece between the 8th and
6th century BC. This led to the colonisation of Asia Minor, the Black
Sea coast, and large sections of the Mediterranean coast — in the west
from Sicily to the Iberian Peninsula, and in the south-east to Egypt
and what is today Syria. Many of these trade centres remain more or
less bustling cities to this very day, among them Marseilles, Naples,
Syracuse and Odessa.

From the very beginning, this colonisation did not, however, constitute solely an expansion of economic relations. Closely linked to this
was the dissemination of the Greek language, Greek gods, customs and
traditions as well as Greek literature, art and science. From an early
stage, Athens probably played a more important role than all other
towns in the field of cultural exports. However, it did not achieve its
outstanding status until the successful foreign and domestic policies
of Pericles had turned the city into a dominant regional centre also in
political, military and economic terms. When Athens finally assumed
leadership of the Delian League in 454 BC, moving the joint war-
chest to the Acropolis, and demanding that the defence contributions
of its allies in future be made in cash only, it at the same time ensured
that its coins became the main currency throughout the entire Aegean
region. It thus not only became the leading sea power, but also the
dominant economic power — at least in the Aegean region.

Disregarding the fact that the Athenian sphere of influence actually fell far short of encompassing the known world at that time, which,
in principle, also included the east coast of Africa and the Indian
Ocean, there are nonetheless a variety of aspects which make the
situation as it existed then similar to the basic phenomenon of globalisation in the wider meaning of the term. In this respect, politi-

cal, social and cultural factors were just as important as economics. Athens' military and economic supremacy was, however, basically limited to Attica, the Greek archipelago and Asia Minor. The colonies in other regions, most notably in the western Mediterranean, acted according to the rules of their respective "parent cities" and multilateral exchange between the various metropolises and their colonies was still relatively underdeveloped. All of this meant that, at least with regard to the central part of the territories settled by Greece, cultural similarities were apparently far more pronounced than economic interdependencies.

Both the empire of Alexander the Great, including the Hellenistic Diadochi kingdoms that succeeded it, and the Roman Empire developed and functioned according to completely different criteria. Initially, the pursuit of hegemony, military success and economic exploitation were at the fore. This too, however, was not limited to the conquest and subjection of other countries. It simultaneously meant colonisation, the founding of cities, military bases and trading posts, as well as the export of the coloniser's own administrative and legal systems. As long as this process also guaranteed peace, it served to foster foreign trade, direct investments and technology transfer; and not just in the strict political sphere of influence, but far beyond it.

Alexandria, even more than Athens under Pericles, was, during the Ptolemaic period and also after its incorporation into the Roman Empire in 30 BC, not only one of the most important metropolises in the Mediterranean region but also a multicultural world trading centre. It linked, via Aden and the Red Sea and the hundreds of ships that sailed from there, the Mediterranean with the Gulf of Oman and India, as well as with East Africa to a point as far south as what is now Dar es Salaam. Although the main flow of goods, especially grain and spices, initially headed almost entirely north and later west, the cultural influence of the Hellenistic world reached in all directions. Not only did Rome increasingly open up towards Greek culture and science — the Orient, too, was, up until the Islamic expansion in the 7th century AD, essentially a Greek-influenced culture.

*The lighthouse of Alexandria. During the early and high Roman imperial era Alexandria was what New York, London or Paris are today, namely a vibrant, multicultural metropolis. Not only Egyptians, Greeks and Romans, but also Persians, Bactrians and even Indians conducted their business there.*

*A map of the world according to Ptolemy (circa 100 to 175 AD). The eastern Mediterranean was the centre of the world economy at this time and the*

*River Elbe at the edge of the inhabitable world. Moreover, the Indian Ocean was evidently better known than the North and Baltic Seas.*

## More than 200 Years of Globalisation under the Leadership of Rome

Most notably in terms of the political and economic integration of the then world, mention must be made of the quite exceptional influence of Rome. Rome was, as the Greek orator Aelius Aristides wrote in the 2nd century AD, the undisputed centre of a "common market", the point at which all trade, shipping and everything else converged. Although local currencies still existed, Roman coinage was the only legal tender accepted throughout the empire. Also, many local languages and dialects were, at least in the early years, still spoken, yet the influence of the administration and the military made Latin the dominant language.

Hellenisation of the world was the first manifestation of globalisation; the spread of the *Roman way of life* the second. Roman law applied to all commercial activities involving Roman citizens, and when Emperor Caracalla granted citizenship to all freemen in the Empire in 212 AD, this deprived any local laws that might till have existed in a few places of their validity. Any town worth its salt built it own forum romanum, a Roman theatre and a Roman temple. The Romanisation of the gods and the Romanisation, to some extent Hellenisation, of customs and mores are further important elements that round out, or complete, the process of globalisation in the then relevant world.

Yet none of this should be taken to mean that the Roman world was not still very much an agrarian society, or that industrial and commercial activity and cross-border trade were the focus of interest in government and society. For the social elite, trade at that time had roughly the same low social status as it did, many centuries later, for European aristocrats. Even the Latin word "negotium" has an inherently negative meaning, i.e. "neg-otium" which, in a pejorative sense, means restlessness or agitation. For the government, however, cross-border trade, especially the import of luxury goods from Greece and

Asia, as well as grain from Egypt, was a welcome spin-off effect of its political, military and administrative activities, contributing to an increase in prosperity and social stabilisation, particularly in Rome.

Rome's wars were indeed not fought for the purpose of economic expansion or the protection of trade interests. The development of ports and roads was strategically, not economically motivated; and the development of the monetary system promoted by the state was principally designed to improve efficiency when collecting taxes and other levies, and not to facilitate economic transactions. There were no policies consciously targeted towards economic development. Apart from the trade in what were then strategic goods, for example timber used in the shipbuilding industry, which was controlled by the administration or military, the Roman government had little interest in international economic activities. In particular cross-border and long-distance trade was predominantly a private business.

But there is no doubt that, over a long period of time, Roman authority, administration and Roman law throughout the Empire, together with many measures motivated by other reasons, created the decisive positive basic conditions required for economic development and integration. Most especially during the almost seventy-year reign of the emperors Augustus and Tiberius, and during the reign of Antonius Pius, Marcus Aurelius and Commodus, the political, economic and cultural conditions in the Roman Empire fulfilled virtually all of the criteria a globalised world economy needs to meet. Yet when, from the 3rd century AD onwards, the "Pax Romana" was increasingly thrown into question by both internal and external turmoil, this early phase of world economic integration came to a relatively speedy end.

## Venice as the New Centre
### of the Globalisation Process in the Mediterranean

After a period of relative stagnation and increased uncertainty, which marked the transition from the ancient world to the Middle Ages, the rise of the Italian cities, in particular Venice, Genoa, Pisa and Amalfi, prompted a new globalisation spurt encompassing the Mediterranean region and, indirectly, large sections of Asia. In principle, the new era commenced with the Crusades, which can be seen not only as wars against the infidels but also as a decisive event in the history of logistics, high finance and economic expansion. Of special importance within this context is the Fourth Crusade (1199–1204).

During the first three crusades, a part of the troops and materials had already been transported to the Holy Land on Venetian ships; in return, Venice, without being actively involved in any battles, was granted rights of establishment and settlement in the newly created Kingdom of Jerusalem, exemption from customs duties and other taxes, as well as the concession that Venetian weights and measures would apply for trade. During the Fourth Crusade, Venice played an even more active role: For the price of approximately 85,000 silver marks, the city agreed to equip an army of 4,500 knights, 4,500 horses, 9,000 squires and 20,000 foot soldiers, and to transport them to Egypt by sea. Moreover, the Doge of Venice assumed control of the operation and used the assembled military might in transit to the Holy Land for his own interests by having first Zadar on the Dalmatian coast and then Constantinople brought under Venetian rule.

Venice was, however, initially not alone with its ambitions to dominate the eastern Mediterranean, having consistently vied for supremacy with Genoa. It was only after Venice had finally, and decisively, defeated Genoa at the Battle of Chioggia in 1380, the last in a series of four wars between the two cities, that it became the absolute ruler of both the eastern Mediterranean and the Black Sea. It remained so until the conquest of Constantinople by the Ottomans in

*Fondaco dei Tedeschi. A testimony in stone to the fact that state over-regulation can lead to the loss of the international competitiveness of a location.*

1453 and the final expulsion of the Venetians from the Aegean in 1470. Even at the end of the 15th century, Venice, with a population of 180,000, was still, after Paris, the second largest city in Europe, and most probably the world's wealthiest city.

Yet Venice's wealth was based not only on its leading position as a trade and maritime power in the Mediterranean, but also on the fact that its geographical location and economic policy, when compared with those of other Italian cities, gave it privileged access to markets in Northern Europe. Via the *Fondaco dei Tedeschi*, the trading headquarters of the German merchants in Venice, it controlled long-distance trade with the large continental trading centres, such as Augsburg, Nuremberg, Cologne and even Hamburg and Lübeck. For a long time, Venice was the central market for spices, silks, drugs and other goods from India and East Asia, not only for the above-mentioned cities, but also for London, Vienna, Bruges, Lyon and Basle. However, monopolies only rarely last forever, and when they return excessively high profits, they eventually arouse the forces which subsequently undermine them. A harsh reality that even Venice could not escape.

Yet the reasons for the end of this last phase of globalisation in the Mediterranean under the leadership of Venice are manifold and of exogenous as well as endogenous nature. The decline began in 1509 following a military defeat at the hands of the League of Cambrai. It was accelerated by the Ottoman expansion, resulting in the loss of Cyprus, Crete and the city's possessions in the Peloponnese. And its fate was sealed almost 300 hundred years later — after 1,000 years of independence — with the Napoleonic occupation in 1797. However, it was not just military conflicts which brought about the demise of Venice as the most important European trading and naval power. On the one hand, the discovery of the sea route to India and the colonisation of America caused long-distance trade routes to shift westwards. On the other, the previous commercial success and wealth of Venice resulted in inflexible policies which prevented the city's economy and society from adapting to new opportunities and challenges.

### The Vikings as Precursors
### of the First Phase of Globalisation
### in Northern Europe

In Northern Europe, too, relations — some hostile, some cordial — between seafarers and merchants and other peoples began to be established in the first century AD. One of the two most significant developments came in the form of the voyages, pillaging and colonisation undertaken by the Vikings; the other starting at the beginning of the second century, was the expansion of the Hanseatic League, which was based mainly on trade.

The Vikings' field of action ranged from what is now Scandinavia to Greenland, Baffin Island and Newfoundland to the west, southwards to Sicily and North Africa, and via Russia to Constantinople and Baghdad in the southeast. Just like the Phoenicians nearly 1,000 years before them, the Vikings were excellent shipwrights and outstanding seafarers. As plunderers and pillagers, they were feared throughout Europe for a period of several centuries, from approximately 800 to 1050. In 845 they burned down a part of Hamburg; in 860, they attacked Constantinople, and in 900 they sailed up the River Seine in 700 longships to ransack Paris. But, according to recent findings, the Vikings were also merchants and settlers. They settled in England, Ireland, Iceland and Greenland, and even in Russia. In 911, finally, the French king Charles the Simple granted Normandy to the Viking leader Rollo to ensure that the latter cease his attacks on Paris and the Ile de France.

It is a matter of some debate as to whether the Vikings were primarily warriors who also conducted a little trade on the side, or whether they were primarily merchants who, whenever it seemed advantageous to do so, did not shy away from violence for the sake of their own enrichment. There is, however, a consensus that the Vikings were not a single ethnic group. They were made up of various tribes and people whose geographical orientation and general motivation for long voyages were remarkably different.

The Norwegian Vikings' original field of action was the west, i.e. England, Ireland, Iceland, Greenland and island groups in the North Atlantic, with colonisation by small groups the preferred approach. The Danes, who were already better organised and operated with larger fleets, headed southwest, i.e. to the German and Dutch North Sea coast, the south coast of England, and France. Their primary aim was to go raiding overseas in order to gain the additional power this gave them at home. For the Swedes, by contrast, trade was clearly the paramount consideration. Their field of action was the Baltic, the Gulf of Finland, the Russian rivers down to the Caspian Sea and Constantinople.

Apart from in Iceland, which was largely uninhabited, there was no real colonisation by the Vikings, largely due to the small number of groups operating collectively at any one time. On the contrary, in

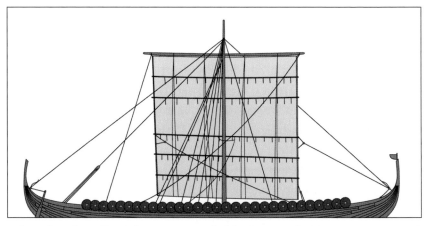

*Viking longship. The Vikings were probably the very first Europeans to reach the American continent after setting sail from Iceland around 1000 AD. They also reached Constantinople and Baghdad by travelling south-east along Russian rivers.*

fact: It was usually the Vikings who adapted to the foreign environment. The Danish and Norwegian Vikings intermarried with the English and Irish; the Normans, primarily of Danish descent, became French; and the Swedish Vikings integrated into the Russian population. Quite remarkable in this context is the strong influence of Islam on the Vikings. In the economic sector, this is reflected most notably in the adoption of the Islamic weight-standard money system.

A number of historians also believe that trade between the Orient and Occident, which had been conducted via the Mediterranean for more than 1,000 years, was, due to Arab blockades, maintained at the time of Charlemagne via a northern route — a trading route that stretched from Constantinople to Central Europe via Russian rivers, the Baltic, the North Sea, the English Channel and the Atlantic Ocean. The central trading towns in the Baltic region were Hedeby and Birka. Slaves were the principal commodity traded from north to south. Only after this came hides, timber, whale's teeth, salted fish and honey. The commodities traded in the return direction were silk, spices, ceramics, jewellery, weapons and wine.

It is nevertheless hard to see the expansion of Viking influence as more than just the precursor of a later Northwest European globalisation process. As with the Phoenicians, and maybe even to a greater extent, what is missing here is the systemic element of an overriding political or institutional regulatory framework. Despite common cultural origins, a common religion, similar shipbuilding and seafaring traditions and predominantly simultaneous developments, there was no common codified legal system and, despite the common Islamic weight-money system, no strategically relevant currency; and, in the end, following the demise of the Norse language, there was not even a common language anymore. The Hanseatic League founded by German merchants in the 12th century can, at least in its later phase, be assessed differently.

### The Rise and Fall
### of the Hanseatic League

The emergence of the Hanseatic League and, most particularly, its contribution to the economic and, in places, cultural integration of Northern Europe as a historical process is another development that cannot be firmly dated. Several founding years, ranging from 1143 to 1161, are named in relevant literature. Yet this is largely irrelevant within the context as considered here. Initially, the Hanseatic League was solely a free alliance of individual merchants whose aim was to protect the group during dangerous journeys and to provide common representation of interests overseas. This early period of the so-called Merchant Hanse already implied the regional expansion of long-distance trade and an increasing presence throughout the Baltic and North Sea region. Once again, however, an overall regulatory framework was still not in place.

This situation changed significantly with the transition from the Merchant Hanse to the so-called City Hanse. Although this alliance also lacked any kind of formal constitution or clear organisational structure, the grouping definitely constituted, in its heyday between roughly 1250 and 1520, a real, albeit multipolar, economic and politico-economic power. All of its members were, in principle, of equal standing. Initially, three towns — Lübeck, Dortmund and Visby — and later four — Lübeck, Cologne, Brunswick and Gdansk — were the primus inter pares in their respective region. The pre-eminence of Lübeck, which, between 1293 and 1298, put an end to Visby's supremacy is illustrated by two specific facts: Firstly, the city's leading role in the so-called Wendish Hanse, which controlled the Baltic and North Sea region and was probably the most powerful alliance at this time, was never really called into question. Secondly, 54 of the 72 assemblies of the Hanseatic cities convened in Lübeck between 1356 and 1480.

The Hanseatic League's sphere of influence ranged from western Russia in the east to Britain in the west, and from Bergen and Stockholm in the north to Northern France and Cologne in the south. It also had major permanent offices in Novgorod, Bergen, Bruges and London. Additionally, there were smaller "Kontors", most especially on the east coast of England and Scotland, among them branches in Edinburgh, Newcastle, Hull, York and Great Yarmouth. On the basis of joint actions, albeit with varying levels of participation, everything possible was undertaken to facilitate profitable trade within a peaceful and legally reliable environment.

Another decisive factor, both for the rise and subsequent fall of the Hanseatic League, was its trade policy. The focus of all politico-economic endeavours, especially at the time of the City Hanse, was the extension and protection of monopolies and privileges. This took the form of restrictions on the economic activity of foreigners in the Hanseatic cities, legal constraints placed on third parties with regard to trading in the Hanse "Kontors", the prohibition of joint trading companies between Hanseatic and non-Hanseatic entities, and all measures taken by the Hanseatic League to prevent the shipping and handling of goods for third parties. Foreigners and even guests permitted to enter the Hanseatic towns and cities did not, for example, usually have the right to conduct business or trade with each other within the towns. Also, the Hanseatic League did everything within its power to prevent Flemish and Dutch ships, which brought cloth from Flanders to the Baltic ports, from returning home with freight.

As long as the Hanseatic League continued to grow, the impact of the disadvantages that these measures potentially also imposed on the merchants of the Hanseatic League was relatively minor. Even the Hanseatic merchants themselves were confident that this policy of eliminating competition could be effectively maintained over a long period of time. Accordingly, the validity of these regulations, which were primarily directed against the English, Dutch, Flemish and merchants from Brabant and Nuremberg, was repeatedly extended. Viewed over the long haul, however, Hanseatic merchants consistently underestimated the power of free market forces. Their competitors found many successful ways to circumvent these regulations. Some of them even found partners in the Hanseatic League who, for fear of missing out on lucrative deals, chose not to comply with the restrictions. Both factors, the market realities and the institutional weakness of the Hanseatic League, ultimately led to the collapse of its protectionist trade system.

In addition to the lack of a constitution and the absence of any formal structures, another characteristic feature of the Hanseatic League was that there was not even a reliable membership list. Apart from a core group, comprising approximately 60 towns and cities, membership changed constantly, and different estimates claim membership figures ranging from 72 to almost 200. With the exception of exclusion from the Hanseatic League, a measure which, for example, actually was applied to Bremen between 1275 and 1358, and the loss of trading privileges abroad and trade relations with the other cities resulting from such exclusion, there were practically no means of taking coercive action. Joint decisions were made on the basis of consensus and peer pressure. All efforts on the part of Lübeck, whose pre-eminence in the Hanseatic League had been officially confirmed in 1418, to eliminate these institutional weaknesses and to give the Hanseatic League a contractual framework failed due to conflicting interests and the heterogeneity of the political situation in individual towns and cities.

The confederation statute, a ten-point declaration of the rights and duties of the members as well as the modalities for permanent financing and a secretariat, adopted by the assembly of the Hanseatic cities in 1557, basically came too late. The Hanseatic League had, to a large extent, already lost its monopoly in North and Baltic Sea trade; the Kontors in Novgorod, Bruges and London had been closed or no longer fulfilled their original purpose, and the external enemies, chief among them Denmark and the German sovereigns, had become much more powerful. Even a defence and consultation pact concluded by Lübeck, Hamburg and Bremen in 1630 for an initial period of ten years, was unable to stop the decline of the Hanseatic League. The last assembly of the Hanseatic cities took place in 1669. And although the aforementioned agreement between Lübeck, Hamburg and Bremen was repeatedly extended, right up until the 20th century, the Hanseatic League vanished just the way it had appeared, i.e. sometime during the 17th century yet on no clearly definable date.

If globalisation is understood as increasingly close political, economic, social and cultural ties between geographically far removed societies across language and cultural borders which are also characterised by an overriding regulatory framework and/or a political power structure, classic Greece under the leadership of Athens, the Roman Empire, the Golden Age of Venice and the Hanseatic League are to be seen as initial examples of this process. These early globalisation phases did not encompass the entire globe, but covered that part of the world which was then relevant in political and economic terms or helped to create and shape that world.

## The Importance
## of External and Internal Peace for
## the Globalisation Process

In the development of all four regional world economies mentioned above, five factors played an important role. These include the general political, economic and social setting, the predominance of cities, the physical and immaterial infrastructure, technical progress and economic policy. These determinants were, however, of special importance not only during the phase of ascendancy but also during the subsequent decline. Both demonstrate the relevance of the historical perspective for the present and the future — for the world economy and also for Hamburg.

With regard to the overall political setting, it can generally be said that the periods of greatest prosperity during all early globalisation phases occurred at a time when external and internal peace prevailed. In the case of Greece, it was after the final victory over the Persians and, in particular, under Pericles from 460 BC onwards, until the Peloponnesian War against Sparta in 431 BC, from which Athens never recovered. The importance of peace for economic prosperity in a globalised world was also highlighted during the era of the Roman Empire. Surely Rome's wealth was initially based on the lavish spoils of war in the shape of slaves, gold, silver, luxury goods and works of art, as well as taxes and tributes from subjugated territories. But it was after its final victory over Carthage in the 2nd century BC that the city advanced to become the most important economic centre in the Mediterranean, alongside Athens and, most particularly, Alexandria.

Nonetheless, the example of Rome clearly shows that external peace alone is not enough to secure long-lasting prosperity. Increasing political and social tension, a widening gap between the rich and poor, as well as slave uprisings — initially in Sicily and then on the Italian mainland — led to permanent unrest and civil wars. Only after Tiberius succeeded in pacifying Rome from the inside in 30 AD did it finally became the capital of the world, not just in military and political but also in economic and cultural terms.

The "Pax Romana" lasted, with brief interruptions, for more than 200 years until the Roman Empire began, from the middle of the 3rd century onwards, to face constantly growing difficulties from both outside and inside its borders. As with the Hanseatic League, it is very difficult to say when the Roman Empire really came to an end. Within the context as considered here, however, the most decisive fact is that, with the division of Rome into the Eastern and Western Roman Empires in 395 AD, the end of the first phase of globalisation in the ancient world had been reached.


## Globalisation and the Protection of Trade Routes

External and internal peace as a basic prerequisite for prosperity also applies to the Golden Age of Venice and the Hanseatic League. Another aspect, well illustrated by these two globalisation eras, is the significance of the freedom and protection of trade routes. Neither Venice nor the Hanseatic League possessed the political weight and military might to control the entire economic region that they dominated. Venice's answer to this problem was to establish a string of colonial bases — similar to those later set up by the Portuguese and the Dutch in the 16th and 17th century. The Hanseatic League, in contrast, operated on the basis of cooperation agreements between towns and cities.

The simplest form such cooperation took was in the conclusion of bilateral agreements, e.g. the treaty concluded between Lübeck and Hamburg in 1241 for the joint protection of the land route between the two cities. At the time of the Hanseatic League, the character of the agreements concerning mutual defence and, to a certain degree, the aggressive pursuit of Hanseatic interests became more and more multilateral. The preferred option was mutual negotiations and monetary payments; where necessary, however, and on a case-by-case basis, the Hanseatic cities also cooperated in terms of trade blockades and military intervention.

Considering the loose organisational structure of the Hanseatic League, the various different demonstrations of power politics are quite remarkable. Trade blockades were, for example, directed against Novgorod in 1277, Bruges in 1280, Norway in 1284, Flanders in 1358 and, again, in 1380, as well as against England and Russia. In addition to the joint battle against pirates and privateers, five wars were fought on the basis of joint military action — three against Denmark and one each against the Netherlands and England respectively.

An excellent illustration of the "Hanseatic cities as the Northern European superpower" is provided by the first two punitive expeditions against the King of Denmark, who initially attacked Visby, then the richest city of the Hanseatic League, in 1361 and subsequently blocked the Sound and thus the sea route between the North and Baltic Sea for Hanseatic shipping. For the first counterstrike in 1362, which actually failed, the Hanseatic League mobilised a fleet of 52 ships, two of which sailed — even though the scene of the battle was the Baltic — from Hamburg. The next, and now successful, intervention, in which, incidentally, the Dutch also took part but not Hamburg, was launched with 37 ships and 2,000 armed men.

## Cities as a Driving Force in the Globalisation Process

Another significant aspect of the various globalisation processes considered here is the importance of cities. Globalisation has never been geographically all-embracing in the sense that the vast majority of the population of the relevant world economy actively participated in it. The momentum of the globalisation process always originated in one or more urban centres. In Graecia Magna, these were primarily Athens and Alexandria. Under the Roman Empire it was Rome, Alexandria, Athens and, prior to its destruction, Carthage. During the next phase, it was Venice, Constantinople, Alexandria and, at the beginning, Genoa. And it is self-evident which important role cities played in the Hanseatic League.

Yet this does not mean that regions outside of the dynamic urban centres necessarily remain unaffected by the economic implications of globalisation. Areas in the immediate vicinity of these dynamic centres usually profit as suppliers of products and services that cannot be obtained more cheaply or easily from afar. Those exposed to growing competitive pressures by long-distance trade, for example peasant farmers in Greece who were increasingly driven to ruin by grain imports from the colonies, have practically no other choice than to adapt to the new circumstances and to innovate. Protectionism can, in individual cases, slow down this process of structural change and mitigate its immediate impact up to a point, yet is basically unable to prevent it.

There are many reasons, interlinked to one another in a complex manner, why cities represent the dynamic centres which normally drive the globalisation process forward. Among the most important are, on the one hand, the fact that, due to the concentration of people, assets and a comparably high average per capita income, they constitute focal points of demand for goods and services. In both Athens and Rome, grain imports to feed the respective city's rapidly growing population became a factor of key importance. On the other hand, high levels of income and assets mean above-average purchasing power and thus lucrative markets for slaves and luxury goods. Interesting in this respect is the demand-induced relocation of production sites, a phenomenon could already be observed in the second globalisation phase considered here. Glass manufacturers from Lebanon, for example, began settling close to Rome, their largest market, on account of the fragility of their products during transportation.

A second reason why cities act as a driving force of the globalisation process is that they are, in the majority of cases, also important transportation hubs. That is, at least, the case with those major cities which, unlike Rome, are not primarily administrative centres but above all trade centres. Usually these are located at points where key trade and transport routes intersect or where goods are transshipped from one means of conveyance to another. Alexandria, for example, was for many centuries the main transshipment point for goods between Asia and the Mediterranean; Venice, in its day, monopolised trade from the eastern Mediterranean to the region north of the Alps; and Hamburg played its dominant role, together with Lübeck, for goods shipped between the North and Baltic Sea.

Venice with its silk production, Bruges after the boom of the Flemish cloth industry and, as will become apparent later on, also Hamburg, which together with Lübeck was the leading producer and exporter of beer at the time of the Hanseatic League, are fine examples of a third element of major importance for active participation in the globalisation process. Since transit alone rarely yields the highest profit in the value adding chain between primary production and final consumption, it is important to own processing capacities whose production exceeds the domestic demand, the local added value that remains generally being far higher if the imported raw materials undergo a further processing stage before being re-exported.

Last but not least, it is the city where industry, trade and finance meet. It is here where advanced and specialized know-how are more concentrated than anywhere else in a county. It is here where people, and in particular experts, find ample opportunities for the exchange of experiences, and this not only from the same profession or discipline. Crossfertilisation of ideas and innovative thinking is the consequence. It is the city where most of the highly paid, high value-added jobs can be found. It is here where the leading schools and universities are located. And it is here where the arts and science flourish. And all this attracts the qualified, and if a city is a top location not only at national, but also at international level. It is no surprise therefore that one of the most dynamic elements of the globalization process is the interaction and networking of vibrant and creative cities.

## The Importance
## of an Adequate Infrastructure

Another important factor, for both the globalisation process in general and the dynamic centres of this development in particular, is the availability of an adequate infrastructure. The underlying motivating forces causing development in this field are virtually irrelevant. The expansion of Athens' port was initially undertaken for primarily military purposes. The foundation of Alexandria by Alexander the Great occurred, as in the case of so many of the towns he established, chiefly out of strategic considerations. The same applies to the construction of roads and ports in the Roman Empire. But all of these infrastructure measures also had important economic side effects without which the early phases of globalisation would have barely been possible. The importance of an adequate and efficient infrastructure for economic development was also recognised at a very early stage in Venice and Hamburg. In both cities, the expansion of the ports and warehouses down through the centuries was pursued with largely commercial considerations in mind.

During all phases of the globalisation process, it is, however, not only the physical but also the intangible infrastructure that plays a decisive role. In addition to the judiciary, the currency system is one of the most important factors in this regard. In Ancient Greece, which encompassed large areas of the Mediterranean, Athenian coinage was the dominant currency of its day. For at least the next 200 years after the monetary reform of 24 AD introduced by Augustus, the sesterce was the predominant currency unit throughout the entire Roman Empire. During the Venetian globalisation phase, gold ducats minted in Venice superseded Byzantine gold coins in the post-1284 period.

Of almost greater interest than the spread of benchmark currencies during early periods of globalisation in the Mediterranean region are developments in the Hanseatic League. By 1225, Hamburg and Lübeck had agreed to issue a common coinage with units of uniform value. This was followed, in 1241, by a first monetary union, with the Lübeck "mark" as the common currency unit. In 1379, an alliance which became known as the Wendish Monetary Union was established. Its members included, in addition to Hamburg and Lübeck, Wismar and Lüneburg, and, for a time, Rostock, Stralsund, Greifswald and Stettin. Also worth noting, incidentally, is the fact that monetary unification between Hanseatic towns and cities was accomplished through negotiations and contracts and not, as in Greek and Roman times or even under the rule of Venice, as a direct consequence of political and economic pre-eminence.

The Hanseatic legal system developed in similar fashion. Here, too, unification did not occur as in the Roman Empire as a result of political or administrative coercion, but on the basis of voluntary co-operation. A particularly interesting example is that of the standard Hanseatic legal provisions, which covered shipping, seaborne trade, freight traffic and mariners. Freight was regulated by the Hamburg Law of 1292, the basic principles of which were accepted by Lübeck in 1299, and later by Bremen, Oldenburg and Riga. With regard to damages and disputes with crews, the Hanseatic legal norms were based on maritime law provisions originating from the Île d'Oléron in France, which were initially translated into Flemish and later Low German.

In the 14th century, the old Hamburg freight laws and the original French maritime legislation were — both in amended versions — combined into one. Under the so-called "Code of Maritime Law (literally: 'Water Law')", this amended version represented the first comprehensive codified maritime law of the Hanseatic towns and cities in the north and, following its acceptance by Lübeck, the Baltic Sea region. Since the most important tribunal for Baltic Sea Law was still based in Visby, the revised collection of laws, which was allegedly also available in printed form from 1505, was called the "Gotland Maritime Code". Acting as a further important legal source were the pronouncements of the assemblies of the Hanseatic cities on shipping-related issues. A collection of some of these rulings had been available since 1482, but a printed version in book form did not appear until the 16th century.

## *Globalisation, Technical Progress and Financial Innovations*

All early phases of globalisation were characterised by new technologies in shipping, harbour construction and, particularly during the Roman Empire, in urban development and road construction. The development of shipping in Northwestern Europe may be taken as an illustrative example of this. At the time when Lübeck was founded there were basically just two types of seaworthy vessels: The narrow and fast Viking ship with low draught, which could be both sailed and rowed, and the Western European sailing ship, which, in comparison to the Viking ship, was shorter, wider and slower. Both of these vessel types had roughly the same load-carrying capacity of approximately 30 metric tons. They only had one mast and were fitted with a side rudder.

The Western European ship was replaced by the cog between the 10th and 12th century. Cogs had a length of between 17 and 30 metres and, in later times, a tonnage of 160 to 200. Since the keel was straight and the bottom flat, they were ideal for dry-docking, which was especially beneficial in areas around shallows and mudflats. As with their predecessor, cogs only had one mast, and the side rudder was replaced by a stern-hung rudder at the beginning of the 13th century. Due to this innovation the tacking of the cog was enhanced to such an extent that it was claimed the ship could sail up to 60 degrees windward. In the 13th and 14th century, this so-called Hanseatic cog was the typical merchant vessel between Novgorod and Lisbon.

In the 14th century, the Dutch developed the hulk type of ship, which displaced the cog in the course of the next century. The first hulks were no larger than the 14th century cogs yet the main advan-

60

tage was their improved seaworthiness. They were more watertight and had an enhanced longitudinal stability; their convex, rather than straight, stem enabled them to cut into the water more effectively; and a later hulk version with three masts had a more favourable rigging with easier-to-handle suits of sails. Further features included a forecastle and an aftercastle, and, by the 15th century, a load-carrying capacity of 300 metric tons or more. The vessels required a crew of 35 to 40. However, by the middle of the 15th century a newer and even larger type of ship emerged: The Atlantic caravel, which was of not only Atlantic but also Italian origin.

The special feature of the caravel was its innovative hull construction, created by planking laid edge to edge instead of overlapping. This gave the ship a smooth outer shell and thus greater speed. Other advantages included its enhanced watertightness, especially when several layers of planks were placed on top of each other, and its good tacking abilities due to the fact that keel and bottom were no longer flat in design. The new design, combined with an increase in size, which now exceeded a load-carrying capacity of 400 metric tons, also posed a series of drawbacks: There were problems with regard to drydocking; hauling vessels ashore was considerably more difficult and the increased draught, which had already been 3 metres on Hanseatic cogs, led to difficulties when entering many ports and, in particular, the upper reaches of rivers.

The result was the final separation of navigation into maritime and inland waterways. The caravel remained the main type of large merchant vessel until the beginning of the 17th century. Only then did the Dutch develop the next generation of ship — the flute — which simultaneously served to promote, in the Hanseatic League at least, the originally non-existing distinction between merchant vessels and warships. A further innovation was the consideration of tonnage criteria specifically designed to take account of the Sound Dues. The growing dominance of commercial considerations was additionally reflected not only in moves to increase load-carrying capacity and speed still further but also — for the first time for this type of vessel — in efforts to reduce sea transport costs by downsizing crew numbers.

As in the case of the infrastructure, technical progress must be considered in terms of both material technological developments and more intangible advances. Of quite particular importance here are new developments in the field of corporate management, business and transaction processing as well as finance and insurance. Even though Venice, when compared with Genoa and, above all, Florence, was clearly less creative in this respect, it was nevertheless during the Golden Age of Venice that, in the cities of Northern Italy, trading companies, double-entry bookkeeping, marine insurance, current accounts, cheques, bills of exchange and credit financing first saw the light of day.

Most notably on account of business contacts made via the "Kontors" in Bruges and London, Italian trade and financial innovations were also introduced into the Hanseatic League at the beginning of the 14th century. This particularly applied to the trading company and credit financing, but not to double-entry bookkeeping. Banking also remained completely underdeveloped in the Hanseatic League. An Italian did establish the first bank in Lübeck as early as 1410, and its initially positive development could have made Lübeck the financial capital of Northern Europe. Upon the death of its founder in 1449, however, the bank was simply closed down.

A similar fate befell the expansion of the bill of exchange and credit financing. After this type of financial transaction had gained broader acceptance chiefly in trade with Flanders and England, there was soon strong resistance to it from the less developed eastern regions of the Hanseatic League. This resulted in an assembly of the Hanseatic cities, held in Lübeck in 1401, banning credit-backed transactions with foreign merchants for three years. This decision against the modern age in business, as well as the consideration of the intangible infrastructure and intangible technical progress in general, takes us directly to the subject of economic policy, and this far beyond infrastructural and monetary policy.

Both during the heyday of Graecia Magna and during the Roman Empire, the positive effects of policymaking on economic development tended to be spin-off effects of government measures taken for non-economic reasons. Also, the end of these early globalisation experiences was, in principle, not brought about by economic policies but, in the case of Athens, by the Peloponnesian War and, in the case of Rome, by external forces on the one hand and, on the other, the unsuitability of traditional government structures for the sprawling empire.

The picture was a completely different one in the case of the rise and fall of Venice, as it was for the beginning and, in particular, the end of the Hanseatic League. In both cases, the impact of economic policy was quite decisive.

## Economic and Social Adaptability
## as Determinants
## for Lasting Success or Decline

In Venice and the Hanseatic League the dynamics of the globalisation process and the prosperity thus achieved were not just the result of the flexible exploitation of market niches but, to a considerable extent, the establishment and initially successful defence of monopolies and privileges. The Venetians, for example, made every possible effort to monopolise trade in the Eastern Mediterranean region; and trade and industry in Venice itself were subject to strict state regulations, primarily designed to deter competition from outside its territories.

German merchants, such as the Fuggers from Augsburg, always had to travel to Venice themselves, as Venetian merchants were not allowed to sell their goods directly to Germany thus by passing the *Fondaco dei Tedeschi*, a sales and storage facility specifically established for trade with German merchants. Venetian entrepreneurs were also banned from opening production sites in Flanders or England in order to take advantage of the far lower wages paid there. Production processes, too, were strictly controlled, meaning that it was impossible to offset the high Venetian labour costs through product and process innovation and rationalisation of production.

As a result of this interventionist and protectionist economic policy, Venetian industry fell farther and father behind its new industrial competitors in Western and Northern Europe. Similarly, the trade monopoly also came increasingly under threat owing to a shift in world trade towards the west following the circumnavigation of Africa and the discovery of America. Spices, silks and drugs from India and Asia could now also be sourced via Lisbon and Antwerp, causing Venice to lose a significant part of its traditional market.

The shift of world trade from the Mediterranean to the Atlantic also contributed to the long-term decline of the Hanseatic League. While a lack of adaptability and the impact of geographical circumstances on the quality of the location could be blamed for the decreasing relevance of Baltic Sea cities, in particular Lübeck, when compared to those of the North Sea ports, most notably Hamburg, this factor definitely cannot be cited with reference to two further Hanseatic cities, of which one, Bruges, became increasingly insignificant, and Antwerp, which experienced a meteoric rise during the same period.

The demise of Bruges was not primarily caused by the increasing silification of the Zwin but by the city's continued adherence to outdated corporative structures and the dogged defence of protectionist brokerage laws, staple right and customs laws. One result was that new investments tended to be made in the relatively liberal Antwerp. Secondly, even the well-established merchants, the majority of whom hailed from the Northern European Hanseatic cities as well as from Britain, Portugal, Spain and Italy, moved virtually en bloc to the increasingly cosmopolitan and dynamic city of Antwerp during the final two decades of the 15th century.

Venice, Lübeck and Bruges are fine examples of how corporatism within the context of globalisation is likely to usher in the process of decline. The same applies to state regulations, which limit the ability of economy and society to adapt to changing world economic conditions. Alexandria in the ancient world, Antwerp until the middle of the 16th century and Hamburg, up to the present day, serve as examples of a contrary approach.

# CHAPTER 2

# Hamburg's Road
# to Becoming
# a Major Hanseatic City

T he origins of Hamburg are, in every respect, shrouded in mystery and legend. Some sources claim that the site of the present-day city has been inhabited "since time immemorial". Other authors believe that settlement began during the Middle Stone Age, a theory that is substantiated by archaeological discoveries, such as ceramic shards and stone artefacts from the so-called Funnel Beaker Culture (approx. 4300 to 2800 BC). Between 1800 and 800 BC, i.e. when the Phoenicians were spearheading the first phase of globalisation in the Mediterranean, Germanic tribes are said to have begun arriving on the shores of the North and Baltic Sea. And it also claimed that, around 200 AD, Saxon settlements appeared north and south of the Lower Elbe. Nonetheless, nothing is known about specific settlement structures and, in particular, about whether the origins of Hamburg actually lie in this period. Europe was still split into two halves, with the border between the civilised south, founded on the art and culture of the Greeks and Romans, and the underdeveloped north, more or less equivalent to the former northern frontier of the Roman Empire.

# Speculation
## about Hammaburg

The topographic advantages of the area in which the first Saxon village and the later Hammaburg might have been established cannot be understated. It is located at the point where the ancient *pathway* along the glacial valley of the River Elbe afforded the easiest crossing of the Alster. Similarly, the historic *Ochsenweg*, a Northern European long-distance trade route that had probably existed since the Bronze Age, may well also have used this crossing point. Moreover, the location of the later Hammaburg was chosen because it was roughly the furthest point upriver at which the tides could be used for early shipping on the Lower Elbe. It was up to here that deep shipping channels for seagoing vessels extended. Over the years, the upper reaches of the Elbe also helped make the hinterland more accessible. It was not until modern times, however, that the Elbe islands facilitated a north-south and south-north crossing of the main river.

Nevertheless, the exact location of the early 9th century Hammaburg, which gave Hamburg its name, remains unknown up to the present day. All attempts to locate and identify the former site of the castle, together with the numerous and often very detailed descriptions of the castle complex must be classified as legends in the face of modern scientific research.

The most recent archaeological investigations, which took place between 2005 and 2007 at the site where the Hammaburg had previously been assumed to lie, discovered twin circular ditches dating to the period between 650 and 750 AD, i.e. before the Hammaburg was built. Archaeologists initially thought they had discovered the Hammaburg when an unusually large circular rampart was unearthed above the ditch. Yet the rampart has, in the light of the various phases of construction, since been dated to the late 9th and 10th century, putting it in the period after the Vikings destroyed the original castle in 845.

However, the fact that the Hammaburg actually did exist at the beginning of the 9th century is definitely not a myth. Documented evidence of the Hammaburg's existence dates from 832, when Emperor Louis the Pious instigated the establishment of the diocese of Hamburg by Pope Gregory IV. The determining factor for this decision was, from a political perspective, the improved defence of the northern frontier of the Kingdom of the Francs and, from a religious standpoint, the continued Christianisation of Scandinavia. The Benedictine monk Ansgar, who had converted the Danish King Harald to Christianity back in 826 and had expanded the footprint of his missionary work — often as companion to travelling merchants — as far north as Birka in Sweden, was first named Bishop and, one year later, Archbishop.

Initially, which means until the partition of the Empire in 843, the Gallic hermitage of Turholt in Western Flanders acted as the basis for economic and, in particular, financial support for the Archdiocese of Hammaburg. However, signs of the independent economic development of what was later to become Hamburg soon became apparent. This was reflected, on the one hand, in the growing number of craftsmen, tradesmen and fishermen settling to the west outside the castle walls and, on the other hand, in the fact that Louis the Pious granted immunity to the Archdiocese in 834 and, from 834 to 845, the right to mint and issue coins.

Incidentally, archaeological finds of Rhenish and Norwegian ceramics, Franconian weaponry, and the remains of corn point to the fact that the first harbour most probably already existed in the 9th century, from where overseas trade was being conducted even at that time.

The subsequent rise to become a major trade hub and Hanseatic city was anything but a continuous process. In 845 the Hammaburg was sacked and burnt down by the Vikings. Subsequent to this, Archbishop Ansgar, who was able to escape, and his successors in this office resided predominantly in Bremen, the Archdioceses of Hamburg and Bremen having been combined in 848. The circumstances prevailing in Hamburg were — quite rightly, as would later be proven — still considered extremely unsafe.

Three times, in 983, 1066 and 1072, Hamburg was attacked by the Slavs, being completely destroyed in each instance. Yet it was always rebuilt — though after 983 not, as would now appear, on the site where the original Hammaburg once stood. Among the other outstanding or noteworthy events which had since occurred were: Firstly, the documented right to hold markets, mint and issue coins and collect taxes instigated by Archbishop Adaldag (937 – 988) and granted by the Holy Roman Emperor Otto I; secondly, the banishment, by the very same emperor, of Pope Benedict V to Hamburg, then still located at the very edge of the civilised world, where he died one year after being elected Pope in 965; thirdly, the appointment of a permanent representative of the Holy Roman Emperor with permanent rights of residence in 966; and fourthly, in February 1164, a severe storm tide which destroyed a part of the new town and, in particular, the harbour.

The most significant of the four events for the long-term future of Hamburg was, without doubt, the appointment of a permanent secular representative of the Holy Roman Emperor, as this was the first step towards limiting episcopal authority. That this did not become effective immediately, but only during the second generation of the Emperor's appointed representative, confirms the beginning of a secular development which continued up until the 19th century. Even the physical face of the city was, from the middle of the 11th century onwards, shaped by the increasing rivalry between temporal and ecclesiastical power. When Archbishop Benzelin Alebrand had a stone tower dwelling built around 1035, this prompted the secular, Duke Bernhard II, to have himself built a castle tower, too, which, to distinguish it from the *Bischofsburg*, was later known as the *Alsterburg*.

As the rivalry between the men of the cloth and the Emperor's representatives escalated further, Duke Bernhard's son finally resolved to erect the *Neue Burg* outside the old town on the right-hand bank of the Alster. Nobody knows whether these castles, which were probably the first secular stone buildings to be erected in the North, actually survived the Slav attacks of 1066 and 1072. The claim that the three towers shown on Hamburg's coat of arms represent the *Bischofsburg*, the *Alsterburg* and the *Neue Burg* and, therefore, remain a symbol of Hamburg to this very day, as certain historians suggest, can, however, be disputed. In fact there are a number of other cities, such as Lüneburg, with three towers in their coats of arms.

## A Fresh Start
## in the Second Half of the 12th Century

The early history of Hamburg proves yet again that dynamic economic development without a peaceful political framework is barely conceivable. This is also true when considering that the craftsmen, tradesmen and fishermen apparently returned to Hamburg relatively quickly after each attack, and that each rebuilding effort was somehow more progressive than what had previously been destroyed. Just how positive an influence is to be gained from the pacification of the surrounding area is illustrated in vivid fashion during the next phase of Hamburg's history.

Just one year before the House of Billung, the first lineage of the temporal representatives in Hamburg, became extinct in 1106, the Saxons dealt a decisive defeat to the Slav tribes that had been so perilous for Hamburg. The resulting Christianisation of the Slavs was a major contribution to the pacification of the entire region. Furthermore, Duke Lothar of Saxony, the later Emperor Lothar III, awarded the House of Schauenburg stewardship of the counties of Holstein and Stormarn, including Hamburg. All this served to secure Hamburg not only some 80 years of peace but also several centuries of continuous economic prosperity, which was, however, occasionally disrupted by fire, pestilence and pirates.

Count Adolf I of Schauenburg gave orders for the *Alsterburg* to be extended. His son and successor, Adolf II, pacified East Holstein and

70

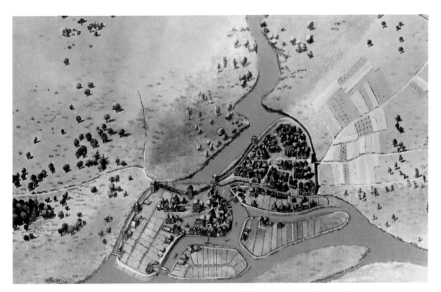

*Hamburg in 1217. The densely populated Old Town stands in clear contrast to the New Town, which was still under construction. The River Alster has not yet been dammed up. The construction of the second Mühlendamm, which led to the creation of the Alster Lake, dates from around 1235.*

pushed back the Slavs, causing Hamburg to no longer be viewed as an outpost permanently under threat. The result was, by the standards of the day, a considerable growth in population. Not only neighbouring Saxons and Friesians, who had already been working in Hamburg as merchants prior to this, but also Westphalians and Dutch decided to take up residence. It was Adolf III (1164–1203), who, in 1188, instigated the re-establishment of the new town and, with great foresight, promoted the development of the harbour. Particularly interesting in this context is that he drew on the services of what could be called a private entrepreneur.

The contractual agreement, which probably dates from 1186 or 1187, was worded as follows: "We hereby declare for all present and future generations that Wirad von Boizenburg has duly been awarded by us Hamburg Castle on the River Alster and the adjacent country to the middle of the River Alster for free settlement in accordance with

*The cog was the seagoing cargo vessel of the Hanseatic League between the 12th and 14th centuries. At this time the ship was already the most cost-effective solution for the long-distance transportation of bulk goods.*

market rights and title of inheritance, enabling him, together with the settlers that he takes there with him, to construct a harbour of sufficient magnitude to accommodate people converging from far and wide."

Boizenburg had the terrain in the Alster bend behind the dyke filled with sand and clay, subsequently allocating 80 construction plots on the new and flood-proof plateau to the settlers working together with him. The new harbour with a crane and weighing machine, which was now installed on the River Alster closer to the Elbe, can well be seen as a targeted infrastructure measure which, most notably, took into account the emergence of a new type of ship with a greater draught: the Hanse cog. If Adolf III can be imagined to have already believed back then that a city in which free rein is given to entrepreneurial forces actually develops more favourably in economic terms, thus potentially generating also higher tax revenues than one in which every single detail is controlled in dirigistic manner, then the economic upswing subsequently experienced by Hamburg is likely to have proved him right.

## Hamburg a Blind Spot
## in World Economic Development

At the beginning of the 12th century there were just two major regions in Europe that engaged in international trade and also exhibited clear globalisation tendencies. One was the Mediterranean and the other was the Baltic Sea. Additionally, four major tradefair circuits played an important role in the promotion of internal trade throughout Northwest Europe: the fairs of Champagne, Flanders, the Lower Rhine and England. Hamburg did not belong to any of these cross-border trading systems, and even the important long-distance trade routes of the period, which crossed the River Elbe from north to south, passed on the one hand through Bardowick, which boasted the last convenient ford before the sea, and, on the other, through Magdeburg, situated even further upriver, but not via Hamburg.

Hamburg, unlike Bremen, was initially not even involved in North Sea trade, which, as a result of the previously described colonisation activities of the Vikings, occurred not only between Flanders and England but also between England and Ireland and Scandinavia, in particular Norway. The same applied to trade between the North Sea regions and the Baltic. In order to avoid the dangerous journey around Jutland, goods were transported along the old Viking routes between Eider, Treene and Schlei, and finally transacted via Schleswig. Until the beginning of the 13th century, Hamburg was, to all intents and purposes, a blind spot on the map of economic development.

It was a privilege granted to the city in 1191 by the Saxon King Henry the Lion that first enabled Hamburg to engage in brisk trade directed towards the upper Elbe regions, most notably with Magdeburg. This also led to an upswing in trade to the west, i.e. to Friesland

and Holland, with the import of woollen cloth from Ghent figuring especially prominently. Nevertheless, Stade was still a more important trade centre than Hamburg. This situation did not change until trade between the Baltic region and the west and south began to be routed through the increasingly important city of Lübeck.


## Hamburg:
## *Lübeck's North Sea Port*

Lübeck, like Hamburg, had to be rebuilt several times after repeated ransacking and devastation and even had to be relocated to a new site, until the city — initially expanded to become a centre of international trade with a secure harbour under Counts Adolf II and Adolf III and Henry the Lion — came under the rule of the Danish King Waldemar II in 1201. Lübeck had established direct trade relations with Visby by the middle of the 12th century, yet it was not until settlers from Lübeck moved to Gotland to engage in direct trade with Russia, Sweden and Norway that they were able to break the Gotlanders' quasi-monopoly of trade in the Baltic region and also to undermine the leading position of Schleswig. This development was favoured by economic as well as political factors.

Decisive on the political front were the imperial ambitions of the Danish King Waldemar II. Not only did Lübeck enjoy greater protection under the rule of Waldemar II than almost ever before. Additionally, peace finally prevailed on the shipping routes of his Baltic Empire. Moreover, Waldemar II evidently pursued a policy of dividing up trade influence, resulting in the Scandinavians, in particular the Danes, controlling the north, and the merchants of Lübeck dominating the south and south-east. Even though Gotland trade was open and free to both, Lübeck gained such an advantage due to the extremely lucrative eastward trade — chiefly with Novgorod in the first instance and later also with Riga — that it gradually became the dominant trade hub in the Baltic region.

The reason why, over the longer term, Lübeck not only displaced Visby in this role, but also overtook Schleswig, is linked to the gradual shifting of trade routes between the North and Baltic Sea occurring during this time. During the reign of Henry the Lion the overland route to Lübeck via Bardowick had already become much safer and, above all, considerably shorter, most especially for merchants from Westphalia engaging in foreign trade. To the extent that it proved possible to make the land route between Hamburg and Lübeck safe, the same arguments applied to Lower Rhenish and Flemish merchants. The River Elbe provided, given the increasing use of Hanse cogs, waters navigable for oceangoing vessels all the way up to Hamburg; this was only partially the case when en-route to Schleswig via the Schlei inlet and the River Treene.

As a result not only Lower Rhenish and Dutch merchants but also those from Westphalia increasingly opted for the route along the River Elbe and ultimately via Hamburg. However, also the fact that ever greater quantities of trade were becoming geared towards bulk goods may have contributed to this development. Even at that time it was far cheaper to transport bulk goods by ship than it was by road. Trade in herrings from Scania and trade in grain from Russia are just two examples.

All of these factors combined to forge closer ties between Hamburg and Lübeck, the latter city having attained the status of imperial immediacy in 1227. In 1230 Hamburg and Lübeck which now had populations of about 4,000 and 8,000 respectively entered into an alliance granting citizens travelling between the two cities the same rights in each. Just a few years later, in 1241, Hamburg and Lübeck signed a further formal treaty to protect the land route between the two cities. This agreement focused on the joint provision of funds for protection against highwaymen and on common principles of punishment for such felons.

## 1266:
## *The Hanseatic City of Hamburg*

In principle the aforementioned bilateral agreements were concluded among equals. But there is no escaping the indisputable truth that the now accelerating ascent of Hamburg was, strictly speaking, based on the fact that it had become the North Sea port of what was then the more important city of Lübeck. For its part, Lübeck had not only become the most important trade centre in the Baltic region; Lübeck's merchants were also playing a prominent role in the foundation of towns along the southern coast of the Baltic Sea. Since many of the immigrants to the new towns, such as Rostock, Wismar or Stralsund, came not only from surrounding areas, such as Saxony or Scandinavia, but also from Friesland and the Netherlands, Hamburg also profited from these developments.

Until the second half of the 13th century, however, the attitude of Lübeck's merchants towards the new towns was ambivalent: They welcomed the benefits of the trade expansion while at the same time fearing the competition. As late as 1249, Stralsund was destroyed by a Lübeck fleet and relations between Lübeck and Rostock are said to have also been strained.

It was not until 1264 that Lübeck, Rostock and Wismar signed a mutual assistance pact, initially for one year, which was subsequently extended for an unlimited period and to include Stralsund, Greifswald and Stettin in 1265. Hamburg joined this league of towns in 1266, and it is herein that the roots of the North German Town Hanse clearly lie. The fact that Lübeck Law applied to all of the league's decisions once again underscores the leading role that Lübeck played at this time.

The rise of Hamburg was, however, not only a result of close cooperation with Lübeck. Internal developments also made a significant contribution to its remarkable success. As early as 1210, residents of the Old Town, which was inhabited mainly by craftsmen, and the

New Town, which represented the merchants and shipping, formed a common "Bürgerschaft" (city parliament). This was a major factor in the process by which the previously separate settlements increasingly became one. One advantage of this development not initially apparent was the emergence of a more differentiated economic structure than that in Lübeck, one in which not only trade and shipbuilding but also manufacturing played an important role.

The first city charter for Hamburg may have already been drawn up in around 1220, and most certainly by around 1270. It not only determined how the Council, today's Senate, was to be elected but also contained first steps towards the establishment of a system of marine and shipping law. The earliest surviving version of the Hamburg town charter originates from 1292. It was followed by an amended and extended version focusing specifically on maritime law in 1301. The preliminary highlight in the codification of Hamburg's system of law was marked by the illuminated manuscript of the Hamburg Code of Municipal Law dated 1497. Divided into 15 chapters covering special areas of law, including maritime law, this version constitutes one of the few systematic legal codes of the 15th century other than the *Sachsenspiegel*.

Another key event in Hamburg's development was that the Old Town — excluding the cathedral chapter, which, to all intents and purposes, remained exterritorial until 1803 — passed from the ecclesiastical rule of the Archbishopric of Bremen to the temporal control of Adolf IV of Schauenburg. From this period onwards the Old Town and the New Town also became one in legal terms. Like his predecessor Adolf III when building the New Town, Adolf IV also believed in the economic momentum of a community driven chiefly by the self-determination of the merchants and craftsmen.

Adolf IV had probably also not forgotten the generous assistance given him by Hamburg in his final victory over Waldemar II in the form of the provision of elite troops as well as 1,200 marks in silver. Be that as it may, he basically limited the exercise of his sovereign powers to jurisdiction, customs duties and the minting of coins. In 1325

Hamburg was even able to acquire the right to mint and issue coins from the Counts of Schauenburg, having paid for this in cash when the latter were facing financial crisis.

## The Wendish Monetary Union: A Common Northwest European Currency

In 1255 Lübeck and Hamburg intensified their relationship by concluding a further treaty which this time not only focussed on the mutual protection of trade routes but also included the common safeguarding of privileges and a monetary union. The new unit of currency — the *Lübeck mark* — was divided into four-pfennig units. The silver content of the coins was binding and effectively policed, resulting in both a simplification of trade and guaranteed monetary stability. For a prolonged period of time these two factors ensured, that this new and stable currency unit became the most widely used coinage in Northern Germany.

Established in 1379 the Wendish Monetary Union, as it later came to be known, included Hamburg and Lübeck as well as Wismar and Lüneburg, together with three other temporary Hanseatic League members. The significance of this monetary union is marked, amongst other things, by the fact that other towns between the rivers Weser and Oder as well as Denmark also used this common coinage — without officially joining the currency union. In the Wendish Monetary Union, which lasted until 1566, the rules governing minting and, in particular, assaying of the silver content were also extremely stringent. As a consequence the *Lübeck mark* represented a hard currency able to promote trade, the likes of which was, at the time, sought in vain in other parts of Europe.

As with the introduction of the Euro in 2002, which has led to a considerable reduction of transaction costs for internal European trade and travel, monetary unification in the Northern European Hanseatic region did not prove beneficial for all market players. The worst effects were felt by the Hamburg moneychangers, who conducted their business on the so-called "Exchange Bridge", which had connected the Old Town with the New Town since 1190. This business was predicated on the fact that, prior to the introduction of the *Lübeck mark*, such a plethora of coins of differing values had been in circulation in Hamburg that only currency experts were able to determine exchange rates and execute exchange business on this basis. As is also the case today, however, this did not mean that the days of the money exchangers were numbered. Even then, a wide range of gold coins not forming part of the monetary union were still in circulation.

A further lesson that, even back then in Hamburg, also had to be learned was the fact that even a hard currency does not necessarily guard against inflation. Food prices, which particularly affected the poor, had been rising for some time, sparking bloody unrest in 1483 and — for a brief period — even the formation of a rival government. The Council, in which chiefly wholesale merchants were represented, was accused of continuing to permit the export of grain in spite of rising prices, bread shortages and a lack of raw materials for local brewers rather than first taking steps to secure an appropriate level of supply for the people of Hamburg. It took the Senate two months to restore order. In response the Council was for a third time — following previous such moves in 1410 and 1458 after internal unrest — forced to give citizens a greater say in decision-making.

Furthermore, the new constitution also considered the possible introduction of restrictions on the export of grain as a new instrument of economic policy. Quite clearly such a measure is a further example of potential and difficult-to-resolve conflicts between free trade and the immediate and short term interests of local populations. In the light of increasing world market prices of commodities, including grain, it is precisely this conflict that is still a very topical one today. Countries such as China, India and Brazil have, after all, been significantly restricting, or even completely prohibiting, food exports since the beginning of 2008 in order to provide an affordable supply of staple foodstuffs at home. These examples, both past and present, once again point up the relevance of national and international distribution problems in the globalisation process.

## The Need for Safe and Free Shipping on the River Elbe

Free and safe shipping on the River Elbe and the provision of the essential infrastructure required by the shipping industry have always been of absolutely crucial importance to Hamburg. To improve navigational safety in the Elbe estuary the first tower was built on Neuwerk Island back in 1310, a structure which served both as a navigational aid and rescue station for ships in distress. The current stone tower, which replaced the original, partly wooden construction in 1377, is now Hamburg's oldest monument.

Further important infrastructural measures designed to secure and maintain Hamburg's competitiveness in international trade and implemented chiefly in the first half of the 15th century, included: Improved marking of the Elbe shipping channels, realised during the first half of that century by the positioning of buoys and landmarks; the construction of the Alster-Trave canal, finally completed in 1529, 100 years after an initially unsuccessful attempt; embanking of the Elbe marshes as well as a link connecting the Norderelbe to the harbour.

Another constant concern faced by Hamburg in addition to the provision of an appropriate infrastructure was to ensure that shipping on the River Elbe remained unimpeded. Not only did Hamburg sign treaties to this effect with countries bordering the river or, whenever necessary—as with the occupation of Emden—use military intervention; it also displayed great skill when enforcing its claims by political or legal means, yet not always in conformity with the actions of an "honourable merchant".

When, in 1259, the Archbishop of Bremen ordered that all ships travelling up the River Elbe had to anchor off Stade for three tides for

*The Neuwerk lighthouse was erected between 1299 and 1310 as a navigation mark, coastguard station and defence tower. From 1648 onwards a fire was lit at night. Since 1814 it has been used as permanent navigational light and to-day still shows ships the way into Germany's largest port.*

customs inspection and the collection of duties, Hamburg referred to a charter granted by Emperor Frederick I Barbarossa on 7 May 1189, which purportedly ensured the city the free transport of people and goods on the Lower Elbe. Even though Hamburg has, for many years now, been celebrating the anniversary of its harbour on 7 May, it is not certain whether this charter really existed or not. Whatever the case, the counterfeit document produced — for want of an original — in the middle of the 13th century was so perfect that it served its purpose vis-à-vis the Church in Bremen. As a result ships belonging to Hamburg merchants were generally exempted from the Stade Elbe duty, which was levied until 1861.

Similarly successful manipulation was engaged in by Hamburg in 1567 before the Imperial Court. In this particular case Hamburg was defending its staple right and its sovereign power over the River Elbe against Harburg, Lüneburg, Buxtehude and, once again, Stade. The decisive evidence was a twelve-metre-long map of the river that displayed all the channel markings erected by Hamburg, together with further relevant details, from Geesthacht located upriver to the mouth of the Elbe. The fact that this otherwise very accurate cartographical document, which was not actually finished until 1568, also contained some discreet but significant corrections in Hamburg's favour should be mentioned only as a brief aside. The exceptionally high fee paid to the cartographer Melchior Lorichs of 850 marks — almost equal to the annual stipend of the highest-paid Hamburg syndic, or seventy times the yearly income of a craftsman — was, with hindsight, therefore more than justified in economic terms.

## The Permanent Battle against Privateers and Pirates

Securing the freedom and safety of trade routes, as well as the preservation and extension of privileges, was a permanent concern not only of Hamburg but of the entire Hanseatic League. This was reflected, inter alia, in the various blockades imposed by the Hanseatic League and the two punitive expeditions against the King of Denmark in 1362 and 1368. To the great vexation of the other Hanseatic cities Hamburg did not actively take part in the second intervention, preferring to pay its share of the costs after the event. The general reason for this circumstance might be that, when in doubt, Hamburg always gave its own political and economic interests priority over those of the Hanseatic League.

Although Hamburg always sought — generally successfully — to resolve problems by contributing cash rather than taking up arms, it was, during the latter years of the 14th century, left with no other choice than to use force when dealing with a further problem. Since 1394, the scourge of privateering and piracy in the North Sea and the Elbe estuary had been getting out of hand to such an extent that trade with Flanders and England was increasingly being disrupted.

*The Charter of Emperor Frederick I Barbarossa. The only authentic specimen is a counterfeit from about 1265. It carries the date of 7 May 1189 and the seal of Emperor Frederick II, a grandson of Frederick Barbarossa, who was, however, not born until 1194. The counterfeit nevertheless fulfilled its purpose at that time, and is still the reason for the world's largest port festival, the 'Hamburg Harbour Birthday Festival'.*

To see off legal action on this exacerbating situation, which was to be brought by Henry IV of England in 1405, the assembly of Hanseatic cities held in Lübeck in 1399 decided to take radical measures against the pirates.

In the years immediately following this, and under the leadership of Hamburg, Klaus Störtebeker's squadron of ships was first sunk near Helgoland and this was followed by victory over the Gödicke Michels fleet. However, the end of piracy in the North Sea did not come until 1528. Although Hamburg's mayor Simon von Utrecht occupied Emden, which had given shelter to pirates, placing it under Hamburg's rule in 1433, it was a further ninety years until Hamburg councillor Ditmar Koel, the commander of the Hamburg flagship, managed to apprehend the pirate and former Danish admiral Klaus Knipphoff who — like Klaus Störtebeker and Gödicke Michels — was executed in Hamburg after looting no less than 172 vessels.

## Hamburg:
### The European Beer Capital

Due to its nutritional value, beer was considered almost a staple food in the Middle Ages, having accounted for roughly eight percent of the daily diet in terms of calorie intake. Beer brewing for home consumption was initially a part of domestic life and widespread throughout Northern Europe. However, this beer, known as "gruit ale", could neither be stored nor transported. It was not until hops were added to ale as a flavouring, while also acting as a preservative, that beer became a tradable commodity — at first to meet local and regional demand but, from the 13th century onwards, also for trade farther afield.

The leading beer producing cities in the Hanseatic Baltic region were Lübeck, Wismar, Rostock and Gdansk, although Lübeck soon lost to Wismar its dominant position as the chief beer exporter to Scandinavia. Bremen and Hamburg were the largest producers in the North Sea region. In the 13th century, Bremen was the leading beer

*"Wappen von Hamburg I". One of the two Hamburg convoy ships which were used in the late 17th century to protect merchant vessels against pirates on routes to Portugal, Spain and West Africa and to accompany whalers to Greenland.*

exporter, most particularly to Friesland and the Netherlands. By the 14th century, it had been pushed into second place by Hamburg, which in fact managed to maintain this strong position until the middle of the 17th century.

With the exception of Einbeck, all the cities involved in the long-distance beer trade were also seaports. As with herrings from Scania or grain from Russia, beer was, in a sense, a mass-market commodity, for the transport of which, even back then, shipping was the cheapest option. At that time, overland transport for a distance of just 100 kilometres would have increased the beer price by 50 to 70 percent. Low transport costs were, however, an essential, but by no means sufficient, prerequisite to being a successful beer exporter. Since domestic beers were available throughout Northwestern Europe, it was important that export beer, which was more expensive due to the transportation costs, was of a higher quality.

As export beer was not only more expensive but also more scarce it was considered a luxury product that served to satisfy prestige consumption needs. In 1320, for instance, export beer from Hamburg accounted for 30 percent of the beer drunk at the court of Countess Johanna in Den Haag but for less than 10 percent of overall beer consumed in the Netherlands. Bremen had obviously not yet realized that competition in the luxury goods market is driven not primarily through price but a product's image and quality. Insufficient supervision of the brewing industry facilitated attempts to cut production costs by, in part, replacing barley with oats and lowering the hop content, which caused the quality of Bremen beers to deteriorate in terms of both flavour and shelf life. As a result Bremen lost its traditional Dutch market to Hamburg and was never able to regain it.

Yet a favourable location and consistently high product quality are just two prerequisites for long term success in international trade. Another important criterion is sufficient delivery capacity. In this respect, too, the development of Hamburg was quite remarkable. The transition from domestic to commercial production had been in progress since the 13th century. The right to brew beer was linked to property ownership. As a result the brewing trade was not organised in guilds, allowing even wholesale merchants to run breweries with salaried employees as a source of additional income. Both factors served to assure greater flexibility in terms of output as it was less important for the business to be permanently working at full capacity.

In 1374 there were 457 brewhouses in Hamburg, 127 of which sold their products in Amsterdam and 55 of which exported their beer to Staveren in West Friesland. By 1517 the number of Hamburg breweries had risen to 531. Annual production, which was approximately 217,400 hectolitres in 1369, rose to around 300,000 hectolitres despite increasing competition from Dutch brewers. Not withstanding this, output is said to have peaked at up to 700,000 hectolitres during the heyday of the Hamburg brewing industry at the beginning of the 16th century.

Approximately 80 percent of Hamburg's beer production was sold outside Hamburg and roughly 70 percent was exported. The main markets were Amsterdam, Staveren and Sluis in Flanders, where Hamburg had special trading offices. Moreover, beer from Hamburg was also drunk in England and Prussia as well as in Russia, Spain and Portugal. Just how important beer exports were for Hamburg's foreign trade is reflected in the fact that, for a long period of time, beer accounted for around one third of all of Hamburg's exports. Against this background it is particularly remarkable that Hamburg, for its part, continued to permit the import of foreign beers, for example from Einbeck, despite the fact that, due to protectionist measures imposed in its existing markets, its own brewing trade increasingly found itself on a downward spiral by the end of the 16th century.

## Advantages
## of a Diversified Economic Structure

Unlike Lübeck, which owed its wealth almost exclusively to long-distance trade and was therefore — if one disregards locally relevant trades and crafts — purely a merchant town, Hamburg was characterised by more multifaceted and, in a sense, complex economic and social structures. This would prove especially beneficial during the decline of the Hanseatic League. Given the importance of Hamburg's beer production the brewing industry supply sectors are deserving of special mention. In addition to suppliers of hops and barley these also included coopers.

The relevance of coopers however, extended far beyond the brewing industry. After all, the barrel was, in addition to the box, the mediaeval equivalent of the modern-day shipping container. It was used to transport not only food and beverages but many other products, too. In 1376 there were 104 master coopers in Hamburg, a figure that probably rose to 200 by 1437, before subsequently falling back to 120. Cooperage products thus became an important export item in their own right. Barrels from Hamburg were traded in Bruges around 1450, and in the 16th century barrel staves were even being exported as far afield as Spain.

A further Hamburg industry which met not only the city's own needs was the milling industry. The first flour mill in Hamburg was built together with a dam at the old ford near the New Town during the final decade of the 12th century. A significant growth in the population meant further mills were already required by 1235. This resulted in the construction of a new mill dam and the Alster reservoir, which subsequently provided the hydropower for not only flour mills but also the textile and metalworking industries. At that time, however, only the flour mills were of any major importance for international trade. Favoured by the crop staple right, which required all ships transporting grain down the Elbe to unload their goods at the port and first offer them for sale in Hamburg, not only grain but, later, also flour became an export product shipped to Flanders and the Netherlands.

In spite of this transit trade was by no means a mere second-string business in Hamburg. The focus in this sector was on trade in textiles and cereal crops. Westphalian linen was exported to Flanders, Holland, England and Scandinavia. Cloth, produced primarily in Flanders using English wool, was marketed locally as well as throughout the Baltic region, partly via Lübeck. The majority of the grain from the hinterland was transported on barges along the Upper Elbe and, if not used for producing bread, beer or flour in Hamburg itself, subsequently shipped from Hamburg to Iceland, Norway, England, Flanders and the Netherlands.

## The Costs of Protectionism

It seems astonishing that Hamburg, a major North Sea port, did not have any shipbuilding activity to speak of at this time. This may have been partly due to the circumstances naturally obtaining in the city's location and partly a result of the city's economic policy. On the one hand, Hamburg had only a few suitable shipbuilding sites and those available close to the water were at constant risk of silting up. Furthermore, Baltic Sea ports particularly active in the shipbuilding industry—Gdansk, say—had much better, and cheaper, access to shipbuilding timber. Additionally, shipbuilding was highly regulated by both the city's Council and the Hanseatic League. A restriction on the sale of ships to non League members passed by the Hanseatic League in 1426 had a particularly negative effect on the long term development of Hanseatic and Hamburg shipyards.

Matters were made even worse for Hamburg following a Council resolution in 1514 stating that the building of a ship required the prior permission of the city authorities and prohibiting the building of any vessels suitable for waters greater than those in Hamburg. It was also stated that foreigners in the city were not allowed to participate in the shipbuilding industry without the Council's express permission. All of these measures, as well as a series of additional regulations imposed by city authorities with regard to employment, production methods and the purchasing of raw materials were, in principle, intended to protect Hanseatic and Hamburg shipbuilders from their competitors. In reality, however, they boosted growth in shipbuilding abroad, most notably in the Netherlands and England, and hampered the development of the industry in Hamburg up until the 19th century.

Shipbuilding was not the only sector whose long term development was obstructed by protectionist measures. After smaller merchants, the grocers, had joined forces to represent their interests as early as the 13th century so-called "trade offices", elsewhere called guilds and crafts, were established around the middle of the 14th century. Even if

89

these institutions did, to a certain extent, contribute to the development of standardised trade practices and thus provide a reliable basis for business their main objective was quite manifestly that of using restrictive conditions to limit market access to a variety of craft industries and to curb competition. When, in 1375, an organized uprising by craftsmen demanded that the Council reduce taxes by 50 percent the "trade offices" gained political significance for the very first time.

As long as economic, social and technological change remained relatively slow in the sectors thus regulated and new activities were able to establish themselves outside the preset structures of the "offices", the overall economic cost of these highly protectionist institutions could be contained. Nonetheless, the increase in the level of "non-unionised" labour by unorganised groups of people offering their services at far cheaper rates and the brutal action taken by the "trade offices" against these illegal workers, so-called *Böhnhasen* ("hares to be hunted"), on whose head, to all intents and purposes, a bounty was placed, sent out an unambiguous message. This quite clearly demonstrates that the focus of all efforts was on the protection of excessive pricing levels and the greater returns to be gained from restrictions on competition.

## Hamburg Thrives – Lübeck Stagnates

As previously outlined, a shift in international trade from the Mediterranean to the Atlantic can, over the longer term, be considered an important factor in the downfall of the Hanseatic League. It should, however, not be overlooked that the gradual decline in importance of this association commenced far earlier due to the power ambitions of regional sovereigns and the divergent interests of the various members of the Hanseatic League. The very fact that Hamburg exercised extreme restraint in the second punitive expedition against the Danish King in 1368 cannot, in all likelihood, be explained solely with the argument that, in the long term, it was important for Hamburg to adopt as neutral a stance as possible towards Denmark. In the short term, there can be no doubt that, to a certain degree, Hamburg even profited from the closing of the Sound.

From the middle of the 15th century onwards Hamburg pursued its own interests even more unashamedly, which clearly conflicted with the traditional customs of the Hanseatic League. Hamburg, together with Bremen, initially got the Norwegian King to grant them the right to sail to Iceland direct, thus bypassing the Hanseatic "Kontor" in Bergen. Later, in 1566, Hamburg granted—in open contravention of common Hanseatic principles—virtually full settlement rights to the English *Merchant Adventurers* who had been expelled from Antwerp by the Spanish—a step that, in highly effective manner, helped to integrate Hamburg into the booming European cloth trade.

Also quite remarkable is the fact that, despite the close political and economic relations between Hamburg and Lübeck, there were only rarely any close personal ties. Very few merchants from Lübeck were successful in Hamburg, with the same applying to Hamburg merchants in Lübeck, and family ties also tended to be the exception. Both cities were, however, quite open to the influx of foreigners and to external family ties—yet in very different ways. Hamburg allowed Frisian, Dutch, Flemish, French, Portuguese and English nationals to live inside its city walls and the City Council considered it important that these immigrants stimulated business. Despite the explicit restrictions specified in the 1603 treaty it was in many instances irrelevant whether they were Catholics, Lutherans, Calvinists or Jews. As early as 1619 Rudolf Amsinck, who was of Dutch descent, was elected to the Council.

Lübeck showed little flexibility when it came to religious beliefs and remained under the conservative influence of the Catholic church for much longer than Hamburg and a number of other Hanseatic cities. The division between the patrician upper class, which represented the Council, and the city's "normal" citizens was much stronger than in Hamburg—in part, no doubt, because Lübeck's economic and social structure was less complex than Hamburg's, yet shaped more by entrenched traditions. Any foreigners settling in the city or marrying into Lübeck families were, for the most part, merchants involved in long-distance trade, which further strengthened the economic monostructure. Relations between Lübeck and Nuremberg figured especially prominently in this respect.

Furthermore, Lübeck continued to defend its staple right and insisted on strict adherence to the Hanseatic laws governing the rights of guests to the city. This meant that a foreigner was not allowed to conduct business with another foreigner within the city or to establish a joint business with local residents, a provision that applied not only to trading activities but also chandlers supplying services and provisions to the shipping industry. Accordingly there was little incentive for non-Hanseatics to settle in Lübeck. In Hamburg, by contrast, it is reported that a ship from Brazil owned by three Hamburgers, two Dutch and one Portuguese entered the city's port as early as in 1590.

# PART II

# Globalisation
# in the Early Colonial Era:
# Increasing Exploitation
# of the Periphery
# by the Centre

*The largest of the three ships with which Columbus sailed to America in 1492 was approximately 25 metres long. The flagship of Admiral Zheng Hé, who commanded the Chinese State Fleet of more than 300 ships on seven voyages to India, the Persian Gulf and East Africa between 1403 and 1433 supposedly had nine masts and a length of roughly 100 metres. How different the history of the world might have been if China had used the sea power it then had in a hegemonic manner as Spain and Portugal, or, later, Holland and England did.*

CHAPTER 3

# From Portuguese Naval Supremacy to Dutch Dominance of the Global Economy

The globalisation process took on an entirely new dimension in the wake of the 15th and 16th century voyages of discovery. This development commenced around 1434 with the Portuguese voyages of exploration along the west coast of Africa. It continued with the circumnavigation of the Cape of Good Hope by Bartolomeu Diaz in 1487 and the first Atlantic crossing by Christopher Columbus in 1492. Some five years later Vasco da Gama crowned the sustained efforts of the Portuguese to reach India by taking the southeast route around Africa. In 1520 Ferdinand Magellan, together with Juan Sebastián Elcano, sailed around the southern tip of Latin America and crossed the Pacific to the Philippines. And it was Elcano who, in 1522, completed the first-ever circumnavigation of the globe. From then onwards globalisation became a process which, due to far-reaching global political, economic and social interdependencies, increasingly encompassed the entire world.

## European Expansion
## Overseas

After the Portuguese explorer Pedro Álvares Cabral had already landed—most probably by chance—in Brazil in 1500 the Portuguese
subsequently occupied Mozambique in 1507, Goa in 1510, Malacca
in 1511 and Macau in 1557. In the period after 1544 Portuguese ships
regularly sailed even as far as Japan. As was the case in China, however, Portuguese expansion clearly ran up against its limits in Japan.
Yet the Portuguese faced difficulties that were not only political in
nature. As the intra-Asian trade in which they engaged increased
rapidly, ultimately exceeding their volume of trade with Europe, conflicts with the native Islamic merchants escalated. This was especially
the case in India and Ceylon.

Between 1493 and 1504 the Spanish dispatched Columbus westwards across the Atlantic a further three times, in the course of which
travels he discovered, in addition to the Bahamas and Cuba, Trinidad,
Venezuela, Honduras and Nicaragua. The Florentine explorer Ame-
rigo Vespucci, working out of Seville in the service of the Medici family, also sailed across the Atlantic, first under the Spanish and later
under the Portuguese flag.

The Portuguese and Spanish voyages of discovery differed not only
in terms of geographical orientation but also—quite apart from their
role in the spreading of Christianity—also in terms of political and
economic objectives. The Portuguese were, first and foremost, seeking
to control trade. From the very beginning the objective of the Spanish was to conquer and colonise: From 1492 onwards in the Caribbean
and subsequently focusing, after 1520, on Mexico and then Peru and,
from 1570, the Philippines.

Yet this was only the beginning. Once the Portuguese and Spanish
had first succeeded in securing the southern routes primarily for
their own interests, leaving the British, Dutch and French to search
for a sea route to India via a northwest or northeast passage, the Iber-

ian monopoly of southern routes increasingly came under greater pressure at the beginning of the 17th century. The Dutch, in particular, were able to break the trade monopoly in Asia, which was controlled and protected by the Portuguese via a network of bases and patrolling warships. Dutch vessels not only refused to call at Portuguese-controlled ports and to pay the customs and other duties levied there; with the help of the United East India Company (Verenigde Oostindische Compagnie), established in 1602, they set up their own bases — predominantly in Indonesia — before subsequently occupying Formosa, Ceylon and Malacca and blocking Goa.

By 1640 the spice and cinnamon monopoly had clearly passed to the Dutch and, from 1663, Portugal finally also ceded its naval supremacy. Yet Dutch supremacy, too, soon began to be questioned. After the Dutch initially succeeded in keeping the ambitions of other European powers in the Asian-Pacific region in check, forcing the British towards India, the monopolistic policy of the United East India Company, primarily focused on spices, became increasingly inefficient. The spice trade, in which the market share of the Dutch was initially around double that of the British, was stagnating. As a consequence of the United East India Company the influence was already progressively waning by the end of the 17th century. The new growth markets were at first in cotton and cloth and later also tea and coffee, areas in which — with the exception of coffee — the English were clearly dominant.

## The Conquest and Colonisation of America

Unlike in the case of European expansion in the Indian and the Pacific Oceans, which essentially remained a "trade project" until the middle of the 18th century, the colonisation of America had been a "conquest project" from its very inception. This applies to both early Spanish colonisation of the Caribbean islands and Latin America as well as to increased Portuguese activity in Brazil once the protection of its spice monopoly in the Indian Ocean had become too expensive.

Spain's main economic interest in its American colonies was to generate sufficient wealth for the Spanish King to finance his European power aspirations, with mining royalties, the mercury monopoly, salt royalties and the tobacco monopoly having helped to achieve these aims. The most important import by far in this respect was silver, even though very little of it remained in Spain. As the silver was primarily used by the king to finance his war loans most of it went to Genoa and Amsterdam. It was then used — inter alia — by these financial capitals of the day to offset the balance of payments deficits of countries which showed a foreign trade gap due to rising imports from India and East Asia. The result was a global payment system based on silver.

During the first phase of colonisation Portugal's economic interest in Brazil focused almost entirely on dyewood exploration and sugar production. Following the discovery of ever more gold deposits in the south of the country and history's first-ever *gold rush* at the turn of the 18th century this situation changed quite fundamentally. In similar manner to Spain before it with regard to silver, Portugal urgently needed these gold imports to counterbalance its mostly structural balance of payments shortfalls. One of the principal reasons for this situation was the Methuen Treaty concluded with England in 1703, regulating — in accordance with Ricardo's theory of comparative advantage — the relatively free import of English cloths to Portugal in return for the similar treatment of port in England. Quite obviously the agreement failed to take account of the fact that cloth has a greater income elasticity than port.

In addition to intercontinental trade and overseas mining the development of Caribbean and American plantations was probably the most important economic trend for the globalisation process in the 17th century. Alongside the cultivation and processing of tobacco the main emphasis was on the production and export of sugarcane. Promoted by the Portuguese and the Dutch in Brazil, this industry

*Torre de Belém. The lighthouse and watchtower at the mouth of the River Tejo, completed in 1521. It is still the landmark of Lisbon and marks Portugal's emergence as the major naval power of the 16th century.*

was initially transferred to the Dutch Antilles, from where it spread throughout the Caribbean to the coastal regions of Spanish America and the southern parts of what later became the United States of America.

The development of plantations, which subsequently expanded beyond sugar to include various other overseas agricultural products, acted in many respects as a quantum leap in innovation within the framework of the globalisation process. Unlike in the case of trade with India and East Asia this led to the establishment of entirely new, dominant and export-intensive production sectors. Furthermore, the American and West Indian plantation economy constituted the first highly-efficient large-scale production of goods prior to the Industrial Revolution. From the point of view of the overseas colonies production and export ultimately brought about their integration into the system of the international division of labour, which — most particulary due to the capital-intensive direct investments this required — reached far beyond simple trading relations.

## Global Economic Aspects
## of the Slave Trade

Another key aspect of this development, which affected not only the plantation but also the mining industry, was the massive use of slave labour — at first indigenous Indios and subsequently huge numbers of blacks from Guinea, Angola and other regions in Africa. It is estimated that roughly twelve million slaves were shipped across the Atlantic to North America, of which, however, due to losses in transit fewer than ten million actually reached their destination alive. Just as an aside, the majority of Brazil's population in 1818 was of African descent and the American Bureau of Census put the value of the four million slaves in America before the outbreak of the American Civil War at 1.5 billion dollars.

In Athens, Rome or Venice or even in 15th century Spain and Portugal slaves were still generally used to carry out household tasks or to work on the land in predominantly small-scale agriculture. Only after the potential of the indigenous Americans had been largely exploited by the Spanish and the Portuguese and, most notably, after the loss of the Spanish monopoly in the West Indies and the demise of Portuguese supremacy in West Africa, did the slave trade really become a major global business. By the 17th and 18th century slaves had, in other words, become the world economy's most important energy raw material.

Not only were slaves shown on the balance sheets of mines and plantations, as current capital alongside material capital and written off in accordance with their diminished service life. Slave prices followed — like the price of crude oil today — short term business trends in the global economy, a fact reflected both during the Brazilian gold rush as well as the West Indian and American tobacco boom. Over the longer term prices for slaves rose permanently as supply was unable to meet the disproportionately growing demand, while the prices of European manufactured goods and of colonial commodities, especially tobacco and sugar, exhibited a downward tendency.

Considered in an economic and social perspective three implications of this development need to be pointed out: Firstly, it boosted the trend towards large-scale agricultural enterprises in the colonies. Secondly, it caused the terms of trade of the slave-exporting nations vis-à-vis the colonial powers to improve in the same way as those of the oil-exporting nations have improved vis-à-vis the industrial powers since the middle of the 20th century. And, thirdly, the development contributed to the increasing decline in the economic importance of slavery over the longer term. This was one of several economic reasons which, in addition to humanitarian considerations, led to the abolition of slavery — in Europe and the United States at least — in the early 19th century.

Of decisive importance in the context of globalisation were not only the evolution towards international commodity markets but, equally, the increasing multilateralisation of trade. In so called "triangular trade", for example, manufactured products, in particular textiles, metal goods, rifles and liquor, were transported from Europe to Africa and African slaves were then carried to the Americas, with silver, gold and diamonds as well as tobacco, sugar and other colonial goods subsequently being shipped to Europe. By no means, however, should this triangular trade be equated with free trade. Trade and shipping were still strictly regulated. Trade between the colonies and the mother country was basically bilateral in character and even the triangular trade from Portugal to Guinea via Brazil and back to Portugal was effected almost exclusively by Portuguese vessels.

Available estimates suggest that the number of African slaves shipped to Brazil by the Portuguese alone amounted to 100,000 in the 16th century, 600,000 in the 17th century, 1.3 million during the mining boom in the 18th century and a further 1.6 million as a result of the coffee boom in the 19th century. Under the agreed terms of the Treaty of Alcáçovas, signed in 1479, Portugal had also secured from Spain a monopoly over African trade and hence also the slave trade. As a consequence demand for slaves in the Spanish colonies was, in the first instance, met by Portuguese slave ships.

## Rising Tensions
## between Portugal and Holland

As had previously occurred in the Indian Ocean and the Pacific Portuguese supremacy in both transatlantic trade and with regard to the colonisation of Brazil was again being increasingly challenged by the Dutch. Not only did the Dutch undermine the Portuguese slave trade monopoly, they also looted Bahia as early as in 1604 and captured the then capital of Brazil, the later San Salvador, in 1624. By 1635 they controlled approximately 60 towns along the Brazilian coast — especially those which were the closest to Europe. In 1636 and 1637, finally, the Portuguese also lost several bases in Africa, and it initially appeared as if the Dutch were going to be as successful with the Dutch West India Company (WIC), founded in 1621, as they had been with the United East India Company in Asia.

Yet appearances can be deceptive. After a long-drawn-out and intense conflict with the remaining Portuguese forces in Brazil blatant errors in Holland's colonial policy, which was primarily geared to trade and proved to be inappropriate in Brazil, and the liberation of Portugal from Spanish rule in Europe resulted in a peace treaty arranged by King Charles II of England and signed in 1661, putting an end to the Dutch adventure in Brazil. As a result Brazil remained under Portuguese colonial rule. Nevertheless, Portugal had to allow Dutch ships to use its colonial ports in the Americas, to acknowledge its territorial losses in Asia and pay considerable war debts. The Dutch West India Company retained Curaçao and its trading rights along the coast of Guinea. As a consequence it specialised in trade between Europe and West Africa and the slave trade to America, a market which the English and French had, however, also since entered.

Despite the failure of the Dutch West India Company, which had to be rescued in 1667 and 1674 yet was finally declared bankrupt after all in 1691, the Dutch had been advancing to become the world leader in international maritime transportation since the middle of the 16th century. After having been granted the right of free passage through the Sound by the Danish King in 1544 they controlled roughly 70 percent of the transport of bulk goods from the Baltic region to the North Sea. Copper and iron from Sweden, grain from the Baltic states as well as shipbuilding timber, predominantly from Sweden and Finland, made up the main part of the freight heading south. In addition to salt, oil and wine, cargo moving in the opposite direction included, first and foremost, silver from Spain and gold from Portugal.

When Iberian agriculture was hit by a serious crisis in the second half of the 16th century and Spain, Portugal and even Genoa became dependent on grain supplied by Amsterdam, the Dutch finally also became the leader of sea shipment in the European Atlantic and Western Mediterranean, commanding a market share of more than 80 percent. And, from here, it was only a small step to call also at Mediterranean ports farther east in order to secure — here too — a larger slice of trade with Constantinople and the Levant.

## Holland's Rise
## to Maritime and Economic Superpower

Of decisive importance for the ascendancy of the Dutch was not only their aggressive trade policy but also the fact that they were, with the help of the Upper German trading houses, in particular the Fuggers, able to squeeze the Venetians out of the lucrative spice trade even during Portugal's heyday and to take control of the European market via Antwerp. For a period of several decades prices and terms in the spice trade, most especially those for pepper, were set in Antwerp. Furthermore, as early as 1568, the Dutch replaced Genoa, as the leading player in the financing of Spain's West Indian trade. The bankers and merchants of Genoa, Europe's financial capital from 1557 to 1627, preferred to concentrate their activities on the then profitable business of extending loans to the Spanish King.

Additionally the Dutch profited from the American-West Indian sugar boom, not only by carrying out roughly two thirds of all transports between 1609 and 1621 but also by making Holland the centre of the European sugar industry. Portugal had decided in favour of Brazil, having all locally grown sugarcane refined in the country of origin. As a result Brazil became, between 1580 and 1680, not only the most important growing region but also, with 350 sugar mills and a total annual capacity of 20,000 tonnes, by around 1629 the world's largest producer and exporter. This role had been increasingly undermined by the Dutch since the first decade of the 17th century. Not only had the focus of the sugar industry shifted to the West Indies, where, besides Dutch traders, and at the expense of the Spanish, the English and French had entered the market. Furthermore, it had been discovered that moisture had a harmful effect on sugar during sea transport and it appeared more expedient to move processing to the countries of consumption. This offered the Dutch another market niche, which they seized upon without further ado.

The supremacy of the Dutch in the global freight markets was further assisted by their maritime capabilities. Their ships, in particular the flyts, were faster, better equipped and therefore safer and more cost-effective than all other ships, all of which implied higher capacity utilization, lower insurance premiums and cheaper freight rates. With the exception of the English virtually every other European nation had become dependent on the Dutch. This applied not only to Spain and Portugal, which were forced to leave the greater part of the maritime transport for the Iberian peninsula to their enemy, namely the Dutch, even during their armed conflicts but in particular also to France. Despite Jean-Baptiste Colbert's great efforts under Louis XIV to secure France a prominent position among the leading maritime powers it was the Dutch who controlled trade along the French Atlantic coast up until the second half of the 18th century. As late as 1756 all 273 ships sailing from Bordeaux to Amsterdam flew the Dutch flag.

## The Geopolitical Ambitions of France

France, too, did not remain completely idle as the process of European expansion advanced. Back in 1535 Jacques Cartier had already sailed around Newfoundland and established a settlement in the St Laurence Bay. Yet it took well over 70 years for Québec and Montréal to be founded, in 1608 and 1642 respectively. The French reached the Mississippi in 1680, gained a foothold in St Louis in 1682, subsequently took possession of Louisiana and founded the city of New Orleans in 1718. In the Caribbean French activity was basically limited to Guadeloupe and Martinique, which they occupied around 1635. In 1643 they began to colonise Cayenne, modern-day French Guiana, which was repeatedly seized from them by the Dutch between 1654 and 1676. The colonisation of certain regions in India commenced around 1673. La Réunion and Mauritius were occupied in 1640 and 1745 respectively, and in the 1870s, finally, the French expelled the Dutch from Senegal.

France's early colonial policy under Henry IV of France and Cardinal Richelieu was, like that of the Spanish and Portuguese, primarily pursued for the glory of God and the King—a motivation never shared by the Protestant Dutch and English, for whom missionary work was, in case of doubt, a cost factor. Not until 1633, under Colbert, did France's strategy change, with politico-strategic ambitions and economic objectives then coming to the fore. France, too, had finally realised that a country with aspirations of becoming a world power needed to have its own merchant fleet and naval force and that colonies and trade in colonial goods would be of major importance within the framework of power rivalries in Europe. As was later to be proven, however, it was easier to formulate objectives than to implement them out on the ground.

The difficulties and resistance France faced were of both an internal and external character. When Colbert wished to establish a French colonial company, the Compagnie française du Nord, modelled on the example of the Dutch and British, he soon had to realise that France did not have any merchants of international standing in the field of overseas trade. Those who were considered as such were either Dutch or dependent on the Dutch. The merchants in Rouen refused to participate in this association and those in Bordeaux had to be forced to join. Yet that was not all: France had neither a sufficient number of seaworthy ships nor enough experienced captains and seamen. By this time the Dutch and the English East India Companies were already multinational corporations with a large network of overseas offices, a distinct, often decentralized bureaucracy and thousands of employees.

The second, and possibly greater, problem hindering France's colonial ambitions in the 17th and 18th century was the fact that the European colonial powers were not only often at war with one other, especially during the formation of nation states, but that there was constant conflict bubbling just below the dividing line where things cross over into outright warfare. Prominent events affecting France were, first and foremost, numerous wars against its hereditary enemy, the English. With France already having lost its entire fleet to the English in a naval battle in 1340 it suffered the same fate once again in 1692 in a battle against a united English and Spanish fleet. Just as the loss of the Spanish Armada in 1588 had heralded the end of Spanish navel supremacy this event finally caused France to fall definitively behind England as the leading maritime power.

## Wars as a Means
## of Enforcing National Economic Interests

Of the vast number of wars in the 17th and 18th century the following six conflicts — besides the Thirty Years' War — are of particular relevance for the subsequent argumentation: Firstly, the wars between Spain and the Netherlands; secondly, a series of trade restrictions and military conflicts between England and the Dutch and/or Spanish; thirdly, the War of Spanish Succession and at least two further wars between England and France; fourthly, the French wars of conquest against Holland and Spain; fifthly, the three Revolutionary Wars between France and Austria and their respective allies; and, sixthly, the Napoleonic campaigns in Europe.

Common to all these wars is the fact that they had a major impact, either direct or indirect, on the further evolution of the globalisation process. Even though the general thrust of foreign and economic policy in Europe's new nation states was moving in an increasingly mercantilist direction it appears that the conflicts in which France was involved almost always had a strong power-political dimension designed to boost the glory of the French nation — *la Gloire de la France* — while the policy of the English was guided by the primacy of economic interest, although the growing international power accruing to the country as a result was surely a not entirely unintentional spin-off effect.

Interesting examples of the French approach are the three Revolutionary Wars and the Napoleonic campaigns of conquest. Illustrative of the British strategy are the wool trade blockades between Spain/Portugal and Flanders, embargos on French wine, manufactured products and luxury goods in 1649 and 1678, the five "Navigation Acts" between 1651 and 1696, which were primarily directed against the Dutch, two Anglo-Dutch naval wars — the first from 1652 to 1654, the second from 1664 to 1667 — and, most notably, the Seven Years' War against France, which, at least from a British point of view, was clearly fought as an economic war. This last-mentioned war involved all the European superpowers of the day, to wit Austria, France and Russia on one side, and Prussia and England together with Hanover on the other. Since this war was, in addition, fought not only on European soil but practically around the globe, including in America and India, it could, in a certain sense, be considered the first "world war". This and — above all — the fact that the war against Prussia was declared an imperial war after its invasion of Saxony made it very difficult for Hamburg, which had been an imperial city since 1510, to uphold its policy of neutrality.

## The Beginnings of English Maritime and Economic Dominance

In the same way that the 17th century could be described as the heyday of the Dutch the 18th century clearly brought with it the maritime and, later, also the economic dominance of the English. The key element in this development, and this applies in particular to the process of increasing globalisation, was the securing of English maritime supremacy. The first step towards this goal was the expansion of the English fleet, which tripled in size between 1629 and 1686 and then again in the period up to 1788. The aggressive pursuit of British interests in transcontinental maritime traffic was a further factor.

The Navigation Acts referred to above prescribed that all forms of transportation to and from the English colonies were to be effected exclusively on English vessels and via English ports. After gaining the sole right to carry slaves to the Spanish colonies in America for 30 years under the terms of the Treaty of Utrecht in 1713 the English — and not, as previously, the Dutch — played the leading role in the slave trade. It has been statistically proven that, in the 18th century, more than forty percent of the slave trade was controlled by Britain, roughly thirty percent by Portugal, almost twenty percent by France and just six percent by the Dutch.

The aggressive expansionist policy of the English was, however, not only restricted to the extension and protection of maritime trade and naval supremacy. After establishing 13 colonies of their own in North America the British began to conquer the colonies of other European countries in the second half of the 18th century. During the Seven Years' War (1756–1763) against France they annexed the French slave station in Senegambia in 1758, occupied Martinique and Québec in 1759 and Montréal in 1760. Under the terms of the Treaty of Paris, signed in 1763, France finally lost all its possessions on the North American mainland.

Yet the Dutch and the Spanish also suffered losses. New Amsterdam, for example, was assigned to New England after the second Anglo-Dutch war in 1667 and has been called New York ever since. Spain lost Cuba and the Philippines in 1762, Trinidad in 1797 and Tobago and Guyana to Britain in 1814. The British also pursued their overseas expansion policy in India, where they conquered Eastern India between 1757 and 1784, annexed Bengal through the English East India Company in 1765, seized French possessions in Southern India and snatched Ceylon from the Dutch between 1767 and 1799.

By the beginning of the 18th century Britain had thus become the world's leading colonial power. Yet some of its new attainments, most especially the complete control over, and related pacification, of North America led to developments that were to have an unforeseen effect on the subsequent course of world history. The decolonisation first of North America and later of Ibero-America, are, in the shorter term, the key events in this respect.

## *The Decolonisation of America*

The United States was the first overseas territory to break free of its mother country and the sequence of actions and successes also discernible in later decolonisation phases was, in a sense, developed during this first white decolonisation. The colony's aggressive need for independence is usually just one element in this process. To this must be added reinforcing processes from the mother country on the one hand and certain conditions within the wider international context promoting this development on the other.

In the case of the United States such factors were the vanishing of competition and a possible threat to New England from the French and Dutch after 1783, the fact that restrictions and burdens imposed on the colony by the mother country were increasingly felt to be unacceptable and the support given to the Americans by the French in their fight against their hereditary enemy, the British, during the American War of Independence. Similar processes would be repeated in the Spanish and Portuguese colonies of Latin America. The outcome, which is of particular interest to globalisation, was the independence of the United States in 1783, of Chile (1810), Argentina (1816), Peru, Venezuela and Mexico (1821) and, finally, Brazil since 1822.

Once the so-called Treaty of Versailles had been signed in Paris in 1783 Hamburg was one of the first to recognise the United States and to propose extensive trade relations. American exports, on which Britain had, up until that point, held a monopoly, consisted primarily of rice, cotton, sugar, and tobacco and were therefore a good way of complementing the range of French colonial goods. Imports from the United States already accounted for a respectable three percent of Hamburg's entire imports in 1788. The extraordinary momentum displayed by Hamburg's trade with America in the following ten years is reflected in, among other things, the number of ships from the USA docking in Hamburg. In 1788 the figure was no higher than 17, but this number increased to an average of 125 ships each year between 1798 and 1801 and a record number of 192 vessels in 1799.

## Economic and Social
## Implications of Globalisation

Geopolitical and economic rivalry, initially between the Spanish and the Portuguese and subsequently between the Dutch, French and British, was one of the crucial driving forces integrating faraway countries and regions into the process of global exchange relations. This extension and, in part, deepening of trade relations led to a further expansion of foreign direct investment and international technology transfer. Equally undisputed is the fact that the colonisation process went far beyond the economic realm to encompass a wealth of political, social and cultural dimensions.

One clear indication is the fact that Brazilians still speak Portuguese while the rest of Latin America speaks Spanish. Further evidence is provided by the legal system in the United States and India, which is still based on the English model and not on a French, Native American, Indian or some other original version of things. Also not to be forgotten in this context is the dominance of the Christian religion throughout America up to the present day and the existence of Christian enclaves in Asia and Africa. The spread of the Christian faith at first in the Mediterranean then throughout Europe and subsequently via European expansion overseas, is, after all, an integral element in the globalisation process.

Colonisation and the globalisation this brought about were thus clearly more than just an expansion and intensification of global trading and exchange relations. Yet the concomitant developments cannot be portrayed in only a positive light. Not only did diseases introduced by Europeans to the Americas result in the death of many millions of indigenous peoples; not only did the Europeans, through the African slave trade, carry out the largest forced migration in history; even economically speaking the early phase of colonisation may have — at least in part — been, a zero sum game for everyone involved. What was won by the one side through the pillaging of existing gold and

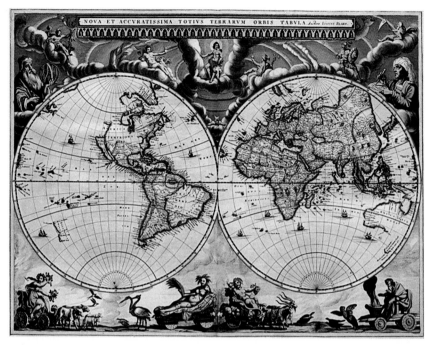

*Map of the world by Joan Blaeu, around 1640. The oceans and continents have taken shape, but the interiors of America, Africa and Asia are still largely "terra incognita".*

silver deposits and through privateering or piracy was lost by the other.

Moreover, there are many examples to show that, even for those who retained the upper hand in war, the costs were far higher than the spoils of victory. The war against the Portuguese for control of Brazil, for example, one largely unsuccessful in the final instance, is said to have cost the Dutch roughly £3.5 million, while having secured them less than £1.5 million. Estimates suggest that, over the course of the 18th century, the English spent £272 million on four major wars alone. And France's state finances were crippled after the war Louis XIV waged against the Dutch.

Both colonisation and the various wars or war-like conflicts during the period as considered here were fought either by the nation states emerging at this time or by the powerful trading companies, such as the English East India Company or the Dutch United East India Company. While towns and cities had been of enormous importance during the early phases of globalisation, the question now to be asked is whether or not this is also true of the early colonisation period and the time during which a policy of mercantilism was being pursued by national governments. The answer is quite unambiguous. During the period of Portuguese supremacy Antwerp became the economic capital of the world. This position passed to Genoa when the Spanish ruled the world. After Genoa's decline in 1630 Amsterdam assumed this role international commodity and financial markets. Amsterdam, in turn, was followed in the middle of the 1870s by London while, from around 1795, Hamburg became the biggest banking and trading centre and the most important port on the European mainland.

## The Heyday
## and Decline of Antwerp

When Antwerp replaced Bruges as the most important Hanseatic base in what was then the Netherlands it had neither its own trade fleet nor local trading houses of international standing. It was the city's geographic location, between the Hanseatic League's principal trading area and the Mediterranean as well as the Hansa merchants and traders from England, France, Spain, Portugal and Italy that made Antwerp great. The city initially profited from the English cloth trade to central Europe and from the fact that the financially strong Upper German trading houses, especially the Fuggers, preferred Antwerp to Bruges. And when the Portuguese King — probably also at the urging of the Fuggers — decided to make Antwerp, and not Lisbon, the new European capital of the pepper and spice trade this ushered in the city's golden age, which lasted from 1501 to 1557, albeit with a ten-year break in the middle of this period.

The reasons for Antwerp's decline, which, after a brief phase of industrial development, accelerated after 1568, were complex. For one thing, Antwerp had been unable to gain a permanent monopoly on the pepper trade, allowing Venice, over the years, to recapture a part of the global pepper market. Two further decisive reasons for Antwerp's increasing difficulties are related to the development of the Upper German trading houses. On the one hand, the output of Germany's silver and copper mines was steadily declining, which meant that, increasingly, resort had to be made to American silver from Seville to finance the spice trade; the first Spanish state bankruptcy of 1557, in particular, after which the Fuggers went into eclipse, constituted, at least in an economic sense, a major threat to Antwerp. On the other hand, Antwerp suffered from the sea blockade by the British, which largely halted all trade with Portugal.

Yet internal causes also played an important role in the decline of Antwerp. In 1564 Emden took in the English *Merchant Adventurers*, who no longer felt safe in Antwerp. The reason for this relocation was, however, not only the increasing "Hispanisation" of the Netherlands. Just as important was the spread of political, social and religious unrest in the Netherlands, partially due to an extreme and widening gap between the rich and poor. Prices and wages, which had risen disproportionately during the golden age of Antwerp, are also likely to have had a detrimental effect on the city's advantages in terms of quality of location. Finally, the sum of all these factors had a negative effect on possible, long-term industrial development, which might, under certain circumstances, have been able to offset the losses sustained in terms of international trade.

## The Rise of Genoa
## and the End of its Leading Role

It might at first seem astounding that, of all places, an Italian city, namely Genoa, succeeded Antwerp as the epicentre of international trade and finance, even though Europe's most dynamic markets were still located in the north. The city's geographic proximity to Seville, together with the Spanish King's credit needs, most probably played a decisive role here. Additionally, Genoa was able to rely on old traditions and, most probably, also on innovative, new practices in the field of lending and international financial transactions, while Antwerp did not even have an efficient banking and credit system. On the Antwerp bourse, established in 1531, government bonds were essentially the only items traded and after bill of exchange renewal, i.e. redemption of one bill of exchange through another, was officially prohibited in 1541 the creation of credit and deposit monies was also subject to drastic restrictions.

When, after 1557, the Upper German merchants ceased to finance Spanish overseas trade or to meet the other credit needs of the Spanish Crown it was thus not really that much of a surprise when the Genoese, who were not only successful traders, navigators and shipwrights but also shrewd bankers, filled the market niche that had thus arisen. In doing so they handled not only simple banking transactions by bundling together the deposits of other Italian cities and individuals, and passing the funds on as loans at higher rates of interest. Decisive were their willingness to take risks and their maturity transformation skills, via which they were able to convert the Spanish King's irregular revenues on the basis of silver imports and tax collection into regular income. Yet this particularly close relationship between the Genoa banking centre and the Spanish state also meant that every financial crisis in Spain spread to Italy's economy in the form of amplified shockwaves; and there were at least six such crises between 1557 and 1647 alone.

Nonetheless, Genoa's reign over Europe's capital and credit markets did not come to an end as a result of the financial turmoil of the day. At least equally important was a side effect of the peace treaty concluded between Britain and Spain in 1630. This treaty specified that all the silver destined for the Netherlands in future had to be transported on British ships. As a result the flow of Spanish silver now travelled north, via English, and no longer Genuese, agents, and most particularly to Amsterdam, a city that had been fast emerging since 1685. Also, the fact that Genoese bankers had focused their loans business primarily on France, thus neglecting the English market, is probably a further reason why Genoa was, even in later years, unable to regain its original market-dominating position.

## Amsterdam:
### The New Centre of the World Economy

Amsterdam is the last example of a city which dominated the world economy yet without being embedded in a politically, economically and militarily powerful nation state. At the same time the rise of Amsterdam marked the final shift of the global economic centre of gravity from the Mediterranean to the North Sea and Atlantic region. And, like Genoa before it, Amsterdam initially owed its rise to a combination of successful trade and the credit business that accompanied this and its subsequent fall to a number of financial crises. It must, however, be emphasised that, unlike in the case of Genoa, the crises afflicting Amsterdam's business and financial sector were not primarily due to major individual creditors defaulting but, first and foremost, the cumulative collapse of an overinflated credit market.

Like Hamburg, at first during the Thirty Years' War and later during the Spanish Counter-Reformation, Amsterdam profited from immigration and the associated population growth. Having numbered just 50,000 in 1600, the population had risen to approximately 200,000 by 1700. Unskilled immigrants, who could be used to perform low-paid work, came mainly from Germany. Immigrants who proved to be especially valuable for the city's dynamic economic development included Spanish and Portuguese Jews, Protestant refugees from France and a large number of experienced and affluent merchants from Antwerp, which had been occupied by the Spanish in August 1585.

Further important factors for Amsterdam's rise were the size and capabilities of the Dutch fleet, the excellent infrastructure available for warehousing of transit goods from all over the world, the efficiency of its port and the successful establishment of certain industries for refining and processing of imported raw materials. Estimates show that, in around 1669, the Dutch merchant fleet boasted roughly 6,000 ships with a total capacity of 600,000 tonnes — a figure likely to have corresponded to the total tonnage of all vessels throughout the rest of Europe. Accordingly, Amsterdam was also the world's leading shipbuilding centre, the hub of the global charter business and the largest market for second-hand ships.

The Dutch set great store not only by the economic superiority of their fleet but also by the outstanding efficiency of the port. The high warehousing capacity was important not only for the merchants, who needed to bridge irregular dockings and to respond flexibly to supply and demand. It also facilitated the rapid loading and unloading of vessels; even at that time, ship-owners evidently considered it important for vessels not to spend too much time in port. One source speaks of an average turnaround period in dock of four to five days. Since entering the sugar industry the Dutch had been pushing the development of this sector with great vigour. By 1622 there were already 29 sugar refineries in Holland, of which 25 were located in Amsterdam. Yet the Dutch were, as Daniel Defoe observed as early as in 1728, "the carryers of the World, the middle persons in Trade, the Factors and Brokers of Europe".

Traditional relations between Amsterdam and Italian cities, most notably Genoa, and the influx of migrant Jews from Spain and Portugal turned Amsterdam, over the course of time, into the world's bank-

The Stock Exchange in Amsterdam. The Amsterdam Stock Exchange was established as a commodity exchange in 1611 and was also trading in securities by 1612. And so the first stock exchange in the world was thus created. The picture above represents an early caricature denouncing commodity and stock market speculation.

ing and financial capital. The Dutch overseas companies, particularly the United East India Company and the Dutch West India Company, were initially founded as joint stock companies whose shares were traded on the regular capital market. Once the city's wealth permitted it to extend interest-bearing loans to third parties, especially to

European dynasties, but also to aspiring cities such as Hamburg for example, dealing in stocks was joined by international trade and speculation in government bonds. Serving as the centre of this activity was the Amsterdam Stock Exchange, established back in 1611 and already residing in its very own building. As is apparent from a so-called "Fund Quotation List" dated 1747, 35 different bonds and six stocks were already being traded in that year. By 1800 the number of securities traded on the Amsterdam bourse had increased to well over 100.

Another important institution marking Amsterdam out as a financial centre at that time was the "Amsterdaamsche Wisselbank", founded in 1609 and modelled on Italian predecessors. The bank's key role was to act as a clearing bank for the extensive transit business of Amsterdam's merchants, i.e. to facilitate cashless payment by making internal transfers between the accounts of its various different clients. However, this bank was not a credit institution; on the contrary, any account overdrafts carried a penalty. The granting of loans was effected via commission business and exchange transactions, whereby, unlike in Antwerp, even high-risk bills of exchange chains formed part and parcel of day-to-day business. The resultant money creation is estimated to have been four to fifteen times higher than the volume of cash in circulation.

## The First
## Pan-European Financial Crises

This enormous and predominantly uncontrolled growth in money supply, as well as the fact that Amsterdam's merchants — like the Genoese some 150 years earlier — were increasingly turning their backs on the commodity trade in order to focus on financial dealings was one of the decisive factors causing Amsterdam to lose its leading global economic position partially to Hamburg, yet primarily to London. As the increasing wealth in Amsterdam had led to a growing imbalance between available financial resources and traditional investment opportunities, the Dutch increasingly began, in the second half of the 18th century, to invest particularly in London — and this not only in business activities, but also in government bonds, something they had, until then, strictly refused to do due to insufficient securities. The fact that, in doing so, they indirectly contributed to the rise of London did not initially bother them that much. In the course of three financial crises following in rapid succession, however, this would come back to haunt them.

The first crisis occurred in 1763, the second in 1772/73 and the third between 1780 and 1783. While the first and third crises were, at least indirectly, linked to military conflicts and the second one coincided with crop failures in Europe, all three still constitute the first modern-day credit crises. Although the collapse of a large company usually triggered the subsequent negative and cumulative spiral, the chain reaction as such was the result of the uncontrolled and increasingly opaque expansion of the credit market. Although Amsterdam recovered relatively quickly from the first crisis, triggered by a currency devaluation in Prussia, its more distant repercussions had a significant impact not only on London, Stockholm, Copenhagen, Berlin and Leipzig but also Hamburg.

The most interesting aspect of the second crisis, which hit Amsterdam much harder than the first, is the fact that it was triggered by the insolvency of a large company in London, not Amsterdam. The third crisis, which finally saw London displace Amsterdam as the world's new financial centre, was brought about by a variety of different causes, including a long period of slow economic growth and the American War of Independence, during which Britain and France were once again at war. Ultimately, however, this was nonetheless a typical financial crisis. The second crisis had already sparked grave social unrest in the Netherlands; right in the middle of the third crisis, in 1781, the Dutch Revolution began. And, with London now the new world economic capital, the next phase of globalisation commenced before the turn of the century.

# CHAPTER 4

# Hamburg: Germany's Largest City and Most Important Port

Having numbered just 5,000 in the 1380s, Hamburg's population rose to approximately 16,000 by the beginning of the second globalisation phase, i.e. the period characterised by European overseas expansion. Depopulation due to plagues and disasters in the 14th century and the Europe-wide outbreak of syphilis in 1498 were offset, or even overcompensated, by a sustained and dynamic process of immigration into the city. While still smaller than Brunswick, Danzig and Cologne during the 16th century, Hamburg had, with more than 40,000 inhabitants, become the largest city in Germany by the end of 1619.

Notwithstanding this, it was clear that Hamburg was unable to play an active role in the global geopolitical conflicts of the 16th, 17th and 18th centuries. Its only realistic option was and remained that of pursuing its proven and largely successful policy of neutrality. This was not an easy task, there always having been a war going on somewhere which — if not directly, then at least indirectly — had a major impact on the development of Hamburg. In addition to the conflicts between the Old Empire and Denmark and the Thirty Years' War, this applied, in particular, to the wars between Spain and the Netherlands, between Holland and Britain and those between Britain and France. The effects these had on Hamburg could be either positive or negative.

# Hamburg and the Chaos of War
## in the Early Modern Period

If one disregards the brief two-month occupation by Danish troops in March 1801 during the War of the Second Coalition, Hamburg became directly involved in just two military conflicts of this period and both times it paid a high price for its involvement. The first was the Schmalkaldic War from 1546 to 1547, in which Hamburg fought alongside the Protestants against the Holy Roman Emperor Charles V. When, despite victory near Drakenburg an der Weser with the involvement of Hamburg, the war was finally lost, Hamburg found itself in a severe financial crisis. It not only had to repay, with interest, the loans taken out to fund the war but was also made to pay a fine of 60,000 gulden to the Emperor. In spite of the then generally favourable economic conditions prevailing and the still strong position of Hamburg in trade with Antwerp, the leading European economic centre at that time, it took many years of great effort to overcome this crisis.

By contrast, Hamburg remained largely untroubled by the Thirty Years' War, which was waged from 1618 to 1648. One could, in fact, almost claim that the city actually profited from it. On the one hand, Hamburg had, in 1608, already joined forces with Lübeck, Bremen, Lüneburg, Magdeburg and Brunswick in the alliance of "corresponding Hanseatic cities" for the purpose of common defence. On the other, Hamburg had, between 1609 and 1627, extended its fortifications to such an extent that it did not seem wise for the warring parties to actually test their strength. In the light of these circumstances Hamburg benefited above all from the fact that the Old Empire required a port that was an efficient hub for both supplies and information.

Trading levels in Hamburg remained roughly the same throughout the entire war despite temporary blockades of the Lower Elbe and slight disruptions in transport to the hinterland. Parallel to this

*Originally planned as protection against Denmark, Hamburg built one of the strongest fortifications in Europe between 1616 and 1625. During the Thirty Years War, Hamburg's armed neutrality, but also its services as an international trading and financial centre, which were appreciated by both warring parties, spared the city from occupation as well as murder and plundering.*

Hamburg's merchants earned good money from the flourishing arms trade — exploiting the city's neutrality to sell to both sides of the fence. Finally Hamburg became a preferred place of refuge, which led to the city's population increasing from 40,000 at the turn of the century to 78,000 by around 1650. It is, by the way, less well known that preliminary negotiations for the Peace of Westphalia took place in Hamburg in 1636 and 1641.

The second instance in which Hamburg became directly involved was during the Napoleonic Wars (1795–1813). Its involvement occurred during three very different phases. The first phase began with the French occupation of Amsterdam and had by and large a positive effect on Hamburg. On the one hand many experienced and affluent Dutch merchants sought sanctuary in Hamburg. On the other, Hamburg was able to strengthen its position further, especially in its trade with England, due to the unavailability of the largest Dutch port. The second phase, which had serious implications for Hamburg, began with the 1803 blockade of the mouth of the Elbe by the British and continued with Napoleon's Continental System, which finally brought shipping to a complete standstill. The third episode was the French occupation of Hamburg, which the city had evidently not expected.

All these were wars whose implications for Hamburg were triggered either by direct participation, by being directly affected or by the city's close geographic proximity to the actual theatre of war. This obviously did not apply to the wars between Spain and the Netherlands during the course of the Counter-Reformation and yet, once again, Hamburg still benefited, both through immigration and the expansion of its trading relations. The first wave of refugees came from Holland as early as 1567, followed after the Spanish occupation of Antwerp by a second wave in 1585. That Hamburg did not always profit from wars between third parties but was also negatively impacted despite its constant efforts to remain neutral, is clearly illustrated by the three wars between England and the Netherlands between 1652 to 1674 and the Seven Years' War, from 1756 to 1763.

## *Limits of the Policy of Neutrality*

As it happened in fact, it was not only the Navigation Acts directed against the Dutch that had a detrimental effect on Hamburg's trade. When, in 1666, four Dutch warships attacked a British convoy abeam of Neumühlen, a fishing village about 3 km west of the city, setting fire to three ships and seizing a further three, the British clearly pointed the finger of blame at Hamburg. In spite of protracted negotiations and in an attempt to remain neutral, the city finally, in 1670, had to pay considerable compensation to Britain.

*Admiralty yacht in 1755. Hamburg not only founded the first German admiralty and used the first German warship in the fight against pirates, the city also had an admiralty yacht, which was so grand that it puts today's Senate launch in the shade.*

During the Seven Years' War Hamburg found itself in what might be described as almost the reverse situation. In August 1760 the city managed to thwart an attack by French citizens living in Hamburg on an English consignment of cash sailing up the River Elbe headed for Hanover and Prussia. France considered this a breach of the city's neutrality, subsequently terminating the trade treaty that had existed since 1716 and refusing to allow Hamburg vessels docked in French ports to put to sea. The ships were eventually released at the end of 1760. However, since France had in the meantime replaced the Dutch as the principal trading partner of Hamburg's merchants, the lack of a trade treaty, which persisted until 1769, was a serious problem for the city.

Despite having, when compared to France or England, only extremely modest resources Hamburg actively sought to defend itself, at least whenever the Council deemed this wise and necessary. After plans to establish an imperial admiralty had failed 50 years earlier Hamburg founded its own admiralty in 1623 — and this not simply to enhance navigational safety but also to secure the Elbe militarily. In 1629 Hamburg attacked Danish warships patrolling the river and subsequently imposed a blockade on Glückstadt, a city further down the river which had been established by the Danish King in 1616 to impede Hamburg's development. Faced with the growing threat to shipping from buccaneers, corsairs and Barbary pirates, Hamburg in 1668/69 built two warships of its own to protect its convoys to Spain and Portugal; these vessels were in fact the first ever German warships. In 1678 Hamburg successfully sank several French pirate ships near the Elbe estuary.

## Hamburg: With Amsterdam, the Major Beneficiary of the Decline of Antwerp

The numerous references made to Hamburg during Amsterdam's period of economic supremacy indicate that these two cities not only shared a close relationship but that there were also certain parallels between them in terms of the opportunities and challenges in the field of economic and social development. Both cities were important ports and trading hubs. Both were located outside the newly emerging nation states and thus highly vulnerable militarily. This applied not only during periods of military action but also with regard to the activities of privateers, buccaneers, corsairs and Barbary pirates. Another key factor was that, to a considerably degree, the economic development of both cities was determined not only by their own policies but also by economic developments overseas and the economic policies of their trading partners.

126

Like Amsterdam, Hamburg too profited from the demise of Antwerp. This was, on the one hand, due to the shifting of trade routes. After the decline of Antwerp even Nuremberg, for example, transacted a substantial part of its trade with Spain and Portugal via Hamburg. On the other hand, both cities benefited equally from the immigration of the Dutch Reformists. From the middle of the 1580s this influx of immigrants also included Spanish and Portuguese Jews, who had previously fled their homeland to find refuge in the Netherlands. Hamburg additionally profited from taking in the English *Merchant Adventurers*, who had originally left Antwerp for Emden before resettling in Hamburg in 1564.

Although the British had, by the beginning of the 16th century, clearly defeated the Dutch in the battle for control of the European cloth trade, they continued to leave the processing and dyeing of the cloth to the Dutch. The latter were obviously superior, not only when it came to mastering the relevant techniques but also when following the latest fashion trends on international markets. In order to remain competitive in the cloth trade, Hamburg's cloth merchants for their part had been poaching Dutch cloth cutters and dyers from Antwerp since 1530. Hamburg was thus able to strengthen its position in this market during the ensuing years. Just a few decades later the absorption into the city of the *Merchant Adventurers*, who controlled the cloth trade between England and the Netherlands, caused the centre of the European cloth trade to shift to Hamburg.

### Economic Growth Dynamics deriving from the Secondary Effects of a Liberal Immigration Policy

In addition to the direct growth momentum deriving from the delocalisation of the *Merchant Adventurers*, there were at least five other important, partially indirect, effects on Hamburg's cloth trade. And these effects were enhanced still further once the first refugees from the Netherlands were taken in around 1567, through the immigration

ein Tolle

ein Kran

Dieß schöne Werck zeigt eigentlich
Die Börse zu Hamburg künstlich
Wie sie ein Ehrnvest hochweis Rath
Den Gewandtschneidern vergünstigt hatt

dem gemeinen nützen zu erbawen
voran fürnemlich zu beschawen,
das sie herlich für dem Rathaus
vnd am Wasser geführet aus,

*The old stock exchange. Trading took place outdoors in the period between its foundation in 1558 and the completion of the first stock exchange building in 1583. The "Commerzdeputation", which was founded in 1665 and moved into an*

*extension of the existing building in 1669, published a weekly stock exchange list with the most important exchange rates, commodity prices and assurance prices from 1735 onwards. Regular securities business did not commence until 1815.*

of Spanish and Portuguese Jews after 1580 and as a result of the arrival of a second wave of Dutch refugees after the occupation of Antwerp by the Spanish in 1585.

Firstly, the demise of Antwerp cut out middlemen who, for Hamburg, had pushed up costs. Secondly, the immigrants brought with them not only capital but, most especially, also their own trade relations, which greatly extended the reach of Hamburg's cloth trade. Thirdly, there were considerable multiplier effects for sectors closely related to cloth processing and the cloth trade. Fourthly, the Dutch and the Jews, who, for the most part, had also fled Amsterdam, were in possession of new technologies and methods which in many sectors — far beyond the world of the cloth industry itself — served as an impetus for innovation. And, fifthly and most notably, cooperation with the *Merchant Adventurers*, which although suspended between 1577 and 1611, lasted until 1802 ensured that long term peace with England was secured.

From an economic policy perspective another important aspect was the fact that the Dutch and English immigrants practised their profession largely outside the existing trade organisation of the guilds. The expansion of the cloth industry therefore led to the break-up of traditional and rigid economic structures, which generally hamper the international competitiveness of an industrial sector or city in the globalisation process. To the extent that the newcomers founded their own guilds or "trade offices" these were at least at that time well adapted to meet current requirements. In practice this meant that they were matched to the technical, commercial and organisational demands of the day, and that their members were not hemmed in by outdated medieval constraints and restrictions.

By the beginning of the 17th century, therefore, Hamburg had become one of the leading European centres of the cloth, velvet, ribbon weaving and calico printing industry. In the industry's heyday there are said to have been more than 1,000 looms in the city. Printed calicos from Hamburg, usually produced on the basis of English preliminaries, were exported around the globe via England. The fact that the

*Hamburg in 1680. In the foreground on the left are the anchored convoy ships "Wappen von Hamburg" and "Leopoldus Primus". The city looks very impressive with its five church spires and the Mariendom (St Mary's Cathedral), demolished in 1806, behind the massive fortification walls.*

number of people working in this industry fell towards the end of the 18th century, from almost 5,000 to a few hundred, was due both to increasing competition, especially from Silesia and the Rhineland, and to the mercantilist policies of the majority of the European trading partners. Prussia, in particular, constantly increased its customs duties, ultimately rendering textile imports from Hamburg a de facto impossibility.

## Hamburg becomes
## the Centre of Europe's Sugar Industry

A further industry that thrived in Hamburg, also initially encouraged and pursued by the Dutch and Jewish merchants from Southwest Europe, was sugar refining. Once again, the origins can be traced back to the 1690s. As was the case with the cloth industry the Dutch who had fled Antwerp brought with them not only the required production technology and know-how but also their trading relations.

For the supply of sugarcane this meant that Brazilian imports were, at least up until 1730, purchased from Antwerp, which had initially retained its position as Europe's main transshipment centre for sugar even after the Spanish occupation. It was not until the Dutch captured the most important, previously Portuguese-owned sugar-growing areas in Brazil that the focus of the sugar trade — and of a number of other colonial goods — shifted to Amsterdam, which subsequently advanced to become the centre of European sugar refining. When, in around 1760, the next wave of refugees from the Netherlands arrived in Hamburg this coincided with the beginning of a far-reaching change in international sugar sourcing structures.

The centre of sugar cultivation shifted from Brazil to the West Indies and despite the fact that Hamburg did not — with the exception of the Caribbean island of St Thomas, a possession of the Danish King which he opened to ships from Hamburg in 1767 — have direct access to colonial trade, the city developed into the then largest sugar-producing and sugar-trading centre in Europe. One of the decisive reasons for this development was the rapidly increasing number of French ships calling at its port. In 1727 there were just 200 sugar refineries in Hamburg; this number rose to 300 by the middle of the century and had reached 400 in 1802. By way of comparison, there are said to have been just 90 sugar refineries in Amsterdam in around 1750 and even fewer — 30 — in Rotterdam.

The number of people employed in this sector — sugar trade, sugar refineries and ancillary sector dependent on the sugar industry — was, incidentally, far greater than it had ever been in the cloth trade. In the 1780s it totalled approximately 8,000, subsequently even rising as high as approx. 10,000 over the next 20 years. Assuming that Hamburg had a population of 100,000 to 120,000 at that time, a comparison with the number of people employed in the sugar industry gives some indication of the significance of this sector for the economy as a whole.

It is, therefore, not surprising that sugar had, by the middle of the 18th century, replaced beer as Hamburg's most important export product. In addition to the immediate hinterland the market for the city's sugar economy initially encompassed the entire Baltic region, from Sweden in the north to Russia in the east. By the second half of the 18th century Hamburg's sugar refiners were acting as suppliers to the whole of Europe and if there still was a serious competitor, then it was the Dutch.

Yet the sugar boom in Hamburg came to an end at the beginning of the 19th century. On the one hand, the supply of cane sugar was at first disrupted by the Napoleonic Wars and the Continental System. On the other hand, a new industry based on sugarbeet was developing on the European mainland and, in this field, too, protectionism was gaining the upper hand.

## Hamburg's growing Significance in the Colonial Goods Trade

While there had, in both the cloth industry and sugar refining business, been close links between trade and locally based production, this was far less the case in the colonial goods trade, which also witnessed a rapid increase from the middle of the 16th century. Hamburg's principal trading partners in this sector were initially the Spanish and Portuguese, followed by the Dutch in the second half of the 17th century, then the British and, from the middle of the 18th century, the French. Since the Dutch dominated maritime trade with the Iberian Peninsula even during military conflicts between Spain and the Netherlands and also controlled international trade along the French Atlantic coast, the immigration of Protestant and Jewish merchants, predominantly from the Netherlands, was of crucial importance for the development of Hamburg's colonial trade. Together with the British they were the specialists for the wholesale trade in coffee, tea, cocoa, tobacco and spices in the 17th and 18th centuries.

This and the circumstances that, along with their capital, the Dutch traders also brought with them excellent relations to the young colonies in the Americas soon turned the merchants who had fled the Netherlands into the wealthiest merchants in Hamburg. Further testifying to the importance of Holland for Hamburg's economy is the fact that more than half of the 1,778 ships leaving Hamburg's harbour in 1647/48 were bound for the Netherlands.

The increasing importance of the transit trade in colonial goods, in addition to the traditional transhipment of grain and wood, is also reflected in the fact that, by 1747, Hamburg had no fewer than 246 coffee and tea traders — a figure that rose even higher, to 267, thirty years later. Incidentally, the first of several flourishing coffee houses opened in Hamburg in 1677 — beating even Vienna by five years.

## Hamburg's Trading Interests
### shift from the Netherlands to France

By 1740 just 390 Dutch ships called at Hamburg while the number of French vessels had risen from just 22 in 1663 to 183. The significance of the French in Hamburg's overseas trade continued to increase once the bilateral trade treaty was renewed in 1769; a secret clause in this contract granted the French reduced customs duties on goods from their West Indian colonies. Almost half of all French coffee exports and more than a quarter of all French colonial goods at that time were traded through Hamburg. If one includes the transhipment of French wine to Eastern Europe, the total French exports handled by Hamburg amounted to what was then the astronomical sum of 25 million marks banco.

A look at the city's import statistics for the year 1788 reveals just how important France was to Hamburg's economy. Hamburg's overall imports totalled 9.4 million livres tournois (= approximately 46 million marks banco), of which 54 per cent were from France, 13 per cent from England, 8 per cent each from Holland and Spain, 4 per cent from Portugal and 3 per cent already coming from the United States. The most important French export port by far was Bordeaux, which handled almost three quarters of all French exports. Hamburg's importance in this respect is underlined by the fact that almost 4.5 million pounds of coffee were exported from Bordeaux to Hamburg in 1751/52, roughly three times more than the volume exported to Amsterdam and Rotterdam combined. The corresponding ratio for indigo was 2 : 1 and Hamburg continued to lead the field in the sugar market.

In addition to this geographical shift of emphasis in Hamburg's overseas trade, there was a further remarkable new development that needs to be mentioned here. Although more and more Hamburg merchants and shipping companies were active in the transit trade they increasingly preferred to use foreign vessels for transportation — most probably as a consequence of Hamburg's inability to protect its ships sufficiently against buccaneers, corsairs, Barbary pirates and other privateers. Not only had Britain, Spain and France since built up a great naval force; these three nations, as well as the Dutch, Danes and Swedes, had also struck a number of deals with the pirates in exchange for deliveries of goods, most notably arms, and monetary payments. Even if Hamburg had had the financial means to afford similar such agreements, it would, in the absence of a powerful navy of its own, never have been able to enforce them.

As a result there were times during the middle of the 18th century when just 100 ships were sailing under Hamburg's flag, yet the fleet subsequently increased in size once again, from 138 to 293 ships, between 1775 and 1800. Yet shipping traffic to Hamburg was constantly increasing — even during periods in which its own fleet was subjected to certain restrictions — and the expansion of the harbour and the further infrastructure required by the port and trade remained an ongoing challenge. Bottlenecks in terms of both the available number of ship moorings and the warehousing capacities for goods on land were already becoming increasingly apparent during the second half of the 15th century. The first large-scale harbour expansion was, therefore, carried out in 1460 and it was at this time that the "Elbhafen" port developed from the cramped harbour on the Alster and Bille.

## Expanding the Physical
### and Intangible Infrastructure

Yet it was not only the number of ships calling at Hamburg but also the size of the vessels that was permanently increasing. Since the shipping channel had, despite the activities of the Düpe Commission, founded in 1548, been insufficiently dredged to ensure enough depth of water for shipping safe passage, most especially between Altona and the harbour entrance required a precise knowledge of the water depths and currents. To prevent ships from running aground or from touching bottom or requiring lighterage off Neumühlen, Hamburg's admiralty introduced compulsory pilotage for vessels on the River Elbe in 1639.

In 1648 the tower set up on Neuwerk at the beginning of the 14th century was converted into a light house to enhance safety of navigation when entering the Elbe estuary at night. Other infrastructural measures of relevance to the port primarily designed to reduce the threats posed to ships by pirates included the construction of the so called "block house" in 1655 and, seven years later, the installation of the "tree house" at the lower port, which used floating tree trunks to block access to the harbour.

Hamburg also profited from the infrastructural measures carried out by third parties. This particularly applied to the Oder-Spree Canal, opened in 1669, which established a directly navigable waterway from Hamburg to Silesia via the Upper Elbe, the Havel and the Spree. The advantages of this link were, however, not only limited to the improved range of the Elbe river system. Considered from an economic perspective, this inland waterway was especially attractive as it comprised, for that time, relatively few — no more than 25 — customs offices along a length of 760 kilometres. By comparison, travelling on the Weser and Rhine was an inordinately costly business.

As previously indicated, when discussing the early phases of globalisation, an efficient intangible infrastructure is just as vital as an adequate material infrastructure. This is particularly true of the financial system as the range and complexity of international trade began to increase. In Hamburg, too, this was recognised at an early stage. In 1558, for example, the Hamburg stock exchange, based on the Antwerp model, opened, making it one of the first in the Old Empire. Up until 1806 this institution even had its own post and courier service to Berlin and Frankfurt and — via Antwerp and Amsterdam — also to London.

The Hamburger Bank, for its part, was founded in 1619 on the Amsterdam model with Dutch and Jewish participation. It, too, was initially a clearing bank effecting non-cash transactions between the accredited merchants. In contrast to the "mark courant", a silver coin-based currency used for day-to-day cash transactions, the clearing unit was called "mark banco". To reduce excessive exchange fluctuations and, most notably, to prevent value impairments, which had been proliferating throughout Europe's coinage system, this accounting unit was secured by silver deposits whose value, in November 1813, was put at 7.5 million mark banco. Until Hamburg adopted the Reich currency in 1875, four years after the foundation of the German Reich, the mark banco was one of the world's most stable and most preferred currencies in international trade.

## Internationality – not only as a Trading and Financial Centre

In the second half of the 17th century Hamburg, too, strengthened its position not only as an international trade hub but also as an international financial centre. One example was the role of mediator that it sometimes played in matters concerning British financial support for

Prussia during the Seven Years' War. In addition to such financial assistance Hamburg's merchants were also very active in the insurance sector.

Inspired once again by a Dutch model a system of marine insurance developed in Hamburg at the end of the 16th century. It encompassed not only issues such as piracy but also the risk of weather-related loss of vessels — a risk that was becoming especially acute on account of the fact that there was no longer any willingness to suspend shipping during the winter months. Incidentally a fire insurance fund, the *Hamburger Feuerkasse*, was founded in August 1676 in the wake of a blaze that destroyed 30 houses and warehouses. Being still in existence today, this institution is most probably the world's oldest insurance company of its kind.

The internationalisation of the economy and society was increasingly also being reflected in foreign direct investment and company relocations. In 1376 Hamburg was already home to 84 merchants from the Netherlands, 40 from Lübeck and 35 from England. Approximately one quarter of Hamburg's 40,000 inhabitants in 1619 were of non-German origin. In the same year 32 of the 42 large Hamburg-based trading houses were controlled by the Dutch. As a result the common language at this time among the merchants, and even some of the craftsmen in Hamburg, was not only Low German but also Dutch and the books of most trading houses were kept in Dutch in accordance with Dutch accounting methods.

A further distinctive feature of Hamburg's relations to its international trading partners was the fact that, for all its love of profitable business, it also displayed remarkable international solidarity. After Lisbon was struck by a disastrous earthquake in 1755 the Council and the merchants association decided to send generous aid to the city, two-thirds of which had been devastated. Once the Portuguese king had accepted Hamburg's support no fewer than four ships with relief supplies, including construction timber, set sail for Portugal.

Yet internationality is not the sole defining feature of dynamic centres in a globalised economy. They benefit, most particularly, from international interdependencies, which can, however, also cause them to be repeatedly caught up in unwanted turmoil. Striking examples of this are growth and innovation cycles, ups and down in the business cycle, interdependencies due to international competition at the level of prices and wages, as well as the cumulative effects of turmoil on international financial markets.

## International Price and Wage Competition

Just as the Venetian textile industry had complained about low wages in England and Flanders in the 15th century, the Spanish cloth industry complained about the low wage levels in India at the beginning of the 17th century. Even back then it was claimed that cheap competition — supported by irresponsible Genoese merchants doing business in Indian calico materials — were damaging the markets and ruining local trade. A similar discussion — also relating to inacceptable wage levels in India — was held in Britain during the second half of the 17th century. Competitive advantages due to wage differences were, however, not a solely intercontinental phenomenon during the said period. In 18th century Europe, for example, there continued to be a wage differential, which increased as one moved eastward and from which Hamburg also profited.

Quite incontrovertibly the rise of Hamburg's sugar industry cannot be accounted for without delocalisations from Holland. This process was accelerated by French producers, chiefly from Bordeaux, shifting the processing of cane sugar they imported into Europe to the metropolis on the Elbe. Hamburg had three decisive locational advantages to offer them: Reliable and low-cost access to the principal sales markets in Germany and Northern and Eastern Europe. The city also boasted comparatively low wage levels which, due to the continuing inflow of cheap labour from the hinterland, seemed unlikely to increase even over the longer term. And it also had access to high quality yet still reasonably priced coal from England, the price of which was artificially inflated in Bordeaux due to high French customs duties.

This once again goes to show that competition between different international locations within the globalisation process is nothing new. Moreover, it becomes clear that this process is driven not only by international, or even intercontinental, price and wage competition. Government policies, too, which influence relative prices due to interventions — for example via customs duties — in favour of certain local products or economic sectors generally result in the specific quality of the respective location also changing for other sectors of the economy. What Venetian merchants had been denied in the 15th century, in other words, also applied in the 17th and 18th century: The fact namely that, besides innovation, the only other option open to an entrepreneur in a globalised economy seeking to remain internationally competitive in the event of certain adverse changes in market conditions and/or the wider setting in terms of economic policy, is that of partially or completely dislocating production abroad.

## New Financial Crisis
### due to Currency Devaluation in Prussia

Quite apart from the difficulties Hamburg had to face with regard to maintenance of its policy of neutrality with England and France during the Seven Years' War, the city was also continuously confronted with new problems from Prussia. Not only had Prussia been hampering Hamburg's trade on the Upper Elbe and Oder since the conquest of Silisea in 1742; tensions also escalated when Hamburg's merchants increasingly refused to accept the Prussian Friedrich d'or, now significantly devalued due to war financing, at a fixed exchange rate. That Hamburg had assessed the situation correctly was proven in 1763 when Prussia minted new coins just a few months after the end of the war, thus effectively abolishing the old devalued currency virtually overnight.

This currency devaluation was, in a certain sense, the epicentre of an economic crisis which subsequently spread to large parts of Europe. It first affected Amsterdam, where two important trading houses that had financed Prussia's war loans ran into great difficulties. The resulting crisis of confidence in Amsterdam's financial centre led to the collapse of the city's excessively inflated credit system. The stock exchange was paralysed; price quotations were suspended and no one was willing to exchange bank deposit money in account for cash. This not only sucked further Dutch banks and trading houses into the vortex but sent shockwaves reverberating throughout Europe. In Hamburg alone, 95 trading houses went bankrupt and the harbour was full of ships vainly awaiting their cargo.

This example clearly illustrates that uncontrolled credit expansion carries the seed of exponential risks. No less apparent is the devastating impact international financial crises can have on the real economy — not only in the country directly affected by the credit crunch but, in a globalised world, far beyond it as well. It is additionally evident that, even during the period under consideration, financial market interdependencies in an interlinked global economy obviously implied much shorter reaction times than was the case in most other markets. Thus the entire process of cumulative destruction and subsequent self-cleansing, which, from an economic perspective must, in part at least, be assessed positively, took just a few weeks to complete.

Wars, blockades and piracy, changes to world trade flows and relocation of production sites, as well as international financial crises, were, however, but a few of the key determinants that shaped the face of Hamburg's economic and social development in the 17th and 18th century. Other significant factors included population development, social unrest and the repeated occurrence of epidemics. By the end of the 17th century the population had risen to 60,000, and in 1769 — even before the first of the several thousand refugees from the French Revolution began to arrive in 1790 — the population had grown to number more than 100,000 inhabitants.

## Social Problems and Internal Security

The security the city offered during the Thirty Years' War, together with its economic prosperity, attracted not only skilled and wealthy immigrants but also, and increasingly, the poor. As their number far exceeded the increasing demand for unskilled workers, the ranks of the unemployed, the needy and the destitute spiralled immeasurably. This led to increasing internal instability and, in light of the hygienic conditions prevailing at that time, a growing risk of epidemics. Between 1618 and 1718 Hamburg experienced three particularly serious epidemics, which, in the absence of better medical knowledge, were always referred to as the "pestilence". In 1628 4,200 people perished; the second epidemic, in 1664, claimed the lives of more than 4,400 people; and the total number of deaths during the third plague outbreak, from September 1712 to February 1714, was between 10,000 and 12,000.

The spread of infectious diseases across international borders is not just a modern-day phenomenon. The third plague epidemic arrived in Hamburg via Constantinople, the Balkans, Courland, Livonia, and Sweden and Denmark. The economic implications well exceeded the direct and indirect costs of the epidemic. Even before the plague had actually reached Hamburg rumours circulating in Amsterdam and London had resulted in ships from Hamburg no longer being allowed to dock in Cadiz, Malaga and Rouen. When the epidemic finally did break out, it almost completely disabled the local economy and the unemployment rate rose to unprecedented levels.

That growing poverty and high unemployment, together with hunger and disease promote social unrest is as true today as it has ever been. Yet this factor alone does still not explain why social tensions in Hamburg in the second half of the 17th century escalated to such a degree that, in the face of the chaotic situation, even the Emperor felt compelled to make a drastic intervention in order to restore peace to the city. At the centre of the conflicts were the growing differences in opinion between the Council and the Parliament about which of these two institutions represented the highest political power and jurisdiction in the city. Matters were compounded by general changes to social structures characterised by the increasing number of craftsmen and wage-earners as a share of the total population, as well as denominational conflicts between orthodox Lutherans and Pietists, which were fought out not only from the pulpit but also on the streets and at the political level.

After several failed attempts to agree upon a new constitution for Hamburg and the repeated escalation of conflicts into running street battles, the Emperor, who had already issued Hamburg with a severe admonition in 1694, finally, after 13 further years of turmoil and mayhem, sent troops into the city to ensure peace and order until, in 1712, a new "main recess" could finally be passed after four years of negotiations. It stipulated that supreme highest authority lay with the Council and the Parliament "in an inseparable alliance". Remarkable is the fact that, in addition to a commission of the Emperor, the Dutch and British envoys to the city were also involved as mediators in the creation of this new constitution. This clearly shows how great an interest there was, on the part of not only the Empire but also the Dutch and British trading partners, in the restoration of the Germany's largest port once again to full operational capacity.

## Inner Peace and Resolution of the Centuries-Old Conflict with Denmark: Paving the Way for a New Economic Upturn

While the denominational conflicts, in which the Catholics subsequently also became embroiled, continued for a number of years, the new constitution did restore the inner political peace over the long term, having remained in force practically throughout the entire 18th century. Political tensions with Denmark, however, still posed a major problem that was not to be resolved until the Treaty of Gottorp

*Map of 1716. The River Elbe near Hamburg with the Elbe islands as well as the Northern & Southern Elbe. One can easily imagine why the first crossing of the River Elbe was not located near Hamburg, but further up-river near Artlenburg.*

was signed in 1768. In return for the cancellation of debts amounting to two million thalers Denmark agreed to a settlement ending a 150-year-old legal dispute and recognising Hamburg as a free imperial city. Along with a few minor territorial concessions relating, in particular, to islands in the River Elbe, a further and innovative element of this settlement was that Hamburg was granted most favoured nation status for its trade with Denmark and Norway.

The resolution of all of these internal and external problems enabled Hamburg to enter a new phase of increasing prosperity once again in the second half of the 18th century. Although trade with Portugal, Spain and the rest of the Mediterranean had almost completely ceased after 1750 due to the permanent threat to shipping posed by the Barbary pirates, this was more than made up for by the shifting of the city's trade interests first towards France and, later, the United States. The previously mentioned financial crisis and wave of bankruptcies in 1763 notwithstanding, port capacities were already seriously overstretched just five years later and new mooring facilities had to be created on dolphins outside the Niederbaum.

Despite its continued policy of neutrality Hamburg still had to face troubled times over the next 25 years — ranging from an unprecedented economic upturn to the greatest humiliation. In 1793 the French placed an embargo on ships from Hamburg and from 1803 to 1805 the English imposed a sea blockade. Hamburg was repeatedly blackmailed into paying large sums of money to France. All of this was testimony to the city's lack of military capabilities. After the Netherlands had been occupied by Napoleon in 1795, Hamburg initially took over the role of Amsterdam as the leading trading and financial centre on the European mainland. Once again many Dutch citizens moved to Hamburg and the volume of trade doubled. However, when a speculative bubble sparked by inflation and the profits of war burst a total of 55 trading houses in Hamburg went bankrupt in September 1799 alone.

### French Occupation and Economic Decline

The biggest misfortune that befell Hamburg at the beginning of the new century was the invasion by Napoleon's forces on November 19, 1806. Hamburg had to endure French occupation for almost eight years and was even incorporated into the French Empire in December 1810. High tax and tribute payments, together with the Continental System imposed by Napoleon, led to the almost complete collapse of the economy. Approximately 60 unrigged ships remained in Hamburg's harbour. Nearly every company that depended on overseas raw materials and British coal had to close down. This led to roughly 10,000 workers losing their jobs in the sugar refining sector alone. The result was mass unemployment, as during the plague epidemic from 1712 to 1714, as well as an exponential rise in poverty and rampant inflation.

When the French finally withdrew their troops after Napoleon's abdication in May 1814 the population had shrunk from approximately 130,000 at the beginning of the century to 100,000. Of Hamburg's previous 280 vessels only 159 remained, the majority of them having left in time or now sailing under a different flag. Almost all of the large trading houses were ruined, unless they had been able to relocate large parts of their inventory and — as for example in the case of Godefroy & Sohn — were able to continue to conduct business from outside the city in the first instance. Even the silver deposits held by the Hamburger Bank had been requisitioned by the French. The total damage, inasmuch as this can even be expressed in monetary terms, was put at 221 million francs and the compensation finally paid by the French — 52 million francs to the citizens of Hamburg and 10 million francs to the Hamburger Bank — bore no relation to this amount. And this sum also did only little to revive the economy.

Most of Hamburg's traditional markets had been taken over by the British. After the systematic plundering of the city by the French it also lacked the capital required to re-establish old trade relations rapidly. Initially, therefore, Hamburg's merchants had no other option than to work on a commission basis for the large number of British traders now settling in the city. Even after Hamburg joined the German Confederation in 1815 it took until around 1820 for the population to regain the level of 125,000. It was only then that the economic conditions prevailing in Hamburg, which had been calling itself the "Free and Hanseatic City of Hamburg" since 1819, returned to normal.

# PART III

# Globalisation on a Global Scale: Industrial Revolution, Free Trade Imperialism, and the Increasing Importance of Overseas Markets

*Hamburg around 1900. The number of inhabitants increased from approximately 130,000 in 1800 to 214,000*

in 1850, and to almost 770,000 fifty years later. The one
million mark was passed in 1910.

CHAPTER 5

# Continental European Rivalries and the Relentless Rise of Great Britain

A series of highly different development trends were the defining features of the globalisation process from the end of the 18th to the beginning of the 20th century. They included: Firstly, the Industrial Revolution, the acceleration of technical progress and advancing urbanisation; secondly, further increases in the integration of international markets and the first global financial and economic crisis; and, thirdly, the trend towards imperial colonialism in India, Africa and the Middle East, as well as enforced free trade, most especially in Asia. Other key determinants that had a decisive effect on the shaping of both the globalisation process and political, economic and social developments into the 20th century were the intensification of the "social question" and the increasing democratisation of society.

## The Beginning of the Industrial Revolution in the Textile Industry

The Industrial Revolution began in Great Britain in the middle of the 18th century. Like many other major historical events it constitutes an extremely complex process in which political, economic, social and technological factors mutually influenced, intensified and promoted one another. It was a period marked by fundamental changes in ideas, behavioural patterns, structures and institutions, albeit one without any clearly defined starting point. Many things suggest that the key catalyst triggering this extraordinarily dynamic development was — at least during the *take-off* phase — of a predominantly economic nature and not primarily technology-driven. Nonetheless, essential requirements for the subsequent traction gained by the industrialisation process included a series of technological innovations, most notably in the textile, metal and mining industries, the majority of which had been already realised in Great Britain at the beginning of the 18th century.

On the one hand, this relates to the steam-driven pump invented by Thomas Newcomen in 1712. This was used to ventilate mining pits and galleries as well as to extract water from the depths of mine shafts. It can be viewed as the forefather of James Watt's steam engine, patented in 1769. At least in Great Britain this new energy source took the place of muscle power, hydropower and windpower at the end of the 18th century. Another example was a new iron casting technique on the basis of coke smelting, a method developed by Abraham Darby as far back as 1709 — yet not adopted for general use until after 1760. Also deserving of mention here is the flying shuttle patented by John Kay in 1733, which led to the development of the *Spinning Jenny* in 1768 and subsequently revolutionised the cotton industry.

In order to turn these inventions into innovations of macroeconomic relevance, however, certain market developments were nonetheless required to make their widespread utilisation commercially viable. Decisive factors for the technological and organisational trans-

151

formation of the British cotton industry were, on the one hand, the strong growth in domestic demand and, on the other, the initial competitive pressures of cheap imports from India. After the latter had been strictly forbidden, except for re-exports, since 1720 import protection opened the door to imitation; the dynamically growing home market and the mechanisation of production allowed the British first to draw level with Indian producers; thereafter mass production and export successes meant that they were poised to overtake.

In terms of globalisation three developments, more than any others, must be highlighted: The conquest of the global market, expressed by the fact that production for export was growing almost ten times faster than that for domestic demand; the fact that large quantities of cotton were being imported, from America and even from India — a development which made cotton the most important internationally traded commodity for many decades to come; and, finally, the fact that international technology transfer spread the new production methods and their application in the early decades of the 19th century from England to the European mainland and to the United States and, in a later development, to the rest of the world.

When compared with developments in England there was a considerable time lag before the Industrial Revolution got underway in Continental Europe and America. Moreover, its progression varied greatly according to the political, economic and social climate prevailing in the various countries and regions. In Germany, for example, the first mechanised cotton mill started operating in Ratingen back in 1764; this was, however, an exceptional event. If one disregards some early applications, most notably in Baden, mechanical spinning machines and looms were not widely used until the 1830s with the relatively new cotton processing industry spreading beyond Baden to establish itself in, above all, Saxony, Brandenburg and the Rhineland. However, throughout the 19th century the continental textile industry never managed to reduce Britain's headstart, and, in Germany in particular, the textile sector never played a leading role in the Industrial Revolution.

## Steam Engine Ascendant

As in the cotton industry the huge expansion of England's metal-working industry was, in the early phase, chiefly driven by economic factors, and it was these which spawned the technological leap forward. Although iron production based on the use of coke had been around since 1709, almost half of all iron production until approximately 1750 was charcoal-based. The iron producing and processing industry was initially able to afford this backwardness for three reasons. On the one hand, no efficient domestic market that could have accelerated the diffusion of the new technology via regional domestic competition and, on the other, there were sufficiently high tariffs in place to act as protection against competition from Sweden. Moreover, exports to other European countries and the American colonies, in which the British initially prohibited the production of iron, was still profitable.

It was only, in about 1760, after growing demand for iron triggered a dramatic rise in the price of charcoal while coal was, at around the same time, becoming less expensive that the industry's technology base changed virtually overnight. After 1775 charcoal proved uneconomical as a fuel for blast furnaces and, once again, it became clear that it was not primarily the new technology as such or the steam engine which powered this change. Steam technology was, nonetheless, an important determinant for the acceleration of this development. Not only did it boost demand for steel and iron; it was also one of the key elements in the industrial mechanisation process and, therefore, the reason for the rapid advances made in terms of industrial productivity during this period. It also made a significant contribution to the simultaneous revolution in transport systems, which found its chief vehicle of expression in railway construction and the use of steamships.

Once expansion of the road system had initially helped to open up those parts of Britain not accessible by river or canal, the railway age commenced in 1825. The first train pulled by a steam locomotive, on the Stockton and Darlington Railway, marked the starting point of a development which, once again originating in England, subsequently spread to the European continent and to America. In 1830 the total length of the global railway network was just 212 kilometres, yet by 1850 it had expanded to number more than 38,000 kilometres, of which 10,000 km were in Great Britain, 13,500 km in continental Europe and no less than 14,600 km in North America. By 1913, the end of the globalisation phase considered here, the global railway network boasted a total length of 1.1 million kilometres, of which three quarters were to be found in Europe and North America. As a result the geographic distribution of economic activity changed quite fundamentally.

## Dynamic Secondary Effects of Railway Construction

In Europe, America and, with a certain time lag, also in Asia and Africa railway construction was the source of major economic expansion effects. Apart from the increase in macro-economic demand due to the construction activities, the availability of a new mass-transport system independent of waterways resulted in the expansion and deeper integration of the domestic market. As a result the combination of increasing industrialisation and the innovative quantum leap in transportation systems facilitated the creation of new agglomeration economies. Subsequently, railway links to seaports led to greater interdependence between the new industries and the global market. The result was growing competition not only with regard to new materials and investment goods markets but also on both domestic and international products markets. Finally — and this appears to be more relevant to Germany than to Great Britain and most other industrial nations at that time — railway construction and its various upstream and downstream linkages constituted, from the middle of the 19th century, one of the most important driving forces in the process that transformed Germany into one of the world's leading industrial nations.

The first railway line in Germany, between Nuremberg and Fürth, opened in 1835. The first economically viable line, with a length of 115 kilometres, was inaugurated four years later between Leipzig and Dresden. In 1840, the German railway network was just 470 kilometres long; by 1850 it had increased to almost 6,000 kilometres and in 1870 it totalled roughly 19,000 kilometres. Even more impressive, perhaps, than total track length as an indicator of the momentum with which German railway construction was developing is locomotive construction. At first, locomotives and other materials were primarily imported from Great Britain. In 1841 Borsig launched the first German-built locomotive; by 1858 the company had already delivered its thousandth locomotive and subsequently advanced to become the world's largest locomotive manufacturer during the 1870s.

As in the engineering sector, other significant feedback effects of railway construction were felt in coal and ore mining, the iron and steel industry and the timber and glass industries. Conversely, the effects of mass production and technological progress had a positive effect on the dynamics of the railway sector. Above and beyond these sectoral amplification effects, which also extended to the banking sector, the other chains of knock-on impacts mentioned previously also applied to Germany. These included national market integration, choice of location, which was becoming increasingly independent of sea and inland waterway transportation routes, and further integration into the globalisation process.

In similar fashion to developments in England the industrialisation process in Germany was more than just a mutually dynamic interaction between technological development and market forces. Here, too, the partially process-inherent and partially politically determined changes to the overall economic and social conditions prevailing played a vital role. From around 1825 Germany experienced strong population growth, which served to stimulate demand. Peasant emancipation, initiated around 1807, and freedom of trade and economic pursuit, which was — in Prussia at least — implemented in the autumn of 1810, created, on the one hand, the labour pool potentials required for industrialisation and, on the other hand, new opportunities for personal initiative and entrepreneurship. Another important factor, most notably for market integration, was the German Customs Union, established in 1834. It is interesting to note, however, that despite the initially external tariffs Hamburg and the two other Hanseatic cities of Bremen and Lübeck consciously stayed out as their economic interests were best served by as free a trade system as possible.

## Internationally Interdependent Commodity and Financial Markets

The general economic upturn of the 1850s commenced in 1851 and, apart from a brief slump in 1855, lasted until the autumn of 1857. It was based on a wide variety of reasons which propelled one another forward. These included firstly the transatlantic wheat trade, which had boomed since the start of the Crimean War; secondly, the dynamic progress of industrialisation and thirdly the global trend towards lowering the level of protectionism. The partially enforced policy of liberalism encompassed not only China, but also Turkey, Egypt, Persia and Japan. A relatively steady annual growth rate of 6.5 per cent on average over a ten year period ensured that 19th century global trade peaked around this time.

If ever proof was needed to show that the globalisation process had become a worldwide phenomenon by the middle of the 19th century and that related economic interdependencies had already gained a considerable degree of intensity, then it was clearly displayed in the second half of 1857. The boom on the international wheat market, which had been caused by, amongst other things, the almost complete loss of Russian wheat supplies due to the Crimean War since 1853, prompted American farmers, in particular, to considerably expand production and to finance this expansion via loans.

*Both the Chamber of Commerce, which grew out of the "Commerzdeputation" in 1867, and the Commercial Library, founded in 1735, were housed in the New Stock Exchange, built between 1839 and 1841. The building was saved in the Great Fire of 1842. It was, however, destroyed during the air raids of the Second World War. The Commercial Library, which is probably the oldest library of economic literature in the world, lost 90 per cent of its valuable stock.*

At the same time the upturn was supported by ongoing industrialisation and the dynamics provided by railway construction; both of which benefited from the new financing facilities in the form of shares as well as from the generous granting of credit by the banks. The establishment of companies based on speculative investments, particularly in the railway and land development sectors, speculative dealings in the stock market and the carefree granting of loans also by the banks made the American economy and society highly prone to crises. But as long as stock prices continued to rise and the credit bubble did not burst, euphoria in the "land of the free" knew no bounds.

The first shock for the American economy came in 1856 when the Russian Tsar Alexander II unexpectedly ended the Crimean War by accepting defeat to the Turks, British and French. The recommencement of Russian deliveries caused the price of wheat to drop so drastically on the global market that a large number of American farmers could no longer compete. Many of these farmers, mainly in the west of the country, ran into financial difficulties. When, in the early summer of 1857, the American balance of payments — not least due to the shortfall of wheat exports — showed a deficit that resulted in massive gold outflows to Europe, the American banks restricted the granting of credit. This led to a huge increase of interest rates, which further compounded the instability of the economic situation.

In this climate it only required a small event to burst the speculative bubble; and this occurred on 24 August 1857 when the New York branch of the Ohio Life Insurance and Trust Company went bust. Ohio Life, as this institution was called on the New York Stock Exchange, had been considered a rock solid company just a few days before. But nobody had known that this institution had invested five million dollars, largely borrowed from other banks, in speculative and highly dubious railway projects. This second shock represented the beginning of the subsequent downward spiral.

The creditor banks of the Ohio Life, which tried to restrict their losses, demanded the immediate repayment of loans. This in turn tipped many farmers and companies into trouble. At the same time share prices, which had already shown a negative trend due to the first increase in interest rates, went into free fall. Even well-known blue chips lost between 8 and 10 per cent of their value within a couple of hours. Within two weeks 20,000 people had lost their jobs in New York alone. But not all hope was lost yet.

Although there were still no central banks to provide additional liquidity, as they did in 2001 after 9/11 or in 2007 and 2008 during the subprime crisis, there were fortunately sufficient gold deposits in California which could be used as additional reserves. The banks on the East Coast thus decided to transport gold to the value of two million dollars to New York as quickly as possible. They thought this would be enough to put the world's third most important financial centre, after Paris and London, back on its feet. But fate had other plans.

## The First Global Financial and Economic Crisis

The last leg of the gold transport to New York was by sea. When the mail steamship *SS Central America* set sail from Panama at the beginning of September, the economic situation had calmed down, since, based on the gold which would arrive in New York by the end of the month at the latest, the banks were already making corresponding arrangements. It could not be foreseen that the ship would sink in a hurricane 200 miles off the Carolinas on 12 September 1857 taking with it not only 426 lives but also the entire gold reserve. This was the third shock which finally plunged America's economy and society into a deep crisis.

Share prices fell drastically without any resistance being offered; one bank after the other had to halt its payments — not only in New York, but also in Boston, Philadelphia, Cincinnati, Chicago and elsewhere in the country; half of all New York brokers had to declare bankruptcy; thousands of companies were forced to close down; most companies had to cease production; warehouses were bursting with goods which could no longer be sold; by the end of October more than 100,000 people were unemployed in Manhattan and Brooklyn alone; then cotton prices fell, which intensified the crisis in the south of the country; the entire American economy — and not only this — was on the verge of collapse.

Europe had also been riding a speculative wave since 1855. In France people tried to get rich quick through railway shares; in Britain the main focus of interest was the railway and wheat; in Scandinavia financial investments in shipyards, factories and mining projects were favoured; many German regions preferred shares in the banking sector and in Hamburg people speculated with coffee and sugar. But no matter how varied the investment projects may have been, their markets were closely interlinked and not just within Europe but, in particular, also with America via London and Hamburg.

The transatlantic telegraph cable had not yet been laid and it took ten days before ships brought news of the serious economic crisis in America to Great Britain, where panic broke out at once. Almost half of all American securities were held by the British. Speculation collapsed; share prices went into free fall; interest went through the roof; commercial bills were no longer cashed; banks could not halt panic withdrawals; the downward spiral took its course. In London, Liverpool, Edinburgh, Glasgow and many other British cities numerous trading houses and banks had to file for bankruptcy. This happened during October 1857; by the end of the month the crisis had reached Hamburg, which, due to its close international trade relations, was the German city affected the most — but there were also other reasons as will be shown later.

In Hamburg more than 200 trading houses and banks, some of which were very renowned, fell by the wayside and even the largest ones eventually owed their survival to the active and preferred intervention of the state. This crisis, of course, not only affected the rich and speculators. Unemployment, poverty and hunger prevailed throughout the world — not only in the United States, Great Britain and continental Europe. This crisis had also dragged trading houses, banks and other companies in Argentina, Brazil, Chile and Uruguay into financial ruin. It even left its mark in India and Indonesia. 1857 was the year of the first real global financial crisis and it took almost two years until the meanwhile truly globalised world economy recovered from this shock and the process of industrialisation and international trade found its way back to its former glory.

## The Second Industrial Revolution

As for the key sectors of industrial development in Germany, the economic dynamics intensified — beyond the further expansion of the railway network, iron and steel industry as well as mechanical engineering — due to the disproportionate growth and the related increasing macroeconomic importance of a series of new sectors. Prominent examples included the chemical industry, the electrical industry, the optical industry, telecommunications and, slightly later, the automotive industry. A decisive factor for this development was, amongst other things, the increasing scientification of economy and society, which at first primarily influenced the technical progress and the organisation of production.

Technology imports, mainly from Great Britain, imitations based on blueprints and the reconstruction of machines acquired from abroad as well as empirical knowledge, which had been the starting point for creating new products and introducing new methods during the first industrial revolution, were now increasingly accompanied by engineering-based calculations. This development in Germany is illustrated by the invention of the Siemens-Martin oven (1864) and the Thomas-Gilchrist process (1879) in the steel industry as well as the electric dynamo (1866) and long-distance electric power transmission (1891) in the electrical sector. The production of synthetic dyes and sulphuric acid determined the upswing in the chemical industry; and the automotive industry also took its first tentative steps during this period. The number of annual patent applications in Germany rose from 4,000 in 1880 to roughly 12,000 in 1912.

However, it was not only the Germans who were playing technological catch-up with Great Britain: The same development could be observed with regard to France, Italy, Belgium, Switzerland and Sweden in Europe and the United States. The comparison between Britain and Germany, in particular, underlines the fact that success in the industrialisation process was not just a question of the overall modernisation of the economy and society. The second half of the 19th century at the latest shows that in addition to entrepreneurial initiative, successful innovation and the basic conditions conducive of economic development, industrial progress and international competitiveness were also determined by the education of the available workforce.

Technical schools, the predecessors of the technical universities which opened at the end of the 19th century, were founded in almost all large German cities in the 1820s — with the exception of the Hanseatic cities of Hamburg, Bremen und Lübeck, which still specialised in trade. Together with the universities, which were also reformed around this time, these institutes guaranteed the availability of a sufficient number of natural scientists, engineers and technicians. Furthermore, there were general and specialist vocational colleges which ensured the training of skilled workers. Both forms of vocational education were highly complementary and decisive catalysts for Germany's growing importance what were then hi-tech industries.

All this was accompanied by a commitment to extend elementary education, especially reading and writing skills which are essential for formal learning. Germany had made great headway in this area since the beginning of the 19th century. Even though compulsory education had been introduced in Prussia in 1763 only about half of the children actually attended school in 1816. However, this number had already increased to 80 per cent in 1846 and by 1860 only four per cent of the Prussian recruits were illiterate; in Saxony and Bavaria the figure was one and seven per cent respectively. In comparison, the number of illiterate and innumerate recruits in Great Britain was still roughly 30 per cent. From today's point of view this was probably an early indicator that, as a result, this nation would increasingly to fall behind in a world of increasing global industrial competition.

## A Turning Point for the Global Economy

In 1870 Great Britain was still world leader in industrial production and international trade. It was responsible for roughly one third of global industrial production and for approximately 30 per cent of global exports. Great Britain's share of global pig iron production was more than 50 per cent at that time; and in 1880 its production of cotton materials and yarns was still greater that of all other European countries combined. Mechanical engineering also played a key role in Great Britain for a long period of time. However, after 1890, the

For a long time, machine power alone was not trusted — at first because steam engines did not achieve sufficient power and later on because sailing in a favourable wind extended valuable coal supplies. Today's high energy prices have rekindled the idea of additional wind propulsion for seagoing vessels.

rate of iron and steel production in the USA was higher than in Great Britain; and by 1893 Germany was also producing more steel than Britain. With regard to overall industrial production, the United States had been top of the league since 1885 and in 1913 Germany moved up into second place ahead of Great Britain.

Predominantly in the second half of the 19th century the dynamics of the industrialisation process also spilled over to the evolution of international trade. The export share of European production rose from 7 to 16 per cent between 1850 and 1913 after probably amounting to roughly one per cent at the beginning of the 19th century. In 1913 European manufacturers still commanded a global market share of more than 80 per cent in the export of industrial products and were almost unrivalled due the low level of exports from the USA. Another significant factor for Europe's leading economic role was that it was far less dependent on energy imports than it is today due to the production of British and German coal.

Meanwhile, Great Britain was not only Europe's first industrial powerhouse. With London and Liverpool it had the largest and the third largest European port respectively, with only Hamburg exceeding the latter in terms of size. Its currency, the pound sterling, had become the key international currency during the 19th century. London was the financial capital of the world; and Britain remained the leading player in global trade right up until the 20th century. Nevertheless it had to deal with considerable market share losses between 1880 and 1913. Its lead over Germany and the United States in particular dwindled drastically over time. In 1880 Great Britain achieved a 23 per cent share of the global export market; Germany and the United States were left trailing with only 8 and 7 per cent respectively. By 1913 however, the respective market shares were 16, 12 and 11 per cent.

The regional focus of global trade changed very little at first. Intra-European trade still dominated, accounting for a roughly 40 per cent of global trade. The percentage of European imports from other European countries was 68 per cent around 1870 and still totalled 60 per cent of all global imports in 1910. Only European imports from North

America increased from 11 to 14 per cent during this period. All other geographical shifts were, at least with regard to the global economy, still irrelevant. This does not, however, mean that all other parts of the world were excluded from the ongoing dynamic development of international trade and the related increase in maritime traffic. What effect trade dynamics had on international maritime traffic and to what extent the German seaports and, in particular, Hamburg profited from this development will be dealt with later.

## Global Market Integration and Worldwide Infrastructure

As with all previous eras of economic development expansion of the transport and communication infrastructure also played a vital role for the long-distance trade and the globalisation processes in the 19th century. In this respect the acceleration and scope of the new developments in this sector, at least in the second half of the century, can almost be classified as a quantum leap. The rapid expansion of railways revolutionised land transport; the introduction of steamships made maritime traffic more efficient and reliable; and a series of large canal systems slashed the sailing distance between Europe and the Indian Ocean and the Pacific Ocean.

The Suez Canal, which opened in 1869, shortened the distance between London and Bombay from 10,667 to 6,274 nautical miles, in other words by 41 per cent. The Panama Canal, which commenced operation in 1914, reduced the route from Liverpool to San Francisco by 42 per cent and from New York to San Francisco by a staggering 60 per cent. This resulted not only in a significant increase in transport efficiency and maritime safety but also in a remarkable reduction of freight costs; a development from which Hamburg obviously benefited.

Together with the continuing technological development of the steamship and a series of other inventions — for example the refrigerating machine — enhancement of the international transport infrastructure led to an unstoppable intercontinental integration of markets at the turn of the 20th century. European industrial products and coal were exported to all four corners of the world. Refrigerated transport allowed Europeans to import beef from Argentina, mutton and milk products from New Zealand and tropical fruit, particularly bananas, from overseas. The economic implications were, however, not only visible in terms of the worldwide physical availability of the various products but also, and in particular, in the price effects. For example, between 1870 and 1913 the price difference for wheat between Chicago and Liverpool, for cotton between Bombay and Liverpool and for steel between Philadelphia and London fell from 58 to 16 per cent, 57 to 20 per cent and 85 to 19 per cent respectively.

All this would surely not have been possible if the opportunity of efficient worldwide communication had not developed at the same time as the global transport infrastructure. After the telegraph, which had been invented in 1837, was installed along railway lines in Europe and the USA a Europe-Asia connection and, after some failed attempts, the first two transatlantic cables went into operation in 1863 and 1866 respectively. Telegraph communication between England and India via a submarine telegraph cable commenced in 1870. The telephone followed around 1878 and wireless telegraphy began its triumphant advance before the turn of the century, even though the first and most important aspect of this technology was communication with and between ships on the high seas. That people even dreamt of wireless mobile telephones can be seen as an illustrative example of the technological pioneering spirit of that time.

As with other previous technological breakthroughs, the telecommunication sector benefited from the complex interplay between technological development on the one hand, and economic and social factors on the other. Increasing intercontinental economic relations required efficient information channels. In 1857 it still took more than one week until news of the New York financial and stock exchange crisis reached London. Now it was possible to transmit share prices and price movements on the commodity markets, for example for wheat and cotton, in a flash even from one continent to the next.

These benefits were, however, not restricted to the economic realm. Press information was being increasingly exchanged on a global scale. After wireless telecommunication systems had initially been installed for marine navigation and safety permanent news services even became a matter of course on the luxury liners that sailed between Europe and America. The world had become a "global village" far beyond the economic sphere even though economic relations played a dominant role. Another aspect which required addressing in light of the internationalisation of telecommunications was the demand for worldwide system compatibility, i.e. the need for internationally harmonised technical standards.

## *From Colonialism to Imperialism*

Apart from Spanish America where conquest, repression, religious proselytisation and exploitation had played a key role from the very start, this did not apply or at least not to the same extent to the trade-orientated base colonisation in the Asia Pacific region or the plantation economy in the West Indies. Imperialist colonialism, which saw local leaders ousted in favour of foreign ones and central sovereignty functions, such as jurisdiction, taxation, police and military forces as well as foreign affairs, primarily determined by the colonial power did not develop until the late 18th century and increasingly in the 19th century. First characteristic examples of imperialist domination can be found in the Netherlands East Indies, where the Dutch had based their trade and financial exploitation on political and military rule, and in British-India, particularly after command of the English East India Company was transferred to the government in London in 1858.

While at the beginning of the colonial period the acquisition of gold and silver, the import of overseas luxury goods and the slave trade were, from an economic viewpoint, the main objectives, the main focus of interest shifted towards the import of plant, mineral and fossil raw materials during the Industrial Revolution and towards the targeted identification and development of new markets when mass production commenced. Missionary work was still being carried out but it was increasingly overlaid with an ideological, partially even racist, sense of mission which aimed to impose European values on the "culturally unsophisticated". However, the most important change in colonial and expansion policy at that time took place in the transition from a policy of an accentuated balance of power between the most important European countries to one of explicit nationalist and rival imperialist power play.

The power-political dimension had once played a vital role for France in particular and, to a lesser degree, for Great Britain, although its economic interests had always come first. The new aspect was that everything was now primarily about power politics and the strategic division of the world. Moreover, not only Britain and France but also Germany, Russia, the United States and even Japan wished to play the leading role on the global stage.

### The Division of the World: Political Prestige and Economic Benefit

The two major colonial powers at the turn of the 20th century were definitely Great Britain and France. Although the mother country only represented two per cent of the world's population at this time, Great Britain possessed 40 to 45 per cent of global industrial potential; it had by far the largest merchant and naval fleet; thanks to its colonies it ruled directly and indirectly over one fifth of the world and had roughly 500 million subjects. In 1913 37 per cent of the country's exports went to its colonies and 20 per cent of its imports came from the colonies. The development of economic relations to the overseas territories was additionally supported by substantial foreign di-

When Hamburg-Süd started services with fast steamers in 1906, the advertising campaigns of the shipping company focussed mainly on emigration. The heyday of cruises started in the 1920s and, in particular, after the commissioning of the new "Cap Arcona".

rect investments and the highly profitable granting of loans via London, the world's leading financial centre.

France, which was able to extend its sphere of influence by nine million square kilometres between 1876 and 1914 during permanent, almost war-like conflicts, still lagged far behind Great Britain. Only 11 per cent of its exports and 9 per cent of its imports involved its colonies; however, the colonial exports of some important industrial sectors, such as the cotton, metal and sugar industry, did reach 40 per cent around 1906. France was also able, although it occasionally involved great effort, to enforce its currency, administrative culture and language in its colonies. Profits for private entrepreneurs and financial investors were, as for the British, in most cases exorbitant; but whether the French colonial adventure actually paid off for the state and taxpayers in light of the high administrative and military expenses as well as the costs for setting up the colonial infrastructure is very questionable.

In addition to a series of internal and external considerations, this last aspect probably contributed greatly to the fact that Germany — even after the foundation of the German Empire in 1871 and as long as Bismarck was Imperial Chancellor — only very hesitantly took part in the colonial expansion race. And even after Bismarck had put a certain number of German possessions, especially the acquisitions of Hamburg merchants, in Africa and in the Pacific region under the "protection" of the German Empire, he at first only recognised them primarily as protectorates whose economic and social development would in future mainly be left to private business. It was only after the Congo Conference held in Berlin in 1884/85, which principally dealt with the future of the Congo, but indirectly also with the modalities for dividing the still available world, first and foremost in Africa, that Germany officially entered the circle of colonial powers.

Despite the aggressive expansion policy with express imperial support after Bismarck's dismissal in 1890 the territorial acquisitions of three million square kilometres made by the German Empire by 1914 were still almost insignificant compared to those of Great Britain and

France. Emotionally highly charged and with broad support from the population, also and particularly in the Hanseatic cities, colonial possession had become a question of geo-political prestige in Germany as well. Its costs for the national budget exceeded the colonial income by far. Whether losses in the public sector were balanced by additional gains in the private sector is difficult to assess, but rather unlikely. Emigration to the colonies was also very limited. In fact there were only 23,000 Germans who decided to relocate to the colonies before the First World War. In contrast, the number of Germans who emigrated to the USA between 1887 and 1906 was one million.

Germany was, however, not alone with its new colonial ambitions. Russia expanded its territory towards the east and south, especially to Central Asia, Korea, Formosa as well as parts of Manchuria, and the United States took possession of the Philippines, Guam, Hawaii and a number of Caribbean islands. Finally it was the United States who, together with the leading European colonial powers, prevented Russia and Japan from dividing up China according to the African example at the end of the century. Apart from the existence of colonial bases it was important that the large Chinese market remained accessible to all via its meanwhile 48 "contract ports" within an "open door policy". It is obvious that this also met Hamburg interests.

## The Social Question
## and the Labour Movement

As in Great Britain since approximately 1750, the first phase of industrialisation contributed to rapid growth of population, rural depopulation and urbanisation, initially resulting in exploitation and social deprivation for large parts of the population on the European mainland. People were expected to work 12 to 16 hours a day, seven days a week, and 11 hour nightshifts were the norm. Pay was often so low that a worker alone did not earn enough to feed a family. Female and child labour, which had always been part of farming, became widespread — but under terrible conditions — also in factories and even mines.

There was no such thing as social laws or labour protection laws. Only the prevention of adverse conditions which negatively influenced production sometimes resulted in the improvement of working conditions. The description of the health of working children in an official report by the Prussian government dated 1824 reads like a menu of misery: "In terms of their well-being and health their pale faces, tired and inflamed eyes, swollen bellies, bloated cheeks, swollen lips and nostrils, inflamed and sore throat glands, terrible skin rashes and asthmatic problems clearly differentiate them from other children of the same social class who do not work in factories."

Deprivation during the early phase of industrialisation in Germany was — as previously in Great Britain — also characterised by the fact that migration from the countryside at first far exceeded the creation of additional jobs in the new industrial towns and cities. Furthermore, and this also applied to the textile industry in France and Switzerland, the mechanisation of certain production processes as well as low-price competition from Britain not only led to mounting wage pressure but also to the permanent laying off of workers. As far as Germany was concerned, the social conditions for workers only improved after the nationwide expansion of the railway network, the upswing in the iron and steel industry and mechanical engineering in the second half of the 19th century as well as after the second industrial revolution, which was characterised by the development of the chemical and electrical industry.

Nonetheless, rising food prices, which represented the major element of expenditure for a worker's household, repeatedly resulted in decreasing real wages also during this latter period. Additionally general business cycles, which could be observed since the Industrial Revolution, led to rising unemployment or underemployment in the downturn phase. Besides such macroeconomic and cyclical developments real wage evolution and the social situation of workers were also influenced by a number of long term trend factors. The first and most important factor was the continuously worsening standard of living conditions. A second factor was that state authorities took little or no responsibility for the social situation of this part of the population. Legislation restricting child labour was not introduced in Great Britain until 1833 and in Prussia and Austria until 1839.

The first workers' uprising in the textile industry in Great Britain in 1811/12 due to unacceptable social conditions was crushed with the help of 12,000 soldiers. A new law stated that the death penalty would be used against anyone found guilty of deliberately destroying machinery. The military was also deployed during the silkweaver uprisings in Lyon in 1831, 1834 and 1848. During the second uprising more than 600 people died and more than 10,000 insurgents were sentenced to imprisonment or even deported. The military and judicial institutions took similar drastic action during the weaver uprisings in Germany in 1831 and 1847. The protests were not only directed against the mechanisation of the individual production sites, but also against foreign competition from Britain, France and Belgium that flooded the German market, weakened prices, increased wage pressure and put jobs at risk.

Continuing industrialisation and the development of large companies resulted in growing solidarity among workers and, due to the exploitative working conditions, social unrest in the form of strikes. One of the first waves of strike action in Germany, which subsequently spread to other sectors and cities, including Hamburg, started in 1865 with a book printers' strike in Leipzig. However, it became quite obvious that such action could not be upheld without sufficient financial backing. Other examples of the increasing intensity of industrial disputes were the miners' strike in the Ruhr in 1889, a two and a half month long dock workers' strike in Hamburg in 1896/97 as well as a mass miners' strike in Rhenish-Westphalia and Upper Silisia in 1904. The events in Hamburg will be discussed in detail later.

## The Beginning of the Democratisation of the Economy and Society

The most important long term result of these protest movements, which spread throughout Europe and later to the United States, was the development of the labour movement. Three dimensions must be differentiated with regard to the characteristics of this new development. The first was a growing feeling of solidarity against the background of comparable economic, social and political experiences. The second was the formation of an intellectual-ideological basis to which — after initial utopian approaches, especially in France — Karl Marx and Frederick Engels contributed, in particular with the publication of the *Communist Manifesto* in London in 1848. The third dimension was the institutionalisation of workers' interests, at first in workers' associations and collectives and subsequently in unions and political parties.

Besides protectionist agricultural groups and the predominantly mercantilist entrepreneurialism in Germany, workers represented a third political power in society through unions and political parties, which would also — at least in the long term — greatly influence the development of the globalisation process. Apart from a few exceptions, such as the weaver uprisings in Germany, the labour movement initially focussed on the improvement of working conditions. The workers' associations had been barred from any form of political activity since 1854 and the Social Democratic Party, founded in 1869, was not allowed to engage in political action outside the Reichstag after 1876.

Their presence in the Reichstag was politically and practically of little significance. After the election of 1881 and with six per cent of the votes the Social Democratic Party held only three per cent of the parliamentary seats. The Empire was, moreover, a constitutional and not a parliamentary monarchy in which Bismarck often simply dissolved the Reichstag whenever he failed to win a majority for his policies. And even Bismarck's social laws, which led to the introduction of a health and accident insurance in 1883 and 1884 as well as an old age and disability insurance in 1889, was in fact initially considered a political tactical manoeuvre against the social democratic underground movement which was becoming increasingly strong. That these measures later became an international role model for industrial nations is a different issue. Bismarck considered unions and social democrats who fought against exploitation and suppression to be "robbers and highwaymen".

It was not until after Bismarck's resignation, practically enforced by Kaiser Wilhelm II in 1890, that the so-called Socialist Laws were finally repealed and free unions allowed. By 1911 almost three million people, roughly 40 per cent of the industrial workers, had become union members. Moreover, the SPD, which assumed this name in 1890, received more than one third of all votes during the 1912 elections, and with 110 mandates clinched 28 per cent of all seats in the German Reichstag. In Hamburg, where the socialists had not been represented in the city Parliament until 1901 and had had just one Member of Parliament before 1904, they won all three seats for the Reichstag with 62 per cent of the votes.

Other European countries also witnessed solidarity movements against the exploitation and impoverishment of workers in the second half of the 19th century. The precise extent of this activity varied, however, greatly from country to country. Great Britain saw the foundation of numerous unionised groups of workers, whose umbrella organisation represented more than 70 individual organisations. The LRC, the political predecessor of today's Labour Party, was not established until 1900. In France and in other Romanic countries, workers initially organised themselves into groups at company level. In 1884, one year after the foundation of unions was also officially recognised in France, the CGT, which is still the most influential union in the country, was founded. However, the political articulation of socialist ideas in France was at first highly fragmented before the establishment of the "Section française de l'Internationale ouvrière" in 1905.

Nonetheless, the political influence of the Labour Party in Britain as well as the SFIO in France was at first negligible.

In the United States the labour movement had been developing since the middle of the 19th century. The period between 1886 and 1894 in particular, saw several important strikes which ended, just as in Europe, in violent clashes with the forces of the state. Despite European immigration socialist ideas did not have a politically relevant echo until after the First World War, and whether Roosevelt's New Deal can be included here is highly controversial. There can, however, be no doubt about the labour movement becoming an active element in the globalisation process thanks to its various international relations. It is interesting, though, that neither the unions nor the closely linked socialist parties demanded the closing of markets to foreign competition. But this was about to change in the not too distant future.

## International
## Trading and Capital Transactions

Advancing globalisation in the economic sector in the 19th century until the outbreak of the First World War can be expressed, amongst other things, by the fact that — at least after the end of the Napoleonic Wars — exports and transnational capital flows grew more quickly than the gross national product. Unfortunately, statistical data regarding international commodity trade for the period between 1820 and 1870 is only available for seven European countries and the United States. With an average annual rate of growth of exports and a national product of 4.5 per cent and 1.8 per cent respectively the export rate, which can be viewed as a rough indicator for the intensity of transnational trade relations, increased from 1.8 per cent in 1820 to 6.5 per cent in 1870. In the ensuing period until 1913 worldwide exports increased by an average of 3.4 per cent and the gross national product rose by 2.1 per cent per annum. The export rate of Central

*With an average speed of 16.5 knots, often achieved over a period of several days, the Flying P-Liner "Potosi" of the Hamburg shipping company F. Laeis, commissioned in 1895, was one of the fastest deep-sea sailing ships of its day. On its journeys to Chile the "Potosi" was usually faster than the majority of steam or motor-powered freighters in the first half of the 20th century.*

and Western European countries, which were the decisive initiators of the dynamics of the globalisation process in the 19th century, increased to no less than 14 per cent in 1913. The total value of international commodity trade was estimated at two billion dollars in 1830 and 40 billion dollars in 1913.

The basic framework of the international division of labour was relatively simple. Western Europe primarily specialised in the export of investment goods, industrial consumer goods and other finished products as well as the global provision of transportation, banking and insurance services. And the rest of the world, if it actually participated in global economic exchange, generally exported food and agricultural and mineral raw materials. Europe's leading position in the global economy was based on this asymmetry in international trade relations but was also supported by the fact that the European countries were altogether far less dependent on the import of important basic raw materials from overseas than they are today. Thanks to their production of coal, Great Britain and Germany provided a large proportion of the energy supply; and three quarters of the iron and steel trade still occurred within Europe's borders.

As there was no such thing as balance of payments statistics in the 19th century, one has to rely even more on the estimated figures provided by historians in this area than when looking at commodity trade. But even if the associated uncertainties are taken into account, the rate of growth of net capital exports was, just like today, greater than the rate of growth of the international commodity trade. While the capital stock invested abroad amounted to roughly one billion dollars in 1820, it hit the 48 billion dollar mark in 1913. With a ratio of 90 per cent European dominance in foreign direct investment was even higher than in the international commodity trade, where it was only 65 per cent. Taking into consideration the stock of foreign direct investment in 1914, Great Britain was by far the largest capital exporter with more than 40 per cent, followed by France and Germany with 20 per cent and 13 per cent respectively.

The significance of international capital flows before the First World War is also emphasised by the fact that British capital exports amounted to 9 per cent of the estimated national product. This figure was not achieved by any country during the last decades of the 20th century. Similarly impressive were the capital imports of the developing nations at the end of the 19th century. For instance, Australia and Argentina's average annual rate of capital imports between 1870 and 1889 was 8.2 per cent and 18.7 per cent of the gross national product respectively. These are dimensions which today's developing nations, including China, which still trails the United States in capital imports, can only dream of.

The reasons for capital exports were numerous. Due to the creation of financial dependencies they were used to secure access to foreign raw material sources. By granting loans for the expansion of production and the infrastructure they opened markets for the export of machines and railway materials. The return on investments abroad was usually also higher than that of investments in the domestic market. However, the type of long term foreign direct investment differed greatly from that prevailing today. Even though there had been certain types of multinational companies for many centuries, the capital exports of the 19th century primarily flowed into portfolio investments. The number of foreign subsidiaries of European and American companies was estimated at no more than 350 in 1913 and their share in global production at between just 3 to 6 per cent.

## *The End of 19th Century Globalisation*

When considering the overall level of international trade relations, transnational capital transactions in terms of the net capital flows and the extent of the cross-border migration of workers, it could be concluded that the degree of globalisation, in relation to the overall level of economic activities of those countries actively participating in international exchange, was probably greater at the end of the 19th century than at the end of the 20th century. The decisive question is whether the end of this globalisation phase can be explained solely or primarily on the basis of the outbreak of the First World War or whether at the turn of the century there were also a number of endogenous factors which tended to weaken of the dynamics of the globalisation process so that it could have possibly been slowed down or even stopped also without the Great War. Even if a definite answer to this question can never be given, there are many reasons to believe that the latter thought cannot be entirely excluded.

The period of free trade did, in fact, not commence until the mid-19th century. In 1842 Great Britain lifted the export ban on equipment. In 1846 the "Corn Laws", introduced to protect British agriculture in 1815, were abolished. And after a provisional suspension in 1847 the then almost 200-year old Navigation Acts were also repealed. Just like the United States exactly 100 years later, Great Britain used its economic and technical supremacy to become the pioneer of free trade and hoped, not least due to the fact that the pound sterling had become the key international currency, to further increase its domination of world trade.

The European continent, apart from a few small countries, such as Belgium, the Netherlands and Denmark, still based its foreign trade and development policies on the ideas of Friedrich List's infant industry argument, i.e. that domestic industries must be allowed to develop behind protectionist trade barriers before entering international markets on a stronger footing. Comprehensive tariff reductions with regard to other continental European countries were not introduced until a trade agreement between Britain and France was signed in 1860 by Napoleon III against the express will of the majority in parliament. Nearly all these tariff reductions were based on bilateral agreements with most-favoured nation clauses.

In spite of this liberalisation not only adding to the expansion of trade but also increasing and accelerating the modernisation of industry on the continent, protectionism clearly underwent a revival, except in Britain, at the beginning of the 1880s. Germany took the first step in 1879, when Bismarck tried to protect the still weak domestic industry — especially in Silesia — and, in particular, the interests of farmers and landowners. The main reason for this political U-turn was the unfavourable development of global economic conditions, which started with the "Panic of 1873" and turned into a real depression around 1880.

The result was, on the one hand, that prices for industrial products dropped as the demand for investment goods as well as for industrial consumer goods declined. On the other hand — and this was probably more important from a political viewpoint — prices for crop imports from America and Australia dropped by more than 50 per cent between 1875 and 1895, and without tariff protection this would have ruined continental European agriculture. In contrast to Great Britain, where the agricultural sector had already become marginalised, no less than 47 per cent of the population in France and 43 per cent of the population in Germany still depended on agriculture in 1880. It comes as no surprise therefore that Britain remained true to free trade while its European neighbours returned to protectionism.

As to Germany it should also be pointed out that the entire agrarian sector was highly indebted so that a collapse in this sector could have led to a banking crisis. Moreover, it could not have been in Bismarck's political interest that unemployed farm workers swelled the numbers of the proletariat in the cities. It was, after all, one of his main domestic political goals, also via the social laws, to keep the revolutionary potential of the workers as well as the political influence of the socialists under control. Even if the parliament did not have a right to control the executive and Bismarck, whenever he thought it necessary, bypassed parliament, he still had to take into consideration the fact that all male citizens over the age of 24 had had the right to vote since the foundation of the German Empire, at least for the Reichstag.

Tendencies towards protectionism and their intensification were, however, not limited to continental Europe. The United States did not participate in the above mentioned trade liberalisation in relation to industrial goods. They continued to impose tariff rates of 40 to 50 per cent of the import value and, at a later stage, raised these high rates even further. Argentina, Australia, Canada, Venezuela and a number of other nations also introduced new tariffs to protect their domestic industries after 1878. And protectionist ideas even circulated in Great Britain, leading to the enactment of a law in 1887 that stipulated the labelling of internationally traded goods according to the land of origin. This is how the label "Made in Germany" came into being and it was introduced as an incentive to promote patriotic consumer behaviour — and definitely not with the idea of turning it into a trademark.

This new wave of patriotism was, however, not restricted to the introduction of trade barriers. The international free movement of labour was also increasingly hampered. Many traditional immigration countries decided to restrict immigration by applying new or stricter quality criteria. These related to a person's education and health — or as in Australia — implicitly also included a racial element. A special characteristic in France was that public contracts were, as a matter of principle, no longer given to companies which employed foreign workers. All this shows that a climate of change with regard to political and social acceptance of the uncontrolled continuation of the globalisation process had already taken place, at least in the economic sector before the start of the First World War and that the question of principle of whether globalisation, national state and the democratisation of society are compatible would also have arisen if the First World War had not broken out.

CHAPTER 6

# Hamburg:
# The European Continent's
# Leading Port
# and Trading Hub

Hamburg's development in the 19th century was characterised by three very different tendencies. To begin with, Hamburg regained its traditionally strong position as the trading hub between Germany and Central and Eastern Europe on the one hand and Western Europe and overseas on the other. In Western Europe, the majority of its commercial activities were geared towards trade with Great Britain. In overseas trade the main focus was initially on the United States and Latin America. It was not until later that the city's interests were expanded to include Asia. During the second half of the century Hamburg recaptured the position it had already occupied at the end of the 18th century. Once again it was the largest port and trading centre on the European mainland. Around 1900 no less than 4.5 per cent of overall world trade was handled via Hamburg.

A second trend which continued throughout the 19th century was the increasing loss of the Hanseatic city's political independence. The city's policy of neutrality came to an end following accession to the German Confederation in 1815 and, even more so, to the North German Confederation in 1867. Incorporation into the German Empire in 1871 and, most notably, introduction of the gold mark four years later resulted in Hamburg relinquishing its own currency and monetary policy. Despite the establishment of a free port the basically coerced membership of the Customs Union from 1888 onwards meant the loss of sovereignty in foreign trade affairs too. Thirdly Hamburg was unable to evade the major sociopolitical changes occurring at the end of the 19th century. The city became the stronghold of the German trade union movement. However it took several outbreaks of cholera before the Senate and the merchants finally realized, in the 1890s, that a sustained improvement in hygiene and living conditions, also including for the workers can be a key factor determining the economic competitiveness of a location. Nonetheless it took a mass strike by dock workers to show many hard-nosed employers that the same also applied in the field of good industrial relations and dialogue with trade unions concerning improved working conditions. When, in 1904, socialists won seats in the Hamburg Parliament for the very first time, the conservative parties were so shocked that, immediately afterwards, negotiations on the subject of stricter enfranchisement laws were initiated.

## *The Revival of Trade Relations, most notably with Britain and America*

Hamburg's traditionally close ties to Great Britain, which were restored immediately after the city's liberation from the French and subsequently fostered by both sides, were beneficial for Hamburg in every respect. The German hinterland, which was slowly recovering from the chaos of the war, was a dynamically growing market for British industrial products. England with its sharply rising number of industrial workers as a percentage of the total population was an ideal market for the agricultural economy of Germany and Eastern Europe. Geographically speaking Hamburg was located between the two and, as a trading centre, it profited from both: Exports to Great Britain via Hamburg consisted mainly of wheat from Prussia and Russia, zinc

*Hamburg's inner port in 1825. In the background, the old stock exchange and the old city hall, destroyed in the Great Fire in 1842.*

from Silesia and wool. Imports from Britain comprised chiefly finished industrial goods and cotton yarn, as well as coal, iron and colonial goods. Due to the ongoing industrialisation of the German textile industry there was an increasing shift of emphasis in the trade of cotton products from finished goods to yarn and, later, to raw cotton.

The average rate of growth in trade between Hamburg and England, for which the annual 2.3 per cent increase in shipping between 1816 and 1831/33 may be taken as a rough indicator, was at first relatively low — and this despite the liberalisation measures implemented by the British between 1822 and 1828 and the trade treaty concluded in 1825. Inasmuch as these measures involved the partial lifting of shipping restrictions through the Navigation Acts, they did not, at least not during the first few years, bring any appreciable advantages to Hamburg. The city had, in 1822, only 114 vessels of its own and, even in 1835, 86 per cent of all ships docking in Hamburg still sailed under

185

other flags. But the reduction of import duties and the easing of conditions in trade with the colonies also had very little positive impact on Hamburg. The British insisted on the principle of reciprocity and Hamburg, as a small city state that profited predominantly from transit trade, had little to offer in this respect.

Remarkably dynamic was, by contrast, the development of trade with America. After a trade treaty was signed in 1827, which also included Bremen and Lübeck, Hamburg's trade in goods with the United States increased fivefold between 1830 and 1840. In 1827 a trade agreement was also concluded with Brazil; this was followed by agreements with Mexico in 1832, Venezuela in 1837, Guatemala in 1847 and a further eight Latin American nations which had all gained independence between 1810 and 1830. The majority of these treaties were based on reciprocity and most-favoured-nation status. They chiefly served to govern the rights of Hamburg vessels in the ports of the partner countries. Furthermore, Hamburg also established its own representative offices abroad in order to protect its trading interests. In 1846 the number of offices in Latin America alone amounted to 162.

In addition to those from Mexico and the West Indies, imports from Brazil showed the highest growth rates. This was largely due to the fact that Britain had, in the interest of its own colonies, prohibited the import of Brazilian coffee and sugar and these goods now found their way to the European continent via Hamburg. Another reason why Hamburg, in particular, profited from British protectionism could be that, unlike in Hamburg, transit goods in Amsterdam, Antwerp and Rotterdam were subject to high tariffs which made these ports comparatively less competitive.

## Problems
## *of International Competitiveness*

However, not all was well with the competitiveness of Hamburg's port. The Stade Elbe Tariff continued — right up until 1861 — to be levied and, considering the large number of incoming ships that did not sail under Hamburg's flag, this proved to be a considerable economic burden on trade with the city. Additionally the duty on transit goods in Bremen and Altona was approximately 2 per cent lower than in Hamburg. Nevertheless, Hamburg's merchants had to exercise significant powers of persuasion to convince the Senate and the Hamburg Parliament ("Bürgerschaft") of the need to reduce this difference by making adjustments to tariffs and other duties. Outdated trade practices were yet another area resulting in significant competitive disadvantages for Hamburg. Not only were the prices of coffee, cotton, linen, sugar, tobacco and many other products calculated in different, sometimes even obsolete currencies; there was also an incredible jumble of different weights and measurement units, obscure discount systems, opacity in the calculation of brokerage fees and inadequacies in the availability of quoted market prices.

It required massive criticism from the city's American trading partners to convince those responsible in Hamburg to implement the reforms required to protect their own trade interests. Notwithstanding this, the reforms were initially incomplete. Sugar producers, who had been experiencing a new upturn in trade due to raw sugar imports from overseas, in particular from Brazil and Cuba, as well as indirectly via England, bitterly opposed the reforms. Together with the tobacco industry, which was also a stubborn defender of the old traditions, they finally had to be provisionally excluded from the new regulations. Hamburg's sugar industry is a striking example of an economic sector which, in an environment of increasing international competition between international locations, accelerated its own demise by refusing to abandon entrenched practices.

In October 1828 Hamburg also signed a trade treaty with Prussia. However, the reciprocal equal treatment, as set forth in the agreement, of Hamburg and Prussian ships and merchandise in the respective ports was of practically no significance as there was barely any direct traffic between Hamburg and the Prussian ports. More important, in relative terms, was the resumption of shipping to the Mediterranean after France had, in 1830, occupied Algeria, thus putting an end to the permanent threat posed by the corsairs. Yet Hamburg's trade with West Africa, which also recommenced in 1832, remained — compared to that with Britain and America — just as insignificant as its trade with East Asia.

## Hamburg opts to stay
## out of the German Customs Union

Even though the Customs Union, founded under the leadership of Prussia and with the exclusion of Austria, initially levied only modest tariffs, there were very good reasons for Hamburg — and the two other Hanseatic cities of Bremen and Lübeck — not to join this basically protectionist coalition. Hamburg's economic interests lay in free trade and just as it had always been at pains to uphold a foreign policy of neutrality prior to joining the German Confederation, it now sought to maintain the neutrality of its international trade policy.

Hamburg's merchants not only feared the potentially protectionist tendencies of the domestic agricultural lobby. Above all, they mistrusted the protectionist attitude of Germany's industrial sector, which was still backward when compared with that in England. That such fears were fully justified was proven by the increasingly prohibitive tariffs on cotton goods as well as the significantly increased tariffs on iron in the 1840s. Relative to the average CIF prices in Hamburg the tariff burden on imports into the territory of the German Customs Union were 27 per cent on pig iron, 51.7 per cent on railway tracks and 68 per cent on Welsh rod iron.

In addition to concerns about the negative impact of this protectionist policy on international trade in general, there were three further aspects which prompted Hamburg to stay out of the Customs Union: Firstly, Hamburg's hinterland, most especially Holstein, Hanover and Mecklenburg, did not belong to the Customs Union either; secondly, Hamburg did not wish to put its traditionally close trade relations with Austria at risk; and, thirdly, there was a quite understandable reluctance to surrender its sovereignty in international trade policy and to become subject to decisions taken by members of the Union, the majority of whom were focused on their domestic markets.

The decisive influence that Hamburg's status as a foreign German customs territory had on the structural development of its own economy would become apparent in the years that followed. No matter how advantageous the neutral policy of the Senate might have been for Hamburg as an international trading centre, the consequences for the city as a business location were that there was no longer a sufficiently sized domestic market to support the manufacturing sector and, in particular, the potential development of industry in Hamburg.

As a result, Hamburg's sugar industry, a sector already facing severe difficulties due to its small-scale structure, lack of capital resources and insufficient innovative capability, was, in its efforts to compete with the newly emerging, state-subsidised German sugar industry, hit by additional tariff burdens which, for refineries, bordered on the prohibitive. For new industries, even if these had been established with capital from Hamburg, it was more advantageous to be located in Harburg, Altona or Wandsbek and not in Hamburg itself. This applied all the more so after these neighbouring areas fell to Prussia in 1864 (Harburg) and 1866/67 (Altona and Wandsbek).

## The Great Fire of Hamburg in 1842

Hamburg continued to thrive as an international trading centre even after the foundation of the Customs Union. Despite Prussia's efforts to promote Stettin and other cities in the Baltic region, Hamburg remained Germany's largest port by far. Hamburg's merchants established a great number of overseas branch offices, most notably in the United States, Latin America and Mexico, but also in Africa and East Asia. On May 7 1842, however, the city was hit by a terrible disaster: The Great Fire of Hamburg.

A total of 70,000 people had to flee the flames; a quarter of the city, including three churches, 1,749 buildings with 4,219 apartments and 102 warehouses, was destroyed by the blaze; 20,000 people were made homeless. The total damage was put at 90 million marks and would probably have been even greater if firefighters had not been sent to help from virtually all of the neighbouring towns — from Harburg, Stade, Altona, Blankenese, Wedel and Wandsbek to Lauenburg, Lübeck and Kiel — and even troops had been provided by Bremen, Hanover and Prussia.

As in the case of the great earthquake in Lisbon 87 years earlier, the Great Fire of Hamburg led to aid flowing in from around the world. Donations alone totalled 6.9 million marks, approximately 1.2 million marks more than the annual public revenues of Hamburg at the time. Among those sending money were Tsar Nicholas I of Russia, Queen Victoria of England, King Louis Philippe of France and eleven other kings and princes — a clear sign of the high esteem in which the Free and Hanseatic City of Hamburg was held around the world.

Even more important for Hamburg's future was, however, the farsightedness of the decisions made with regard to the city's reconstruction. Not only was the task of rebuilding the city tackled with great determination and a minimum of delay; more than 100 years later it would prove advantageous that the city was not restored to its former layout but completely modernised in line with urban planning principles. The fact that the first-ever compulsory expropriation law in Germany had to be adopted in order to widen roads and alter the layout of many properties and premises testifies to the progressive political commitment of the Senate and Parliament. Before this, the protection of private property had otherwise always been one of their prime concerns.

## Scepticism Towards Technical Innovations

When it came to the acceptance and introduction of new technologies, Hamburg's merchants were far less progressive than the city's urban planners, and not as successful as they were when expanding overseas trade relations. A first example of this was the suggestion of an entrepreneur from Altona, made in 1836, to set up a telegraph connection between Cuxhaven and Hamburg that could act as a ship signalling system. Even after this idea was, despite a negative assessment by the Commerzdeputation, realised in 1837, it took another three years until the benefits of the installation were generally acknowledged and appreciated.

Things were not that much different in the field of steamship navigation. After a number of distinguished Hamburg merchants and shipowners, among them August Bolten, Adolph Godeffroy and Ferdinand F. Laeisz, established the HAPAG (later Hamburg America Line) in 1847 the New York route initially commenced operations with three sailing ships. Yet this decision was probably based not only on the persisting mistrust of steam technology but also on commercial prudence. The later Cunard Line had already started a regular steamship service between Liverpool and New York in 1840, but this service was supported by high state subsidies on the American side. The same applied to the first steamship that sailed from New York to Bremerhaven in 1847, for which Prussia had paid a considerable subsidy.

Although steamship navigation had, at least in intra-European shipping services, already become well established by the middle of the 19th century Hamburg's maritime fleet still consisted, in 1855, of 457 sailships and just nine steamships. It should, however, be borne in mind that steamers in those days consumed huge amounts of coal and that not all nations had their own coal mines. This limited the efficiency of steamships on many routes, since coal first had to be transported by sailing ship to the coal stations established around the world, further increasing transportation costs as a result.

Similarly, Hamburg's merchants were initially also very sceptical about the idea of connecting the city up to the rail network. The first railway link from Hamburg to Bergedorf, using locomotives and tracks imported from England, was finally established in 1842 and the line was extended to Berlin at the end of 1846. The late integration of Hamburg into Germany's railway network was, however, due not only to the many and varied reservations in Hamburg but also to strong opposition from its neighbours.

Denmark was not interested in a rail link between Hamburg and Lübeck as this would have reduced revenues for the Danish ports and from the levying of the Sound Dues. At the same time the Danes decided that the terminus of the railway line from Kiel was to be not Hamburg but the competing Danish port of Altona. As early as 1824 Brunswick had suggested the construction of a line to Hamburg via Hanover and Celle. Yet Hanover feared significant competitive disadvantages for its port in Harburg. When the northbound line from Hanover finally was built, some 15 years later, it was decided that that it would terminate in Harburg and not be continued to Hamburg.

Given the close ties between Hamburg and Britain it might have been expected that the city would have been one of the first in Germany to pick up on the early industrial development in England. Even back then, however, Hamburg was already going its own way, deciding to focus on overseas trade instead. This also applied to the beginning of the next phase of the Industrial Revolution, which was driven by the development of the railway and the coal and steel industry. The fact that the first British steamship had already sailed to Hamburg in 1816, is — in the event of doubt — to be seen rather as an expression of the technical and industrial advances made in Great Britain than as a manifestation of the Industrial Revolution in Germany.

## International Trade Continues to Thrive

Despite these problems encountered in the expansion of the shore-side infrastructure, Hamburg recovered from the Great Fire more rapidly than had generally been expected. As in the mid-1830s Hamburg profited from the positive economic developments in England, which, between 1843 and 1846, was posting an average annual economic growth rate of 5 per cent. Further reasons for the continued upswing in the Hamburg economy were the consolidation of trade with the United States, the strong expansion of trade with Latin America and the intensification of new trading relations, most notably with East Africa, India, China, and the Pacific islands.

Worth pointing out in connection with the increase in trade and shipping with North America is not only the constant expansion of trade but also the structural change in cargo types. Inward freight still consisted chiefly of cotton, tobacco and rice. Yet, due to the increasing industrialisation of the United States, finished commercial products as a share of outbound freight were increasingly being replaced by emigrants. Initially the latter were — subject to availability of passage — classed as additional cargo; later, they accounted for a significant part of the core business. For a long time, however, Hamburg lagged far behind Le Havre, Antwerp, Liverpool and even Bremen, as a port of embarkation for emigrants.

The dynamic development of trade with the Americas, including Latin America and the West Indies, was basically the result of a favourable cycle in the global economy, with momentum accelerating once again after a period of stagnation between 1847 and 1850. The expansion of Hamburg's economic interests in Africa and the Pacific islands was fostered primarily by the entrepreneurial spirit of Hamburg's merchants, for whom overseas trade was the main focus of their attention. As far as relations to India, China, Hong Kong, Singapore and Australia were concerned, economic policy decisions in both Great Britain and these far-flung regions of the world also played a decisive role.

In this context specific mention should be made of the First Opium War, waged by the British against the Qing Dynasty empire from 1839 to 1842 with a view to making up for the growing deficits in British trade with China by enforcing the unimpeded import of Bengali opium. Although Hamburg was not directly involved in this war it benefited from it indirectly, as China was not only forced to pay huge reparations and cede Hong Kong to Great Britain, as stipulated in the so-called "Unequal Treaty"; it also had to open its five treaty ports — Canton, Amoy, Foochow, Ningbo and Shanghai — to foreign traders and vessels.

A further event of major political and economic importance that proved advantageous for Hamburg, opening up new prospects for the city's merchants and shipowners, who, unlike in 1822, now had their own fleet, was the initially provisional, in 1849, and then, in 1857, final and complete repeal of England's Navigation Acts. For a period of almost 200 years these Acts had prevented Hamburg ships from sailing directly to and between Britain and its colonies. After the Navigation Acts had been repealed Hamburg ships were now also able to earn money on the outbound journey to Hong Kong and Singapore by first loading up with coal in England. Additionally Hamburg shipowners now also had access to the important rice trade between the British colonial ports of Akyab (now Sittwe), Singapore and Hong Kong.

Yet the most astounding new route for Hamburg ships was the so-called Chinese Coastal Run, which was in fact not restricted China but also included Bangkok, Saigon, Singapore, Batavia, Makassar, Manila and, since the first Australian Gold Rush in 1851, also Sydney and Melbourne. While just seven ships from Hamburg were plying their trade on permanent deployment in the Far East in 1853, their number had risen to 33 by 1857 — and this despite the excellent development of the economy in Northwestern Europe and North America and the related earnings potentials on the transatlantic route. In 1864, following a short period of stagnation in Europe, the number of Hamburg ships earning money on a permanent basis in the Asia-Pacific region increased even further to 85. Also highlighting the significance of Hamburg's engagement in this territory is the fact that, in a number of major East Asian ports, including Hong Kong, the Hamburg flag ranked second only to the British ensign during the 1860s.

## Measures to Enhance
## International Competitiveness

Britain continued to lead the world at the level of both industrial output and international trade. Nevertheless, Hamburg was now not only Germany's largest port but also the most important trading and transshipment hub on the European continent. The only city in Europe to surpass it in this respect remained London. Yet Hamburg had achieved this status not only by slipstreaming in the wake of positive world economic trends. As cities vied, nationally and internationally, with one another for supremacy as business centres and industrial locations Hamburg itself had put in place a series of policy measures serving to strengthen its own competitive position. Not only did the majority of trade agreements and representative offices abroad now cover the entire world, rather than being restricted to the Americas; in both Hamburg itself and the city's immediate environs — and including with respect to the relations to its close neighbours — a number of urgent problems were resolved during this period.

Apart from the need for reforms to the political constitution and the efficient linking of the city and the port to the hinterland, factors that were of relevance to Hamburg's success as a business location

*Dry docks already existed in Ancient Egypt and Greece, and they were also used for large Chinese treasure ships at the beginning of the 15th century. Floating docks, on the other hand, were not invented until the middle of the 19th century. A floating dock still made of wood — here with the first Flying P-Liner "Pudel" — was commissioned at the Stülcken shipyard in Hamburg in 1858. It was in service until 1911.*

most specifically over the longer term, the following three challenges called for resolute action: Firstly further expansion of the port's infrastructure and improvements to navigational safety on the Elbe; secondly the reform of the customs system and increasingly anachronistic trade practices, and thirdly the permanent rivalry not only with Bremen, Amsterdam and Antwerp but also, and most notably, with Harburg and Altona.

Between the end of the 1820s and the beginning of the 1840s the volume of goods passing through Hamburg's port had already more or less doubled and it continued to rise steadily in the years that followed. In 1856 more than 500 vessels docked in Hamburg, a quarter of them steamships. This demanded not only the expansion of the port, for which Grasbrook was ideal, but also considerable innovation in cargo handling techniques. The loading and unloading of sailing ships was still effected on the river using lighters and barges. To boost handling efficiency and to reduce port turnaround times, quay walls had to be built for the steamships. After a construction period lasting several years Hamburg's first steamship port was finally inaugurated in 1866. In light of the growing size of vessels, which made hauling them up the slipway increasingly difficult, the first dry dock had already been taken into operation in 1851 and the first floating dock was constructed in 1857/58, enabling repairs to be carried out in particular also below the waterline. Other infrastructural measures of relevance to shipping related to the Elbe fairway. In 1814 the navigational light on Neuwerk was put into permanent operation; in 1816 the first lightship was positioned in the Elbe estuary and the increasing draught of the ships approaching Hamburg had already made reliable fairway buoyage and lighting and, most especially, the deepening of the Elbe a recurrent problem.

Even after a massive reduction in export tariffs and the preliminary reform of a number of trade practices in 1823/24 Hamburg's external trade was still suffering from certain competitive disadvantages which were, on the one hand, due to the city's import, shipping and transit tariffs, and, on the other hand, to a number of outdated trade customs. As Hamburg's state finances were in an especially parlous state after the Great Fire of 1842 the Senate was extremely reductant to make major concessions to the merchants in terms of tariffs during the 1840s. Yet this attitude changed in the mid-1850s, when worries about Hamburg's competitive position, most especially vis-à-vis Harburg, increasingly came to the fore.

By contrast, with the weights and measures system already having been overhauled in 1826, the reform of trade customs was, from the very beginning, a much speedier process. In 1844 a new corn law came into force, despite bitter resistance from the city's bakers. Modified regulations for the grain trade, which was of ever-increasing importance for Hamburg, were introduced in 1846. The previously excluded reform of sugar trade practices was implemented in 1847.

And, finally, in the marine insurance sector the "Assekuranz- und Havarieordnung" of 1731 was replaced — also in 1847 — by the "Hamburg Standard Form of Marine Insurance Policies", a model subsequently adopted by numerous other German seaports.

Many of these measures had been under discussion for many years in the "Commerzdeputation" and had also been put before the Senate; yet they were only actually implemented, as in the case of the first major reform package of the 1820s, in response to growing external pressures. One of the first events to intensify competitive pressures on Hamburg's port at the political level was the signing of a trade treaty between the German Customs Union and Belgium in 1844, the terms of which implied considerable advantages for Antwerp. A further aspect was the increasing competition from Altona and Harburg, which was no less political in nature. Quite apart from the fact that Denmark and Hanover were blocking Hamburg's connection to the northern and southern railway lines respectively, Hanover in particular engaged in considerable additional efforts to obtain further competitive advantages for the port of Harburg.

Not only was the port of Harburg rapidly expanded and the harbour waters deepened further; ships docking in Harburg had, since 1850, also been exempted from the Stade Elbe Tariff, which still constituted a considerable financial burden on all ships not sailing under the Hamburg flag that berthed in Hamburg. Grain imports handled via Harburg were subject to only 50 per cent of the tariff, while the full rate was payable on those arriving in transit via Hamburg. After the Kingdom of Hanover joined the German Customs Union in 1854 every effort was undertaken to make Harburg the leading overseas port of the Customs Union.

From a short term viewpoint Hamburg most probably considered these political manoeuvrings by Prussia, Denmark and, most notably, Hanover as annoying and, in part, unfair. Over the medium term, however, the reactions these induced in Hamburg, which strengthened the city's competitiveness via institutional modernisation, higher efficiency and greater flexibility, proved to be very advantageous.

Most strikingly this was demonstrated during the first "global economic crisis", which hit Hamburg quite unexpectedly in the late autumn of 1857.

## 1857:
### The First Global Economic Crisis

The first global financial and economic crisis, which had originated in the United States in the late summer of 1857 and reached Hamburg via London by the end of October of the same year, affected the city's economy in a variety of different ways: Firstly, wheat trade with the United States was suspended. Secondly, high foreign payment obligations, especially to Britain, the United States and Latin America, had to be met. Thirdly, Hamburg's merchants were sitting on an incredibly large amount of merchandise, including speculative stocks of coffee and sugar, for which there was no longer any market. Even the ships in the harbour could no longer be unloaded since nobody would have been able to pay the purchase price and the freight costs. Fourthly, Hamburg merchants and bankers, too, held a variety of US securities. Fifthly — and this might, alongside share losses, have been the most painful fact — Hamburg's trading houses had extended large amounts of loans to Scandinavia. These loans were initially used to fund illicit and black market trade with Russia conducted via Sweden during the Crimean War. Yet the credit business continued even after the end of the war, with the money having found its way into speculative projects which, ultimately, could only be written off.

Nevertheless the crisis in the United States should primarily be considered as an unexpected gust of wind that caused an already fragile house of cards to collapse completely. Hamburg, unlike many other cities and regions in Europe, did not have state-paper money and the two private banks — Norddeutsche Bank and the Vereinsbank zu Hamburg, founded in 1855 and 1856 respectively — were expressly prevented from issuing their own banknotes. However, these restrictions did not hinder the creation of a considerable volume of money surrogates, mainly in the form of the three-month promissory notes common in Hamburg at that time. While the value of such notes in circulation stood at 162 million marks banco in 1855 this figure had already risen to 225 million by the first quarter of 1857 and is believed to have reached no less than 340 million by autumn of the same year. In the light of this credit expansion, which had, by now, clearly uncoupled itself from the development of the real trade flows, there could no longer be any talk of responsible business practices. By the spring of 1857 critical voices could in fact — completely independent of speculation in shares in America — be heard in Hamburg expressing deep concerns about the possible bursting of this credit bubble pumped up with promissory notes,.

When the crisis did then hit Hamburg with a vengeance and a first rescue attempt by the "Commerzdeputation" had failed, Hamburg's leading banks and trading houses — as the banks in New York before them — developed a second, far more comprehensive rescue scheme to avert the worst consequences. To get Hamburg's financial market functioning again a "Garantie-Disconto-Verein" with subscribed capital of 12 million marks banco was set up in November of that year, primarily with a view to refacilitating normal bill transactions, as common chiefly among merchants. But it was already too late to restore the confidence already lost and to get the crisis under control. In a first step a number of trading houses engaged in trade with England had to file for bankruptcy. Others followed — and now it was predominantly those with close business ties to Denmark, Norway and Sweden. Remarkable is the fact that the Senate refused to take part in this second rescue plan. The principle reason it gave was that any state involvement "in the interest of what might even be a large part of the population would be most disquieting both internally and also on account of the possible consequences and can be justified only if the conditions were to become so severe that their effects would imperil the existence of all citizens in the most direct manner".

What began as a financial crisis in the United States increasingly developed into a crisis of the real economy, and not only in America and England but also on the European continent, with Hamburg — amplified by the local speculative bubble — having been particularly badly affected. Once the city realised how big a threat it was facing, and in contravention of every tradition in Hamburg regarding the subsidising of ailing sectors and companies, the Senate finally became actively involved in the crisis management — even then, however, only in response to massive pressure from the city's merchants and most certainly not without some reservations. Interesting in this connection is the assessment of this state intervention by one of the leading economists of the day, Adolph Wagner, as his criticism and fears basically still apply today: "Whatever one may choose to think, this decision by the exchequer to vouch for the losses and sins of individuals will always remain a highly dangerous precedent."

## State Intervention
### to overcome a Systemic Crisis

No matter how correct Adolph Wagner's assessment of direct state interventions in the market process may have been and still is in principle, it has to be acknowledged that the financial problems of 1857 had, even if they were caused by the misconduct of a multiplicity of different individuals, resulted in a far-reaching systemic crisis. Decisive was the fact that there was a complete lack of trust in any type of trading transaction that could not be effected in cash or silver. On December 4 the bill discount rate exceeded an all-time high of ten per cent. Quotations of the rate were subsequently suspended. It had become impossible to convert bills into money. Just six days later, on 10 December, the crisis spilled out onto the streets as people queued up in front of the savings bank (Sparkasse) to take out cash. The orderly withdrawal of deposits totalling 70,000 marks courant was possible only with the help of police protection.

The idea behind a third, now state-backed, rescue plan was that of creating a fund of 15 million marks, of which one third was to be financed via the issue of a Hamburg government bond and two thirds via silver borrowed from abroad. However, private creditors for such a large sum could be found neither in London, Paris, Amsterdam nor any other European city. Hamburg requested help from a number of possible state creditors, which even included Denmark; yet Prussia was initially the only one to show a certain willingness to provide the required funding. Unfortunately, however, Prussia withdrew its offer once the gravity of Hamburg's situation also became known in Berlin. In the end it was Austria that came to the rescue. On December 15 13 railway carriages carrying silver worth 10 million marks banco arrived in Hamburg from Vienna. At that time it would not have been sufficient to give the Hanseatic city a guarantee by simply securitising the silver; the metal had to be made available in physical form.

In all probability the positive decision of Emperor Franz Joseph I was, once again, a sign that Hamburg's traditional policy of neutrality had borne fruit. Similarly, it may be seen as a further reflection of the history of rivalry between Austria and Prussia. Testifying to the fact that Berlin also saw things this way is an official letter to Prussia's representatives abroad by the then Prussian prime minister, who, in a reference to Hamburg's merchants, could not resist making the following comment: "It is increasingly becoming apparent, and increasingly being acknowledged everywhere, that some houses became involved in speculative trading that was out of all proportion to their means or true market demand." A clearer indication than this to the effect that Hamburg's merchant and banks had brought about their own downfall due to unsound business practices can barely be imagined in diplomatic language and the reactions in Hamburg were correspondingly sharp.

For Austria, however, the granting of the loan was not only a political demonstration but also an extremely lucrative deal. The National Bank in Vienna possessed large silver deposits designed to meet the demands of the German Coinage Convention from 1 January 1859 onwards, and to re-establish the silver reserves required to cover its paper currency. Under normal conditions these silver deposits would not have yielded a profit. However by lending it to Hamburg the Austrians earned a good rate of interest and, with hindsight at least, the risk turned out to be relatively low. As in 1799 Hamburg's economy recovered within a few months, and six months after it was taken out, the loan was repaid to Austria in full. The normalisation of conditions in Hamburg was reflected, inter alia, in the fact that the discount rate, which had averaged 6.5 per cent in 1857, returned to just below 2 per cent between 1858 and 1860. That this normalisation was, in part, accompanied by a certain stagnation of business activities was due to the continuing weakness of the global economy.

It is impossible to put a figure on the total cost of this crisis. One source puts the city's financial losses alone at roughly 400 million marks banco. More reliable are, however, the details of the state financing provided, including the silver borrowed from Vienna, which amounted to no less than 35 million marks banco. This figure was five times higher than Hamburg's planned public budget for 1857 and almost equal, in nominal terms, to the fire insurance fund for the reconstruction of Hamburg after the Great Fire of 1842. However only 20 million marks banco were actually disbursed in the form of state aid. Remarkable, too, is the fact that, taking into account all intervention-related expenditures and revenues, the net burden on the state is said to have totalled less than 200,000 marks banco.

Up until beyond the middle of the 19th century Hamburg had essentially focused on its trade interests, playing only a marginal role in the process of industrialisation taking place elsewhere in Germany.

This situation changed significantly during the next phase in the city's development. Characteristic features of this new period of political, economic, technological and social evolution, which commenced in Germany around the middle of the 19th century, were the scientification of technology, the development of new leading sectors of eco-

nomic activity, growing social polarisation, the trend towards urbanisation and the increasing political integration of the small German
states, leading to the formation of a nation state.

## Hamburg becomes
## Part of the German Empire

For Hamburg, whose interests were still predominantly international
in orientation, it was becoming more and more difficult to follow the
"special path" that had hitherto served it so successfully. After joining
the German Federation the city largely had to abandon its policy of
neutrality and as a member of the North German Confederation
being at odds with Prussia was not even really an option. Yet its sym-
pathies tended, not least on account of the generous financial aid
that Austria provided to help it weather the first global financial and
economic crisis, towards Vienna rather than Berlin. Hamburg finally
yielded to Prussia's demands only after lengthy negotiations in 1867,
and even, albeit only in the final phase, participated in the war against
Austria. This decision probably saved it from being absorbed into
Prussia the way the Kingdom of Hanover, Schleswig-Holstein, Kur-
hessen, Nassau and the Free City of Frankfurt am Main had been.

That Hamburg subsequently became part of the German Empire
was the logical continuation of political developments in the years
before. From an economic point of view emphasis must be given to
two events that marked the end of an era. The first was the introduction of the reichsmark at the beginning of 1875 and the incorporation
of the Hamburger Bank into the Reichsbank. This meant that Hamburg no longer had its own currency, a fact of particular significance
in terms of the internationally accepted mark banco. The second and,
in the long term, possibly more important, event for Hamburg's economy was the city's accession to the protectionist German Customs
Union, a step taken in order to allow it to retain its free port status.
Although the Empire Constitution stipulated that the Hanseatic cities

of Hamburg and Bremen could remain outside the common customs boundary until they themselves applied to join, the Empire had enough clout to force the Hanseatic cities to come to the negotiating table.

Following tough negotiations, which lasted nearly a year, the Senate and the Parliament approved a compromise deal attained by the later mayor, Johannes Versmann, in Berlin in May 1881. This saw Hamburg's urban area integrated into the German Customs Union but at the same time made Grasbrook and the southern Elbe islands a large new free port. Investments in the new harbour installations amounted to 106 million reichsmarks, of which 40 million marks were a subsidy provided by the Empire. Both processes — integration into the German customs area and the opening of the free port — were completed in 1888. In order to realise this project, most notably for the construction of the Speicherstadt, some 1,000 buildings had to be demolished and roughly 24,000 people resettled. As an aside it may be noted that little or no help was given to these people in their search for a new place of abode.

From an economic viewpoint and, therefore, also for the working population over the longer term, expansion of the free port was a considerable success. Four aspects are of key significance in this respect. Firstly, this measure led to a significant expansion in the moorage capacities, which were again failing to meet demand. Secondly, large quay sheds and warehouses required to accommodate the increasing volume of exports and imports could be built at the new site. Thirdly, the free port status facilitated the processing of international transit goods without the imposition of tariffs or taxes. And, fourthly, the free port allowed Hamburg's economy, which still consisted of largely small-scale businesses, to make a late but very dynamic entry into the industrialisation process, which was already much further advanced in other parts of the country.

*Blohm & Voss around 1900. Shipbuilding in Hamburg can be traced back to 1380. The oldest still existing company is the J.J. Sietas shipyard, founded in 1635. At the beginning of the 20th century roughly 20,000 people were employed*

## Hamburg's Advance to become an Important German and European Industrial Location

Hamburg was not only successfully able to defend its status as the largest port on the European mainland, a position it had regained in the middle of the 19th century. Due to the settlement of industrial companies, it also became one of the key German and European industrial locations at the beginning of the 20th century. Shipbuilding,

*in Hamburg's major shipyards. Blohm & Voss, with more than 10,000 workers at that time, is the only large shipyard that has survived the various ship-building crises until today — although with a workforce of just 1,700.*

mechanical engineering and manufacturing, whose raw materials and products remained duty-free, were the core industries in Hamburg's harbour. The year 1840 witnessed the foundation of the Stülcken ship-yard, with Blohm & Voss following in 1887; and in 1909 the Stettin-based Vulcan shipyard established a branch office on the Elbe as the Oder estuary placed size constraints on the shipbuilding business. Two years later the company moved its head office to Hamburg.

Nonetheless, Hamburg's shipbuilding industry developed far more slowly during the first years than the founders had most probably expected. Blohm & Voss, for example, had to build its first vessels at its own expense and survived on repair work until well into the 1880s. Hamburg's shipowners continued to place their orders in England, whose shipyards were still considered more experienced and less expensive. The breakthrough for shipwrights in Hamburg and elsewhere in Germany did not come until 1885 with the passing of the "Imperial Mail Steamer Subsidy Law", which offered subsidies to German shipyards building vessels for use on routes to East Africa, East Asia and Australia.

Having stood at roughly 1,200 in 1887, the number of shipyard workers employed by Blohm & Voss rose over the 15 years that followed to 13,000, equivalent to almost 13 per cent of all industrial workers in Hamburg. By 1905 the company had increased the size of its premises to 560,000 square metres with a three-kilometre-long waterfront, making it the world's largest shipyard housed on a single site. The first peak in Hamburg's shipbuilding industry was marked by the construction of what was then the world's largest express steamer. The Vulcan shipyard built the *Imperator* in 1913 with 52,117 GRT (gross registered tonnes) and a length of 277 metres. This vessel was even bigger than the *Titanic*, which had sunk the previous year, and had had a capacity of just 46,329 GRT and a length of 269 metres. Blohm & Voss matched this by building two even larger ships one year later, the *Vaterland* with 52,282 GRT and the *Bismarck* with 56,551 GRT. Once the *Deutschland*, a vessel built at the Vulcan shipyard in Stettin back in 1900, won the Blue Riband for what was then the fastest Atlantic crossing the shipbuilding industry in Germany, and most notably that in Hamburg, was, together with its suppliers, finally ranked among the world's best.

Other industrial sectors that profited greatly from the free port status were the chemical and pharmaceutical industries, together with a variety of companies active in food and raw materials processing. On the one hand, these companies produced finished and semi-finished products on the basis of domestically sourced raw materials, the majority of which were exported. On the other hand, a thriving refinishing industry developed for numerous imported goods, which were subsequently either sold in Germany or re-exported. Hamburg was able to establish itself as one of the world's leading centres for trade in oriental rugs as well as for the transhipment and finishing of colonial goods, such as coffee, tea, tobacco and spices. Overall this positive evolution was already the result of the establishment of the free port, which contributed to the promotion of overseas trade and, since the turn of the century, had also been handling more and more industrial and, most notably, investment goods manufactured in Germany.

## Hamburg's growing Merchant Fleet

The expansion of trade and enhancement of the port's infrastructure obviously also had a major impact on the development of Hamburg's merchant fleet. Having already stood at 539 units with a total capacity of 187,847 GRT in 1866 the number of vessels registered in Hamburg, among them 22 British-built steamers, rose to no less than 1353 units in 1913. More than half of the vessels — 792 to be precise — were steamships. In the meantime HAPAG, founded in 1847, had become the largest shipping company in the world, owning 175 seagoing vessels with aggregate capacity of 1.3 million GRT.

Hamburg-Süd, established in 1871, was the second largest shipping line in Hamburg, with 61 ships and 347,000 GRT. Other important shipping companies were the Levante Line with 59 ships, the Woermann Line with 39 vessels and the Deutsche Ost-Afrika Line with 26 ships. Additionally the Laeisz shipping company, which sent the first sailing ship to Valparaiso in 1862 and started the first regular service to Chile in 1878, enjoyed an excellent worldwide reputation. With a fleet of 18 deep-water sailing ships, the legendary *Flying P Liners*, F. Laeisz was not only the largest private shipping company in Hamburg in 1913 but most probably also the last major shipping company in the world not to have owned a single steamship.

*Three Flying P-Liners at anchor in Hamburg's port. Today, only one is still in use, namely the former "Padua", built in 1926 as the last large cargo-carrying sailing ship. It now sails as the training ship "Krusenstern" under a Russian flag. Three other surviving Flying P-Liners can be found as museum ships in Travemünde, Mariehamn and New York. The invention of ammonia synthesis and its industrial application in fertiliser production made the nitrate trade unprofitable at the beginning of the 1930s and the wheat trade between Europe and Australia ceased upon the outbreak of the Second World War.*

Apart from the shipbuilding subsidies and the free port status Hamburg's merchants, and most notably the ship owners, also hoped to benefit from the rapid expansion in trade due to Germany's imperialist colonial policy. However the profits Hamburg derived from the country's colonial ambitions should definitely not be overestimated. Even in 1913 Europe still accounted for more than 50 per cent of the port's transhipment activities, with America taking some 25 per cent and Asia just under 10 per cent. Trade with Africa amounted to a little more than 5 per cent; and the share of the German colonies in Africa, with exports and imports reaching no more than 1.8 per cent and 0.5 per cent respectively, were not much greater an concerning imports, even smaller than those of Australia and Oceania.

If one disregards the state-funded shipbuilding programmes and profits of individual companies active in Africa and the Pacific region, German colonial policy was thus of little importance for Hamburg's economy as a whole. Politically this is also reflected in the fact that Hamburg flatly rejected, in order to protect its own global trade relations, all attempts to favour the exchange of goods with the German colonies through preferential tariffs. On the other hand, Hamburg pinned great hopes on a renewed increase in emigration, in particular to the United States, which had witnessed a sharp decline after the global economic crisis of 1857 and during the American Civil War between 1861 and 1865.

## New Business with Emigration

Between 1836 and 1850 no more than 40,000 emigrants left Hamburg to seek their fortunes in the New World. The corresponding figure for Bremen was 235,000; and this was definitely not only a consequence of Hamburg having failed to spot the opportunities offered by this new business in time. Due to an emigration law enacted back in 1832, which forced shipowners to provide a minimum amount of space on their ships, Bremen had gained an excellent reputation as an emigration port. The opposite applied to Hamburg. In the 1860s hygiene on board ships of the Hamburg-based shipping company Sloman was still in such a scandalous state that it sparked a series of critical newspaper reports throughout Europe.

It took, in fact, until 1891 for Hamburg finally to overtake Bremen as Germany's main port of embarkation for emigrants. The reasons for this new development were manifold. In 1842 Hamburg's Senate, which had banned the emigration of larger groups of people from Hamburg in 1832, passed a first package of measures to protect the welfare of emigrants. Until approximately 1870 Hamburg always took guidance from the provisions applying in Bremen; after 1870 this situation was reversed. Furthermore, unlike Bremen, Hamburg also

*Between 1850 and 1939 roughly five million people emigrated to the United States via Hamburg's port. Since most of the pre-1934 passenger lists have been preserved the "Links to your roots" project, which makes the data accessible online, is a treasure-trove for genealogical research.*

profited from its closer proximity to Russia and Eastern Europe, the traditional homelands of the second wave of emigrants after 1880.

In addition to direct emigration Hamburg also offered the possibility of an indirect but less expensive route to the United States, primarily via Hull and Liverpool. The number choosing this option between 1850 and 1914 is estimated at almost 700,000. HAPAG finally became involved in a bitter competitive struggle with Bremen-based Norddeutscher Lloyd, a battle that focused not only on the price and comfort of the passage but also on the recruitment of emigrants in the hinterland, the overall quality of service, including processing and interim accommodation at the port of departure. However this rivalry did not prevent the two shipping companies from joining forces whenever the lucrative transit business was endangered by third parties — as, for example, in 1892 when Prussia imposed an immigration ban due to health concerns.

Nonetheless the majority of measures taken to improve the conditions of emigrants were not guided primarily by humanitarian concerns. Repeated health examinations and the construction of the first reception centres, which HAPAG was itself obliged to set up, were first and foremost aimed at protecting Hamburg's population from a cholera epidemic that had allegedly been brought in from Russia. Improved health precautions and enhanced hygiene conditions, both prior to departure and on board the ships, were also of benefit to the shipping companies, since sick emigrants were refused entry by American immigration authorities and had to be shipped back to Europe at the ship owners' expense.

Technical progress, especially the replacement of sailing ships with steamships and the subsequent deployment of passenger liners, was also advantageous to emigrants. The time it took to sail from Continental Europe to New York was cut from six to two weeks and the interplay of state regulations and market-driven competition also brought with it an improvement in travel conditions. All of these factors and, in particular, the dream of leading a better life in the New World ultimately made the emigration one of the largest growth segments in maritime business during the late 19th and early 20th centuries. Between 1880 and 1910 almost 17 million Europeans emigrated overseas, with one quarter of them having embarked in Hamburg.

## Harbour Modernisation, Deepening of the Elbe, Lighthouses and Leading Lights: The Beginnings of Intensified Cooperation across National Frontiers

While total transhipment volumes at Hamburg's port amounted to approximately six million tonnes upon the opening of the free port in 1888 this figure rose to 15.9 in 1903, subsequently climbing even higher — to 25.5 million tonnes — by 1913. If Altona and Harburg are included, total volumes in 1913 topped even 29.6 million tonnes, which meant that Hamburg was still the most important port on the European mainland. There are at least three good reasons to justify this aggregation: Hamburg's accession to the German Customs Union, the increasing blurring of lines between the three cities and the so-called Köhlbrand Agreement of 1909. Hamburg's biggest competitor was, however, now Rotterdam and no longer Antwerp.

The prerequisites paving the way for the remarkably dynamic growth in transhipment were, on the one hand, the rapid expansion and related modernisation of the port facilities and, on the other, the permanent deepening of the Elbe fairway required due to constantly increasing size of vessels and guaranteed navigational safety not only during the day but also during hours of darkness. The size of the free port was therefore increased from 426 hectares in 1881 to almost 1,000 hectares in 1910. The area of the quay sheds, which was roughly 68,000 square metres before 1883 and 112,000 square metres in 1894, grew no less than 516,000 square metres by 1910. The partial mechanisation of loading and unloading operations, which, however, advanced only relatively slowly due to the varying nature of mixed cargo and a plentiful supply of cheap labour must be added to this.

It was not only the necessity of keeping vessel turnaround as short as possible but also rising labour costs and downtimes due to strikes that accelerated technical progress in the field of cargo handling and logistics. In the pre-WWI period Hamburg was one of the world's leading ports in technological terms. By 1905 approximately 600 steam-driven or electric cranes were already in operation, the largest of which — also the world's strongest — was able to lift 150 tonnes. No less interesting from a technological point of view was the development of the petroleum port. After the first petroleum port for the handling of barrels had been constructed relatively close to the city in Grasbrook in the 1870s the 1909 Köhlbrand Agreement permitted — after several dissatisfactory interim solutions - the final relocation of the handling of petroleum products, a segment that was growing much faster than all other port activities, to Waltershof. This simultaneously involved a shift towards tank storage.

That the construction of the new petroleum port led to increased capacity and tank storage is, however, merely the technologically relevant dimension of this measure. In the petroleum trade Bremen had, due to the limited storage capacities in Hamburg, initially become the main German oil port before eventually — as was previously the case in the emigration business — being outstripped as Hamburg rapidly caught up and overtook it. At the outbreak of the first world war the Hamburg-based Deutsch-Amerikanische Petroleum-Gesellschaft (today's Esso Deutschland GmbH), founded in 1890, already had a fleet of 36 tankers carrying petroleum and gasoline in from the United States. Imports from Southern Russia, most notably Odessa, and the Middle East played only a minor role at this time.

With regard to the rising safety requirements for navigation between the North Sea and Hamburg's port there were two major problems to contend with: Firstly guaranteeing a sufficient fairway depth in both the Elbe and the port basin. While 4.3 metres and 8 metres had still been considered sufficient at high tide in 1840 and 1897 respectively, the depth required after the turn of the century was at least 13 metres; and this was not simply due to the increasing size of vessels but also to permit tide-independent navigation. Since this could no longer be achieved through dredging and the installation of fairway buoys alone extensive river training work had to be additionally carried out, including bank enforcements, training walls and groynes.

The second problem was navigational safety during the hours of darkness. Initially this problem was solved by using a flare-lit shallop which went ahead of the merchant vessels, piloting them from buoy to buoy. Around 1850, approximately 50 navigational lights were then installed. These were complemented, from 1890 onwards, by an array of leading lights, which, to a large extent, are still in use today. The technical realisation of all these measures was, however, but one dimension in efforts to maintain the competitiveness of Hamburg's port. The other was that Hamburg depended — as it does today — on political cooperation with its neighbours. The increasing size of the ships and the correspondingly greater draught required by vessels did, from

Turbinen-Schnelldampfer (HAPAG)
„Imperator"
Länge 268 m, Breite 29,5 m, Höhe 19,5 m
Rauminhalt 50,000 Tons
Platz für 4000 Passagiere
Besatzung 1200 Mann
Schornstein 21 m hoch, 5,5 m Durchm.

*Until the middle of the 20th century, overseas travel was conducted on passenger and multi-purpose ships. The passage from Hamburg to New York took approximately nine days. Today the flying time is just nine hours.*

the middle of the 19th century onwards, bring about an increasing convergence of interests, at least with regard to navigational safety on the Elbe.

As early as in 1866 the first Köhlbrand Agreement was concluded between Hamburg and Hanover and this was subsequently acknowledged by Prussia in 1868. This agreement entitled Hamburg to make a further and, unlike that made in the 1560s, official modification to the Bunthäuser Spitze, enabling more water to be fed into the Norderelbe, and to broaden and deepen the part of the Köhlbrand that belonged to Prussia. The second Köhlbrand Agreement, concluded in 1909, allowed Hamburg to expand its harbour, including the facilities at the new petroleum port at Waltershof, quite significantly. In principle the groundwork for a joint Hamburg-Prussian port development policy had now been laid. Yet the First World War temporarily halted port expansion and any closer cooperation designed to promote this aim.

## *Social and Public Health Deficiencies force Political Change*

From around the turn of the century until the outbreak of the First World War Hamburg experienced a period of political upheaval and social change. This was, on the one hand, reflected in the growing strength of the labour movement and, on the other, in conflicts with new political groupings and, following the repeal of the anti-socialist laws, most notably with the social democrats. Irrespective of these factors, however, the city's elites were increasingly realising that the long term prosperity of Hamburg also depended on basic minimum living conditions and hygiene standards for the general population The key event for this change in attitude was the cholera epidemic of 1892, which, with a total of 17,000 affected by the disease, resulted not only in approx. 8,500 fatalities but also significant economic losses for Hamburg's merchants.

The squalid living conditions of the majority of the people working at the port had already been denounced by the Hamburg physician Johann Bökel in 1597. Nevertheless the poor were still, 300 years
after his accounts, living in the cellars of buildings in the low-lying
Gängeviertel, which was soon under water whenever flooding occurred. Nevertheless not even the descriptions and admonitions
delivered in 1801 by the Hamburg-based physician Jacob Rambach
and the Berlin-based journalist Garlieb Merkel, who pointed to the
inhumane and moist cellar dwellings, as well as to the overcrowded,
dilapidated houses above them, along with the filth and dirt in the
narrow alleyways as a major and serious problem, had any effect on
large sections of the middle classes. In 1872, for instance, the Senate
continued to reject a proposal to build a water treatment plant despite
health authority warnings that the drinking of unfiltered tap water,
which came largely from the River Elbe, posed a serious health risk.

It therefore comes as little surprise to hear that Hamburg witnessed
a total of seven cholera epidemics between 1822 and 1873. The worst,
however, was the epidemic of 1892 — probably not, as originally assumed, originating in Russia but brought to the city by a ship from
Le Havre — which spread through drinking water pipes to large parts
of the city, its effect being greatest in the poorer quarters. In light of
the catastrophic situation in Hamburg Robert Koch, the discoverer
of the cholera bacillus, who had been commissioned by the German
Emperor to report on the measures taken in Hamburg to prevent
the further spread of the epidemic, described the situation as follows: "Never in my life have I encountered such unhealthy dwellings,
plague-infested hovels and breeding grounds for every type of infectious germs, as in the so-called Gängevierteln…". Yet the rapid spread
of the epidemic and the Emperor's threat to place Hamburg under
the guardianship of the Empire in view of this "wanton sloppiness"
were just two of the motives prompting the Senate to take action.

At least as important in terms of the influence it had was the fact
that news of the scandalous conditions in Hamburg spread throughout Europe and also much further afield. Apart from the reputational

The grand town houses of the ship owners and important merchants, as well as their elegant summer residences on today's Elbchaussee, stood in stark contrast to the Gängeviertel, where workers and the poor lived in cramped conditions. The intolerable hygienic and sanitary conditions made these districts the ideal location for all types of infectious diseases to spread rapidly. In the worst cholera epidemic of 1892 nearly 17,000 people became sick, of whom 8500 died.

damage this brought with it, the main concern was the financial consequences for the city. Very few foreign vessels were now docking in Hamburg, which caused cargo handling in the port to come to a virtual standstill. Similarly the lucrative emigration business ceased entirely and emigrants stranded in Hamburg had to be provided for by the city. Hamburg's own ships were placed under quarantine in foreign ports. Rail traffic to Cologne, Vienna, Prague and Copenhagen was discontinued. Other rail connections were subject to rigorous restrictions and most of the trains arriving in Hamburg were more or less empty. Even letters sent from Hamburg were often burnt without being read by their recipients. For the dockworkers the consequence of the economic collapse was — unless they found work in one of the disinfection crews or as gravediggers — unemployment and for the merchants it meant millions in losses.

The most important immediate measure taken was the accelerated construction of a filtration plant that had already been approved in 1891. Other steps that followed in the years thereafter included the redevelopment of the Gängeviertel; a law against the building of squalid and unhealthy dwellings; the establishment, at long last, of a port health and medical service, and constitutional reforms giving large sections of the population a say in political affairs. Finally, for the sake of completeness, it should also be mentioned that the so-called "Housing Maintenance Act", passed in 1898, prompted bitter resistance from many landlords, just as the redevelopment measures implemented after the Great Fire had once done.

## The Stronghold
## of the German Labour Movement

For Hamburg the second half of the 19th century was not only a period of strong economic growth but also of increasing social polarisation. Journeymen had opposed exploitation by their masters in 1791 but rigorous state control, including a requirement to register with the police and a ban on public assemblies as well as on the first employers' organisations formed between 1820 and 1825 helped to block virtually almost any social demands, however justified they might have been, until the middle of the century.

The sole employee organisations which the Senate and the employers refrained from quashing were the health insurance companies and burial funds of the journeymen. By 1850 there were 127 such organizations in Hamburg and by the 1870s their number had risen to 249. The nation-wide links maintained by these institutions, together with the fact that they were at least able to obtain moral verdicts against, and sometimes also impose material penalties on, certain masters or even a city's Chamber of Crafts, made them the first institutional weapon in the incipient labour disputes. A second organisation that became a nucleus of the workers' opposition to excessively long hours, exploitatively low wages, child labour, unbearably squalid living conditions and exclusion from any political decision-making processes was the "Bildungsgesellschaft für Arbeiter zu Hamburg", founded in 1845. This organisation gained political clout and even support from certain sections of Hamburg's bourgeoisie after becoming associated, one year later, as an educational society with the already reputable Patriotische Gesellschaft.

From 1849 onwards Hamburg's workers became organised in trade unions and co-operatives, to call strikes designed, although with little success, to achieve better working conditions. From a very early stage the strikers realised that their fight came at a cost, for example in lost wages, and therefore set up a relief fund for striking workers at the beginning of the 1860s. In the years that followed Hamburg increasingly became the centre of the German labour movement. Not only were representatives of Hamburg's labour movement always very vociferous speakers whenever and wherever a labour congress was held in Germany. The above-mentioned seven-month-long wave of strikes in 1865, which in Hamburg spread from one craft to another, also became a model of successful labour disputes in many other cities.

Yet Hamburg did not turn out to be the undisputed capital of trade union activity in the German Empire until after Bismarck's resignation and the repeal of the anti-socialist laws. One clear indication of this was the great dockworkers strike which involved almost 17,000 workers and lasted from November 1896 until February 1897. The spark that lit the fuse in an already tinderbox-like atmosphere was the arrest and deportation of a British trade union leader who had come to Hamburg to convince the city's dockworkers -like their counterparts in Rotterdam before them — to join the "International Federation of Ship, Dock and Riverside Workers", an organization founded in Britain.

The real reasons for labour discontent were, however, falling real wages due to increasing food prices and purchase taxes, the increase in rents following accession to the German Customs Union in 1888 and the greater distances to travel between the home and the workplace. Other reasons included deficiencies in the organisation of labour referrals and the placement of workers, unsatisfying regulations with regard to the hours worked, and no, or insufficient, industrial health and safety. Although the "Allgemeiner Deutscher Arbeiterverein" (General German Workers' Association) was founded in Leipzig in 1863 Hamburg became the headquarters of the "Generalkommission der Gewerkschaften Deutschlands" (General Commission of German Unions). Furthermore, 25 of the 58 individual trades unions in Germany were now based in the Hanseatic city.

## Social Dialogue and Balance
## as Determinants for International Competitiveness

The question could certainly be posed what all this has to do with globalisation and international competition between different economic locations. Complex though the answer may be two aspects seem to be of quite particular importance. The first is the circumstance that the development of the labour movement was itself subjected to strong international influences. Before returning to Hamburg the founder of the aforementioned Bildungsgesellschaft für Arbeiter had spent 19 years living abroad, in London and Paris among other places, where, upon coming into contact with revolutionary emigrants, he had embraced the then still new socialist and communist thinking. Karl Marx, who at first belonged to the "League of the Just" in Paris and later drew up the statutes for an international communist movement together with Friedrich Engels and two compatriots from Hamburg, spent time in the Hanseatic city in 1845 and 1849. In the 1860s both Friedrich Engels and Karl Marx published their works in Hamburg, and it was here that the first edition of Marx's seminal work, "Das Kapital", also appeared in 1867.

The second aspect is the impact the labour movement had on the international competitiveness of Hamburg's industry and port. One example of the industrial effects wrought by an approximately two-month-long strike was the fate of the Hamburg firm of coachbuilders Lauenstein. The intransigence of the management, which refused to back down and reconsider an unacceptable wage cut, resulted in the company — despite having full order books — going bankrupt in 1870. It was unable to absorb the lost production costs resulting from the self-inflicted industrial action. Another example was the strike by dockworkers. Although the decline in the volume of goods moved initially remained lower than expected as the employers were able to recruit replacement labour, both from other German cities and from England, it is hard to pretend that Bremen and Rotterdam were not the major beneficiaries of the strike.

More generally the dock workers' strike sent out a clear message. Despite numerous negotiation attempts the Senate was still on the side of the employers, and these seemed to be quite happy to be locked in a power struggle which they, in principle, actually won mainly due to the long duration of the industrial dispute. Nonetheless this first mass strike made politicians and the Senate sit up and take notice that the welfare and the long term economic interests of the city also included the legitimate demands of its workers. As a result a port inspector, who was responsible for improving occupational health and safety, was appointed in 1904/05; the foundation of a port operation association enhanced recruitment procedures and the payment of wages in 1906; and shift work and the nine-hour day were introduced in 1907 and 1913 respectively.

Considering the still hard-nosed attitude of the employers it is quite obvious that none of this would have happened without permanent pressure from the trade unions, including a renewed wave of strike action between 1905 and 1907. However, the long and arduous path from increasing, partially uncontrolled labour unrest to social dialogue and employee representation can still be seen as a key element in strengthening the international competitive position of Hamburg's port.

## Hamburg's Concept of Democracy: Free Expression: Yes – Sharing Power: No

Since 1860 Hamburg's Senate had consisted of 18 members, of whom at least nine had to be lawyers and seven merchants. Its members were appointed for life by the Senate and the city's Parliament. The fact that the Parliament usually accepted the proposals of the Senate led to the de facto continuation of the co-option procedure of the so-called Council. Every three years half of the Parliament's members were elected by those citizens entitled to vote. Of the 192 representatives, 48 were appointed by the landowners, 60 by the notables and 84 by the voting public. To be allowed to vote a member of the latter group had to be a citizen of the city, in other words male, above the age of 25 and verifiably paying tax on at least 1,200 marks per annum. A notable who was also a landowner and met the tax payment conditions was entitled to three votes. The number of citizens entitled to vote comprised no more than 3.5 per cent of the city's total population.

After reducing the number of Members of Parliament to 160, incorporating rural communities into the circle of those entitled to

The City Hall, built between 1886 and 1897, is the seat of the Senate and the Hamburg Parliament. Boasting 647 rooms it offers more space than Buckingham Palace in London. The fact that the City Hall is structurally connected to the Chamber of Commerce and the Stock Exchange testifies to the special attention which political decision-making in Hamburg has always paid to the economic development of the city.

vote, some minor changes to the voting right and, in particular, making it easier to become a citizen of the city, 5 per cent of the population were eligible to vote in 1896. However women and all lower social classes were still completely excluded from political life. Hamburg was, as a French observer remarked after the turn of the century, ruled by 160 citizens and 18 kings who could not be knocked off their thrones. Even though the Social Democratic Party had more than 10,000 members in Hamburg at the turn of the century it was still not represented in the Parliament in 1900.

This changed in 1901 when the social democrats succeeded in winning at first one and three years later 13 seats in the Parliament. After the social democrats claimed 62 per cent of the vote, winning all three of the city's seats in the Reichstag, in 1903, the result of the 1904 parliamentary election sent such shockwaves through the middle class that the Senate and the middle-class majority immediately took steps to restrict the right to vote. Their declared goal was to secure the reign of the propertied class and to keep the influence of the social democrats under control. "Free Expression: Yes — Sharing Power: No" is probably the most fitting description of the middle class concept of democracy at that time.

After proposals for an income-related three-tier voting system had been initially discussed an extremely restrictive two-class voting system was finally adopted in 1906 against the wishes of the Mayors Johann Heinrich Burchard and Johann Georg Mönckeberg as well as the then Member of Parliament and later Senator and Mayor Carl Wilhelm Petersen. Yet this only applied to the city but not the rural communities. The idea of this system was to allow the election of 24 and 12 Members of Parliament every three years by those citizens who, on average, had paid tax on more than 2,500 marks and on between 1,200 and 2,500 marks respectively during the previous three years. Together with the 80 parliamentary members appointed by the landowners and notables the middle-class majority in the city's Parliament seemed to be safe forever; especially as the rural districts, which elected eight Members of Parliament, usually voted in favour of the middle classes. Despite this new voting system it was impossible to stop the process of democratisation. In 1907 and 1910, socialists won 19 and 20 seats respectively. By 1913 the SPD (Social Democratic Party of Germany) had almost 62,000 members in Hamburg alone; a figure which the middle-class party and the united liberals could only dream of.

## *Hamburg on the Way*
## *to becoming a Modern Metropolis*

The four decades prior to the outbreak of the First World War were, on the one hand, characterised by strong economic growth due to the expansion of the port industry, more general industrial activities and international trade. On the other they were marked by the fundamental modernisation of urban planning as well as the development of a metropolitan infrastructure. After the city had witnessed an initial phase of conscious modernisation after the Great Fire a land development plan was approved in 1892 specifying general rules for the development of the inner city, setting out residential and commercial areas, including public parks, as well as planning important traffic routes.

The economic boom demanded the construction of new and functional office buildings. By 1881 Hamburg had a public telephone network with as many as 206 participants. The network installed in Berlin two months before this had just eight connections. In 1882 — and only three months after Berlin — Hamburg introduced electric street lighting with a number of arc lamps at the Rathausmarkt Square. After 1911 the common horse-drawn cabs were replaced by motorised ones, so-called "stink pots". And even private transport changed from horse-drawn to motor vehicles. The growing number of rich foreign visitors promoted the building of luxury hotels. Increasing wealth — not only in the city, but also further afield — turned Hamburg into a shopping paradise in which, in addition to traditional shops, the first department stores opened between 1896 and 1912.

The fast growing population, the continuing settlement of Hamburg's outlying districts and their incorporation in the city as well as the increasing distance between a person's place of residence and place of work — partially due to the large-scale resettlement of residents for the development of the free port — required an efficient local transport system. Therefore the horse-drawn omnibus to Wandsbek, established in 1839, was replaced by a steam tram connection in 1879. A similar development occurred in 1883 on the route from Hamburg to Blankenese and Wedel via Altona. Two years previously a railway connection had been established to Cuxhaven, which actually belonged to Hamburg until the "Greater Hamburg Act" was passed in 1937.

Urban traffic was, in the strict sense of the term, enhanced by putting the first electric tram into operation as a circle line by the mid-1890s. The plan to construct a partly elevated and partly underground railway system intended to travel across the inner city, the port and large areas of the working-class districts with 23 stops was tackled in 1906. In the first 12 months after its inauguration in 1912 it transported 24.8 million passengers. One year before that the Elbe Tunnel, based on British and American examples, became the first river tunnel on the European mainland. This project was also a huge success since numerous dock and shipyard workers no longer had to depend on the less reliable ferry service.

Hamburg's onshore long-distance transport infrastructure was also further enhanced in the later decades of the 19th century. A line between Altona and the various train stations in Hamburg opened in 1866. The construction of a railway bridge across the River Elbe ensured that the line from Hanover to Harburg could finally be extended to Hamburg in 1872. In 1906 the main central station was inaugurated, bringing together the individual lines which until then had terminated in four different stations. This made changing trains and catching connections much easier. Although the number of air travellers was insignificant compared to the number of people travelling by rail and ship Hamburg's airport opened its doors in 1911. The construction of a special zeppelin hanger was completed one year later. But very soon the airship's new rivals, the first aeroplanes, took possession of the site, too.

Apart from modernisation of the traffic infrastructure Hamburg, which was the largest city in Northern Europe in 1910 with more than one million inhabitants, had to invest greatly in other urban facilities. As the hinterland refused to accept the increasing amount of urban waste after the cholera epidemic a waste incineration plant was put into service in 1896. It was the first of its kind on the European continent. The city's water supply was improved, too, first by constructing further filtration plants, after 1905 also by drilling of deep wells. The Eppendorf hospital was built in 1884 and the Harbour hospital was inaugurated in 1901. After Hamburg had turned a blind eye to the hygiene and health care issues for a large percentage of the population for more than 300 years many of these new urban facilities were exemplary for that time.

## Schools, Education, Research, Information and Culture

Schools and education more generally also experienced dynamic development during this period. After the school system had finally broken away from the church as a result of the constitution of 1860 a supervisory school authority had been established in 1865 and compulsory education for all children aged 6 to 14 years was introduced in 1870. In terms of secondary education a vocational school for girls was inaugurated in 1867. In addition to the Johanneum, founded in 1529, and the Akademische Gymnasium, which offered its pupils lectures in history, natural sciences and languages, but closed down in 1883 after 270 years of service, the Wilhelm-Gymnasium was established in 1881.

Beyond that the beginning of the 20th century was characterised by the greater emphasis being placed on theoretical aspects of vocational education. Although there had been a navigation school since 1749, a school for seamen since 1864 and a state vocational and trade school since 1864 the Hamburg Scientific Foundation for training young merchants was not founded until 1907. The following year saw the opening of the German Colonial Institute, where civil servants were prepared for their future careers in the colonies; particular attention was paid to teaching languages, history, economics and the natural sciences.

Although the "Commerzbibliothek" (Commercial Library), the world's oldest specialised library in economics, was established as early as 1735 the research landscape in Hamburg was relatively underdeveloped compared to other big cities. The most remarkable exception was the Institute for Maritime and Tropical Diseases, founded by the then naval physician Bernhard Nocht in 1899. As in the case of Commerzbibliothek with its rare treasures dating back to the 16th and 17th century, this institute still enjoys a reputation of excellence for its research both nationally and internationally. Apart from this Hamburg had been home to the German Observatory since 1887. Early in the new century it had been able to boast a physical, chemical and two botanical institutes. And since 1908 the German Colonial Institute which systematically collected and prepared information on overseas regions, was also located in Hamburg. A university, however, was not founded until 1919.

The development of the press and communication was in stark contrast to that of scientific research. Thanks to its worldwide trade relations and various postal links Hamburg was already an important centre for national and international information exchange in the 17th century and, in particular, the 18th century. By the 1620s it was not only possible to obtain regular local newspapers in Hamburg but, due to close links to the Netherlands, also newspapers from Amsterdam and Haarlem.

The *Hamburgische Correspondent* was supposedly the most read business newspaper in Europe throughout the 18th century. It was printed four times a week and had a circulation of 30,000 copies around 1800. These figures become more impressive if compared to *The Times*, which at that time had a circulation — even though daily — of just 8,000 copies. Also an English-language newspaper was available in Hamburg between 1828 and 1834.

The city's cultural life also boomed during this period. Hamburg had had an opera house since 1678 and several theatres since the middle of the 18th century and renowned poets and writers, such as Gotthold Ephraim Lessing and Heinrich Heine, or famous composers, such as Georg Philipp Telemann, Johann Sebastian Bach and Johannes Brahms, temporarily lived and worked in the city. But as Hamburg was a city of citizens and not a royal seat it clearly lacked the glamour. In addition and, probably even until the late 19th century, those in power had neither the will nor the insight to ensure that highly gifted musicians, such as Bach, Brahms or Gustav Mahler, resided permanently in the city.

Nevertheless the new art gallery (Kunsthalle), mostly financed by private donations, the concert hall (Musikhalle), donated by Laeisz in 1906, as well as numerous new large museums ensured a period of prosperity for Hamburg's cultural life.

Today one of these, the Museum of Arts and Crafts, is among the leading museums for cultural history and arts and crafts in Europe. Another, the Museum for Hamburg History, is the largest city museum in Germany.


## Hamburg
### on the Eve of the First World War

Although it was not as common in Hamburg to display wealth and social status as it was in other major cities it was still difficult to conceal that the city was one of the richest in Europe and probably the world at the beginning of the 20th century. Allegedly there were five or six families whose assets were estimated at between 20 and 30 million reichsmark. They were all internationally successful ship owners, merchants and/or private bankers. The number of families whose assets amounted to several millions was also remarkable in every respect. And the number of families who had at least one million marks was so great that they were not really considered special. The main source of the city's wealth was trade, port industry in the narrower sense and increasingly also port-oriented industry.

But not only a number of very rich people and a broad bourgeois middle class lived in Hamburg before the First World War. Expansion of the port industry as well as advancing industrialisation in the free port and Hamburg's outskirts ensured that the number of workers rose permanently. While roughly 45,000 workers were employed in the 1,400 industrial companies in the city in 1900, their number increased to approximately 115,000 by 1914. Together with the 40,000 to 50,000 employees in skilled trades more than 155,000 people were employed in the commercial sector alone; which corresponded to roughly 43 per cent of the total workforce. Apart from the approximately 17,000 dock workers most of the population worked, if they were not unemployed, in trade, banking or insurance companies as well as other service sectors.

Important events also effectively promoting economic growth and employment in Hamburg at the end of the 19th century were the opening of the Kaiser-Wilhelm Canal, today known as Kiel Canal or North Sea-Baltic Canal, and the Elbe-Trave Canal in 1895 and 1900 respectively. Both waterways supported Hamburg's position as the key overseas port for the Baltic region — a function which Hamburg once again fulfils today just as it did during the period of the Hanseatic League. Moreover, the importance of the River Elbe for the port was heightened by the fact that the canalisation of the connection between Prague and Aussig resulted in a large percentage of Bohemian international trade being handled via Hamburg instead of Triest.

The dynamic development of Hamburg as a trade and economic metropolis as well as the growth of the population to more than one million inhabitants turned Hamburg into the main city in Northern Europe at the turn of the 20th century. Another important fact was that Hamburg had not been so gravely affected by the business downturn crisis of 1873 and at least the middle classes, borne by self-confidence and trust in technological progress, were captivated by a sense of euphoria and looked optimistically towards the future. The fact that, unlike business activity in other German cities, Hamburg focussed on the wider picture and not simply on Germany and the fact that 5 per cent of its inhabitants were not German ensured that the city was one of the most important cosmopolitan urban centres before the Great War.

However despite economic success and the almost unlimited support provided by the city's merchants for the Kaiser's expansive colonial and fleet policy, some people in Hamburg were still very concerned about what lay ahead. One man who observed the political developments with great scepticism was the Mayor of Hamburg Johann Heinrich Burchard, who declined a government post in Berlin in 1909 despite his close ties to the Emperor. Among other things he was not willing to share Germany's aggressive stance, in particular towards Great Britain.

Another man who viewed German foreign, colonial and fleet policy at the beginning of the 20th century with a great deal of distrust and fear was Albert Ballin. He had already discussed the possible risk of a war between Germany and Great Britain with Bismarck in 1901. Asked by Great Britain to act as a negotiator Albert Ballin tried to achieve a German-British fleet agreement in 1912. But all his efforts were in vain as the size of the German naval fleet continued to grow. He is said to have watched the launch of the Imperator, the world's largest ship at that time, in May 1912 with a very concerned look on his face. They said he thought it was too good to last and unfortunately for Germany, Hamburg and himself he was to be proved right.

# PART IV

# Globalisation of War, an Illusory Boom, Economic Crisis and Reconstruction

# CHAPTER 7

# World Economy and International Economic Policy from 1914 to the Middle of the 20th Century

T he period between 1914 and 1945 was overshadowed by two world wars. But the interwar period, too, was marked by a number of very different yet interdependent developments that proved to be extremely detrimental to the future of the world economy and the globalisation process. Following an illusory boom directly after the end of the First World War, North America, England and France experienced the first serious recession in 1921. This was followed by German hyperinflation in 1923, the stock market crash in the United States in October 1929 as well as the Great Depression and worldwide mass unemployment in the second half of the 1930s. Further increases in protectionism and state interventions designed to protect national interests were partly the cause, partly the effect of the crisis. Prevailing opinion considers the war and interwar years to be a period of de-globalisation.

Nevertheless, the question arises as to whether this period can, in an historical sense, also be seen as a period of continuity with a renewed shift of the world economic centre. All of these phases of fundamental changes in international relations and power constellations were, in the past as now, characterised by political, economic and, no less frequently, social turmoil. Another possible interpretation could be that the previously prevailing nature of the globalisation process, which had been based chiefly on private initiative since at least the 17th century, came to an end with the outbreak of WWI, and the worldwide political and economic interdependencies now additionally — and in some sectors even predominantly — became the responsibility of the governments of the nation states. This would mean that the globalisation process in principle continued, yet was subject to a fundamental qualitative shift due to increasing state interventions.

This last-named aspect is underlined not only by increasing state interventions with regard to macroeconomic developments and in the areas of structural and distribution policy. The institutionalisation of a new world economic order, carried out under American leadership after WWII, can also be viewed within this context. It is important to note, however, that key principles of this new system, i.e. the simultaneous realisation of fixed exchange rates, the free movement of goods and capital as well as national autonomy in matters of economic policy, were incompatible with one another. As a consequence, due to its inherent contradictions, the system was, despite its remarkable initial successes, ultimately doomed to failure over the long term.

### Increasing Disintegration
### of the International Goods, Capital
### and Labour Markets

The thesis of de-globalisation between 1914 and 1945 is supported primarily by economic factors. Not only did, with the exception of the exports of goods, services and capital from the United States, international trade and movement of capital come to an almost complete standstill during the two world wars. In the interwar years, too, world economic development and, most notably, international economic relations lacked the positive momentum that had characterised the 50 years prior to WWI. With economic growth reaching 4.7 per cent in the United States between 1922 and 1929 and averaging 3 per cent in European countries — with the exception of Britain — and 2.8 per cent in Japan, growth in international trade, which, together with the Industrial Revolution, had been the engine of economic growth before the First World War lagged behind growth in production for the first time since the middle of the 19th century.

Moreover, the European economies were not only weakened by the enormous war efforts but also highly indebted. On the one hand, this resulted in a significant reduction of their import capacities; on the other, they were as yet unable to resume traditional capital exports. Both factors had their greatest impact on raw material exporting colonies or developing countries, which were hit by a steady decline in the price of their export products. However, even trade between Europe and the United States did not help to eliminate existing world economic imbalances — on the contrary. Repayment of the loans taken out by France and Great Britain in the USA during the First World War was hampered by the persistence of the US trade barriers imposed in the 1870s. At the same time, the leadership attained in the field of industrial technology by the United States during the war led to a structural American export surplus.

The de-globalisation thesis could also be supported by the trend towards restrictions on immigration, which was already to be observed before WWI. Particularly apparent in the United States it also applied to a number of other traditional immigration countries, such as Canada, Australia, Argentina and Brazil, which, slowly but surely, began to seal off their borders from the beginning of the 1920s. While the number of Europeans seeking their fortune overseas was approximately 1.5 million between 1909 and 1914, the figure fell to less than 700,000 in the 1920s and to roughly 100,000 in the 1930s. Thus at the same time as the global economy fragmented, the free international labour market not only temporarily peaked but had already passed its zenith.

Despite increasing state intervention in both domestic and foreign economic affairs, international market interdependencies were, however, not completely severed during the 1920s. At one level this was reflected in the steep fall in prices on national and international markets caused by surplus capacity in heavy industry and the commodities markets as well as by overproduction in the agricultural sector. Equally the fact that the New York stock market crash of October 1929 and the subsequent depression in the United States triggered a worldwide economic crisis serves as confirmation that international economic interdependencies had not, as yet, been suspended. In fact, it could even be argued that the scale and intensity with which the crisis spread around the world is a clear indication that global commodity and financial markets were, for all the politically determined distortions, still part of a globally interconnected system as the world entered the 1930s.

## Fundamental Trend Reversal versus Historical Continuity in the Globalisation Process

To assert that the process of world economic disintegration during the war and interwar years represents a general trend reversal with regard to the lines of developments evident in the pre-WWI period would, in many aspects, be too one-sided. Even without the First World War the United States would most probably still have become the world's leading industrial nation in the first half of the 20th century. Occurrences during the war merely accelerated this development — without the USA having systematically planned it in any way. Yet a further shift in the world economic centre — this time from London to New York — and the progressive emergence of the American dollar as a serious challenger to sterling as the key international currency was, even back then, only a matter of time.

Similarly, globalisation should not be understood solely as a phenomenon of international market integration. Even in the 1930s, when

240

the economic sector was increasingly being determined by national policies favouring national interests and internal economic stabilisation over the stability of external economic relations, an intensification of globalisation tendencies was definitely taking place in many other sectors. One example is international knowledge and technology transfer — as principally reflected in the adoption of modern American production methods in Europe and Japan. A second example is the globalisation of cultural trends, a process that intensified further during the 1920s — both in the motion picture industry, where France gradually had to surrender its leading role to Hollywood, and in the music industry, where American musicals and jazz increasingly came to dominate the European scene.

Yet between 1914 and 1945 the process of globalisation had taken on a different quality to that seen in the 19th century. Decisive was, in this context, not so much the circumstance that many new developments in the process of international exchange were no longer originating in Europe but in the United States. Equally that Europe lost its political and economic supremacy after the First World War and was unable to regain this during the interwar years was basically also just one dimension of change, but probably not the most important one. Truly decisive was the fact that the destruction of the geopolitical world order prevailing during the prewar period, as occasioned by Europe's growing loss of importance, had, in the interwar years, been replaced neither by any purposefully targeted American policy of hegemony nor by a collectively organised system of governance.

The League of Nations, founded in 1919 and based, inter alia, on the notion that any restriction of national sovereignty is unacceptable, was not an appropriate forum for the establishment of a generally accepted new world order or, even less so, a world economic order. A series of international negotiations at which an attempt was made to solve at least some of the world's economic problems on a multilateral basis failed to yield any tangible results. Moreover, the United States, which would have probably been able to fill the power vacuum left by the Europeans, chose to pursue isolationism and continued protectionism. The sole exception were efforts to ease German reparation payments and the British and French war debts through the Dawes Plan of 1924 and the Young Plan of 1929, together with the monetary policy of the Federal Reserve Board. As a result, other governments also decided to gear their economic policies almost exclusively to national interests and sought—wherever possible—to "unload" the costs of the internal balancing of interests onto foreign countries.

## Cumulative Amplification Effects due to the World Economic Crisis

Since the end of the First World War the leading industrial nations had witnessed three to four more or less distinct economic cycles. Accordingly, the beginning of a new downturn, which commenced in Germany in 1927, in England in 1928, in France in February 1929, and in the United States in the summer of 1929, initially appeared to be a quite normal development. Of increasing concern to some observers was solely the New York equity market boom, which, having begun in 1926, continued to build momentum and was, to a considerable extent, now fuelled by credit-financed buying. The Federal Reserve Board, in particular, looked on with growing unease as escalating speculation caused the Dow Jones Index to rise by almost 100 per cent between 1926 and 1928.

Initially, however, the Federal Reserve Board was unable to decide on the hike in interest rates that this situation really demanded. For one thing, Britain and Germany had, in the light of the accelerating economic downturn in Europe, requested the US to keep interest rates on hold in order to prevent them, in turn, from being forced to adopt a restrictive, procyclical monetary policy in line with the rules of the gold standard. For another, prevailing opinion in the United States— and not only there—was that the market would, over the longer term, itself correct untenable imbalances, even those in the financial sector. Yet the all-important factor that made the Federal Reserve Board keep interest rates too low for too long was, however, massive pressure from the New York banking industry. In the case of the National City Bank this even went so far as the threat to offer its own cheap loans to neutralise any credit squeeze on the part of the central bank.

By the time the Federal Reserve Board finally decided, at the end of 1928, to adopt a more restrictive monetary policy to end the huge speculative disconnect between stock prices and actual company valuations it was basically already too late. From the middle of 1929 at any rate, rising interest rates intensified the downward momentum and the stock market crash of October 1929, with the so-called "Black Thursday" and "Black Tuesday" on 24 and 29 October respectively, constituted little more than a few especially glaring flashes of lightning in a storm that was already fast approaching. The number of new orders in the construction sector had been declining since the spring of 1929. March saw automobile production peak at 622,000 units, with the figure falling to fewer than 450,000 units in August and September and subsequently plummeting to 169,500 units in November and just 92,500 in December.

The banking sector, buffeted by a combination of restrictive monetary policy, the stock market crash, falling property prices and non-performing loans, suffered such a severe liquidity crisis that not only small players but also large banks became insolvent. Even the easing of monetary policy instituted on 31 October of the same year was unable to halt the deflationary spiral. The money supply shrank at a speed equivalent to an annual rate of 31 per cent. In October 1931 alone 522 banks in the United States collapsed; four months later the total number of banking industry failures had risen to almost 1,400. The number of commercial and industrial bankruptcies increased from 26,000 in 1930 to more than 28,000 in 1931 and over 31,000 in 1932. Similarly, the jobless figures hit fresh highs as each month went by, finally rising to 37.8 per cent at the height of the Great Depression.

An awareness that the New York stock market crash might spread beyond the United States to become a turbocharger for a global economic crisis did not, however, develop until the end of 1930. In Europe at least the sharp falls on the New York market were, in part, even received with a certain sense of relief. It was hoped that this would open the door for an expansionary monetary policy — an assessment that very soon proved to be very short-sighted. It failed to take account of the various economic interdependencies that continued to exist and, most notably, the potential of international transmission due to the gold standard. Moreover, the purely economic interaction dynamics were additionally burdened by political agreements and constantly being further aggravated by interventions at the level of economic policy.

A striking example of political agreements with a negative impact were the provisions regarding German reparation payments and the obligations requiring France and England to repay their war debts to the United States. Germany depended on U.S. loans to honour its commitments, which significantly exceeded its own economic potential. The other two countries, for their part, needed Germany's reparation payments to pay off their own war debts. Since the American market remained practically closed to European exports, a large part of these payments had to be financed with capital imports from the United States. The economic, banking and liquidity crisis in the USA not only brought this cycle to a halt but also led to considerable capital outflows in Europe.

Astounding highlights in a succession of irresponsible foreign trade policy decisions included the devaluation spirals, which commenced following the abandonment of the gold standard in 1931, as well as the worldwide proliferation of protectionism. Particularly severe in this context was the so-called Smoot-Hawley Tariff Act, enacted in 1930 by the US Senate. This act not only raised the average tariff burden on imports into the United States to almost 60 per cent, provoking countermeasures, including quantitative import restrictions, in many other countries; it also documented that the US had, with this initiative, clearly decided to become a negative role model, finally indicating that, quite evidently, nobody any longer felt responsible for the stability and smooth functioning of the world economy as a whole. The upshot was the globalisation of state intervention and protectionism, the globalisation of economic decline and mass unemployment, the globalisation of despair and fear of the future, the globalisation of nationalism and xenophobia and, ultimately, the globalisation of rearmament, hate propaganda and war.

## Germany at the Epicentre of World Economic Turmoil

Although unemployment figures in Germany had not yet fallen to the pre-war level, there was much at the end of the 1920s which recalled the euphoric mood at the turn of the century. Even the fact that Germany was still labouring under the high reparation payments and the peak of the economic cycle had been passed back in 1927 initially failed to give rise to fears that, beyond what appeared to be a quite normal cyclical slowdown, a major economic and, later, also a major political disaster was approaching. Subsequently, however, the devastating economic earthquake that shook the United States developed into a powerful tsunami with fatal consequences for the entire world economy. Yet the economic burden and, above all, the long-term political consequences were indisputably far more serious for Germany than for the United States.

In Germany, unemployment had already exceeded five per cent by November 1927 and a decline in private investments, most notably inventory investments, commenced in 1928. The reasons for this were manifold. Wage increases had, due to state intervention in the interest of political and social stabilisation since 1925, clearly become detached from productivity development. Together with high taxation and other levies this was placing considerable strains on the international competitiveness of companies and the investment climate. Additionally, the then German Chancellor Brüning continued, despite being frequently urged to consider an anti-cyclical financial policy, to pursue a policy of tough budgetary consolidation even during the downturn.

All this served to weaken the German economy long before the deflation shock from the US reached the country. The fact that Germany was hit particularly badly by the global downturn, which intensified cumulatively after 1930, thus had a lot to do with the specifically German pre-history ahead of the world economic crisis. Part of this history is the fact that Brüning initially adhered strictly to the international treaties specified in the Dawes Plan and, subsequently, in the Young Plan. The latter also demanded the maintenance of exchange rate stability within the framework of the gold standard, which obliged the Reichsbank to adopt a restrictive monetary policy and led to a tightening of the supply of credit.

Even the renowned British economist John Maynard Keynes, in a speech delivered at the Übersee-Club in Hamburg on 8 January 1932, recommended — albeit in rather veiled manner — that Germany, like Britain, which had implemented this step in 1931, should abandon the gold standard. However, Brüning's highest political priority was that of proving Germany was unable to honour its reparation payments and that these should, therefore, be cancelled. The revival of the economy and the battle against unemployment were, quite obviously, only his second concern.

As a result, national income in Germany declined by more than 42 per cent between 1928 and 1932 and gross domestic investments hit an all-time low in 1931. At the height of the crisis, during the winters of 1931/32 and 1932/33, approximately six million people were out of work, a figure equivalent to an unemployment rate of more than 30 per cent — and this despite the Reichsbank having already, in its pursuit of an anti-cyclical monetary policy, cut the discount rate from 7.5 to 4 per cent between the spring of 1929 and September 1930.

Yet this shift towards an expansionary course could only be maintained until August 1931. The increased share of the vote gained by the NSDAP in 1932 and 1933 triggered a massive outflow of foreign capital, a circumstance that was compounded still further by a banking crisis in Austria and Germany. In a matter of just a few weeks the Reichsbank lost more than half of its gold and currency reserves, forcing it to return to an extremely restrictive monetary policy. From that point on both monetary and fiscal policy were markedly pro-cyclical and the subsequent economic crisis and political disaster were just waiting to happen.

## A New World Economic Order
## under the Leadership of the United States

Not until America entered the war in 1941 did it become clear that it now saw itself as the new global champion seeking to shape global political and economic development in accordance with its own national interests and to prevent key strategic and economic regions from falling increasingly under the control of foreign states. Unlike in the case of the foundation of the League of Nations, which they never joined, the United States played an extremely active role in the creation of its successor organisation, the United Nations Organisation.

As early as in August 1941, US president Roosevelt and British prime minister Churchill met to proclaim joint political principles in the so-called "Atlantic Charter", which was designed to secure a better future for the world once the war was over. The majority of these principles, above all the idea of collective measures to preserve world peace, the equality of all nations, the right to self-determination of all peoples, the promotion of human rights as well as the obligation to cooperate to solve international problems, were enshrined in the UN Charta passed by 51 nations in June 1945.

As far as the postwar world economic order was concerned, for which decisive elements had also already been prefigured in the Atlantic Charter, the first concrete ideas had been emerging in Britain since 1940 with the participation of John Maynard Keynes. Equally, independent approaches had, increasingly, been undertaken in the United States, too, after 1941. As a result, two very different concepts confronted one another at the Bretton Woods conference in 1944, which was attended by representative of 44 nations: A British concept, reflecting the interests of a debtor nation with high unemployment, and an American concept, which was an expression of the interests of a creditor nation with highly competitive production capacities.

At the heart of the British proposal was the possibility of pursuing an independent national employment policy, the defence of which even permitted exchange rate adjustments and the introduction of trade restrictions. The promotion of world trade was to be assured through the generous provision of international liquidity via a supranational central bank. The United States, for its part, gave priority to the lifting of existing trade barriers and the re-establishment of a multilateral payment system based on the full convertibility of all participating currencies and essentially fixed exchange rates. At the same time, the Americans were assuming that they would, even in the foreseeable future, remain the dominant creditor nation for the rest of the world. The final compromise reached at the Bretton Woods conference was basically a reflection of the US ideas.

The US dollar was linked to gold at a fixed rate of 35 dollars an ounce. This meant that the US Department of the Treasury was required to buy or sell any amount of gold at this rate. For other currencies the exchange rate to the dollar was set with a fluctuation margin of ±1%. With controls on the movement of capital initially still in place, participating countries committed themselves to making their currencies convertible as soon as possible within the framework of a multilateral payments system. To provide loans to states with temporary balance of payments deficits and a possible lack of monetary reserves related to this, the International Monetary Fund (IMF) was established. In the event of more fundamental balance of payments deficits there was a provision permitting an adjustment of exchange rates — up to 10 per cent following consultation with the IMF, and anything beyond this only with the approval of a three-quarters majority of all its voting members.

In addition to the International Monetary Fund the World Bank was also founded at the Bretton Woods conference. Its task was to make available long-term loans, initially for the rebuilding of Europe and, later, for development projects in the Third World. A third organisation whose creation was conceived but not negotiated in any detail in Bretton Woods was the International Trade Organisation (ITO). The remit of this organisation was, in addition to that of providing a system of rules governing international trade, to include international aspects of employment and internationally relevant issues relating to commodity agreements, restraints on competition, international direct investment and the service sector.

However, despite the fact that it was primarily the US government which pushed ahead with this project, and despite the signing of the so-called "Havana Charter" by 45 UN member states, including the United States, in November 1947, this organisation never actually came into being. There was no chance that the US Congress would ratify the ITO agreement. What remained was the "General Agreement on Tariffs and Trade" (GATT). This referred only to international trade in goods and did not have the formal status of an international organisation, being merely a trade agreement. As such, it could be adopted within the framework of the as yet still existing powers of the US president, which were to expire in November 1948, allowing trade agreements to be concluded by the executive without the involvement of Congress.

The institutionalisation of the new world economic order was thus complete. However, it applied only to the so-called Western part of the world, which, for these purposes, included Japan. China had shut itself off from the rest of the world. The Soviet Union, for its part, did not even participate in the negotiations on the establishment of GATT, preferring to form its own system, one which also encompassed its satellite states, based on dictatorship and command economy. The demarcation line, later known as the Iron Curtain, did not just run straight through Europe; it also divided Germany into two parts. For Hamburg, located just 30 kilometres west of this demarcation line, this meant the loss of its entire economically relevant hinterland.

For the free market economies of the Western world the most visible success in the field of monetary policy was the fact that, by 1958, all currencies of the IMF members had become convertible. De facto there was now only one reserve currency, the US dollar. And since, following the 1948 devaluation of the French franc and the devaluation of the Deutschmark, the British pound sterling, the Japanese yen and the currencies of some smaller nations in 1949, virtually no further use of the exchange rate adjustment option was made. The only exceptions were a renewed devaluation of the French franc in 1957/58 and a revaluation of the Deutschmark and the Dutch gulden in 1961. In principle, it could be said that, via the fixed exchange rate to the US dollar and that currency's linking to gold, the gold standard had been reinstated.

Major progress has also been made in the area of trade policy. In the course of the first five liberalisation conferences between 1947 and 1962, average import tariffs in the GATT member states had already been cut from 40 to 15 per cent—despite the fact that agricultural products and textiles were, until the so-called Kennedy Round between 1964 and 1967, de facto excluded from negotiations. Even under these conditions, however, world trade increasingly regained its traditional momentum. Accompanied by revolutionary developments in both the transportation and communications technology sectors, trade volumes climbed from 58 billion dollars in 1948 to almost 600 billion dollars in 1973. From 1950 to 1973, the average annual rate of growth in global exports was, at approximately 8 per cent, far higher than that of global production, which grew at an average rate of 5 per cent per annum during the same period. The last time such figures had been seen was, in fact, before 1914.

## The Rebuilding of Europe
## and the Beginnings of European Integration

The lessons drawn — by the Americans in any event but also by some Europeans — from the abortive developments after the First World War and the counterproductive economic policies pursued during the interwar years went far beyond the institutionalisation of a new world economic order. There was also a growing awareness that US demands for repayment of war-related debts, most notably from Britain and France, and the enormous reparations Germany had to pay under the terms of the Treaty of Versailles, had played a considerable part in the creation of global economic instability during the interwar period and, indirectly, had even led to the outbreak of the Second World War. As a result, America this time not only cancelled some 50 billion dollars in war debt owing from the Allies but also — in addition to a variety of immediate aid measures — provided an additional non-repayable 12.4 billion dollars for the reconstruction of Europe under the Marshall Plan.

Particularly interesting in this respect is the circumstance that, upon officially unveiling the plan during his famous Harvard speech on 5 June 1947, US Secretary of State George C. Marshall expressly emphasised to his fellow US citizens that it would not only help Europe but would, over the longer term, also prove to be of particular benefit to the United States. And how right he was. Not only was this financial injection — of which Germany, incidentally, received only 1.5 billion dollars — an important pump-priming measure for the reconstruction of war-ravaged Europe and, as intended by the Americans, a decisive foundation stone in the fostering of intergovernmental European cooperation via the OEEC; it also created, as the European economies became stronger and as anticipated by Marshall, the dynamic new sales markets urgently required by American industry. Not intended in the original plans for the post-war period was another important political spin-off effect for the United States. In line with the terms of the Truman Doctrine of March 1947, the Marshall Plan also made a significant contribution to the establishment of an effective bulwark against the spread of communism.

The notion of an integrated Europe was, however, not only of American origin, having already been discussed in Europe for a quite considerable period of time. Very early visions of this are to be found in the works of Immanuel Kant (1795) and Victor Hugo (1849). And, as early as in 1922, the Austrian Count Richard Nikolaus von Coudenhove-Kalergi, founder of the Paneuropean Union, whose members included, amongst others, Albert Einstein, Thomas Mann and Konrad Adenauer, proposed a European confederation of states which, as a special-purpose political and economic association, would prevent another world war, the domination of Europe by Russia and the dependence of Europe on America. Aristide Briand, who served several times as French foreign and prime minister, also a member of the Paneuropean Union and a fierce critic of the harsh terms of the Treaty of Versailles, presented a plan for the establishment of a federal European union in October 1930. Similarly, Charles de Gaulle was, in late June 1940, already urging Robert Schuman, his subsequent foreign minister, to give some initial thought to a European peace and economic order in the postwar period and possible reconciliation between France and Germany.

Primarily the brainchild of Jean Monnet, the proposals to emerge from this French plan were presented to the international press in Paris on 9 June 1950 by French foreign minister Robert Schuman: The foundation of the European Coal and Steel Community (ECSC) as the first step towards a long term and more far-reaching European integration process which could even lead to a political federation. Institutionalisation, in 1951, of the ECSC, whose members included Germany, France, Italy and the Benelux countries but not Britain, was followed in 1957 by the foundation of the European Economic Community (EEC) and the European Atomic Energy Community (Euratom). In the first instance, the members of these new European institutions once again included only the six above-mentioned states.

Since France had initially vetoed accession requests from Britain in 1963 and 1967 enlargement did not occur until 1973, when Britain, Ireland and Denmark formally joined the EEC.

The European integration process was anything but smooth from the very start, as difficult compromises repeatedly had to take their cue from what was deemed politically feasible. Notwithstanding this, the integration of EEC, ECSC and Eurotom was effected in 1967 and the establishment of the customs union in 1968. Last but not least, the economic successes, too, were impressive in every sense of the word. Due to the dynamics of reconstruction and a favourable phase in global economic development, but also following the creation of a large continental European internal market, which most notably opened up the German market for French agricultural produce and the French market for German industrial products, gross national product in the EC rose from 0.8 billion dollars to 2.6 billion dollars between 1950 and 1973. Average real economic growth during this period was thus in excess of 10 per cent. This figure puts all previous boom periods of comparable duration in the shade yet is also one that has never been attained since.

During the same period the average annual increase in aggregate EC exports was running at over 30 per cent. The share of EC internal market trade rose from approximately 35 to roughly 50 per cent, which — even when taking certain stimulating effects of geographical proximity into account — clearly points to the first positive implications of European integration. To this one must add the fact that, since 1973 and despite its great heterogeneity, the EEC had, within the framework of further GATT liberalisation rounds, been speaking with one voice through the vehicle of the European Commission. In negotiations with the United States and Japan this body lent greater weight to the European position, even though the latter was itself generally the result of a laboriously negotiated compromise, than would have been the case if all six member states had negotiated individually.

## Germany: From "Zero Hour" to Economic and Currency Reforms and the Division into West and East

The consequences of war were particularly tough for Germany. Regions east of the Oder and the Lusatian Neisse had to be ceded and the country, together with its former capital Berlin, was divided into four occupation zones. Most of the larger cities, especially their manufacturing facilities, had been devastated. And, once hostilities had ceased, large tracts of industrial plant that had not been damaged by bombs or direct acts of war were either been dynamited to render them inoperative or dismantled and taken away. Yet it should be pointed out in this context that the Soviet and, in parts, also the French occupation zones suffered more substantial losses than the American and British zones due to the varying intensity of the dismantling activities and other postwar burdens.

The situation of the population was alarming and, during the bitterly cold winter of 1946/47, even desperate. When the Hamburg trade union leader Adolph Kummernuss, speaking in front of 120,000 people protesting at food shortages, stated that it was a matter of life and death, nobody considered this to be an exaggerated claim. And even representatives of moral institutions, such as Cologne's Cardinal Frings in his famous New Year's Eve speech of 1946, did not hesitate to issue a public justification of the illegal procurement of vital commodities on the black market, of foraging trips, and even of "coal pilfering" — yet only, however, when committed as petty theft of comestibles or household items designed to ensure inhabitants' very survival and not when it involved organised crime or large-scale racketeering.

In the Western zones the major turnaround came with currency reform and the simultaneous economic reforms of June 1948. Currency reform, largely conceived by the Americans without any attempt to consult either the other occupying powers or the Germans, gave little or no cause for controversial discussions. Yet the picture was an entirely different one in the case of the economic reforms drawn up by the Germans. The most contentious issue here was the extent to which the economy should be regulated by state and administrative controls on the one hand, or guided by market forces and free price mechanisms on the other. Since it was the German "ordoliberals" centring around Walter Eucken, Wilhelm Röpke, Alfred Müller-Armack and Ludwig Erhard who gained the upper hand in this discussion, prices controls—not all but the greater part of them—were lifted on the day the currency reform came into force. The shops filled up overnight and it once again became worth people's while to go out to work and earn money again.

After just a few months, however, the experiment embarked on by Erhard without the consent of the occupying forces was threatening to fail. Prices rose dramatically; the number of people out of work increased instead of declining; economic growth, which had at first been dynamic, faltered. It was not possible to manage entirely without government stimulation of demand and other economic policy measures for enhancing the investment climate and eliminating bottlenecks, especially in the infrastructure. In September 1949 the currency was devalued by 20 per cent. Additionally, 3.4 billion Deutschmarks' worth of additional demand, mainly for housing construction, was pumped into the economy at the beginning of February 1950 within the scope of a job creation programme. Due to generous depreciation allowances and, shortly afterwards, by lowering the very high income and corporate tax rates specified by the Allies private investments were made attractive again. After that things improved rapidly and continued to do so, although not always at the same rate.

No matter how successful the realisation of economic and monetary union in the Western zones might have been from an economic point of view, it had serious drawbacks in a political sense. Although the resolutions of the Potsdam Conference to maintain Germany as a single entity still applied—apart from certain territorial cessions— there had been signs of a longer-term division of the country ever since the expropriation of private property, the nationalisation of most of the enterprise sector and the imposition of a centrally planned economy began in the Soviet occupation zone at the end of 1945. This development reached possibly its most visible manifestation with the rapid succession of currency reforms in both the Western zones and in the Soviet zone within three days of each other, the Berlin Blockade of 1948/49 and the incorporation of the GDR, founded in October 1949, into the COMECON in 1950. All this can be viewed as one of the first major crises of the Cold War. However, it also established the fact that after the foundation of the Federal Republic of Germany and the German Democratic Republic there were *de facto* two German states.

## *The German Economic Miracle*

Only the Federal Republic of Germany took part in the highly dynamic globalisation process that followed the principles of the market economy and free trade within the framework of the new world economic order. By 1950 production in West Germany had reached the pre-war level of 1936/37 and the average annual rate of economic growth remained at more than 7 per cent during the next ten years. Wages also increased after 1952. Private consumption was expressed in the first instance by the so-called wave of gluttony. This was followed by a wave of clothes buying and a wave of furniture buying. There was then a wave of motorisation and a wave of travelling.

The Deutschmark became one of the hardest currencies in the world and first came under revaluation pressure in 1957/58. The country enjoyed full employment after 1961. And by 1962 German exports had reached the 10 billion dollar mark. In spite of considerable growth in the population the real national income per capita rose from 850 Deutschmarks in 1950 and more than 1480 Deutschmarks in 1960 to 2300 Deutschmarks in 1973. The prevailing mood of the day was characterised by broad economic optimism and euphoria based on the successful reconstruction of the country.

The institutional preconditions for the remarkable economic resurgence of West Germany were created with the dual and parallel reform of the economic and currency systems, which only later became embedded as a single unit in the collective memory. Moreover, a series of material preconditions contributed greatly to the widely unexpected success of the shock therapy described above. To begin with, the West German economy had a very well motivated and highly qualified potential labour force, which was continuously boosted until 1961 by the immigration of roughly 2.6 million people from the Soviet occupation zone or the GDR. The lower wage level compared to international averages and the restraint of the trade unions in demanding higher wages, at least in the 1950s, contributed to the reduction of unemployment and secured international competitiveness when recapturing export markets. By 1958 the Federal Republic of Germany — just like the German Empire prior to 1914 — was only second to the United States as the world's most important export nation.

Two important advantages in comparison to other nations must be mentioned in this regard. On the one hand, many German companies were relatively quickly able to restore their production facilities damaged during the war via reparation investments and realise high capacity increases with relatively few resources. On the other hand, and partly also due to the Allied dismantling of West German industry, the possibility arose of rapidly adapting to new market requirements, in terms not only of quantity but also of quality thanks to the introduction of advanced American technologies and management methods. Furthermore, the German economy was remarkable for a favourable sectoral structure of industry. The traditionally high proportion of investment goods production in particular, which encountered rapidly growing domestic and international demand, turned the domestic market as well as foreign trade into the vital element of an increasingly dynamic growth process.

A further aspect that was particularly important for the continued integration of the West German economy in the next phase of the globalisation process was an increase of foreign direct investment.

The Federal Republic of Germany had, to a certain extent, regained its credit-worthiness on the international capital markets under the London Debt Agreement of 1951. West Germany with its liberal economic system, growing mass demand, relatively low wage levels and, in the first instance, still existing trade barriers now represented an interesting investment location and there is no doubt that foreign direct investment also contributed to a considerable extent to the modernisation of the German economy. But no matter how much successful economic reconstruction filled West Germans with pride and was admired around the world, the path the country travelled at that time contained the sources of a number of political, economic and social problems in the future.

Apart from the Investment Aid Act of 1952, which imposed a forced loan of billions of Deutschmarks on the overall industrial economy in order to provide funds for urgent investments in the coal and steel industry, the electricity and water industry and the Federal Railway, little consideration was given to the systematic development of the infrastructure until well into the 1960s. In spite of an increase in the relevant expenses from 24 per cent in 1952 to almost 35 per cent of the total public budget by the end of the 1960s, the situation in the areas of education, healthcare and transport was in stark contrast to the image of wealth which characterised many other areas of life in the Federal Republic of Germany. There could be no doubt that increasing bottlenecks in the infrastructure and insufficient investment in human capital, which, as measured by the gross national product, were even less than during the German Empire and the Weimar Republic, would put pressure on Germany's future competitiveness at least in the longer term. This was particularly critical in view of the looming trend towards a primarily knowledge-intensive society.

A number of other side effects of the post-war years of the economic miracle which would have a negative impact on the international competitiveness of the German economy in the future were of an institutional nature or concerned the social atmosphere. One aspect in this context is the revival of a politically highly influential net-

*What the Tin Lizzy had been in America at the beginning of the 20th century, the VW Beetle became in Germany in the 1950s and 1960s. Both cars revolutionised production methods and consumption patterns. And both were sold in record numbers: Roughly 15 million Tin Lizzies were purchased between 1908 and 1927, more than 20 million VW Beetles up until 2002.*

work of industry associations and other types of corporatism which had their origins partly in the 19th century and partly in the Weimar Republic. There is no question of all types of corporatism being counterproductive: Employers' associations, trade unions and chambers of commerce, to name just a few of the relevant organisations, have important functions in modern-day society. However, industry associations often see one of their major tasks as lobbying for vested interests and demanding state subsidies to support economic sectors that are no longer competitive. As long as they are successful in this — and there are numerous examples, the most impressive of which probably being the German Farmers Association (DBV)— they prevent the structural changes that are so important to the economy as a whole and the adaptation of economy and society to the world of tomorrow.

## The Revival of Japan

Another nation whose economic development after the Second World War excited general admiration was Japan. Japan too had had to suffer considerable territorial losses. In 1945 its agricultural production had fallen by 40 per cent compared to before the war; industrial production totalled just 20 per cent of the pre-war volume and foreign trade had practically ceased. Even more than Europe, Japan profited from the Korea boom. Economic reconstruction had been more or less completed by as early as 1953/54 and what followed in terms of economic growth made the successes of the Federal Republic of Germany appear rather limited. Between 1953 and 1973 the average real economic growth rate in Japan was no less than 10.1 per cent while in Germany it was "just" 5.8 per cent.

Nevertheless, this comparison should take into account that the Japanese revival took place on a much lower level. While the nominal national product per capita was 740 dollars in the Federal Republic of Germany in 1953, it was only 230 dollars in Japan. And even almost 20 years later in 1970, the absolute difference had not decreased but increased. The Japanese per capita income had reached 1,910 dollars and was thus already higher than the Italian one. However, the German per capita income had in the meantime risen to 3,020 dollars. Moreover, living conditions in Japan still failed — at least from a Western point of view — to meet international standards: Not only was the domestic living space per capita extremely limited, the quality of living conditions still lagged far behind those of Western industrial nations.

As in Germany there were considerable bottlenecks in Japan's infrastructure despite the country's remarkable economic growth. This applied particularly to transport and communication systems as well as to electricity and water supply. In contrast to Germany, these bottlenecks were not in the first instance the result of a politically determined insufficient increase of public spending in the respective areas.

*Ginza Tokyo. Economic recovery in Japan after the Second World War also led to the creation of a rampant consumer society.*

Rather, they were predominantly caused by the fact that, due to the low starting point, the expansion of the infrastructure was simply not able to keep up with the requirements placed on it by high economic growth.

Japan's economy nevertheless experienced a steep upward trend and, just as in Germany, reintegration into the global economy also played an extremely important role in Japan. Nevertheless, the external economic development of both countries was fundamentally different in several respects. Japan had no raw material base of its own and therefore depended, more than Germany, on a successful export strategy. Also, since it is an island Japan was at the same time considerably more dependent on maritime transport. As a consequence Japan—especially through the Ministry for International Trade and Industry (MITI)—followed a policy targeted at the reconstruction of the iron and steel industry and the rapid development of an effective shipbuilding industry. The huge demand for shipping, underlined by the doubling of the available domestic shipping tonnage between 1964 and 1968, as well as the import and independent development of new technologies turned Japan into the world's leading shipbuilding nation in just a few years. By 1968 Japan produced with approximately 16 million GRT roughly 50 per cent of the additional shipping tonnage in the world.

As with Germany, Japan's export success was based mainly on the export of industrial goods. But while Germany enhanced its competitive position internationally in the investment goods sector and automotive industry, Japan's range of exports initially included traditional sectors, such as textiles and clothing, followed—in addition to iron, steel and ships—in particular by products of the motorcycle industry, optical industry and consumer electronics, also because of the strong influence of the MITI. In 1969 the export ratio, i.e. the share of exports in total production, was 65 per cent for ships, 60 per cent for cameras, 45 per cent for motorcycles and almost 40 per cent for television sets. With just nine product groups in 1969 Japan achieved more than one third of the corresponding exports of all OECD countries.

Since Japan had an overall export share of only about 10 per cent of the national product — the respective figures for Germany and Great Britain were 19.2 per cent and 18.7 per cent respectively — this concentration should not have caused any problems. That problems still arose can be explained by the simultaneous regional concentration of Japanese exports. Almost one third of all Japanese exports went to the US and in the first instance these were concentrated on the American west coast. Therefore 75 per cent of all television sets, 60 per cent of all radios and tape recorders and, although the absolute number was still small compared to later years, already almost 50 per cent of all the automobiles exported by Japan were shipped to the United States. That this development would eventually lead to serious tensions between Washington and Tokyo was not difficult to predict. Additionally a number of quantitative import restrictions as well as foreign exchange and capital flow controls still applied in Japan. All this, together with the undervaluation of the yen, contributed to the fact that Japan had, except for 1967, recorded a permanent export surplus since 1963 and, at least since 1968, also a persistent imbalance in its overall external economic relations.

## The Rise
## of the Asian Tigers

The rise of the Four Asian Tigers — Hong Kong, Singapore, South Korea and China/Taiwan — is also one of the great and partly unexpected economic success stories during the first phase of globalisation after the Second World War. Although these four remarkable new players on the global economic stage are often referred to in the same breath as the so-called "small tigers" due to their export-oriented growth strategy, it should not be forgotten that — apart from their high macroeconomic savings ratio — they started from decidedly different positions and that Hong Kong in particular chose a different orientation in economic policy from the other three.

Hong Kong, under British sovereignty since the middle of the 19th century due to the "unequal treaties", had been China's main foreign trade port since the middle of the 18th century. After the Japanese occupation during the Second World War it was largely able to regain this position before two global political events completely changed the situation. Firstly, Hong Kong lost its position as the depot for Chinese exports as the People's Republic of China, founded in October 1949, redirected the focus of its economic relations towards the Soviet Union. Secondly, the United Nations imposed an almost complete embargo on Chinese trade after China's entry into the Korean War in December 1950. As a result, China's exports handled by Hong Kong sank from roughly 35 per cent in 1951 to just 1 per cent in 1960.

Hong Kong's rise as an industrial location commenced when the predominantly English textile producers — mainly from Shanghai, but partly also from Canton — dismantled complete industrial plants on the mainland and rebuilt them in the British Crown Colony as predominantly modernised facilities. Just like Amsterdam and Hamburg in the 17th and 18th centuries, Hong Kong benefited from capital inflow on the one hand and from the experience and business connections of immigrants on the other. The industrialisation process was supported by the "positive non-intervention" of the administration, low wages and the permanent immigration of cheap labour, as well as weak trade unions. Another advantage was that Hong Kong became by far the most favoured place for foreign direct investment in Southeast Asia due to Communist agitation in Malaysia, Indonesia and Indochina.

In the course of these developments Hong Kong's textile industry became so successful in the export market that the United States, the European Community and even Britain finally reacted with import restrictions. Apart from the already existing and equally flourishing plastics industry this led to a further acceleration of the diversification of the economic structure and this in particular favoured work-intensive light industries. Within this context it is remarkable that it was precisely American investors who built up the electrical and later also the electronics industry in Hong Kong in order to protect themselves against increasing Japanese competition in their domestic market.

In contrast to Hong Kong, the industrialisation process in Singapore, Taiwan and South Korea was, as previously in Japan, driven by largely authoritarian and targeted state interventions. Singapore, which had also been in English hands since 1818, was of little interest as a possible location for foreign industrial projects after liberation from Japanese occupation at the end of the Second World War due to its high wage levels, the Communist influences on its economic policy and its federation with socialist governed Malaysia in 1963.

This did not change until Singapore withdrew from Malaysia in 1965, becoming completely independent and introducing a basic shift in its economic policy. Drastic wage cuts, improved investment protection, the legalisation of the transfer of profits overseas, the successive elimination of sales tax and capital gains tax and the abolishment or reduction of almost all import tariffs, particularly for raw materials and semi-finished products, turned Singapore into an internationally attractive investment location—in the first instance for multinational industrial companies and—like Hong Kong—over time into an international logistics and finance centre.

In addition their own endeavours South Korea and Taiwan owed their meteoric rise primarily to the United States. In Korea, however, important foundations for the later economic boom had already been laid by the Japanese colonial and occupying power which had not only promoted industrialisation since 1910 but had also smashed the traditional, extremely rigid agrarian-feudal social structures. This process was then successfully continued by post-war Korean governments within the framework of land reforms in 1947 and 1949/50 in spite of strong political opposition.

After the division of the country a ruthless programme of modernisation was of decisive help to the government in quickly turning the essentially agrarian South Korea, 80 per cent of whose industries had been completely destroyed, into an aspiring industrial nation from the mid-1970s onwards. Nonetheless, this was not simply achieved through their own efforts according to the motto "reconstruction first, distribution later" but was supported by roughly 13 billion dollars of American economic and military aid. Other elements which contributed to the sharp rise of the country included efficient government economic planning under the leadership of a notably competent bureaucratic elite as well as an extremely protectionist and simultaneously export-promoting foreign trade policy that was tolerated by the United States. South Korea achieved the final breakthrough after changing its industrialisation process from import substitution to an export oriented growth strategy in the mid-1970s.

Just like Korea, Taiwan had been under Japanese rule for 50 years. Here too the Japanese created important preconditions for successful economic development after the Second World War in that they improved the infrastructure, modernised certain areas of agriculture and set up the basic structure for efficient administration of the state. After the Second World War Taiwan also profited from American economic and military aid, which at only 5.9 billion dollars was much less than the amount South Korea received. A state-mandated land reform as well as several development plans pushed through by the government laid the foundations for the subsequent economic upturn.

In many respects, however, Taiwan's foreign trade policy was completely different to South Korea's. At least after it overcame the severe economic crisis at the beginning of the 1950s thanks to American aid Taiwan pursued—following an initially very protectionist phase—its integration into the global economic division of labour, predominantly on the basis of free trade and openness for direct foreign investment. Both were decisive prerequisites for investors, including indigenous ones and the roughly 1.5 million Chinese who had come across from the mainland, as well as foreign ones—mainly Americans and Japanese—to generate a booming textile and clothing industry and, shortly afterwards, become active in other sectors, such as electronics, telecommunications, chemistry and mechanical engineering.

Further important driving forces for this development were initially low wage levels combined with a relatively highly qualified workforce as well as targeted export promotion.

## *Revolutionary Developments in the Communications and Transport Sector*

As always in the history of globalisation, developments after the Second World War were not determined simply by a process of widening and deepening of global economic integration, by changes in the supply and demand for goods and services, by regional, sectoral and corporate restructuring or by increasing international financial transactions. Once again the intensification of international trade, the extension of investment activities, including foreign direct investment, and the continuing internationalisation of capital markets went hand in hand with a revolution in the communications and transport sector, which was in principal both the cause and effect of the economic development.

The most striking events in terms of intercontinental goods transportation occurred initially in shipping. These included, firstly, the development in the size of ships; secondly, the trend towards specialised ships; and thirdly, the efficiency of conveying goods from land to ship and vice versa. The continually increasing demand for crude oil in Europe and Japan, the closure of the Suez Canal from 1967 to 1975 and the fact that the United States was increasingly becoming an oil import nation combined with advances in shipbuilding resulted in an increase of the load-carrying capacity of tanker ships from 100,000 to 500,000 tons deadweight. The introduction of specialised bulk carriers for ore, grain and coal, which, following the oil tanker trend, also reached new dimensions in size. The development of gas tankers, refrigerator ships, ro-ro ships and heavy lift ships were further examples for increasing specialisation and diversification in maritime transport.

But the change that was probably the most radical and far-reaching was the progressive replacement of traditional general cargo vessels with container ships. This started the large-scale industrialisation of maritime transport. The basic idea was born in the United States: Initially it came from the U.S. Army, which used small transport containers, so-called "conex" boxes, to supply its troops at first during the Second World War and then in the Korean War. It was subsequently introduced in the civilian sector by a shipper from New Jersey called Malcolm McLean, who shipped 58 large aluminium containers on a converted tanker from Port Jersey to Houston/Texas for the first time in April 1956. Container traffic between the American east coast and Europe commenced at the beginning of the 1960s.

Over 10 million standardised 20-foot containers (TEUs) are today transported on approximately 4,800 seagoing container ships; and the total capacity of global transhipment is estimated at roughly 500,000 million units. The world's largest container ports are Singapore, Shanghai, Hong Kong and Shenzhen, which together handle more than 20 per cent of global container traffic. The dynamics of this new form of transportation can best be illustrated with the rough rule of thumb often quoted in the logistics sector which says that if worldwide industrial production rises by one per cent, international trade will increase by two per cent and global container traffic by three per cent. At the same time, containers in general cargo handling, just like large tankers in the global oil business, not only serve as a means of transportation but also as intermediate storage facility which is unusually cheap despite the large distances which have to be overcome. For example, the freight costs from China to Hamburg for a tin of food were 0.10 Euros, for a video or DVD player between 1.50 and 2 Euros and for a TV set less than 20 Euros and that was even before the freight rates plummeted due to the 2008 economic crisis.

Besides rail, road and sea transport, air travel also became increasingly important for business trips, tourism, parcel and mail deliveries during the late 1950s, initially on internal European and American medium haul routes and soon after also between the continents. Reg-

*Concorde, the first and, as yet, only supersonic passenger airliner, was used in regular service from 1976 until 2003. The average flight time from Paris to New York: 3 hours, 45 minutes — faster than a train journey from Hamburg to Cologne today.*

ular transatlantic and transpacific transport on large passenger steamers still continued up to the end of the 1960s. Especially after the introduction of jet planes, for example the Boeing 707 in the autumn of 1958, the reduction in travelling time became, however, so great and, in the end, the price difference so small, that passage by ship scarcely had any attraction, at least for business travellers. Already by the mid-1960s more passengers were opting to fly over the Atlantic than sail across it. The next big technology leap in air traffic was marked by the deployment of wide-bodied aircraft, in particular the Boeing 747, from 1969 onwards.

From an economic point of view this new generation of commercial aircraft turned aeroplanes into a cheap and widely accessible means of mass transport, even for long-distance travel. Moreover, the introduction of wide-bodied aircraft led to the so-called "hub and spoke system" in air transport, i.e. route planning in which long-haul routes concentrated on an ever smaller number of major airports while other airports — such as Hamburg — rapidly lost their overseas connections and in this market sector provided scarcely more than a shuttle service. A further technical highlight in the air traffic revolution was the commercial deployment of Concorde, the first, and for the time being last, supersonic airliner, which from 1976 reduced the flight time between Paris or London and New York to less than four hours. However, the high noise level and high fuel consumption of this aircraft meant that its deployment was restricted to the transatlantic route.

Intercontinental air cargo traffic also experienced a sharp upturn. Besides mail deliveries this included the transportation of goods with a high value, small weight and limited volume as well as perishables, such as fruit and flowers. The result was the development of new global markets with products that were previously predominantly traded on local markets. A particularly striking example of this is the international flower market in Aalmeer near Amsterdam's Schiphol Airport. Every day roughly 20 million flowers are auctioned here. These flowers — if they were not grown in the Netherlands — are flown in early each morning from countries like Columbia, Kenya, Zimbabwe, Israel, Tanzania or South Africa and subsequently sold to flower shops not only in Europe but also in New York, Tokyo or Sydney.

Advances in the communications sector affected, on the one hand, the bilateral exchange of opinions and information via telephone, fax and e-mail and, on the other, the worldwide distribution of general news about politics, the economy, society, culture and sports initially via the radio, then via television and today also via the Internet. From an economic point of view all this has not only contributed to the faster and more precise transmission of information about developments in various national economies and markets. Together with the liberalisation of global capital flows—in particular including short-term financial transactions — technical progress in the communications sector has also encouraged the application of new tools and instruments in international financial markets. The first consequence was that real economic developments were amplified in the financial sphere and, on top of that, in the later phase that the real economy and the financial economy became increasingly separated. The period

270

between 1990 and 2000, in which world production rose by 46 per cent, international trade by 88 per cent and international financial transactions by no less than 1,236 per cent, is an impressive illustration of this.

## *Global Free Trade with Industrial Goods and increasing Foreign Direct Investment*

All these new technological developments and their implications for economy and society, the economic upturn in some leading national economies, especially in Europe and Asia, as well as the new world economic order created under the leadership of the United States introduced a new phase of globalisation at the beginning of the second half of the 20th century. Just as before the First World War, the main driving forces of development included the reinvigorated dynamics of international trade, the rapid increase in foreign direct investment and the associated cross-border transfer of technology and management knowledge as well as the continually expanding stream of international capital transactions.

The essential difference between the globalisation process before 1914 and the one after 1945 was, however, a clear shift from a primarily functional economic order of informal conventions and unwritten rules towards an institutionalisation of transnational economic relationships based on cross-national agreements and international organisations. In terms of trade and monetary policy these were—at least among the members of the IMF and GATT—and with the regional associations—for example the EEC and the EFTA—mainly multilateral agreements, while foreign direct investment outside the EEC was still almost exclusively regulated by bilateral accords.

Despite this institutionalisation of international economic relations, which often prioritised a number of national political goals such as full employment, certain industrial interests or the protection of sovereignty over free trade, global trade experienced a rate of expansion between 1950 and 1970 that, compared with past experience, was without parallel. Not only did global exports rise nominally from 60 to 310 billion dollars during this period; it is even more remarkable that world production had an annual real growth rate of 5 per cent during these 20 years, while the respective real growth rate of world exports was roughly 8 per cent. This was complemented by a roughly equally high growth of foreign trade relevant services, such as international transport and insurance, and an explosion in tourism at least from the end of the 1960s awards.

The reasons for this astonishing development of international trade were manifold. While economic reconstruction was initially in the forefront, particularly in Europe and Japan, a remarkable momentum gathered in international economic relationships from the beginning of the 1960s, which was due to at least three factors. First, worldwide growth in income not only accounted for an increase but also for an increasing diversification of consumer demand, which usually also stimulates the purchase of imported goods. Second, strong growth of domestic and foreign demand is, as a rule, associated with a high level of investment. In return, high investments normally promote foreign trade, since in many cases the import of products manufactured abroad is necessary. A third factor in the expansion of global exports was that high economic growth increased the demand for imported raw materials.

The most forceful dynamics originated from the export of goods by the industrial nations, so that the structure of internationally traded goods shifted more and more from raw materials and foodstuffs to industrial semi-finished and finished products. While the exports of the industrial nations were still approximately 60 per cent of world exports in 1950, their share rose to over 70 per cent by 1970 and the corresponding share of the developing countries fell from more than 30 to less than 20 per cent. The shift is even more striking in the structure of goods in international trade, where the share of industrial goods rose from approximately 40 per cent to 65 per cent during the same period.

To a large extent these developments could be attributed to the differences in the economic dynamics, the rising prices for industrial goods and, after the end of the Korean War, to the dramatically falling prices for raw materials. A further influential factor was the decline of trade between former colonial powers, especially England and France, and their former colonies. But the fact that trade liberalisation within the framework of the GATT focussed mainly on industrial products and initially largely excluded agriculture as well as vital work-intensive commercial goods, such as textiles and leather goods, from which developing nations in particular would have had a competitive advantage, may have had a strong influence in this context.

After the Second World War and from the mid-1950s onwards the globalisation process was also greatly accelerated by the almost explosive rise and a shift in the regional redistribution of foreign direct investment, in particular on the part of the United States. The US had invested abroad previously but these investments, except for Canada, were primarily aimed at securing the supply of crude oil and raw materials from the Middle East and Latin America. The reasons why US foreign direct investments, which had experienced a meteoric rise of roughly 40 per cent since around 1960, now concentrated on Europe were: The rapidly developing and large dynamic domestic market, the highly qualified labour force potential with an initially low wage level, the possible by-passing of still existing trade barriers, the political stability and finally the increasing overvaluation of the dollar, which made the purchase of European companies relatively inexpensive. Sectoral preferences focussed mainly on the oil industry, the automotive industry, the chemical industry as well as the high technology fields, such as electronics and information technology.

Japan's doors were still closed to American investors. A reorientation of U.S. direct investments towards Asia commenced in the mid-1960s and in particular after 1968, when the industrial nations granted the Four Asian Tigers as well as other developing countries certain tariff preferences. This, combined with the extremely low wage levels, prompted even more American companies to relocate their production to sites with the lowest costs and, if possible, at the same time to realise their profits where the tax burden was the smallest. A further advantage which at least Singapore, Hong Kong, Taiwan and South Korea offered foreign investors was a relatively high level of political stability—an advantage in terms of location which most other developing nations in Asia and Africa that had become politically independent within the context of decolonisation after the Second World War could not offer.

The increasing globally oriented exploitation of political and commercial location advantages by multinational players led to a number of extremely negative reactions in the host countries, but also in the United States. Europe in particular was afraid of becoming technologically dependent on the Americans. Many developing nations in which multinational companies played a leading economic role felt that the independence they had won after the Second World War was in danger. And in the USA itself the foreign direct investments of American companies resulted in a permanent increase of the balance of payments deficit as well as in the fear of cheap competition from overseas and concerns about the stability of the dollar.

## *The End of Bretton Woods*

Increasing tensions in the new world economic order were, however, not only caused by growing external economic imbalances caused by due to international trade, the expansion of foreign direct investment and the widely accepted, politically motivated objection to possible exchange rate adjustments. The exceptionally sharp increase in short term international capital transactions was another factor which led to an intensification of problems in international economic relations and, in particular, in the international monetary system. There were two reasons why this new variant of international capital flow became more and more attractive: Firstly, the exploitation of interest differentials and, secondly, speculation regarding changes to currency parities.

When the Bretton Woods system was created the United States of America was not only the largest but also the most competitive national economy in the world. With a permanent balance of payments surplus, the USA could afford to supply the global economy with the required international liquidity via capital exports — initially in the form of reconstruction aid, especially for Europe, and later mainly through foreign direct investment — without causing major problems for the development of America's domestic economy due to the associated balance of payments deficits. It was, rather, the other members of the system, in this case especially Germany and Japan, who had difficulties with regard to their own economic policy. In the light of their growing current account surpluses they were forced to buy US dollars in order to stabilise exchange rates. As long as this contributed to the strengthening of national currency reserves without resulting in imported inflation due to the linked increase in domestic monetary circulation this development was at first perhaps even desirable.

Yet during the 1960s the construction faults of the Bretton Woods system became increasingly visible, not only for the United States but also for the partner states. A particular concern was that the foreign dollar reserves of the latter had reached a level that far exceeded gold reserves in the United States. The United States' obligation to redeem foreign dollars in gold as originally specified in the Bretton Woods agreement therefore only existed on paper. The price of gold on the London gold market rose to 40 dollars, which prompted the U.S. government under President Kennedy to introduce capital export restrictions for the first time. Nevertheless, capital flight from the United States could not be stopped.

Germany in particular, due to its continued balance of payments surplus as well as for speculative reasons, registered such an influx of dollars that it had to revalue the Deutschmark by 5.5 per cent in 1961 in order to reduce inflationary pressure — a measure that was promptly copied by the Netherlands. But this was not something that could bring a resolution of the inherent problems of the Bretton Woods system any closer. On the contrary, real turmoil was just around the corner, especially after the United States failed to play by the rules around the mid-1960s.

In the same way that the partner states had to accept certain restrictions in the autonomy of their economic policy, in particular regarding monetary policy, the system presupposed that the United States as the reserve currency nation should give its own economic policy a strong focus not only on domestic economic objectives but also on global requirements. It was exactly this obligation that the United States no longer could or would meet in 1964. Instead of following the restrictive economic policy that was needed from an international point of view, the United States chose an expansionist monetary and financial policy that was on the one hand defined by increasing military spending as a result of the Vietnam War and on the other by rising social expenditures for the realisation of the "Great Society" proclaimed by President Johnson.

Apart from the fact that in particular countries with a permanent balance of payments deficit — such as Great Britain — generally failed to meet or were late in meeting their devaluation obligations due to reasons of political prestige, this conflict between the United States' international and domestic economic policy requirements was most probably the weakest point of the system, which eventually caused its collapse at the beginning of the 1970s. Against the background of rising inflation and the deteriorating international competitiveness regarding the US as well as Germany's and Japan's refusal to yet again revalue the Deutschmark or now to revalue the yen, renewed speculation against the dollar commenced in 1967.

As a result gold was increasingly in demand so that in 1968 the U.S. government decided to restrict to central banks only the obligatory redemption of dollars at a price of 35 dollars per ounce. However, at the same time it expected these banks either not to make use of this right or, inasmuch as they did, to invest the gold in the United States in order to boost the appearance of the American balance of payments. As before, speculation about a further upward revaluation of the Deutschmark intensified and this was then carried out at the rate of 9 per cent in 1969, while France—following Great Britain's 14 per cent lowering of the exchange rate in 1967—at the same time devalued the franc by 11 per cent. Nevertheless, even these adjustments could not restore the balance on the international currency markets. As early as 1970 Germany and Japan had to undertake further interventions with the goal of stabilising the parity of the Deutschmark and the yen with respect to the dollar.

The peak of this new wave of speculation came during the first months of 1971. The German Federal Bank had to accept the influx of five billion dollars, two billion of which during the last two days before the closure of the international currency markets on 5 May. Four days later the Federal German Government decided to temporarily float the exchange rate of the Deutschmark. The Netherlands followed suit as previously with the revaluation of the Dutch guilder. Other countries such as Switzerland and Austria initially opted for revaluations of 7 and 5 per cent respectively, while France and Belgium chose the course of tightening exchange controls. When, on 15 August, the U.S. government finally announced that it was suspending the convertibility of dollars into gold even for foreign central banks the European states, with the exception of France, switched to restricted floating. Only Japan still tried to stick to the old system, but after just one week it was practically forced by political economic pressure from the United States to join the temporary floating initiated by Germany.

A further attempt to rescue the Bretton Woods system in 1972 by fixing the price of gold at 38 dollars per ounce, expanding the bands for exchange rate fluctuations to 2.5 per cent and keeping the original dollar gold standard simply as a dollar standard failed at the beginning of 1973. As in 1971 the German Federal Bank had to buy another five billion dollars. In February Germany and Japan closed their currency markets. The United States devalued the dollar again by 10 per cent. But all this was to no avail. In March the general system of flexible exchange rates gained acceptance. Six member states of the EEC (excluding Great Britain, Ireland and Italy) formed a floating block together with Norway and Sweden after a further revaluation of the

Deutschmark by 3 per cent, but the Bretton Woods system was finally dead. A period of erratic exchange rate fluctuations followed. Between 19 March and 9 July 1973 alone the American currency had to accept a further loss of 15.5 per cent of its value against the floating block. It became more and more apparent that the financial system had detached itself from the real economy even though the origins of the crisis could clearly be traced back to the different growth dynamics of the major industrial nations at the time and the lack of internationally coordinated inflation management.

# CHAPTER 8

# Hamburg:
# The Largest City
# in the European Union
# which is not also
# a Capital City

It was never clearer than during the First World War and after the National Socialists came to power that Hamburg had finally lost its political independence by joining the German Empire. During the First World War all key decision-making powers were transferred to the General Command of the military region. The Senate and Parliament felt demoted and degraded to nothing more than minions. As with all other German state parliaments in the Third Reich, the Hamburg Parliament was dissolved by a Reich law (Reichsgesetz) after a short transition period during which the NSDAP became the strongest parliamentary party. Once the Gauleiter appointed by Adolf Hitler had seized all power for himself as the Reich Governor, the Senate, which in the end only consisted of NSDAP members, became an institution whose sole concern was to implement decisions made by the Reich Government in Berlin and to exercise power on behalf of the party without opposition.

In the period between 1914 and the second half of the 20th century Hamburg's economy was also influenced more by external factors than by decisions of the Senate or the merchants. On the one hand, this applied to economic debates at a world level and the development of the global economy; and on the other hand, the economic policy of the Reich Government in the pursuit of its real and supposed macroeconomic interests triggered numerous side effects which proved to be disadvantageous to a city whose economy was mainly based on international trade, shipping and the processing of imported raw materials. The worst events for Hamburg were the two World Wars. Apart from the direct effects of war, the division of Germany and of Europe into East and West after the Second World War meant that for approximately 50 years Hamburg also lost the hinterland which was economically so important to it. Just as at the time of the official foundation of the port in 1189 Hamburg found itself once again far from the centres of world economic development.

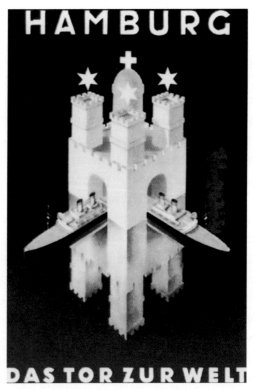

*"Hamburg. Gateway to the World". A 1920s poster advertising Hamburg. Shanghai, Hamburg's Chinese twin city, is also referred to as the gateway to the world.*

280

Hamburg's return to normality, the largely successful race to catch up with its traditional competitors Rotterdam and Antwerp and its reintegration into the rapidly accelerating globalisation process were the result of the will of the people to reconstruct the city and a result of the policies of the Senate, which not only promoted reconstruction but also a flexible adaptation to the rapidly changing economic and technological environment. As in earlier times, Hamburg focussed on close cooperation with neighbouring states—in this case Schleswig-Holstein and Lower Saxony. That this was beneficial for both sides was illustrated by the fact that during the subsequent years the dynamic economic development of Hamburg increasingly included the hinterland beyond the city's borders.

## *The First World War and its Economic Consequences*

As in the rest of Germany, the outbreak of the First World War was received enthusiastically by the majority of Hamburg's population. With the exception of an extremely small political and economic ruling elite, everyone—the middle class as much as the working class—believed in a short war and, first and foremost, in victory. It is difficult to determine to what extent nationalistic and patriotic fervour also concealed worries and fears. However, in the Hamburg Parliament a temporary truce was called between the political parties—as it had been earlier in the Reichstag. For the duration of the war the Social Democrats abandoned their right of opposition and even voted for war loans. Similarly, the trade unions decided not to call strikes throughout the war years even though they did not share the warmongering patriotism of the bourgeoisie.

However, in spite of all the solidarity and in spite of the first news of the initial victories of German troops, the change of mood came sooner than generally expected and in Hamburg probably earlier than in other parts of Germany. The British sea blockade brought maritime trade to its knees. The last ship from overseas called at Hamburg's port on 13 August 1914. The throughput of goods in Hamburg's port fell from 25.5 million tonnes in 1913 to 1.3 million tonnes in 1915 and never achieved more than 2.6 million tonnes during the following three years. By as early as September 1914 30,000 dock workers were unemployed—even though many men had been called up for military service. The majority of trading houses, the activities of which were based on imports and exports, ran into severe difficulties and had to cut wages and jobs. The same applied to industrial companies which depended on imports and exports, in particular to those that were not—as for example shipyards and certain engineering works—directly involved in war production.

Shipping companies' business also came to a complete standstill. Not only had German foreign trade collapsed, with many ships in Hamburg and other German ports stuck, unoccupied, at the quays, but a large number of ships which had been in Germany at the outbreak of the war had also been requisitioned by the Imperial Navy and deployed as auxiliary cruisers, troopships or hospital ships. Even the German ships which had been in foreign ports when the war broke out stood little chance of escaping the war. If they were located in enemy territory they were detained and later declared to be booty. After the War had finally been lost in November 1918 Germany had to hand over all seagoing vessels above 1,600 GRT, half of all its ships between 1,000 and 1,600 GRT, as well as a quarter of its fishing fleet as reparation payments under the Treaty of Versailles. Hamburg alone lost 764 steamers and all of its tall ships. Moreover, the Allies granted themselves a number of privileges along German sea shipping routes and inland waterways, i.e. also on the Elbe, without offering anything in return.

The material damage to Hamburg as a result of the First World War was only surpassed by the human misery and suffering. Soon after the outbreak of the war, deficiencies in the supply chain became apparent; bread and flour had to be rationed from an early stage and a large part of the population were already suffering from hunger by the end of 1914. At the beginning of 1916 70 war kitchens were feeding more than 100,000 people who would otherwise not have had a warm meal. Due to the low pay for soldiers as well as unemployment and inflation, many families were no longer able to pay their rent and were therefore forced out of their homes. Already in the late summer of 1914 the number of homeless rose from approximately 5,000 to more than 16,000.

At the turn of 1916/17 the initial enthusiasm for the war turned into public protests. Although the Senate and private aid organisations were able to increase the volume of distributed meals from three to six million litres between January and April 1917 protests about the food shortages did not cease. And anyone who had expected that the war would result in a social rapprochement as the precondition for social balance was proven wrong. The complete opposite occurred. In many respects the middle classes, which were predominantly in a better position than the majority of the workers, had completely lost touch with reality. In July 1917 the Senate and the Parliament decided on a reform of the electoral laws which was not only politically insufficient and moreover too late, but which also had no relation to the real concerns of Hamburg's population. What really troubled the people could be heard in the large strike meetings of the shipyard and industrial workers in January 1918.

When the war ended on 11 November 1918 Hamburg had lost roughly 35,000 of its sons in action. In part due to the helplessness of the Senate and the Parliament during the last years of the war, revolutionary movements had also risen up in Hamburg and power was at least temporarily exercised by a workers' and soldiers' council. Only after the SPD had defeated the communists and gained an absolute majority in the elections for the constituent parliament of March 1919 was it possible to hope for a return to normal life. However, Spartacist revolutionaries once again occupied the city hall in July of the same year. The Senate was forced to ask the Reich Minister of Defence to send in government troops. This restored law and order, but only for a short period.

A mere nine months later, in March 1920, the Republic was again put into question in Germany and in Hamburg too. This time the threat came from the right wing and included high ranking military personnel. To stave off this threat the social democrats and trade unions, supported by the progressive middle class and other groups representing the basic interests of the state, called a general strike in Hamburg. The right-wing coup was ended and the Senate and the Parliament could finally turn their thoughts to the long-term future, including the measures required to revive Hamburg's economy. Politically speaking, the social democrats had already gained credit by having entered into a coalition with the left-wing liberal, progressive middle class despite their absolute majority. They even turned down the position of Lord Mayor as they thought it was useful for this post to be held by someone with close ties to the old Hamburg families. And indeed, the economic situation of the city required the coordination of all available forces.

Apart from the loss of the trade and fishing fleet, Hamburg's merchants, shipowners and bankers had lost all their overseas branches and foreign financial assets as well as to a large extent their business relationships, which had been established over decades. Furthermore, the global economic environment had changed during the war. In the United States and Japan, which had been important customers for German industrial products before the war, new production capacities had been developed so that these markets — apart from the effect of protectionist barriers which had already existed before the war — became considerably more competitive for German exports. Finishing industries and trade networks had been established in numerous countries which had supplied Germany with raw materials before the war. Even in the shipping sector there were new companies which would never have been classed as significant competitors prior to the war. As so many times before in its history Hamburg's economy therefore faced the challenges of a completely new beginning.

## From an Early Illusory Boom
## to Galloping Inflation

During the first years of reconstruction Hamburg's merchants and shipowners were helped by a development which would later lead to a new economic disaster, namely rising inflation. As long as wages stayed relatively low due to the high rate of unemployment, loans could be taken out to increase domestic capacity and revenues were achieved with relatively constant exchange rates against foreign currencies, by preference the pound sterling or the U.S. dollar. The short term result was not only considerable profits for Hamburg's export companies and shipowners but also a fall in the number of unemployed people from roughly 70,000 in 1919 to just 8,000 two years later.

In 1919 Hamburg-Süd was able to resume services to South America — if only with a small sailing ship at first. After losing their own fleets, other shipping companies, in particular Hapag, had to operate their businesses using charter ships. On top of this, Hapag reached cooperation agreements with American and English shipping lines very soon after the war. The Americans transferred passenger check-in on the Hamburg-New York route to Hapag, which also fulfilled similar tasks with regard to the East Asia service for its British partners. Hapag hoped that this cooperation would help to re-establish and, for the meantime, maintain its presence on these routes.

A good two years after the end of the war the shipping company F. Laeisz recommenced its traditional nitre trade routes. The majority of the company's tall ships had been located in Chile at the outbreak of the war and had been interned there. Just like approximately 35 other German sailing ships, in 1919 they had to be transported to Europe at the owner's expense to be handed over as the spoils of war. After difficult negotiations with the commission responsible for reparation issues in London, Laeisz and some other shipowners managed to extract from the allies the concession that the ships could return fully loaded. Since nitre was in extremely short supply in Europe at that time the profits from the return journey were so high that between 1920 and 1924 Laeisz was able to repurchase six ships requisitioned under the Treaty of Versailles at prices ranging from 3,000 to 13,000 pounds sterling. A further Flying P-Liner which participated in this return journey jointly organised by German shipowners was a new ship, completed immediately after the end of the war, which had transported materials and crews to Valparaíso.

In 1921 shipowners received additional aid from the Reedereiabfindungsgesetz (Law Regulating the Compensation of Shipowners), which provided them with the option of re-purchasing their former ships — as Laeisz had already done — or even to some extent of constructing new ones. In the course of the same year Hapag used the first three new ships constructed after the war on passenger routes to New York. In February 1922 Hamburg-Süd's Cap Polonio, which had been bought back from England, set out on her first trip to South America. In the summer Hapag celebrated the launch of the first ship of the Albert-Ballin class; and by the end of the year the Hamburg-Süd fleet boasted 16 ships.

In 1923 maritime traffic in Hamburg's port regained its pre-war level for the first time. However, only 40 per cent of the ships calling at the port were German, compared with 60 per cent before the war. A new development for Hamburg's port was that a large proportion of the ships coming to Hamburg now sailed under the American flag. Even Japanese ships, which had not been handled via Hamburg before the war, were now frequent guests. Both these facts can be seen as a sign of structural changes in the global economy. Despite the changed global economic environment, it had evidently taken Hamburg a surprisingly short period of time to achieve economic reconstruction and re-integration into global trade with goods and services.

But appearances were deceptive. Hamburg was part of the German Empire and could not escape the economic difficulties Germany faced, in particular due to the high reparation payments specified in the Treaty of Versailles. Hamburg was also dragged down when creeping currency depreciation turned into galloping inflation, causing the German economy to collapse once more. In Hamburg, too, prices rose so quickly that wages paid in the morning were almost worthless by the evening. As in the rest of Germany normal business relationships were practically no longer possible.

Moreover, a foreign trade orientated city like Hamburg suffered more under the inflation-determined exchange rate changes than the interior of the country. While the dollar exchange rate was still 8.02 Marks in 1919 compared with 4.20 Marks before the war, it was already 49.10 Marks one year later and rose to 74.50 and 188 Marks in 1921 and 1922 respectively. Under these conditions, the export and import business was devoid of any reliable basis for calculations. German foreign trade came to a complete halt with the dramatic acceleration of this development in 1923, when the dollar exchange rate of 7,500 Marks in January rose to the record level of 58 billion Marks by October.

The hyper-inflation, during which many companies went bankrupt and the majority of the German population lost its savings held in nominal form, only affected Germany and had not yet acquired an international dimension. Yet the question was already being asked whether monetary value and currency stability were not in some way a public good. Galloping inflation not only made a well-ordered business life impossible: through the uncontrolled increase in food prices it also prevented sufficient supplies from reaching the population. And as shown by the communist uprising in October 1923, it also represented an acute threat to the political system. In light of the desperate situation in Hamburg, the Senate and the merchants finally tried to find a solution which, in going beyond the practice generally accepted in the rest of Germany of printing emergency money, would at least temporarily restore normal conditions to the city.

## Single-Handed Against Hyperinflation:
## The Hamburg Bank of 1923

As during the period of the Hanseatic League and again in the 18th century, the answer to this challenge was Hamburg's *de facto* disassociation from the prevailing inflationary environment by establishing its own stable currency. After the Hamburg Chamber of Commerce had invited representatives of the Senate, the banks, the mercantile community and industry to a meeting about the untenable situation in Hamburg's banking sector on 9 September 1923, the plenum decided on 14 September to commission the Chamber's banking department to develop proposals for the introduction of a stable currency. At the plenary meeting on 21 September, Carl Vorwerk, partner of Vorwerk Gebrüder & Co and chairman of the banking section, reported that the solution lay in the "foundation of a Hamburg bank for market-resistant (meaning: internationally stable) bank transfers with the option of subsequent equally stable banknotes".

The foundation of this bank took place on 24 October. The 103 founding shareholders, each holding one share, included 64 banks and banking businesses, 15 firms from the import and export and wholesale and retail sectors, 13 shipping companies, 8 industrial companies, including 2 shipyards, as well as 3 insurance companies and brokers. A further 17 shares were initially held by the association of Hamburg banks and bankers for subsequent distribution. The purpose of the Hamburg Bank of 1923 was specified in Paragraph 2 of the shareholder contract as follows: "The bank has the task of facilitating payment transactions, in particular by establishing gold mark accounts, and is entitled to carry out any operations related to the establishment of gold mark accounts. It may also take on the task of balancing the securities and goods trades. The United States of America dollar divided by M 4.20 equals one gold mark."

Moreover, the bank was authorised to issue vouchers in gold marks in exchange for foreign currency holdings or foreign currency until the introduction of a new stable currency by the Reich Bank. The denominations of these so-called settlement orders were half a gold mark, one gold mark, two gold marks and five gold marks. Additionally, 7.5 million coins, so-called settlement marks, were minted with the approval of the Senate as small change. This ensured that the Hamburg gold mark could also be used for wage and salary payments. In general the founders of the bank showed great loyalty towards the Reich by regarding the issuing of the settlement orders and settlement marks as a purely temporary measure and, in expectation of the Rentenmark, by not initially applying for the right to issue banknotes.

A development of this kind was, however, not out of the question since Hamburg viewed with great concern the danger of a possible disintegration of the German Reich. The reasons for this were: Firstly, separatist tendencies in Bavaria; secondly, the compulsory detachment of the Rhineland occupied by French and Belgian troops; and thirdly, a communist government in Saxony. If this negative scenario of a disintegration of Germany had become reality, one would have had to expect the introduction of the Rentenmark to fail. Hamburg wanted to at least be prepared for this eventuality and to have an institute available, as it did in the Hamburger Bank of 1923, which could guarantee an independent Hamburg currency in the case of an emergency.

The currency reform of the German Reich was enacted in October 1923 but was not actually implemented until 15 November, when the Rentenmark was issued with an exchange ratio of one billion Rentenmarks to one U.S. dollar. Twelve months later the Rentenmark was replaced by the now stable and internationally recognised Reichsmark. The Hamburg gold mark as well as the settlement orders and settlement marks had thus lost their right to exist. The Hamburger Bank of 1923 also ceased operations after completing the final transactions on 1 October 1926. It was nevertheless not legally dissolved until December 1939 after an interim involvement in the export credit business.

Once the reparation payments had been adapted to the economic capability of Germany under the Dawes Plan, the preconditions for a positive economic and social development were also created in the rest of Germany. The upturn in Hamburg was additionally supported by the fact that the internationally operating shipping companies as well as most of the larger trading houses could now, using their still existing relations with the United States and Great Britain, finance the expansion of their activities on favourable terms not only in Germany but also overseas.

### Massive Structural Changes
### During the Upturn

After the acute problems on the monetary and currency front had been resolved, reparation payments had been spread out and a foreign loan amounting to 800 million Reichsmarks had been granted, economic recovery in Germany, and in Hamburg too, was additionally fostered by a positive development of the global economy. Economic growth in the most important foreign markets of the German Reich in Europe, North and South America as well as in the Asian-Pacific region was on average about 3.5 per cent between 1924 and 1929. In 1928 German exports exceeded their pre-war level for the first time. The same applied to the handling of goods in Hamburg's port, which rose from 22 to roughly 29 million tonnes between 1925 and 1929 — a record level which was only achieved again in 1960, i.e. after the Great Depression and 15 years after the end of the Second World War.

Meanwhile qualitative, not merely quantitative, aspects played a decisive role in the reintegration of Germany and Hamburg into the process of the international division of labour. The United States and Japan in particular, but also numerous other countries with which Germany had traded prior to the First World War, now had their own industrial production facilities. This meant that German industry and, with it, Hamburg's exporters had to attune themselves to completely new conditions in many parts of the world which had been their major markets before 1914. On the one hand, there was now local competition in these markets, at least for industrial mass products, and, on the other, this competition was additionally promoted by protectionist measures. In order to remain competitive in these markets it was clearly necessary to move higher up in the chain of value creation and specialise more than ever before in technologically high-grade products.

For Hamburg's port this meant another structural adjustment. The higher value of the goods traded required a further improvement in performance with regard to reliability, speed and security in the transhipment of cargo. Quayside equipment had to be extensively modernised. The old steam cranes were generally replaced by electric ones. The increasing volume of high-quality general cargo demanded larger and more modern warehouses. As a result of the new construction and reconstruction of buildings, approximately 30 per cent more warehouse space was available in 1927 than before the Great War. The construction of special warehouses, for example for tropical fruit and combined shipments, was also groundbreaking. The increasing weight of the individual items demanded changes from simple push-carts to fork-lift trucks and other mechanised floor conveyors. Even the hinterland connections and supply routes to the port faced fundamental structural changes. As transhipment shifted from mass goods to valuable general cargo the percentage of rail and, later, road vehicles for inland transport rose considerably in comparison to inland water vessels.

Hamburg's shipping companies played a full part in this new upswing. By 1926 Hapag had 175 ships with a capacity of 1.1 million GRT. In 1930 the total size of Hamburg's fleet amounted to approximately 600 vessels with a total capacity of 2 million GRT, thus far exceeding the pre-war level, not with regard to the number of units but with regard to the overall tonnage. Quite remarkable in this context was the strong tendency of the shipping business towards concentration. A first wave of mergers or takeovers could be observed immediately after the end of the war. Thus at the beginning of the 1920s, a whole series of medium and smaller-sized shipping companies — such as

*In the 1930s the "Flying Hamburger" was what the "Transrapid" could have been in the first decade of the 21st century, a sensationally fast railway connection between Hamburg and Berlin. However, economic considerations put an end to this dream in 2000. Today the only commercially operated line is located in Shanghai and connects the airport to the financial centre of Pudong.*

for example the Levante Linie, Kosmos Linie or the Afrika Linien — lost their economic independence even though some of them were able to retain their former owner's house flag and funnel colours while trading under the name of Hapag. A second wave of concentration took place during the 1923 economic crisis due to inflation; and once again it was Hapag that was able to continue expanding.

However, this concentration process would most probably have also taken place without the crises caused directly and indirectly by the First World War. Competition in the international passenger and sea freight markets had become ever fiercer and the German shipping lines had to survive against the large English, American and Dutch shipping companies. Furthermore, the increasing size of ships combined with the latest and therefore more expensive technology as well as the trend towards specialised vessels led to higher capital expenditure. In 1926 Laeisz built the last tall ship. The company subsequently specialised in refrigerator ships for the transportation of bananas and tropical fruit. In 1929 Hapag put the first specialised cruise liner into operation in keeping with a tradition started by Ballin in 1891 with what was probably the first ever Mediterranean cruise.

### Moving into Tomorrow's World
### once more

Technical progress and the related structural changes also determined many developments on land and in the air. In 1931 a Rail Zeppelin travelled from Bergedorf on the eastern edge of Hamburg to Berlin in just 94 minutes, achieving a maximum speed of 230 kilometres per hour. And a regular Hamburg-Berlin service with a high-speed train, the so-called "Flying Hamburger", commenced in 1933, taking just two hours and 20 minutes. The modern-day ICE connection, with a journey time of one hour and 39 minutes, is only just a third faster. In the same year the first teleprinter link was established between Hamburg and Berlin. Two years after a broadcasting service had gone on the air in 1924 there were already roughly 40,000 listeners in Hamburg. A modern broadcasting centre was built in 1929 that remained in operation until 2008.

From today's point of view it is remarkable that when cars were introduced Hamburg initially only permitted electric vehicles to travel on its roads, as the exhaust fumes created by petrol engines were considered unacceptable for the city's citizens. Nonetheless, 420 vehicles were already registered in Hamburg by 1907. Even then road construction could not keep up with things, and the number of accidents, especially collisions between cars and horse-drawn vehicles as well as cyclists, took on an alarming dimension. But it was not until after the First World War that private motor transport became so popular that not only road construction but also automated traffic control systems came to be regarded as the state's responsibility. A spectacular event in this context was the installation of the first traffic lights at Stephansplatz in 1922. By 1929 the number of vehicles registered in Hamburg had risen to 10,854 cars and 4,777 trucks.

Another modern means of transport which gained increasing importance after the First World War was the aeroplane. At least for wealthy travellers, air traffic gradually became a competitor for rail and sea transport. Before the First World War Hamburg had had one of the first airports in Europe and in 1919 the first regular service between it and Berlin commenced, using former military aircraft. At the beginning of the 1920s the city took over the airport, extended it and made it suitable for night flights. Through scheduled departures—in particular with Deutsche Lufthansa—to Scandinavia and the Netherlands, Hamburg airport became the major hub for air services in the North. The number of passengers rose from just 2,032 in 1924 to more than 11,000 in just one year and had reached almost 18,000 by 1929. Air freight achieved an even higher rate of growth. Freight traffic including airmail rose from 18 to 600 tonnes during the same period. Finally, Hamburg together with Lübeck and the Reich built the "Sea Airport Travemünde" in 1926, once more illustrating the traditional positive cooperation between the two Hanseatic cities that goes back to the 13th century.

Intellectual and cultural life were also carried along by the upswing in the economy and the mood in the post-war period. After long debates a university was finally founded in 1919, based on the General Lecture Series as well as the lecturing and research activities of the now defunct Colonial Institute. The Institute's collection of literature and information was continued as the Hamburg Archives of International Economics (HWWA) which represented the largest library of economic literature in Germany at the time. Hamburg has always been considered—quite wrongly, according to many—as the city of moneybags, where even theatres have to be self-financing like businesses, but a rich stage and music scene developed there in the 1920s, though admittedly overshadowed by Berlin and other former royal capital cities, such as Dresden or Munich, and it therefore remained internationally insignificant. Moreover, there was a new and forceful competitor for the theatre: The cinema. In 1929 alone 14 million people went to the movies in Hamburg.

## Hamburg
### and the Great Depression

In Hamburg, too, the economic and social dynamic came to an abrupt end in the first half of the 1930s due to the Great Depression. However, the economic downturn commenced considerably later in Hamburg than in other parts of Germany; but it lasted longer and was much more severe. On the one hand, this delayed start can be explained by the fact that Hamburg was first and foremost still a trading city and the collapse of investment, which mainly affected industry, was felt less strongly at the beginning. On the other hand, German foreign trade displayed positive growth rates up until 1929 and even the first slowdown in 1930 of approximately 17 per cent could still be considered as within what was normal for an economic cycle. The real crash came in 1931. The collapse amounted to 25 per cent, and that in the following year to 35 per cent. More than 30 per cent of the German merchant fleet lay idle in Hamburg's port. Averaging the years 1933 to 1935, the development of Germany's foreign trade stabilised at a level that corresponded to only a third of its 1929 value.

This long, drawn out stagnation of Germany's foreign trade, which was considerably more marked than that of global trade, is the main reason why Hamburg was hit harder and longer by the world economic crisis than the rest of Germany. This was complemented by the politically motivated withdrawal of foreign capital and, in September 1931, the devaluation of the pound sterling. Since the British currency still determined freight rate, its devaluation had an extremely negative impact on Hamburg's economy. A further burden for Hamburg were the implications of German policy, which was essentially orien-

*Shipping line Hamburg-Süd's "Monte Rosa" with the old Kaispeicher A, built in 1875, in the background. Until 1934 the time ball on the spire dropped at exactly 12 noon each day, allowing the ships in the harbour to check their*

*chronometers. Today the remarkable landmark does not exist anymore. Yet the site will be serving for an equally imposing marker: the new "Elbphilharmonie".*

tated towards the interior. The Reich's protectionist agricultural policy had a negative influence on crop imports through Hamburg, while the job creation programmes concluded in 1931 had little relevance for Hamburg's economy, at least in the short term. Finally, the exchange controls introduced in July 1931 also caused major problems for many of the city's shipping and foreign trade companies.

For Hamburg the real scope of the world economic crisis was expressed by a dramatic drop in economic activity and an extremely high level of unemployment. After Germany's foreign trade was slashed to approximately 60 per cent of its 1928 level the port's transhipment activities fell from almost 30 million tonnes in 1928 to less than 20 million tonnes between 1932 and 1935. In 1931, 100 ships were already laid up in the Waltershofer port. Two years later it was 146. This corresponded to approximately one quarter of the German merchant fleet. This situation meant that the shipbuilding industry and its numerous supplier industries were brought to a complete standstill and the repair business was also severely reduced. At Blohm & Voss alone the number of employees was cut from 10,700 in 1929 to 2,449 at the end of 1932.

When the unemployment rate in Hamburg almost reached the 40 per cent mark in 1931 and was thus 10 percentage points higher than the German average, one third of the public budget had to be spent on benefits. As a result, the Hanseatic city was very close to bankruptcy by the middle of the year despite all the savings implemented in the investment budget and in personnel expenses. And, indeed, it required a loan from the Reich to avert the city's insolvency. Nonetheless, the continued payment of benefits, completely inadequate as they usually were, was not a real solution to the problem. Even workers who were still officially employed had to accept pay cuts that often forced their wages well below the minimum living wage.

As in the rest of Germany hostility grew towards the established parties and the parliamentary system, as they were evidently incapable of finding a way out of the crisis. As a result Hamburg's population, too, turned more and more towards the extremes and in the end — after a short interregnum without a stable democratic majority in the Parliament — Hamburg was also finally taken over by the Nazis in the middle of 1933, with the Senate basically becoming the henchman of the party leadership.

## *From the so-called Köhlbrand Treaties*
## *to the Greater Hamburg Act*

Hamburg has always been reliant on finding compromises with its neighbours in order to secure the international competitiveness of its port. Illustrative examples of this are the so-called Köhlbrand Treaties concluded between 1866 and 1909. However, concepts that go beyond contractual agreements between basically still competing partners are only to be found after the First World War. For example, Altona had been interested in a political and territorial merger with Hamburg since 1919. However this proposal was absolutely unacceptable for Prussia. Hamburg was therefore hindered by its state borders not only with regard to further port developments. Given the constantly growing population the physical constraints of the city inevitably also led to housing problems.

In 1921 the Senate explained in a memorandum to the Reich Ministry of the Interior why it would be beneficial not only for Hamburg but also for the international competitiveness of the largest German port to incorporate the Prussian communities of Altona and Harburg-Wilhelmsburg into a future Greater Hamburg. This proposal was supported, among other things, by the Achsenplan (axis plan) created by the then Hamburg city planner and architect Fritz Schumacher in 1919. As a concept, this plan already anticipated many of the issues that were discussed in 1969 within the framework of a development model for Hamburg and its hinterland and were only actually implemented when the current metropolitan region of Hamburg became a reality.

It is no surprise that this plan was not welcomed with open arms by Prussia. But Prussia's reaction was not limited to passive resistance.

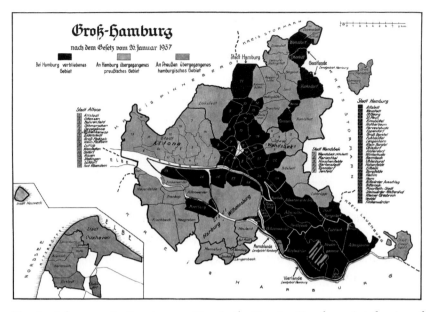

*Territorial reorganisation in 1937. Due to the Greater Hamburg Act the size of Hamburg increased from 41,500 to 74,700 hectares and the population rose from 1.2 to 1.7 million. Hanover received the Amt Ritzebüttel and Neuwerk.*

Since there was no possibility of incorporating Hamburg into Prussia, the latter's response in 1927 consisted of raising the towns of Altona, Wandsbek and Harburg-Wilhelmsburg to the category of cities by means of incorporation of the surrounding communities. Only after long and tedious negotiations was the Hamburg-Prussian Regional Planning Committee formed in 1928 with the aim of joint urban and regional planning within a radius of 30 kilometres of Hamburg's city hall. The first concrete result of the planned closer cooperation was a treaty between Hamburg and Prussia concerning the foundation of a port alliance for the three ports: Hamburg, Altona and Harburg. However the Great Depression and radical political change in Germany meant that these plans were never actually realised.

Moreover, the reason why Prussia, which was represented in the treaty negotiations by the later Mayor of Hamburg Herbert Weichmann, was so uncompromising is also interesting. In a letter written by the former Prime Minister of Prussia, Otto Braun, to the then First Mayor of Hamburg, Max Brauer, in 1951, Braun confirmed that he had at the time understood Hamburg's desire to expand and believed it to be in principle legitimate. However, given the various other difficulties at that time he had not been prepared to take the risk of Hamburg causing the collapse of his three-party coalition, which would not have permitted an entirely satisfactory and appropriate solution. As a result people had to wait until after 1933 for the Greater Hamburg project to be taken up again and then actually realised—this time without the consideration of democratic principles.

The solution to this problem in 1937 was then, however, not a treaty between Hamburg and Prussia, which is what would have been expected under normal circumstances, but a Reich law. Greater Hamburg now consisted of the former four large cities Hamburg, Altona, Wandsbek and Harburg-Wilhelmsburg, as well as 27 communities of the adjacent Prussian districts Pinneberg, Stormarn, Harburg and Stade. Hamburg had for its part to cede the town of Geesthacht as well as the communities of Großhansdorf and Schmalenbek to the province of Schleswig-Holstein and the town of Cuxhaven with Neuwerk Island and the five communities of the Amt Ritzebüttel to the province of Hanover.

Following this territorial reorganisation Hamburg's population rose from 1.2 to 1.7 million. The area of the city was almost doubled and was now 74,500 hectares. Henceforth one third of the German fishing industry, one quarter of all shipyards and one fifth of the German oil industry belonged to Greater Hamburg. Since this time Hamburg has been the largest city in today's European Union that is not also a capital city. What is, however, remarkable is that the new borders of Hamburg more or less corresponded to those which had been granted to the city as its area of influence at the time of the first Alster port in 1188.

## Complete Destruction
## and the Beginning of Reconstruction

Although, after centuries of disputes with its neighbours, territorial reorganisation finally created the preconditions for fuelling new, dynamic growth for Hamburg based on planning for an extended geographical area, the changed political environment did not encourage links with the positive old traditions. Hamburg had lost the remains of its independence and become the first "Reichsgau" within the framework of the enforced coordination planned by the Nazis. The historically important adjective "Free" was deleted from the now official name "Hanseatic City of Hamburg". The Parliament had been dissolved since 1933 and all power was now held by a Reich Governor who received his orders directly from Berlin and was simultaneously Gauleiter and head of the municipal administration.

The majority of Hamburg's population attributed the positive results of the job creation programmes, the temporary revival of trade after the slowdown of the world economic crisis as well as the restoration of Germany's international recognition to the success of the new government. Rearmament brought with it new contracts and, thus, work for Hamburg's shipyards and supplier industries. It additionally led to the siting of new industries, such as oil refineries and engine construction, and to a further expansion of aircraft production. As a consequence only a few were really concerned with the political evolution. The persecution of Jews and the repression of dissenters took place almost without protest, even though it resulted in Hamburg losing a part of its economic and scientific elite. What the new regime really meant only became clear to many when the war came to be conducted not only at the front but also at home and air raids became a permanent threat.

The first air raid on Hamburg took place on 18 May 1940 and was followed by a further 127 before the end of 1942. The climax of these raids was the so-called "Operation Gomorrha" in July/August 1943 when 3,000 British planes dropped roughly 9,000 tons of incendiary and high explosive bombs, creating a huge firestorm that made even the Great Fire of 1842 look insignificant in comparison. The death toll was 35,000 and 62 per cent of all homes were either completely destroyed or became uninhabitable, so that almost one million people were homeless. But since the British bombers, in contrast to the American ones, did not primarily attack the industrial installations that were important for the war approximately 80 per cent of Hamburg's armaments industry was back in full operation just five months later. Despite the widespread use of forced labour the real limiting factor was the insufficient availability of workers.

The bombings continued until the end of the war. However, in 1944 and 1945 they cost fewer lives than previously since they were increasingly concentrated on industrial targets and the port. On 3 May 1945 the city surrendered unconditionally to the British without a struggle. People's live were characterised in the following years, too, by great hardship, in practice up until the currency reform of 1948. Food and homes were scarce and the economy was on its knees: 90 per cent of all the quay sheds, 79 per cent of all the cranes, 72 per cent of all the warehouses, 68 per cent of all the railway tracks, 55 per cent of all the landing installations and 42 per cent of all the bridges had been destroyed in the port. The number of vessels sunk was estimated at 2,300.

Furthermore the occupying powers made use of their dismantling rights laid down in the Potsdam Agreement in Hamburg. On the one hand, this meant that a great number of useable machines in industrial plants which had not been fully destroyed were dismantled and transported to England. On the other hand, industrial facilities which could not be transported, for example the launchways at Blohm & Voss, were wilfully demolished. No less than 40,000 people lost their jobs due to dismantling and intentional destruction, most of them at Blohm & Voss.

Apart from the construction of 100 small fishing vessels, approved by the Allied Control Council in November 1947, the construction of

*The result of more than 200 air raids on Hamburg. 48,600 deaths, 900,000 homeless, more than 40 per cent of all homes completely destroyed, a further 30 per cent in part severely damaged, 379 office buildings, 277 schools, 58 churches and 24 hospitals bombed. By the end of the war almost 70 per cent of all Hamburg citizens had lost either everything or nearly everything they once owned; 42,000 people had to be housed in Nissen huts.*

seagoing vessels was strictly prohibited in Germany until the Petersberg Agreement was signed in 1949. The restrictions with regard to the size and speed of ships — set at a maximum of 1,500 GRT and 12 knots — were not fully lifted until the spring of 1951. The capacity of the shipyards nevertheless remained under Allied control and their expansion was still strictly forbidden. These restrictions were finally removed only in the spring of 1952.

Repair work at Hamburg's shipyards was also severely limited. Before the war 23 ships could berth at the simultaneously in Hamburg's port. The total lifting force of the docks was 268,000 tonnes and the two largest docks each had a load-carrying capacity of 45,000 tonnes. After the already severely damaged dry dock Elbe 17 was made completely inoperative by demolishing its west wall in March 1950, in 1951 Hamburg's port only had a dock capacity of 63,000 tonnes and the largest dock a capacity of no more than 20,000 tonnes. As a result numerous potential and lucrative repair contracts had to be turned down when maritime traffic resumed in Hamburg's port.

Port transhipment, which in the first post-war years consisted mainly of importing supply goods for the occupying power and exporting reparation payments, recovered very slowly. In spite of the currency reform implemented in 1948 the liberalisation of foreign trade, which had taken place in the meantime, and the start of a dynamic rise in German industry, exports handled via Hamburg had by 1951 reached only 56 per cent of their pre-war level. Apart from coasters German shipowners had only approximately 3 per cent of the tonnage registered in 1939 and, just as after the First World War, had in the first instance to act as agents for foreign shipping companies.

Hamburg's trading houses also faced great difficulties in restoring their traditional trade relations abroad. Those who primarily exported finished products had lost their traditional sources of supply since the former producers and their export goods were now located in the Soviet Zone or the GDR. In addition, many of these companies exported mainly consumer goods for which production facilities had in the meantime been established in the former customer countries, a similar fate as befell companies after the First World War. Import trade, too, if it had previously dealt with raw materials, also found that many of the former raw material suppliers now carried out the first stages of processing in-house. And those whose speciality had been importing foodstuffs were confronted, except in the cases of coffee, tea and spices, at first with German and later with European agricultural protectionism.

## On the Road to Normalisation

The German economic miracle which began to develop in the second half of the 1950s was the prerequisite for the restoration of normal living conditions for the people of Hamburg. However, this development was arduous and by no means straightforward. The population of Hamburg had fallen to 1.1 million by the end of the war. Despite suffering an acute lack of food and unimaginable housing shortage, the city registered a steady influx of people even between 1945 and 1947. Some of them were Hamburg citizens who had left the city in order to avoid the bombing and were now returning; others were refugees and expellees from the former eastern territories of Germany, whose number was estimated a few years later at no less than 275,000. Hamburg had become the "expellees' capital". In spite of an official ban on people moving to the city, Hamburg's population had risen again to 1.5 million by the end of 1947. The accommodation available was hopelessly overcrowded and roughly 200,000 people were housed in emergency shelters.

After the economic and monetary reforms in 1948 the food situation improved in Hamburg and throughout the Western zones. The number of houses being constructed increased substantially after the spring of 1949, and completion figures rose year by year. Nonetheless, more than two thirds of all homeowners and main tenants were still forced to share their living accommodation with lodgers in the autumn of 1951. 110,000 people were still housed in emergency accommodation, and another 60,000 lived in emergency shelters or summer houses. Even in the middle of 1954 numerous families were still accommodated in temporary housing or camps and the already difficult situation was further aggravated by an influx of East German refugees.

The greatest challenge of the immediate post-war period from the social point of view was, besides overcoming the housing shortage, the reduction of unemployment. In the first ten years after the war the unemployment rate in Hamburg was considerably higher than the average level in the Western zones and, after 1949, the Federal Republic of Germany. The reason for this was not only the destruction of production sites, which had either been bombed or dismantled, but also the high immigration rate. The average level of unemployment in Hamburg remained at 11.6 per cent between 1950 and 1953 — while the national average, including Hamburg, was just 7.3 per cent.

In the course of the almost unimaginable dynamic rise of Hamburg's economy the employment situation in the city also improved faster than anyone could have anticipated. The unemployment rate fell to just 1.9 per cent in September 1956, thus making good the difference between Hamburg and the national average. Just as impressive was the fact that Hamburg's economy basically faced the phenomenon of overemployment in 1961, boasting an unemployment rate of 0.5 per cent despite its population climbing to more than 1.8 million. The consequence was that Hamburg companies had to recruit additional workers not only from the neighbouring areas but also more and more guest workers. In 1968 the total number of foreign workers employed in Hamburg was approximately 28,000. Five years later this number had risen to 69,000, including almost 16,000 workers from Turkey, 14,000 from Yugoslavia and roughly 6,000 from Portugal and Spain.

The expansion of the transport infrastructure was considerably slower than the upturn in the private economy. Although a central bus station had been opened close to the main station in 1951 and the Neue Lombardsbrücke (New Lombard Bridge) — today's Kennedy Bridge — had been inaugurated two years later, the focus was almost entirely placed on the restoration of the cityscape and the pre-war transport infrastructure — a complete contrast to the future-oriented decisions made after the Great Fire of 1842. The only exception was the construction of the then extremely controversial East-West Street. That the number of cars in Hamburg would quadruple between 1950 and 1959 had not been foreseen.

The south-east motorway bypass completed in 1963 helped to reduce transit traffic. But major road traffic investments, for example the Köhlbrand Bridge, Kattwyk Bridge and the New Elbe Tunnel with the respective motorway routes to the north and south, which made a great improvement to port traffic as well as westbound transit traffic, were not completed until the 1970s.

Development of the city during the first 25 post-war years was, however, not only characterised by the problems of economic reconstruction; there were also a number of other challenges. Probably the most dramatic event was the Great Flood of February 1962, which killed 317 people, made 20,000 people homeless and which, according to the available estimates, caused almost 3 billion Deutschmarks worth of damage. The comprehensive flood protection measures carried out after this catastrophe prevented Hamburg suffering further damage when an even larger storm tide threatened the city in 1976.

## The "Gateway to the World" Without a Hinterland

Due to the exceptional dynamics of world economic development observed between 1950 and 1970, Hamburg's port achieved the highest annual transhipment volume in its history in 1960 with 31 million tonnes. The extremely positive development of the port and the port-related economy was, however, not only limited to Hamburg. Rotterdam and Antwerp in particular but also Bremen together with Bremerhaven profited from the economic upturn that had seized Germany, Europe and the then most important other regions of the global economy. All these competitor ports initially had a higher transhipment growth rate than Hamburg.

The reasons for this were clear. On the one hand, ever since the foundation of the European Economic Community, to which initially neither Great Britain nor the Scandinavian countries belonged, Hamburg had been, economically speaking, situated completely on the edge of things. On the other, Hamburg had lost its hinterland through the division of Germany and Europe. Before the war Central and Eastern Germany represented 60 per cent of the imports and 40 per cent of the exports handled via Hamburg. Hamburg had also been an important transit port for the former Czechoslovakia, Poland, Hungary and other East European countries. Instead of via Hamburg, Central European inland water navigation now was primarily directed to the Eastern Block ports of Gdansk, Gdingen and Stettin. Since both Hamburg and the ČSSR had a substantial economic interest in reopening the Elbe connection the Hamburg Senate attempted in the mid-1950s — in part independently of the Foreign Office in Bonn — to conduct its own Elbe policy. A certain change in favour of Hamburg then became apparent from 1958 onwards.

The ports in Hamburg and Bremen suffered additionally under politically motivated distortions of competition in favour of the Benelux ports. Apart from different tax burdens for diesel fuels it was mainly a question of disadvantages with regard to connections to the hinterland. The first set of problems included issues of differences in freight charges for inland goods transport. In the Benelux countries the prices for transportation services were generally determined by the market, while transportation tariffs in the Federal Republic of Germany were subject to strict regulations. And the special seaport tariffs of the German Federal Railway only partially compensated for existing transportation cost disadvantages for Hamburg, particularly as each adjustment to changed realities required lengthy negotiations. The second set of problems, which affected Hamburg more than Bremen's ports, concerned the infrastructural deficiencies in the connections between the seaport and the interior.

Competitive disadvantages for Hamburg's port arose firstly as a result of the delayed construction of the motorway link to the south of Germany leading on via Hanover and Göttingen to Switzerland and Austria; secondly, as a result of bottlenecks in the rail link to the south and its relatively late electrification; and thirdly, as a result of the fact that Hamburg had for many years been the only German North Sea port not connected to the German canal system. Emden's connection had occurred relatively early via the Dortmund-Ems Canal; and Bremen profited on the one hand from the Coastal Canal and its connection to the Dortmund-Ems Canal, and on the other from the canalisation of the Mittelweser, which had already commenced and would soon open up access to the Mittelland Canal. The problem of motorway and rail links could be considered as largely solved by the mid-1960s but Hamburg had to wait until 1968 for construction of the Elbe Lateral Canal to begin. The canal was eventually inaugurated in the mid-1976.

## Structural Adaptation
## in the Light of Geopolitical Changes

Due to the forward-looking policies of the Senate, which was democratically re-elected in 1946, Hamburg — initially under Mayor Max Brauer and later under Mayor Herbert Weichmann — very soon not only caught up with its pre-war development as a major modern city but due to the systematic expansion of the port in the 1960s became the most important industrial city in West Germany. Once again the economic success of Hamburg was based on a direction of policy that was in clear contrast to certain inherited traditions. An 1867 report on Hamburg joining the German Customs Union stated: "Even if the favourable situation of Hamburg after entering the Customs Union makes the establishment of grand factories possible, we ask ourselves whether this situation, and the proletariat it inevitably brings with it, would be a blessing for our hometown. However, there is just one thing that should guide us…, that Hamburg, the emporium of world trade, never becomes a city of factories."

Dynamic industrial settlement, which effectively benefited from the support of the Hamburg Senate, matched the economic policy challenges of the 1950s and 60s. Apart from the shipbuilding industry and its suppliers and the traditional coffee, tea and cocoa processing industry, the main focus of the post-war industrialisation process was initially placed on sectors which were to some extent port-orientated and connected to historical developments in Harburg and Altona.

This included the oil industry, copper, tin and aluminium smelting, steel production, vegetable oil mills and animal feed production as well as the rubber and asbestos processing industries. The growing demands of Hamburg's metropolitan area led additionally to the reconstruction, resettlement and expansion of consumption-oriented sectors, such as the food, beverage and tobacco industries and the pharmaceutical and cosmetic industries.

The first phase of this industrialisation-orientated development plan was supported by rapidly increasing domestic demand and a dynamic international economy. The success of this strategy was expressed, among other things, by the fact that Hamburg together with its adjacent municipalities was distinctly ahead of the urban agglomerations Frankfurt, Stuttgart and Munich. Despite a continued positive industrial development Hamburg was, however, unable to further extend its position — on the contrary. This was, on the one hand, a consequence of an extremely dynamic development in other regions of the Federal Republic and, on the other, a result of a number of critical structural problems in Hamburg's economy. That these were not only caused by the loss of traditional supply and sales areas in Eastern Germany and Eastern Europe is shown by the examples of the shipbuilding and oil industries.

## Rise and Fall
## of the Shipbuilding Industry

In 1952, when restrictions on shipbuilding were finally lifted, German shipyards produced around 290,000 of new Gross Register Tonnage: Deutsche Werft contributed with 13 vessels, Hamburg Howaldtswerke with seven and Stülckenwerft with five. From this point in time there was a sharp upturn in the fortunes of the shipbuilding industry, which had at that time at first specialised primarily in cargo ship construction. Boosted by state subsidies it was in particular freighters and refrigerator ships that German shipowners initially ordered. For foreign customers the German shipyards primarily built tankers. The 1953 launch of the Tina Onassis, built at Howaldtswerke as the world's largest tanker, boasting a length of more than 236 metres and a load-carrying capacity of about 46,000 tdw, was especially symbolic for the renewed upturn of the German and Hamburg shipbuilding industry. Another highlight was the launch of the Esso Deutschland in 1963, which, at the time, was the largest ship in the German merchant fleet with 90,000 tdw. In the same year Blohm & Voss made its mark with the delivery of the largest German mass goods freighter and commenced construction of the first container ship for Hapag in 1968.

However, even in the first half of 1960s a crisis started to emerge for European and, therefore, also Hamburg shipwrights. The Japanese shipyards had become unquestionably more competitive and not only due to targeted government support. Apart from considerable wage advantages the superiority of the Japanese competitors was achieved through technological innovations, geographical advantages of location, including proximity to the steelworks, and through the size of the companies, which made even the leading West German shipyards look like medium-sized enterprises. Added to this the West German shipbuilding industry, by contrast with its foreign competitors, had to cope with several upward revaluations of the Deutschmark; and international competition for the building of new vessels was generally between Asian and European shipyards. The United States industry was completely sheltered from foreign competition via protectionist measures — supposedly due to reasons of national security.

The relocation of shipbuilding from Europe to Asia is documented by the following statistics. In 1955 roughly 85 per cent of all new vessels were still being built in Europe. Great Britain, the Federal Republic of Germany and, considerably further behind, Japan were the three world leaders with 26.7, 19.4 and 11.3 per cent respectively. But just 13 years later, in 1968, Japan achieved approximately 50 per cent of worldwide production for the first time and retained this leading position — apart from slight economic fluctuations — until the beginning of the shipbuilding crisis in the mid-1970s. Europe's share of the

The Hamburg harbour scene in the second half of the 1960s was still characterised by conventional freighters and brisk shipyard activity. In the foreground the Howaldtswerke, where the "Tina Onassis", the world's largest tanker
at that time, was launched in 1953 and where in 1968 the largest container ship
in the world was also built, under the construction number 1000. However shipbuilding ceased here in the middle of the 1980s, and even repair work stopped
in 1988.

market decreased accordingly, and in particular the number of ships manufactured in West Germany and Great Britain had dropped to approximately 5.2 per cent by 1973. Despite the immense growth of the global shipbuilding industry this meant not just a relative but also an absolute downturn for Germany by comparison with 1971, when tonnage deliveries peaked.

However, the reduction of the labour force employed in the West German shipbuilding industry had commenced several years prior to this. The peak was reached in West Germany in 1958 with roughly 113,000 blue- and white-collar workers and in Hamburg in 1957/58 with 33,500. The corresponding values for 1973 were 72,000 (down by 36 per cent) and 17,400 (down by 48 per cent). Hamburg was thus unquestionably harder hit by the downward trend in employment than all the other German shipbuilding locations put together — and this despite the extremely strong commitment of Hamburg's Senate within the framework of the shipbuilding aid provided by Germany for shipowners. Within just one decade one major Hamburg shipyard alone is said to have profited to the tune of double-figure millions from this subsidy policy. Nevertheless, the costs of shipbuilding in Hamburg were higher than in other major German shipbuilding towns.

The first and, in 1962 probably the most modern major shipyard in Hamburg which had to close down was the Schlieker-Werft. In this particular case, however, the lack of orders due to international competition was not the decisive factor but primarily undercapitalisation. A temporary state or state-secured private liquidity support of just seven million Deutschmarks would probably have prevented the 170 million bankruptcy and saved the shipyard at least in the medium term. But the competition knew how to prevent this. In 1966 the Stülckenwerft was close to bankruptcy and it was taken over by Blohm & Voss.

In the same year the Deutsche Werft merged with the federally owned Howaldtswerke in Hamburg and Kiel, which subsequently operated under the name Howaldtswerke-Deutsche Werft (HDW) with its headquarters in Kiel. Production at the former Deutsche Werft in

Hamburg ceased in 1973. Apart from two container ships, which were delivered in the late 1980s under special circumstances, the construction of merchant ships at Blohm & Voss ceased as early as 1978. The shipbuilding activities of the former Hamburg Howaldtswerke, which primarily specialised in repair work after the merger, came to an end in 1983.

## Relocations in the Oil Industry

Another industrial sector beside shipbuilding which initially experienced a sharp upturn in its fortunes during the post-war period and then moved with most of its key areas of production to new locations as a result of further economic and technological developments was the oil industry. In this sector, too, Hamburg was able to take up its old traditions and in the 1950s the petroleum ports in Harburg and Waltershof as well as the Shell, Esso and BP refineries were not only rebuilt, but their total capacity was even extended. Also taking into account also the small companies which, beside German Shell, were mainly active in the production of lubricants, at the beginning of 1950 Hamburg was home to more than 43 per cent of the West German oil refineries, 54 per cent of the fuel redistillation companies and 80 per cent of the lubricant refineries. From just under two million tonnes in 1952 and almost nine million tonnes in 1963 Hamburg's refinery capacity reached its absolute peak in 1972, with more than 15 million tonnes. In spite of this increase in absolute capacity, Hamburg's share in the overall refinery capacity of the Federal Republic of Germany had been decreasing continuously since 1966, when it was still almost 15 per cent.

The initially unforeseen developments which led the oil sector to have to adapt constantly to new practices were, on the one hand, the trend towards large tankers which, despite the deepening of the Elbe shipping channel to 12 metres in 1961, due to their draught could no longer call at Hamburg when fully loaded. On the other, the use of

*Petroleum harbour. When the world's first machine-powered tanker, the "Glück-auf", called at Hamburg harbour in around 1890 with a freight of American crude oil the Unites States was an important oil exporting nation. Today the USA is the biggest oil importer in the world.*

pipelines made it unnecessary to refine crude oil where it landed. The landing of oil for West Germany increasingly occurred not only in Rotterdam but also in Wilhelmshaven, and, compared to other locations, Hamburg's importance as an oil import port and a refinery location gradually declined. The new refineries, which obtained their crude oil mainly from Rotterdam and Wilhelmshaven, were in the first instance built in the Ruhr region and in North Rhine-Westphalia.

But also in the south of Germany, first and foremost in Bavaria and Rhineland-Palatinate, new refinery capacities came on line from the mid-1960s and their raw materials were supplied via pipeline from Triest, Genoa and Lavéra. Although a pipeline from Wilhelmshaven to Hamburg was put into operation by BP and Esso in 1983, the Hamburg based refineries of these two companies closed down in the mid-1980s due to global overcapacity. In terms of the mineral oil industry Hamburg was left with the Harburg Shell refinery, which was still supplied with crude oil via tankers, and the production of lubricants by Shell and BP, as well as a number of long-established small companies. After being idle for 18 months the former Esso refinery was sold in 1988 and is now run as the Holborn Europa Raffinerie, which is supplied via the Wilhelmshaven to Hamburg pipeline.

It is difficult to say from today's point of view whether things would have developed differently if Hamburg had built a deep water port in the Wadden Sea, as proposed in a forward-looking plan for securing new industrial sites in the 1960s. What is certain is that it would have been possible to take into account future trends in sea transport, which were already forseeable. Tankers with 250,000 tdw and buck carriers for ore and coal of 200,000 tdw, which have a draught of roughly 20 metres when fully loaded, could easily have called at the planned harbour. There would also have been no cooling water problems for the operation of a new large power station, meaning that the energy supply for large and even energy intensive industrial complexes could have been secured without major problems. It is nevertheless uncertain whether the establishment of steelworks, aluminium smelters and other industries that depended heavily on imported raw materials would in the long term have been worthwhile from an economic point of view. After all, it should not be forgotten that there were worldwide overcapacities in these particular areas in the 1970s. Moreover, the landing of oil merely to supply pipelines headed for the interior would have resulted in only minimal added value for Hamburg.

## The Problems
## of Post-Industrialisation

The shipyard crisis as well as the foreseeable decline of the oil industry put the Senate under considerable political pressure to counter the de-industrialisation of Hamburg. Initially it was still possible to implement this process of post-industrialisation directly in Hamburg's port. The two striking examples in this context are the settlement of the Hamburger Stahlwerke (Hamburg Steel Works), belonging to the Korf Group, and the construction of the Hamburger Aluminiumwerke (Hamburg Aluminium Works), built and operated by the U.S. Reynolds Group. In both cases, Hamburg's Senate not only had to invest considerable sums to prepare the site but also undertook certain obligations during the following years to ensure the survival of the businesses.

Hamburger Stahlwerke was founded in 1969. Hamburg spent approximately 20 million Deutschmarks on preparing the site and the transport links. However, this may be seen as justified since the land remained the property of the city and, like other port companies after 1970, Stahlwerke was responsible for the investment and operation of the superstructure. Although a relatively small and, by comparison, environmentally friendly electric steel plant based on direct reduction seemed quite suited to the existing port landscape, it is possible that the degree to which in a globalised steel market such a plant is susceptible to business cycles was seriously underestimated.

In 1974 the Hamburgische Landesbank und Girozentrale (HLB) had to take over 49 per cent of the shares on a trust basis to secure its own as well as other state liquidity and investment loans. The running losses amounting to 204 million Deutschmarks between 1969 and 1981 were still borne by the shareholders, but when the Korf Group had to file for bankruptcy in 1983 due to further losses totalling 172 million Deutschmarks, primarily caused by the collapse of the U.S. market, but also by the economic downturn in Germany, Hamburg invested another 93 million Deutschmarks of tax payers' money for the purpose of stabilisation. The Senate's aim was to secure the 1,500 jobs by carrying on the business while at the same time minimising its own financial losses as well as those of the HLB, which were due to loans totalling 184 million Deutschmarks that had previously been granted.

It is now no longer possible to find reliable figures on how much the bailout of the steelworks actually cost the city's tax payers at the time. Following a period of political and economic turbulences the Hamburg facility has been owned since 1995 by the multinational ArcelorMittal Group, the world's most important producer by a long way, and is the fourth largest strip steel plant in Germany. Since, despite temporary difficulties, the company has supposedly been in the black in most of the years following its foundation it is reasonable to assume that the tax revenues collected by Hamburg more than outweigh the financial aid of the 1980s.

The successful recruitment of Aluminiumwerke was hardly less problematic for Hamburg. The Senate had to begin by investing 91 million Deutschmarks in the development of the site, which complied with usual practices. Additionally, 40 million Deutschmarks in the form of investment aids were paid—however, not directly to Reynolds, but to the Hamburgische Elektrizitätswerke (Hamburg Electricity Works, HEW), which gave a 20-year long electricity price guarantee. The economic possibility for this arose from the opening of the nuclear power station near Stade, for which a supply guarantee was simultaneously obtained. Since the electricity generation costs for HEW, which held one third of the shares in the Stade nuclear power station, were significantly below the guaranteed price, it could be assumed that a large part, if not even the entire amount, of these indirect subsidies for the aluminium plant was flowing back to Hamburg as profits at HEW. By contrast, the fact that the Senate additionally gave Reynolds securities against possible losses worth up to 600 million Deutschmarks should be seen as much more problematic.

As early as 1975, two years after the start of production, Hamburg had to take over the plant with debts amounting to 150 million Deutschmarks. One substantial reason why the company was not able to operate cost-effectively from the start was that fluorine emissions damaged a field of gladioli belonging to a local market garden, whereupon a court decided that the aluminium plant should initially only be operated at one third of its overall capacity. Since the fluorine emissions in question clearly fell within the permissible pollution budget for Hamburg it would certainly have been wiser, from a macroeconomic point of view, to pay the market garden adequate compensation and allow the aluminium plant to work at full capacity. All the offers of the Senate in this respect were, however, turned down by the market gardener so that in the end it was necessary to turn to a compulsory order for the public benefit.

Ownership of Hamburger Aluminiumwerke has changed several times over the years. After the foundry had been operated by the E.on subsidiary VAW, the Austrian AMAG and the American Alcoa Group, which each had a one third share in the company, VAW sold its shares in the foundry and rolling mill to Norsk Hydro at the beginning of 2002. Norsk Hydro then managed to achieve a shut-down of the plant in 2005, supposedly due to excessive energy costs but possibly also with the aim of a market shake-out. The plant has been owned by the German Trimet Group since 2006 and has now been started up again. The fact that Hamburg was actually able to escape the much quoted subsidy trap and was repaid the whole investment including interest had at least two reasons. Firstly, after the issue of the plant's accumulated environmental pollution was settled it was possible to reach an acceptable handover agreement even though the site had been shut down; and secondly, the aluminium stocks, which had been included in the initial takeover, could be sold at a considerable profit after the global aluminium market had recovered from the price collapse.

## Profound Structural Change
### in the Shipping and Port Industry

In 1961 the Hamburg Parliament passed a special port expansion act, which had been presented by the Senate and was based on a plan agreed the previous year for the entire territory. Among other things this act also provided for extensive reserve sites for the further development of the port: Beside the expansion of general cargo handling in the free trade zone provision was made in the first instance for the construction of additional large-scale facilities for bulk handling and the preparation of new, more extensive areas for the siting of port industries.

However, during the following years the increase in bulk handling could be managed without great difficulty on the available sites and the settlement of important new port industries also remained very limited. Apart from the steel and aluminium works it was principally the Norddeutsche Affinerie, today Aurubis AG, which doubled the size of its premises in 1967. Essentially traditional quaysides with sheds, cranes and the requisite transport links were constructed for general cargo handling. The only things that were truly innovative were: The first quayside for ro-ro ships, inaugurated in 1966; the construction of a highly specialised transhipment facility for bananas, where the cold chain between ship, shed and land transport was no longer interrupted; and the Overseas Centre, opened in 1967, which at that time was the largest sorting and distribution centre in Europe for aggregated shipments.

The really revolutionary innovation in sea transport lay, however, elsewhere: In the introduction of the container. And once again, just as with the emigration business 100 years earlier, Bremen was the first German port to discover this new area for business before it was overtaken by Hamburg roughly ten years later. The first containers, actually non-standardised boxes with which the U.S. Army transported its supplies to Germany, were being handled in Bremerhaven as early as the beginning of the 1960s. The first regular commercial service to a German port—Bremen and not Hamburg—began in April 1966 and was operated by Sea-Land Service Inc.

In Hamburg those responsible for the port went to great lengths to protect traditional working practices—justifying their actions not least with the argument that the container could become competition for the conventional transhipment business. Voices which claimed that the state-owned HHLA (Hamburger Hafen und Logistik AG) feared nothing as much as competition could also be heard. It was not until April 1966 when Helmuth Kern became the Hamburg Senator for Economics and Transport that the city administration finally realised that the container business had enormous growth potential. In the spring of 1967 the Senate and the Parliament decided to transform Hamburg into a highly efficient container port.

The first specialised container terminal was built at the Burchard Quay, which had previously been used for shipping VW Beetles to the USA. As ships loaded with containers and normal general cargo had been handled here — although using conventional cranes — since the middle of 1966 the first container bridge was put into service in the spring of 1968 after a further berth was created. In May of the same year the first full container ship of the United States Lines docked here. In the following years the Burchard Quay was repeatedly adapted to growing demand and new container terminals, including by private investors, were built in several other areas of the port.

The adaptation of the port to dynamically growing container transhipment required immense investments. In order to realise this new port regulations came into force in 1970 which withdrew all sovereign functions from the state-owned HHLA, putting it on a level footing in terms of competition with other transhipment companies active in the port. Moreover, it was decreed that the city of Hamburg had to provide the infrastructure while the transhipment companies were responsible for the construction and operation of the superstructure. This basically meant that the city was responsible for the expansion of the port basin, the construction of its land transportation links, the provision of sites, as well as energy and water supplies and waste removal and disposal. The private transhipment companies, on the other hand, had to provide the production halls and warehouses, the container bridges, the cranes, the transport equipment required for quayside operations, etc. in competition with the HHLA.

These regulations of the port industry resulted in a new and almost unexpected dynamism. It was not just that the share of containers involved in general cargo handling in Hamburg increased from 5 per cent in 1970 to 20 per cent in 1975 before reaching more than 60 per cent in 1987: the industrialisation of overseas cargo handling enabled the loading of the most varied goods in standardised boxes, the pro-

*Hamburg's harbour has a total of four container terminals. The Burchard Quay, inaugurated in 1968 with an area of 1.4 million square metres, a quay length of 2.8 kilometres, ten berths and 27 container cranes, is the largest facility in terms of the number of containers transshipped.*

tection of goods against damage and loss and their shipment from seagoing and vessel to the hinterland using inland waterways, rail and road from factory to factory, from warehouse to warehouse and from door to door. The integrated transportation chain considerably accelerated procedures and additionally reduced freight costs but it also destroyed many jobs — especially those which required only minimum qualifications.

In the 1950s roughly 115 workers were required per shift for the physical transhipment of 1,000 tonnes of general cargo; the same tasks were managed by no more than ten people 30 years later, with container transhipment. Nonetheless, the transition to container transport also created many new fields of activity and jobs. This applies to new kinds of port business, such as depots for empty containers or

323

workshops for container repair work. But probably the most important change invoked by the container revolution was that the largely fragmented transportation and handling chain, where freight documents were often forwarded by errand boys, has become a fully integrated logistics service due to modern information technology, where added value is principally achieved through highly qualified services and not primarily through hard physical labour.

## Industry and Port Activity is not Everything

The tertiary sector also profited from the upswing in industry and in port activity. This applied particularly to many traditional areas, such as the export/import trade, banks and insurance companies, as well as transport and logistics. Hamburg also made a name for itself in two other areas which could draw on successful developments in the past but were largely independent of the new wave of industrialisation and the revival of the port: On the one hand, aeronautics, and on the other, the media and communication sector.

Outstanding entrepreneurs and publishers — for example Axel Springer, Rudolf Augstein, Gerd Bucerius and Henry Nannen — were able to build on Hamburg's centuries-old tradition as a media and information centre and make the city the Federal Republic's most important location for newspapers and magazines. The German Press Agency, dpa, formed by the merger of the three Western zone agencies, also chose Hamburg as its headquarters. The numerous complementary competencies which Hamburg also possessed became continuously more effective as the press and media landscape developed. Examples of this are print shops, the graphics industry, printing plate and reproduction agencies, and advertising agencies, as well as institutes specialising in opinion polls and market research.

Besides radio and television, music publishing houses and the film industry were important sectors which characterised Hamburg as a leading media and communications hub. For example, three of the six largest German record and music cassette producers, responsible for roughly 50 per cent of Germany's revenue in this sector, were based in Hamburg. In permanent competition with Munich Hamburg also developed into one of the most important production locations for the German film industry in the 1950s and 60s: 126 feature films were shot in Hamburg between 1948 and 1960. Studio Hamburg, the most modern studio in Europe at that time, was founded in 1960. Today, more than 50 years later, this company is still one of the leading producers and service providers for the German film, television and new media industry. With its studio facilities in Hamburg and Berlin it covers the whole range from high-quality fiction production over documentaries and nature films to enter- and infotainment. The publicity-oriented TV productions of Studio Hamburg and some smaller producers have turned Hamburg into the capital of German advertising films.

After air traffic had completely ceased during the Second World War Lufthansa had to wait until 1954 to be able to resume its regular air services. However, it was only after the Federal Republic of Germany was granted air sovereignty under the Paris Treaties one year later that Lufthansa began the continuous expansion of its routes. In 1955 it launched the first direct service from Hamburg to New York. Moreover, Hamburg was a destination flown to by a further 25 airlines at this time. The first jet plane landed in Hamburg in the middle of October 1959, and after 1960 there was a real boom in the deployment of jets .

Besides Lufthansa, PanAm and SAS also offered flights from Hamburg to New York. SAS additionally started a service to the Middle East. Air France and Japan Air Lines flew the North Pole route from Hamburg to Tokyo. In view of the steadily rising number of flights, increasing protests by local residents about the higher levels of noise pollution and the fact that the Fuhlsbüttel Airport could scarcely continue to be expanded in the longer term, Hamburg and Schleswig-Holstein signed a contract in 1968 on the construction of a major new airport north of Hamburg in Kaltenkirchen. Hamburg held a 64 per cent stake, Schleswig-Holstein a 10 per cent stake and the Federal Government a 26 per cent stake in the planning company. The first stage of development was estimated at a cost of 800 million Deutschmarks.

But even back then the realisation of infrastructure projects of this dimension faced numerous hurdles. Not only was the project delayed by a flood of administrative court proceedings on the part of local residents and environmentalists: There were also a number of economic questions, at least regarding the short term aspects of the project, which threw serious doubt over Hamburg's future as the main hub for air traffic in the North.

Of particular importance in this context were, on the one hand, the problems of financing the project, which were still unresolved, and on the other, the threat by Lufthansa Technik to subject Hamburg to a reassessment. On top of this there was an unexpected slump in air traffic growth after the first oil crisis in 1973, which raised serious doubts on the demand projections on which the plans for the project were based. The serious long-term consequences of the decision not to build the airport have only become apparent since Copenhagen became the main air traffic hub in Northern Europe instead of Hamburg and Lufthansa decided to make Munich its second German hub after Frankfurt.

## Emerging
## into the Mass Consumer Society

The mass consumer society took off in the United States in the 1930s and did not reach Europe until after the Second World War. It spread throughout the Federal Republic of Germany and thus also Hamburg in the 1960s. New standards for the quantity and quality of private consumption were set during this period. Many things which the majority of the population had considered luxury goods in the 1920s and 1930s suddenly became normal consumer goods. Wages rose steadily and reductions in the number of working hours per week and increases in holiday entitlements meant that workers had more free time.

Both factors, the increase in available income and greater leisure time, led to a permanent sectoral shift of private consumption patterns. Initially these changed from essential goods, such as food, clothing and shoes, to semi-luxury goods, the kind of thing that could enhance living conditions, for example the purchase of furniture and household appliances. This was soon followed by the purchase of a first car and private expenditure that was related to personal preferences which helped to fulfil "the dream of a better life". This included expenditure for leisure activities and hobbies, entertainment and education and, first and foremost, holidays. It became evident that as wealth increased the classification of the various goods and services to categories such as essential goods, semi-luxury and luxury goods was subject to major revisions. While the ownership of a car, a television set, a washing machine, a dishwasher or going on a long distance holiday were still considered a luxury even at the beginning of the 1960s, these things had increasingly become the norm by the 1970s.

The crucial point is that, as a consequence of these developments, there new dimensions for the attractiveness of a city, town or region came into being, which also played an increasingly important role in the competition between locations, especially with regard to the availability of qualified labour. This included the quality of shopping facilities and opportunities for education and recreation. In terms of shopping facilities, an attractive range of shops developed in Hamburg during the 1960s and increasingly at the beginning of the 1970s. On the one hand, there was a concentration of shops selling luxury goods in the city centre and certain up-market districts. On the other hand, shopping centres with large numbers of individual shops emerged alongside re-opened department stores in the inner city. The Elbe Shopping Centre was, for example, opened in 1966, and the shopping centre in the Hamburger Strasse and the Alster Shopping Centre both opened in 1970. Specialist shops, particularly in the areas of food and furniture, and DIY stores also began to appear around this time.

The first multi-storey car park was built in the city centre in 1955, followed by many others. Since the mid-1960s it has gone without saying that every large shopping centre should have its own parking facilities. After all, the number of passenger cars registered in Hamburg had gradually risen from 23,473 in 1950 to 433,079 in 1970. During the West German economic miracle, and in Hamburg too, the VW Beetle became what the Ford Tin Lizzy had once been in the United States during the 1920s and 30s. It soon became almost normal to go shopping in one's own car. Characteristic of this development was that the number of people using the public transport system in Hamburg fell slightly and did not increase, as one might have expected, despite the population growing from 1.6 to 1.8 million and the expansion of the metropolitan and underground railway systems.

## Culture, Entertainment and Sport

In parallel with the consumer revolution in a narrower sense, the increase in disposable income and free time provided people with greater opportunities for culture, entertainment and sport. The new cultural interest was demonstrated by a new trend towards specialist educational trips, at first mainly to Italy, Spain and Greece, and later also to destinations on other continents. It also made a decisive contribution to the revival of the local cultural scene. As in the past, Hamburg today is especially characterised by the fact that its rich cultural life is supported not only by state subsidies but also to a large extent by foundations as well as by the material and financial donations of private patrons.

The Hamburg State Opera initially came to prominence between 1946 and 1956 under the artistic direction of Günther Rennert and then from 1959 to 1973 under Rolf Liebermann. The guest performances of the State Opera overseas, especially at the Metropolitan Opera in New York, further enhanced the reputation of Hamburg far beyond Germany's borders. The fact that Maria Callas gave her first concert in Germany in 1959 in the Musikhalle Hamburg and that Placido Domingo has performed several times at the State Opera since 1967 underlines the fact that Hamburg has indeed been able to reconnect with the "golden" years before the First World War. Today the international reputation of the Hamburg State Opera rests particularly on its extensive repertoire of modern operas and its ballet, which under artistic director John Neumeier has won itself an undisputed place among the best in the world.

Other highlights of Hamburg's cultural life in the 1950s and 60s were marked by the theatre scene. In this context it is important to emphasise the heyday of the Deutsche Schauspielhaus under — and including — Gustaf Gründgens between 1955 and 1963. Later directors included many famous names, such as Oscar Fritz Schuh and Ivan Nagel. The Thalia Theater also celebrated great successes, starting in 1969 under Boy Gobert and later (until 2009) under Jürgen Flimm and Ulrich Khuon. Another theatre which made a name for itself during the post-war period, not only in Hamburg but also in the other German-speaking countries, was the Hamburger Kammerspiele under Ida Ehre.

Beside the opera and these three theatres there was also the Operettenhaus and a long list of further, predominantly smaller stages in Hamburg. Although the financing of private stages has become ever more difficult over the years, the theatre landscape of Hamburg today with more than 45 stages in 35 theatres, including the internationally renowned Kulturfabrik Kampnagel, is extremely lively and multifaceted. By contrast with the music scene, which includes the Philharmonie Hamburg, currently directed by Simone Young, and two other classical groups, spoken theatre is basically of local and national significance due to the inevitable language barriers.

In the entertainment sector movies, musicals and the concerts by U.S. jazz, rock and pop stars have, in particular, enjoyed great popularity. Hamburg's outstanding "individual" contribution to the enrichment of the international music scene in the latter field is without doubt the discovery of the Beatles, who set out from here in 1962 to conquer the world. After Louis Armstrong in 1952, Bill Haley in 1958 and the Rolling Stones in 1965, the Beatles, now world famous, returned to Hamburg for one last time in 1966. Today, too, Hamburg is an attractive location for musicians from the jazz and pop scene as well as other styles of non-classical music. This distinct music scene not only has committed support from amongst the Hamburg population, it also attracts many fans from surrounding areas. Beside London, Hamburg is one of the two European strongholds of the musical.

In the field of sport and recreation two tendencies began to appear in particular during the post-war period and the following decades. Firstly, increased leisure time and probably also the trend towards healthier living resulted in more active participation. A side effect of this development, partially caused by increasing income, was that many sports previously reserved for a minority, for example tennis, sailing or golf, became sports for the people. Secondly, a number of sports, in particular football, attracted more than ever a mass audience.

The prime example of this was Hamburg football club HSV, which was soon able to recapture the heights of its pre-war performances. Thanks to its national and international success in the 1960s the club became one of the most successful advertising mediums for Hamburg at that time. Today HSV is the only club that has never been relegated from Germany's top league, the Bundesliga, since its inauguration. The club is well known outside Germany due to its frequent participation in Europa Cup and Champions League matches. If you ask the man on the street abroad what he knows about Hamburg, it is quite possible that you will hear the answer: Reeperbahn, harbour and HSV.

# Globalisation as Race to Prosperity: On the Necessity of Positive Adjustment Policies in a stable Macro-Economic Environment

# CHAPTER 9

# Globalisation
# at the Crossroads?

The globalisation process in the years from 1950 up to about 1970/73 can be seen as a race to prosperity that is unparalleled in the history of world economic development. Never before had economic growth in the industrialised countries reached such a high level over such a long period; never before had the entire population benefited from such a gain in wealth; never before had the gap in per capita income between rich and poor nations decreased to such a degree as during the immediate post-war period. But all those who assumed that these developments would continue without interruption over the longer term future were wrong. This applied not only to the majority of economic experts but also to the large international organisations, such as the OECD and the IMF. While actual results exceeded most economic projections for the post-war years, quite the opposite was the case with regard to longer term forecasts for the 1970s and 80s.

## The "Golden" Post-War Years and the Collapse

The average annual growth of global production between 1950 and 1973 was 4.9 per cent, compared to 0.9 and 2.1 per cent achieved in the earlier periods of prosperity from 1820 to 1870 and from 1870 to 1913 respectively. Worldwide the real per capita income roughly doubled between 1950 and 1973. In the United States it rose from 9,600 to almost 17,000 dollars, in Western Europe from approximately 4,600 to 11,500 dollars, and in Japan, which had an average annual growth rate of 9.3 per cent, from less than 2,000 dollars to nearly the same level as in Western Europe. Furthermore there were significant qualitative gains in wealth that cannot be measured in monetary units, such as the improvement of living conditions and hygiene or the considerable reduction of infant mortality.

The increase in international trade, illustrated by the average annual increase in the export of goods, was no less than 7.9 per cent compared with 4.2 or 3.3 per cent in the two above mentioned periods before the First World War. The share of world exports in the global gross domestic product rose from 5.5 per cent in 1950 to 10.5 per cent in 1973, which is a first indicator of increasing international economic integration. Even in the first liberal phase of global economic development before 1914 this value lay at only 1.3 per cent. Beside the quantitative development it is also relevant to consider the qualitative aspects of the deepening and widening of the international division of labour. The process of deepening was expressed, among other things, by the fact that foreign direct investment no longer primarily related to the supply of raw materials but contributed more and more to the internationalisation of production. The widening of the international division of labour was characterised by the increasing integration of new countries into the international network of trade and production.

Additionally, the international trade of services, for example in the form of journeys to foreign countries, cross-border transportation, transnational communication and international finance services, experienced an almost meteoric rise. All this—together with increasing foreign direct investment—contributed to the faster diffusion of modern technologies, management methods and new ideas. This led in turn to further increases in productivity around the world and as a consequence once again to higher economic growth. Even international migration re-intensified. The United States, historically the world's most important immigrant country, accepted roughly eight million immigrants between 1950 and 1973; and even in Western Europe, which had been the traditional region of emigration prior to the First World War, the balance of migration amounted to approximately 9.5 million immigrants, of which seven million came to the Federal Republic of Germany.

Other positive attributes of the "golden" post-war years were, at least in the industrialised nations, price stability and later also full employment. The average price increase for private consumption between 1950 and 1969 was 2.2 per cent—a figure which was not to be achieved again until the second half of the 1980s. The unemployment rate, which as a consequence of the Second World War was still at 10.4 per cent in 1950, stabilised during the course of the 1960s at 1 per cent—a level which all of today's politicians can only dream of. All this describes the historically unique success story of the post-war period, which was also characterised by the historically unique fact that the gap in per capita income between the richest and the poorest nations decreased from a ratio of 15:1 to 13:1 between 1950 and 1973.

Nothing tells the story of the collapse of the economic boom years better than a series of bare figures. Gross national product growth, which had been almost 5 per cent worldwide between 1950 and 1973, ran at only 3 per cent between 1973 and 1998, the fall in Europe and later also in Japan being appreciably sharper than in the United States. A comparable trend applies to per capita income. The unemployment rate, which had averaged 3.1 per cent in the seven largest OECD countries between 1960 and 1973, increased from 4.9 per cent between 1974 and 1979 to 6.9 per cent between 1980 and 1989. The global unemployment rate then stabilised at roughly 7 per cent and in Western Europe at almost 10 per cent. A similarly strong upward trend could also be observed with regard to inflation rates. After a massive leap from approximately 4 per cent in the 1960s to more than 10 per cent between 1973 and 1979, the rates of price increase remained stable in the OECD region at about 9 per cent before falling back to 5.2 per cent in the 1990s.

The reasons for the downturn in economic growth, the increase of unemployment and the rising inflation since the beginning of the 1970s were closely interlinked. Moreover, their interaction was so complex that in practice it seems impossible to assess the significance of the individual determinants for global economic development and the globalisation process separately. Nevertheless, there is little doubt that the relevance of some factors is greater than others. An initial plausible explanation for the slow-down in global economic activity lies in the fact that the pace with which Western European countries and Japan caught up with the technology of the United States, which encouraged growth, was bound to slow down with increasing success. This is shown particularly strikingly by the progress of Germany and Japan in catching up with U.S. labour productivity. In 1950 the gross national product per working hour in the USA was three times higher than in Germany and approximately six times higher than in Japan.

In the early 1950s the Federal Republic had profited from recommissioning existing production plants with relatively low capital expenditure. Thereafter—since the 1960s—it was the availability of a qualified and mobile labour force that allowed the absorption of high rates of technological progress and structural change in the economy. A significant element in this respect was the introduction of advanced American production and management methods. By 1973 productivity levels in the Federal Republic of Germany and Japan constituted 62.2 per cent and just 50 per cent of the U.S. level respectively.

## Growing Problems with Regard to International Competitiveness and Structural Adjustment in the U.S. Economy

In 1998, i.e. 25 years later, the Federal Republic and Japan achieved 76.9 per cent and 65 per cent of U.S. productivity respectively, even though levels had almost tripled in the United States during this period. It must also be pointed out, however, that the rate at which labour productivity and per capita income increased in the United States slowed down considerably over time, at least in the 1970s and 80s. Between 1950 and 1973 the average annual growth rate of U.S. labour productivity was no less than 2.8 per cent. The corresponding value for the period between 1973 and 1990 was just 1.4 per cent.

In contrast to continental Europe and Japan, the Second World War had hardly changed the social structures and, in particular, the patterns of corporate interest groups in the United States. This situation, together with the fact that full employment was reached in the US in the late 1950s and thus considerably earlier than in Western Europe and Japan, triggered a noticeable intensification of conflicts over income distribution sooner than in most other OECD countries. Indeed, the figures speak for themselves as the number of lost working days due to strikes and lockouts in 1959 was four times higher than in 1957. The result of these social conflicts was a significant increase in unit labour costs and, after making use of remaining opportunities for rationalisation on the cost side, a reduction in the international competitiveness of U.S. industry.

Furthermore, U.S. companies had to accept increasingly shorter life cycles for their products. Important determinants in this respect were, firstly, the intensification of foreign competition due to the industrial recovery of Germany and Japan; secondly, the activities, usually related to technology transfer, of U.S. companies abroad and their exports, including those to the United States; thirdly, the dynamic construction of new production capacities in the newly industrialis-

337

ing countries, especially for textiles, household appliances and consumer electronics; fourthly, the further strong fall in communications and transportation costs; and fifthly, the trade liberalisation promoted by the Americans themselves.

If well-established U.S. companies wished to remain competitive in their home market, they had to continuously accelerate the internal innovation process and restructure or rationalise production processes. This resulted in growing resistance to the required changes, increasing demands for protectionism and continuous income distribution conflicts, which further weakened market competitiveness and the capacity of the affected companies for innovation while further slowing down economic growth in the United States. In view of the importance of the US in the global economy at that time it was inevitable that this development would also have an effect on economic growth at global level.

Beside the dire consequences resulting from the reduced international competitiveness of American companies and the repercussions of the first U.S. trade deficits on the international monetary system, the economic and social developments in the United States — and not only there — had further implications which may have had a negative effect on global economic growth. As long as the United States experienced high economic growth and American companies did not have to fear any real competition from abroad, negotiations about further liberalising international trade were predominantly an issue for technocrats. Trade policy was "low policy"; it attracted hardly any interest from the general public and was used by U.S. industry to open new foreign markets. The same applied to U.S. policy on foreign direct investment.

Trade policy became "high policy" when the exports of European and, in particular, Japanese competitors resulted in appreciable sectoral employment problems in the United States. Not only had the United States adopted a less aggressive policy stance on trade liberalisation since the mid-1970s, at least in the area of finished industrial goods; against the background of reduced space for domestic political manoeuvring they also increasingly took refuge in bilateral and frequently protectionist international trade agreements instead of — as previously — vigorously promoting the further development of the multilateral free trade and investment system. This resulted in fundamental changes in the systemic framework of the globalisation process.

## Increasing Resistance to Economic and Social Change in Western Europe

A growing gap between necessary structural adjustments — within companies as well as in the economic and social macrostructures — and the capacity of the economy and society to respond to the new challenges in a positive manner was not only apparent in the United States. The US was hit by this phenomenon just a little earlier. Increasing economic and social rigidities, for example in the Federal Republic of Germany, were only to be seen from the second half of the 1960s onwards. Nonetheless, there are numerous indications that the negative effects on economic growth, employment and inflation in Western Europe were not only more distinct than in the United States but were also longer lasting. On the one hand, the major problems in this respect related, firstly, to the widespread misconception that high economic growth, full employment and price stability could be achieved primarily through macroeconomic demand management and, secondly, to the expectation that product and factor markets, including the labour market, would guarantee macroeconomic efficiency even with increasing government intervention and regulation. Furthermore, there was the questionable assumption that increasing government intervention and state-organised social security always, that is to say, regardless of the resulting burden for the economy, represent a necessary and desirable complement to the market economy.

The limitations of macroeconomic demand management soon became apparent. The basic idea of this strategy, which was even enshrined in legislation as the so-called "Stability Law", is relatively simple. Tendencies towards inflation should still be combated by a restrictive monetary policy; furthermore, the government should be responsible for smoothing out possible economic fluctuations via an anticyclical fiscal policy, based on short-term variations of tax burdens as well as of public expenditures. In reality, however, the fiscal policy in particular, which was intended to be anticyclical, often had procyclical effects and contributed — even though unintentionally — to the continuous increase of the state's share of the national product.

The worst legacy of the exaggerated trust in the possibility of demand management was the false impression of security that it gave with regard to political and economic feasibility of macroeconomic fine-tuning and into which it lulled entrepreneurs, employees, trade unionists and politicians. Since economic growth and full employment were now the responsibility of the government, certain safeguards which, particularly in the labour market, usually ensured that wage increases were by and large in line with the development of macroeconomic productivity were no longer functional. As in the United States the intensity of income distribution conflicts in Europe increased with the achievement of full employment. Developments in the Federal Republic of Germany may serve as an example.

The Federal Republic achieved full employment in 1960 with an unemployment rate of just 1.2 per cent. Apart from a one-off increase to 2.1 per cent in 1967, the unemployment rate remained at the — from today's point of view — unbelievably low level of just 1 per cent until 1973. The reality of full employment was therefore not only considered normal for the past, but also for the future. This problematic view was encouraged by certain statements from leading politicians, including the then German Chancellor, which were often interpreted as a guarantee for full employment, even if they were not intended as such.

After the trade unions had, in the 1950s and 1960s, accepted remarkable wage restraint, they pursued a notably aggressive redistribution strategy from 1969/70 onwards. This can be seen in the changes in the ratio of wages and salaries to the national product and also in the rising wage costs per unit of output. The latter increased on average by 2.8 per cent between 1950 and 1969 and then rose sharply by an average rate of 8.2 per cent between 1970 and 1974. The fact that the unemployment level remained at approximately 1 per cent in the first three years after the wage cost increases can surely only in part be attributed to existing reserves of rationalisation in the economy.

It is considerably more likely that statutory protection against dismissal, which had become more and more stringent over the years, made the labour market less flexible and/or that entrepreneurs still believed that even this severe increase in wage costs could be shrugged off by increasing the prices for their products. The trend of creeping inflation, which had been accelerating significantly since the beginning of the 1960s, and the fact that wage increases had always followed price developments with a certain delay could have justified such expectations.

### The Global Economic Implications
### of the First Oil Crisis

Gradually sinking rates in the growth of productivity, intensifying conflicts over income distribution, increasing rigidities not only, but predominantly, in the labour markets, increasing subsidies for various uncompetitive industries, the growing intensity of government intervention and regulation as well as accelerating inflation meant that most OECD countries were sitting on a number of time bombs that, in their combination, would have sealed the fate of the "golden" postwar years even without being detonated from outside. The first oil crisis, which hit the global economy on 17 October 1973, became the decisive trigger for a sustained trend reversal in global economic development. It is surprising that this event was probably not foreseen by anyone except for a small group of experts at Shell International in London despite the increasingly aggressive behaviour of the OPEC group since 1970.

341

While the growing demands of the OPEC cartel had in the past been primarily economically motivated, for example as protection against global inflation and/or against the devaluation of dollar reserves, the price of oil was now being used for the first time as a foreign policy weapon, putting pressure on Israel's Western allies. This was clearly reflected in the distinction of three main country groups with regard to the intended severity of the measures, namely hostile countries, such as the United States and the Netherlands, neutral countries, such as the Federal Republic of Germany and Japan, and friendly countries, such as France and Great Britain. The fact that the oil market is a global market and that large oil companies were able to redirect oil from non-OPEC countries to those with an embargo on deliveries meant that this distinction was of no real significance except in the subsequent bilateral negotiations that France in particular strove for. The price shock was the same for all oil importing countries. It definitely contributed to a further increase in global inflation but does not by itself explain the whole extent of its acceleration.

The OPEC cartel's ability to more than quadruple the price of crude oil between October 1973 and January 1974 — from approximately 2.5 dollars to almost 12 dollars — arose from the fact that crude oil is a raw material and an energy source that cannot be substituted in the short term and that the global oil market had shifted from a buyer's to a seller's market around 1971/72. The effects of this price shock must be considered in terms of its global economic, country-specific and its sectoral aspects. From a global economic perspective a historically unique transfer of resources took place from the industrialised nations to the OPEC oil-producing countries. The relevant estimates for 1974 alone were between 40 and 75 billion dollars, though a figure in the order of 60 billion dollars is regarded as most likely. Since the OPEC countries could only use a small part of this money for the additional import of consumer and investment goods a considerable gap in demand developed on the global market as a whole, which was initially bound to have a negative impact on global economic growth, even if the majority of these financial means eventually flowed back to the industrialised countries in the longer term in the form of foreign direct investment or loans.

The effect on the individual industrialised countries, too, was as a whole negative, but varied greatly depending on their economic starting points and the economic policies they subsequently pursued. All countries initially experienced a slowdown in economic growth, a rise in unemployment and an additional burst of inflation. The overall effect on particular countries varied according to their dependence on oil imports and their external trade balances. In Europe it was in particular France, Italy and Great Britain that reacted to the inflationary supply shock with an expansive monetary and fiscal policy. This resulted in a vicious circle that led from inflation to high wage agreements, to a further increase in the balance of payments deficit, to a collapse of exchange rates, to more expensive imports, including oil — and then began at the beginning again. The countries of the European floating block, including the Federal Republic of Germany, which were more oriented towards stability were clearly better off.

France, Italy, Great Britain and a few smaller European countries, such as Norway and Sweden, had given priority to short term growth and employment stimulation over price stability. By contrast, the countries more oriented towards stability believed that monetary stability would in the long term also promote economic growth and therefore create jobs likewise. After Germany's restrictive economic policy was initially relaxed in the light of the start of the economic downturn in December 1973, the Deutsche Bundesbank (German Federal Bank) and the Federal Government decided from the middle of 1974 on an anti-inflation programme which was based on both monetary and fiscal policy.

The reason for this was, however, not simply the burst of inflation due to the price of oil. Trade unions, in particular, were not willing for employees to bear the burden of their share in the global transfer of income and pushed through wage increases of 12 to 15 per cent despite the worsening situation — clearly with the aim not only of keeping with inflation but also of achieving further successes in their policy of redistribution. In actual fact the result was that earned income increased in all sectors by roughly 4 per cent more than would have been compatible with macroeconomic productivity growth. As a result economic growth in Germany fell from 4.7 per cent in 1973 to −1 per cent and unemployment rose from 1.2 per cent to 4.6 per cent during the same period. This was the highest level since 1955. Apart from 1979 and 1980, when it briefly fell to 3.6 per cent, the unemployment rate would never fall below the 5 per cent mark again during the next 25 years.

## Lessons for Caping with the Second Energy Crisis and Beyond

Countries like the Federal Republic of Germany, which pursued a rigorous anti-inflationary policy and basically left adjustments to market forces, coped much better with the oil crisis than countries which reacted by taking recourse to direct government intervention in market mechanisms in the form of rationing and wage, price and foreign exchange controls. In most cases currency devaluations did not provide the solution either. Instead of the expected international competitive advantages, the high dependency on oil imports resulted in such drastic increases in import prices that the potential positive effect on exports, on which in particular Japan and Great Britain had banked, was cancelled out by higher internal inflation rates. In spite of the negative experiences gained from tackling the first energy crisis with an expansive growth and employment policy as well as direct government interventions in the pricing process, the corresponding lessons were learned only occasionally or even only after the second oil crisis, which hit the global economy in 1979.

A stability-oriented policy was adopted in Great Britain under Margaret Thatcher in 1979. It became quite apparent that once macroeconomic stability has been put at risk it requires high social costs to

344

return to a path of stable and, in particular, non-inflationary equilibrium. Even after the resistance of certain social interest groups, for example the trade unions, to the restrictive monetary policy and public spending cuts had been broken, this policy initially produced a dramatic rise in unemployment before inflation could also be brought under control. France, which initially pursued a traditional expansive policy agenda under François Mitterand, had quite a different negative experience. Here it was demonstrated that a policy of expansion in a stability-oriented international environment initially increases the balance of payments deficit, endangers currency stability and promotes inflation before it — much later and only maybe — also has positive effects on employment. The policy in France was changed in 1981.

In an increasingly interdependent and integrated European and global economy with free currency convertibility the isolated pursuit of a stability-oriented economic policy was, however, not without problems either. As far as the Federal Republic of Germany was concerned external as well as internal implications arose that often led to long-lasting consequences. The inflation difference to other countries initially led to speculative capital inflows, which either had to be neutralised by increasing the amount of money in circulation, which would have kindled imported inflation, or by further intensifying the restrictive monetary policy. When these two processes reached their politically acceptable limits there was, apart from the introduction of foreign exchange controls, which would have meant a direct intervention in the market, only the option of revaluing the Deutschmark.

An upward revaluation of the mark was, however, initially only possible against third party currencies, in particular the U.S. dollar. There had been relatively fixed exchange rates within the EC since 1972 in the framework of the so-called "floating blocks". But since the German economy was characterised by a high level of foreign trade, with two-thirds of exports going to third party countries, it was unavoidable that each upward revaluation of the Deutschmark triggered

345

new structural shock effects. This particularly affected the shipbuilding industry, which, including in Hamburg, was already suffering from Japanese competition, and companies which were in direct competition with the Four Asian Tigers. As a result general structural adjustment pressures intensified further. And to a certain extent this development partially created temporary exchange rate related benefits even for other European competitors when the original European Exchange Rate Mechanism (ERM) evolved into a reduced Deutschmark bloc between 1974 and 1978, which, in the end, in addition to the Federal Republic of Germany only included the Benelux countries and Denmark.

However anyone who thought that the permanent upward trend of the Deutschmark would contribute to a sustainable reduction in the West German export surplus, which in principal entailed the same effects in terms of inflation as the speculative capital inflows, was disproved by reality. Both oil crises had not only led to a global redistribution of incomes but also caused a global shift of demand from consumer goods to investment goods. And this is where German industry was in many areas a technological leader and internationally almost unrivalled. A price increase based on currency revaluation did not therefore have a sufficient braking effect on German exports — except in sectors which were already hardly competitive on the international market. Apart from the political consequences in inflationary, monetary and currency terms, which originated from export surpluses and speculative capital inflows, another long term effect was important in this context, namely a tendency towards the over-industrialisation of the German economy, something which has still to be overcome.

A final aspect of the world-wide economic development that became increasingly apparent at the beginning of the 1970s and was intensified by the oil crises was the phenomenon of stagflation which characterised the economy of industrialised countries practically up until the beginning of the 1990s. This was not simply a question of weak economic growth and inflation developing at the same time but also of each new economic upturn starting from relatively increased levels both of unemployment and prices. Apart from a markedly increasing gap between the qualifications of job seekers and the specifications of the new jobs that were created in the context of economic restructuring, there were at least two other reasons for this: On the one hand the almost complete downward inflexibility of labour costs and, on the other, an increasingly half-hearted anti-inflationary policy, even in Germany at that time, which would not allow a further rise in unemployment with the goal of reducing the mainly wage-determined "cost base". Added to this was the fact that the combination of these two factors — as well as the simultaneous proliferation of government intervention, growing public deficits and the increasing tax burden — had a negative effect on companies' inclination to invest, so that the way back to higher employment was also blocked from this point of view.

## On the Way to a Multipolar World Economy: USA, European Union, Japan?

The collapse of the Bretton Woods system, which commenced at the beginning of 1971 and was complete by the March of 1973 at the latest, resulted in significant changes to the geopolitical environment of global economic development. Great Britain, together with Denmark and Ireland, had also joined the EEC in early 1973. At the same time Japan had increasingly reduced the gap between it and the United States and Western Europe. As a result the world of the industrialised nations now consisted of three powerful economic blocs that comprised 50 per cent of the world's gross national product but held only 15 per cent of the world's population.

Besides the clear slowdown of economic growth and rising global inflation in the early 1970s, there were a number of further developments which decisively changed the environment, in terms of both the world economy and economic policy. One of them was the increasing global synchronisation of business cycles which made a policy of national stabilisation significantly more difficult. In the 1950s and 60s global economic stabilisation was assisted as a rule by the fact that a slowdown of economic growth in Europe coincided with a boom period in the United States and vice versa. The increasing integration of European and American national economies led more and more to a transatlantic synchronisation of economic development. That is the reason why the idea of a transatlantic coordination of anticyclical monetary and fiscal policies was taken up more than once in the hope that it would counter the effects of this synchronisation. However, all initiatives of this kind failed for one reason or the other.

Two further events of global economic relevance which characterised the 1970s were, on the one hand, the growing competitiveness not only of Japan but also of the Four Asian Tigers in the global markets for industrial goods, and, on the other, the more aggressive approach adopted by the OPEC cartel after 1971, which initially led to the complete or partial nationalisation of significant foreign direct investments of the large oil companies and then to the first oil crisis in 1973. One unexpected side effect was that the high oil prices after 1973 and 1979 may also have strengthened, at least temporarily, the economic and — connected with it — the military position of the USSR during the "Cold War", since it benefited from the increasing profits of its crude oil exports.

The consequences of all these developments for the future of the global economy and, particularly, the design of the future world economic order were profound. The United States was still the dominant force, both politically and militarily, but was too weak in terms of international competitiveness and related domestic politics and, as a result, economically no longer willing or capable of bearing the particular burden of being the global economic leader. Europe was economically strengthened but although integration was gathering pace it was politically still too disunited to be seen as a full partner for the United States. Japan, finally, had risen to become the leading economic power in Asia but was still not on the same economic level as the United States or the European Communities. It had no political ambitions and it is highly unlikely that the US and the EC would have accepted any sort of claim for leadership in international economic policy matters from Japan.

The systemic overarching political framework of the globalisation process had thus become relatively instable compared to the 1950s and 60s. This is demonstrated very clearly by the fact that due to the oil crisis two important American initiatives, both aimed at enhancing world governance with regard to monetary policy and international trade policy and staking—in certain respects—America's claim for leadership, were not at first seriously pursued. The desired reform of the international monetary system, for which a "rough draft" was submitted in September 1973, was adjourned *ad calendas graecas*. And the so-called "Tokyo Round" of GATT negotiations turned into a marathon of negotiations conducted at a snail's pace. The only thing which progressed dynamically in terms of trade policy was the expansion of non-tariff trade and investment barriers which were not, or not sufficiently, subject to GATT disciplines. Apart from speaking with one voice in the Tokyo Round, which concluded after seven years of negotiations in 1979 with tariff reductions amounting to a further 33 per cent, the European Communities' influence on international economic policy remained insignificant until well into the 1980s. There was too much self-preoccupation. The internal monetary policy of the EC is a clear example of this. The result of the fundamentally different approaches to policy on economic growth, employment and stabilisation was that neither the Exchange Rate Mechanism with reduced band widths between the community's currencies concluded in 1972 nor the European Monetary System (EMS) created in 1979 was able to put an end to Western Europe's monetary turmoil. By 1983 the central rates had already been adjusted 21 times, including four upward revaluations of the Deutschmark and three devaluations of the French franc. The foundations for Europe becoming a fully fledged player in international economic policy were only laid after the focus of economic policy across Western Europe turned towards stability at the end of the 1980s, when Great Britain also joined the EMS in 1990 and the criteria for the establishment of an economic and monetary union were codified in the following year.

## International Economic Policy without Systemic Orientation

After the United States lost its hegemony at the beginning of the 1970s the world economy was therefore only multipolar in terms of the economic potential of the United States, the European Community and Japan, but not in the sense of a systemic trilateral political leadership. Nevertheless, in the 1980s a gradual normalisation of the economic growth, employment and inflation trends — promoted by multilateral policy dialogue in the OECD and IMF — took place and the worst external imbalances were reduced. This course was set by a slowly emerging paradigm shift in economic policy. The principal starting point of the new policy orientation was a consensus that each country should clean up its own act and that the international markets would then eventually balance themselves — a position which could, from the point of view of the world economy, be interpreted as a further indication of a leadership vacuum.

The most important elements of the new guiding principle for economic policy included: Firstly, the fundamental reorientation of the macroeconomic policy of the OECD countries towards stability; secondly, the shift away from an attempt at macroeconomic fine tuning towards a policy of creating a macroeconomic framework that was as robust and reliable as possible; thirdly, the acceptance of flexible adjustment to global economic and technological change; and fourthly, retention of the regime of flexible exchange rates. This new strategic orientation of economic policy laid the foundations for the global economy's escape from the stagflation phase.

If there really ever was anything like a triad that played a relevant part in economic policies, it most probably existed within and alongside the G7 process. It is interesting to note, however, that the G7 heads of state failed miserably in their initial attempt to establish international coordination of economic policy in 1978, mainly in the field of international monetary policy. Much more successful in this area was the close cooperation, particularly in crisis management, between the responsible ministries of finance on the one side and the U.S. Federal Reserve Board, the Deutsche Bundesbank and the Bank of Japan on the other side. The so-called "Plaza Accord" reached in 1985 for the controlled devaluation of the U.S. dollar is still regarded as a prime example of successful cooperative exchange rate intervention. It was not only important to stop the continuously increasing overvaluation of the U.S. currency but also simultaneously to fend off the ever intensifying demands of American industry for protectionist measures. 400 protectionist measures are reported to have been brought before the U.S. Congress for consideration in 1985 alone, all aiming to protect American industry from foreign competition, particularly from Japan and the Southeast Asian industrialising economies.

The Louvre Accord signed two years later, at which the signatories agreed that the dollar parity rates now reached reflected economic fundamentals, must, however, be assessed more critically. Some of the measures concluded at that time were indeed never realised. The initially planned long term cooperation was partially neglected as early as 1987 and was finally abandoned when the Iron Curtain fell in 1989. Moreover, the longer term consequences of some of the decisions which were implemented as agreed proved to be very problematic. This applies in particular to the expansive monetary policy of the Bank of Japan, which was adopted in order to stimulate Japan's domestic demand. The Japanese Central Bank could not bring itself to change its policy even when the economy started overheating in the autumn of 1987. This not only created the preconditions for the speculative boom which later soared out of control. The brutal crash of the stock market in 1990 and of the housing market in 1991 were thereby also in practice pre-programmed.

In the 1980s, and even more so after the collapse of the Soviet Union, the United States believed it was politically powerful enough to be able to decide case by case whether the enforcement of its national interests could be realised more effectively on a multilateral, bilateral or even unilateral basis. This last variant was well documented by a number of unilateral protectionist measures against increasing imports from Japan and the Asian Tigers. A common commitment to a new systemic and effective concept for a future-oriented world economic order was initially, apart from a few partial aspects, almost non-existent.

Beside international monetary policy, other positive developments during this period included the conclusion of the Uruguay Round and the establishment of the World Trade Organization (WTO) in 1994. Amongst the failures must be counted the unsuccessful attempt to reach a multilateral OECD agreement on foreign direct investment, due, however, mainly to France and Canada, not the United States. This initiative would have had the potential to translate more than 1,300 bilateral investment agreements into a multilateral framework and create long term international legal security in the area of foreign direct investment. The negotiations were abandoned in 1998 and within the WTO, too, there has been only one further attempt in this direction but no substantial progress has been made.

## Continued Deepening and Widening
## of the Economic Globalisation Process and the Special Role
## of Multinational Enterprises

The widening of international exchange relationships implied that more and more countries and regions were participating in the ongoing process of economic globalisation. Apart from the expansion of global trade this particularly referred to the expansion of foreign direct investment and technology transfer, not only by the US but also by many other countries of origin, in particular Great Britain, Germany, France, the Netherlands and Japan. Parallel to this it meant the integration of a number of newly industrialising countries, first and foremost in Asia but also in Latin America. In the Asian-Pacific region these included Thailand, Malaysia, the Philippines and Indonesia; and in Latin America it was primarily Mexico, although its exports went almost entirely to the US. From the mid-1980s the circle of key players widened with China, India and Brazil joining the ranks. Russia only started to play a role in this context after the collapse of the Soviet Union.

The most important aspects of the deepening of the globalisation process concern not only the inclusion of many new products and services in the global system of exchange which had never before been traded internationally or over longer distances. They also included, in particular, the formation of multinational, often globally operating companies which in turn contributed to the regional expansion of the globalisation process due to their location policy. Moreover, they also promoted the continued dynamic development of a whole range of global goods, services and capital markets. This is characterised by the fact that, according to available estimates, roughly one third of today's international trade of merchandise takes place within the internal networks of multinational enterprises.

During the 1950s and 60s the country of origin of foreign direct investment was primarily the United States and the recipient zone, except when it was a question of raw material extraction, mainly Europe and since the second half of the 1960s, though only to a relatively small degree, also the Asian Tigers. Japan still remained closed. The characteristics of developments since the beginning of the 1970s have been a rapid acceleration of foreign direct investment growth as well as the increasing regional diversification of locations. In 1968 the annual transaction volume was still approximately 5 billion dollars, by 1974 it had increased to 13 billion dollars, and between 1989 and 1994 it stood at more than 200 billion dollars. The annual figures quoted for 1995 and 2000 are more than 340 billion and 1,400 billion dollars respectively. This had risen to an unbelievable 1,800 billion dollars by 2007. More than 80 per cent of foreign direct investments are transnational corporate mergers and acquisitions.

The continued change in economic motives for foreign direct investment is remarkable. The initial objective was to secure raw materials. The next period was characterised by developing new markets and here local presence and local production played a role, as well as overcoming trade barriers. The third phase was marked by the targeted optimisation of a company-specific procurement, production, sales and finance strategy based on an orientation towards the global market and costs. The fact that the international division of labour within companies was further deepened, particularly in the operative functions, led finally to new innovative business models. On the one hand, this related to new functional processes, such as worldwide outsourcing, insourcing and supply chains; and on the other, the increasing intensity of global competition simultaneously required a strategy of location optimisation from the point of view of global efficiency.

Viewed superficially, the last mentioned aspect could, in particular, support the widespread public opinion that foreign direct investment, especially by multinational companies, lead to de-industrialisation and a loss of jobs in industrialised countries due to the geographical redistribution of production. Given the fact that the percentage of foreign direct investment going to developing countries was still less than 20 per cent in 2000, this thesis seems very questionable. By far the largest part of foreign direct investment promoted the deepening of the international division of labour within the triad. Since the first phase of the eastern expansion of the European Union and therefore the integration of European low-wage countries did not take place until 2004, the argument which claims that moving production sites to Eastern Europe is to blame for the big loss of industrial jobs in the European Union is of very limited validity, at least for the period before this date. By the way, in 2007 almost 70 per cent of worldwide foreign direct investments were still made in the industrialised countries.

354

*Hyundai Heavy Industries, Korea. This is one of the leading Asian shipyards for large container ships and bulk carriers with which European shipbuilding locations can scarcely compete.*

In fact, analyses carried out by the OECD as well as the European Commission and other institutions confirmed that the great majority of job cuts in industrialised countries up to now are related to technical progress and not to low-wage competition from developing countries. The relationship of unemployment to foreign direct investments in low-wage countries is thus primarily a sectoral phenomenon. It essentially concerns labour-intensive production processes characterised by low qualification.

The sectors which most clearly displayed protectionist tendencies were therefore predominantly the so-called old industries. Prominent examples of this could be found in areas such as textiles and clothing, the leather processing industry, shipbuilding, crude steel, toys, household appliances and soon also simple electronic consumer goods. All these were typical problem sectors which faced ever stronger competition in the 1970s, at first primarily from Japan and somewhat later also from the emerging Asian countries. The shipbuilding industry in Northern Germany and Hamburg is also a clear example of this trend. Since these old industries were additionally often characterised by strong regional concentration, the United States and Europe increasingly experienced vociferous demands for protectionist measures due to the resulting regional problems.

As tariff increases would have violated international GATT regulations the main focus of protectionist industrial policy was either on the payment of subsidies or in the area of non-tariff trade barriers (NTBS). According to available estimates the percentage of subsidies in the gross earnings of industry in the OECD countries rose from 4.7 to 8.7 per cent between 1970 and 1983; in other words, it almost doubled. The share of industrial goods imported that were covered by NTBS rose from roughly 6 per cent to almost 13 per cent in the United States and from almost 11 per cent to roughly 15 per cent in the EC during the same period. If agriculture is also included roughly 27 per cent of all industrialised country imports were obstructed by some sort of grey area protectionism in 1983.

## The BRIC States

Just as the term Four Asian Tigers was used in the past without giving much thought to the fact that the economies had very little in common apart from a certain freedom for entrepreneurial initiative and a successful strategy for investment and export-oriented growth, it has become common practice to call Brazil, Russia, India and China the BRIC states. In this case, too, it is difficult to identify basic similarities between the four nations except for their large geographical area compared to other countries and the fact that they failed to utilise their potential for economic development up until the late 1980s. The only thing that links them is their geopolitical and, increasingly, also economic claim to play a greater role in international politics, including the politics of international economics.

A few striking figures are sufficient to underline the differences between these four countries. The largest and smallest of the four countries are Russia and India with 17.1 and 3.3. million square kilometres respectively. China and Brazil are somewhere in the middle with 9.9 and 8.5 million square kilometres respectively. The countries with the largest population are China and India, each having more than one billion inhabitants. Brazil has 184 million inhabitants, while Russia's population is estimated as no more than 143 million people. India and Brazil are characterised by a functioning democracy. China is a dictatorship controlled by a communist party and the actual form of government in Russia is rather difficult to assess. In 2010 the per capita income — based on purchasing power parity — was 15,600 US dollars in Russia, followed by Brazil with approximately 11,300 US dollars. In China it is as much as 7,500 US dollars and in India it is somewhat more than 3,400 US dollars. In recent years, however, China in particular, but also India, has been able to free millions of people from the shackles of poverty. Today both countries have a middle class of 250 to 300 million people — which roughly corresponds to the population of the United States or the Eurozone.

Apart from differences in the form of government, the area they cover, the size of the population and the per capita income there are further economically crucial dimensions which make the diversity of the four BRIC states even clearer. These relate firstly to the availability of agricultural, mineral and fossil natural resources; secondly to economic structure; and thirdly to integration into the international division of labour and intensity of participation in the globalisation process. China has followed the Asian model of development. The basic orientation focused, as previously in Japan and the Four Asian Tigers, on rapid industrialisation based on investment and export orientation. This has turned the country into the world's largest factory in less than 25 years. The share of investment in the gross national product is 43 per cent. China produces more than a million tonnes of steel, more than 14 million pairs of shoes and roughly 50 million pieces of clothing every day. Today companies such as Haier in the field of electrical household appliances and Levono in the computer industry are world leaders.

With the exception of foodstuffs and coal China is heavily dependent on the import of mineral natural resources as well as of crude oil. In addition, China has a strong import demand for investment goods, certain high-quality components and semi-finished products. Both foreign trade and foreign direct investment are largely liberalised. In 2010 China was the world's largest exporter ahead of Germany and the United States and the second largest importer behind the United States and ahead of Germany. Additionally, China, including Hong Kong, is the world's second largest recipient of foreign direct investment after the USA.

In India almost 60 per cent of the population still depend on agriculture. The share of the agricultural sector (including forestry and fishing) in the added value of the economy as a whole was approximately 18 per cent in 2009; the comparable figures for China, Brazil and Russia during the same period were 11, 6 and 5 per cent respectively. To a certain extent this structural feature of the Indian economy could also be viewed as an indicator of underdevelopment — a judgement that is supported by the fact that 80 per cent and 35 per cent of the population still live on less than 2 dollars and 1 dollar a day respectively. The comparable figures for China are 47 and 17 per cent.

Apart from the comparatively very high proportion of agriculture in the added value of the economy as a whole, the share of services is 52 per cent which is also very untypical for a country at this stage of development. In fact, in terms of its contributions to the film industry, globally networked applications of information and communications technology and software development India is one of the world's leading producers. In the meantime India has become the home to large industrial companies such as Tata. It is, however, characteristic that India's most successful steel tycoon Lakshimi Mittal, originally based in Calcutta, owes his expansion almost exclusively to having purchased companies outside India and today he controls his business from London and Rotterdam.

The situation in Brazil is completely different. The economy is highly diversified and since denationalisation, currency stabilisation and, in particular, since turning away from import substitution policy in the 1990s, almost all economic areas are tied into global economic exchange relations. Agriculture, which has since profited from the import of fertilisers and agricultural machinery, has witnessed great increases in productivity in recent years. It is also important to note in this context that agriculture, including agro-industry, is not primarily oriented towards domestic demand as in China and India. The most important agricultural export products are soya, coffee, sugar, meat and increasingly also biomethanol.

Additionally, Brazil is an important exporter of mineral and fossil natural resources. It is the global market leader in the export of iron and iron ore and also exports natural resources and semi-finished products, such as steel, aluminium, tin and crude oil. Industry, which has a 30 per cent share in the added value of the economy as a whole, contributes a roughly 55 per cent share to Brazilian exports. The proportion of high-tech goods in the overall export of industrial goods was 12 per cent in 2006 and 2007. Today the Brazilian company Embraer is the world's third largest aircraft manufacturer after Airbus and Boeing.

With regard to international politics and the global economy Russia is the most important state of the 15 successor states of the former USSR and was an integral part of the Soviet planned economy up until its collapse in 1991. The economic problems caused by the system-based slowdown of economic growth since 1970 and by the arms race with the West prompted Mikhail Gorbachev to increase the level of political freedom in the Soviet Union between 1985 and 1990, largely to release the Eastern European satellite states into independence, and to dismantle the planned economy system, without, however, replacing it with a new economic system.

It was Yeltsin who introduced the market economy after 1991 and dissolved the USSR after a secret conference with the political leaders of Ukraine and Belarus. The abrupt transition to a market economy without first establishing the required institutions and without a monetary and fiscal policy that was sufficiently oriented towards stability led to hyperinflation, a downward spiral of falling income for the majority of the population and growing poverty. In 1998 the gross national product was 42 per cent and investments 92.5 per cent less than in 1990. Moreover, former Soviet state-owned companies were sold for next to nothing during the privatisation process. The obverse side of the poverty that affected 50 per cent of the population between 1993 and 1995 was the emergence of a new class of economic and financial oligarchs. Russia's integration into the global economic division of labour is now primarily characterised by the export of natural resources, especially natural gas.

The average annual growth rate of the real gross national product between 1993 and 2007, the 15 year period before the 2008 economic and financial crisis, was 10.2 per cent in China, 6.9 per cent in India, 3.2 per cent in Brazil and 2 per cent in Russia. It is possibly these differences in the dynamics of economic development which represent the largest and most far-reaching differences between the four BRIC states with regard to their integration in the globalisation process. And as with the Asian Tigers it is obvious that to a great extent it is the differences in economic policy approaches pursued by the individual nations that provide a possible explanation. Another aspect is that the Asian Tigers enjoyed nearly equal success despite having different development strategies. This can, at least at present, not be said of the BRIC states.


## Lessons from the Economic Reforms in China and India

Although China had practically isolated itself from the rest of the world since the end of the 15th century, its gross national product in 1820 was still about 30 per cent higher than that of Western Europe and a good 20 per cent higher than that of Europe and North America combined. For China the middle of the 19th century marked the beginning of its economic decline — even before it became the playing field of the colonial powers. At the same time Europe and North America experienced a clear acceleration of economic development as a consequence of the Industrial Revolution and the intensification and expansion of the globalisation process. In 1973 China was insignificant in the global economy. Compared to the gross national product of Europe that of China only reached 20 per cent and in comparison with the combined GNP of Europe and North America it only achieved 10 per cent. The average growth rate of the real national product between 1820 and 1973 was 0.8 per cent; in other words, this means 150 years of stagnation.

The end of 1978 saw the start of the reform policies under Deng Xiaoping, China's opening to the world and thus its integration into the global economy and the globalisation process. Economic growth, which had been less than 5 per cent in the 1960s and 1970s, reached 9 per cent in the 1980s and 1990s and more than 10 per cent after the turn of the millennium. Besides reforms that were oriented towards a market economy and the so-called "open door policy", which permitted foreign trade as well as foreign direct investment, there were at least six further decisive factors which shaped China's economic upturn:

*Firstly,* the availability of capital and foreign exchange as well as agricultural resources; *secondly,* a huge and motivated workforce with a relatively high literacy level; *thirdly,* accelerated absorption of foreign technology and modern management practices through large-scale foreign direct investment; *fourthly* an economic system based on efficient combination of market forces and state intervention; and *fifthly,* sufficient control over social tensions so that the political system had the capacity to create a stable environment for investment, including foreign direct investment. And finally *sixthly,* the open international trading system allowing China to adopt an export-led growth strategy.

Today China is the workshop of the world, admired and feared as a competitor around the globe. Its share in global exports rose from less than 4 per cent in 1998 to more than 10 per cent in 2010. It overtook Germany as the leading world exporter in 2009. China's exports consist predominantly of industrial finished goods, of which 30 per cent can already be regarded as high technology products. Its most important import category is integrated circuits, followed by crude oil and iron ore. This proves that China's industrial production within the framework of the international division of labour has already set its sights on high-quality products despite the almost unlimited possibilities of expanding labour-intensive production. It should nevertheless be pointed out that 55 per cent of China's overall exports originate from the Chinese production facilities of foreign multinational companies, whose market share in China itself is just 13 per cent.

Ever since its independence in 1947 and particularly after 1954 under Nehru, India had chosen to be politically and economically isolated from the outside world. A socialist planned economy based on the Soviet model and protectionism with tariff rates of up to 350 per cent had resulted in the so-called "Hindu rate of growth" of roughly 3.5 per cent over a period of approximately four decades. The declared goal was self-sufficiency. However, the actual result was inefficient and inadequate production, a completely underdeveloped infrastructure, double-digit inflation rates and — except for corruption and tax fraud — the end of any entrepreneurial initiative. A gradual experimentation with market reforms at the end of the 1970s lifted India's economic growth rate to 5.5 per cent. But it required a severe balance of payments crisis — which would have led to a complete collapse of the Indian economy without a loan from the International Monetary Fund amounting to 2.2 million dollars — to finally bring about a programme for economic policy reforms in 1991.

The success of the new economic policy, especially the opening of the Indian economy to foreign trade and foreign direct investment, was in every respect remarkable. After just two years currency reserves had risen from 1 billion to 22 billion dollars. The stimulation of economic growth, however, took rather longer. Nonetheless, industrial production increased at a rate of 11.3 per cent and 12.7 per cent in 1994 and 1995 respectively; and exports rose by 18.4 per cent and 20.3 per

*Shanghai. 25 years ago the shoreline of the River Huangpu was still a meadow landscape with isolated villages. Today the financial and trading centre of Pudong, which sits opposite the historical old town, has a skyline to rival New York, Tokyo, Hong Kong or Dubai.*

cent. Foreign direct investment in India totalled 1.2 billion dollars in 1994 and 2 billion dollars one year later; and the real gross national product increased by 7.3 per cent during both years. Apart from slipping due to the global economic downturn in 2002, the "Hindu rate of growth" was definitely a thing of the past — even though the government repeatedly had to make political concessions and compromises regarding its reform programme. India is yet another example which shows that an effective and sustainable reform policy within a democracy is not possible without political and social acceptance.

As a result many of the required reforms have either not yet been completed or not even started. Import tariffs are still much higher than in the other BRIC states. This applies not only to finished goods but also to intermediate industrial products, with the consequence that Indian industry is hardly competitive on international markets. On the one hand, there is no competitive pressure from abroad. And on the other, protectionist measures force Indian industry to work

363

with overpriced semi-finished and other products on the input side. Moreover the rigidities of the labour market have not yet been reduced. For example, it is still in practice difficult for companies with more than 100 employees to dismiss workers. Additionally the Indian economy is highly over-regulated and therefore suffers from the complexity, the time wasting and to some extent the arbitrariness of bureaucratic decision-making processes.

All these factors contribute to the fact that, in contrast to China, the Asian Tigers or Japan, there has been no labour-intensive industrialisation in India, that foreign direct investment in India is still 75 per cent less than in China and that the integration of India into the international division of labour has, apart from exports in the area of "low technology", primarily taken place in the form of services in the information and communications technology sector. In China, too, the reforms are far from being completed and they are becoming increasingly complex. Yet the negative effects on the dynamics of economic growth are considerably less problematic, including from a social perspective. The imbalance between the employment of skilled and unskilled people is less marked. And the potential for social unrest is probably also considerably lower in China, unless there is suddenly a dramatic slump in economic growth.


## From Web 1.0 via Web 2.0 to the "Global Village"

Similarly to the transition from agricultural to industrial society, it also became apparent with the diffusion of information and communication technologies and their associated networks that new and groundbreaking technology developments can lead to profound changes in all areas of life. Particularly remarkable was and still is their influence on the working environment, on the organisation of production and distribution, on settlement structures as well as on economic and political power relations, indeed even on family structures, social behaviour and human value systems. Just as with the profound waves of innovation in earlier eras, information and communications technology also display an interdependency in reverse order. Usually, groundbreaking new technologies can only completely develop once the changes and adaptations of the institutional and social structures have set the stage for this process. The experiences of the 20th century have also shown that these changes, including modifications in patterns of social behaviour and values, have a great impact on the speed and direction of developments and innovation in technology.

It was in 1991 that British computer scientist Sir Tim Berners-Lee created the first website, based on the World Wide Web which he had conceived. And it is less than 15 years since Netscape launched its first commercial browser on the market, which in practical terms made the Internet accessible to everyone. This was the beginning of a truly explosive development that is by no means completed today. The estimated number of 8.5 million Internet users in 1995 rose to 361 million by the end of 2000 and to 2 billion in 2010. The six countries with the highest number of Internet users are China (452 million), the United States (244 million), Japan (102 million), India (88 million), Brazil (82 million) and Germany (67 million). However, the highest user density with over 85 per cent of the population can be found in Denmark, Finland, Iceland, Luxembourg, the Netherlands, Norway and Sweden.

Global networks in general and the Internet in particular have extremely different fields of application. For personal and private use the Internet is a means of gathering information (Google, Yahoo, Wikipedia), of exchanging knowledge and thoughts (email, Skype), of accessing culture and entertainment (television, films, music, games), of achieving self-fulfilment (personal websites, blogs, podcasts, YouTube, Facebook, Twitter, MySpace), of purchasing products and services (Amazon, Ebay, banks, insurance and tourism services) and of controlling electrical household appliances remotely (alarm systems, heating in holiday homes, intelligent kitchens). Never before has the individual had better direct access to such an extensive range of products. Never before has it been so easy to compare the prices of various suppliers. Never before has the knowledge of this world been more readily available than today. And the user-friendliness and performance of search engines and other devices will continue to improve.

But there are also downsides. When Napster began its story of web success in 1999, it turned millions of otherwise law abiding Internet users into digital shoplifters through its music exchange programme. When Napster was banned by a U.S. court two years later due to copyright infringements, it was probably the most successful website ever, with roughly 60 million visitors a month. Even today the dispute about effective copyright protection for the Internet is still waiting to be resolved. Moreover the criminal potential of the Internet is almost unlimited. It ranges from virus infection and identity theft to credit fraud and the exchange of illegal contents. At the same time the Internet is a highly effective instrument for spreading propaganda, ideological positions and half-truths. And the combination of new technology and extensive coverage gives even emotionally charged irrationalities an inappropriate credibility.

The comprehensive networking of society has resulted in a profound change in the daily life of the individual, particularly since the transition from the initially one-way information flow (Web 1.0) to bi-lateral and multilateral interactivity (Web 2.0). Today fundamental changes are already apparent with regard to how, when and where people work; what, how and where they produce and consume; how they structure their day, their leisure time, even the various stages of their lives; and how they develop their social relationships with their family, friends, workplace and wider social environment. The Internet and its various services allow interactive dialogue across all geographical distances and across all borders. They enable active participation in discussion groups with participants from home and abroad whom one will never meet in person. All this offers almost unlimited possibilities for the global exchange of opinions and information as well as unprecedented spaces for individuality, diversity and self-development.

However, the new opportunities of the digital world have already led to the creation of new polarisations both nationally and internationally: Firstly, between those population groups with access to the new technologies and those without; secondly, between those who are capable of selecting data from the flood of information in a targeted manner and then interpreting and using this data constructively and those who are not; and thirdly, between those who are capable of following new developments or even driving them on as a result of their initial and ongoing education and those who are excluded from this process. Additionally, the universal validity of many traditional and ethical standards has come into question during the current transitional phase in the movement towards a society in which information and knowledge are globally networked. This often results in increased resistance to the new and the foreign, even if there is no realistic chance of decoupling from them.

## The Implications
## of a Networked World Economy

Developments in transport and in information and communications technology have caused the world to shrink and have at the same time intensified the globalisation process. While it took ten days for news of the New York Stock Exchange crash to reach London in 1857, information about the Wall Street crash in October 1929 spread within just a few minutes, and it took only a fraction of a minute in the case of the electronically triggered stock exchange collapse in 1987 and the so-called dotcom crisis in 2000. Speed and coverage were additionally complemented by the quantity and density of information and data exchange as well as the quality of the interaction, which has gradually turned from a unilateral flow of information into a bi-lateral and multilateral dialogue.

Just as for private life, the transition from an industrial society to the knowledge-intensive society has both national and international implications for the economy. Fundamental changes of orientation can initially be observed in the structures of production, of markets, of corporations and of organisation. After the industrial age invented mass production and mass consumption, modern information and communications technologies open up new opportunities for small production runs and bespoke production. They simultaneously allow the further expansion of the international division of labour and, above all, its deepening. Basic changes in the chains of value creation were initially seen in economic sectors, where business relationships could be dematerialised and digitalised. These included, in particular, traditional service sectors, such as banks, insurance companies and tourism. A special feature in these sectors is, besides higher market transparency, the drastic reduction of the intermediate steps between producer and consumer.

Another sector which was seized by the new technological revolution at a relatively early stage was retail trade in standardised products such as books, CDs and electronic equipment. Here it became possible to process orders and payments electronically while the products were dispatched by delivery services. Probably the most prominent example of this trend is the worldwide success of Amazon. Founded in 1994 the world's most important online bookshop already offered 1.3 million titles by 2003. At that time customers of the largest bookshop in New York could choose from 180,000 titles. Amazon's current online database contains several million titles, more than 250,000 different CDs and 200,000 films and entertainment programmes. Today customers can purchase almost anything that is relatively easy to ship by means of a delivery service from Amazon. In addition to many other online suppliers Ebay, the world's largest online auction house, and Hamburg-based Otto Versand, the world's largest multi-channel dealer, can also be included in this category of rapidly growing electronic retail trade.

Apart from the electronic provision of traditional services and the electronic retail trade, the outsourcing of special service functions that could be digitalised soon played a vital role. A typical example of this development is the establishment of call centres — initially in Ireland and later in Morocco and India. Today between 250,000 and 300,000 Indians answer calls from around the globe including after-sales services, active telephone marketing and reminders for outstanding invoices. Other examples relate to the outsourcing of accountancy services, flight reservation systems and routine work procedures regarding tax returns. In 2002 25,000 U.S. tax returns were partially processed in India. By 2004 the figured had risen to 100,000, and estimates for 2006 suggest 360,000.

The long term trend clearly indicates the external processing of increasingly higher quality functions. Indian digital service centres are now able to process complete tax returns and annual accounts. Companies such as Cisco, IBM, Intel or GE have increasingly outsourced their research and development activities to India and even China. The majority of these laboratories and research centres work in permanent digital cooperation with the corresponding development teams in the US. Certain activities, for example in the field of software development, utilise the different time zones and are constantly being forwarded from one development team to the next through a global digital network. Even in the field of evaluating of computer generated tomography scans outside hospitals the various time zones form the basis for global cooperation. Many American hospitals send their images to Australia and even India. Apart from the cost advantages due to lower wages, another decisive advantage is that the evaluation of images taken in the late afternoon is available the next morning.

The fourth development in this respect was, to conclude, the breakdown of physical production processes into separate elements, thus enabling the production of a product's individual components at the most cost-effective locations and their assembly as an end product at a central location. For many years it has been common in the automotive industry to manufacture engines, gearboxes and axles at various sites belonging to the same company. The same applies to the aircraft industry, where individual components are not only acquired from the most cost-effective location but often from facilities where it is possible to make use of specialist experience and related research and development.

A rather extreme example of the component-oriented breakdown of the production process, which, by the way, can also be used to illustrate a fifth tendency in the development of the international division of labour, is the production of Dell laptops. The parts for the twelve main components of a Dell computer can come from 44 different suppliers in twelve countries including three OECD countries (Germany, Japan and South Korea), two Latin American countries (Costa Rica and Mexico) and the rest from Asian countries (mainly China, followed by Malaysia, Taiwan and Thailand). Important components are provided by multiple suppliers in order to ensure that local supply bottlenecks do not disrupt the flow of production. The same applies to the place of assembly, which can be in China, Malaysia or Mexico. The supply of components and the delivery of finished products are carried out by leading logistics companies that are, in a spirit of insourcing, not only responsible for transportation and storage but often also for packaging, customer services and related repair work.

### Renewed Strength of the United States: Endless Economic Growth?

A new geopolitical situation had arisen after the collapse of the Soviet Union, inasmuch as there was now only one military and economic superpower, namely the United States of America. On the one hand, this meant that, apart from regional conflicts, another world war was unlikely to break out in the foreseeable future. On the other hand, the rivalries between the still relevant players shifted increasingly towards the economic and technological sector. Many people believed that democracy and the market economy had finally been victorious in the centuries-long competition between political, economic and social systems. Some observers even let themselves be carried away into labelling the uniqueness of the new situation the "end of history".

Others were confident that the economic upturn which took hold of the US at the beginning of the 1990s after a brief recession was simply the start of a never-ending boom.

Indeed, between March 1991 and March 2001 the United States experienced the longest economic boom period since the 1960s. It lasted ten years compared to the average 49 months during the previous 25 years. At the same time this phase of expansion was characterised by a new dynamic in the development of American productivity. Even after Europe and Japan had made considerable progress in catching up with America after the Second World War, the annual increase of labour productivity in both Japan and Europe was still almost twice as high as in the US, which averaged little more than one per cent between 1973 and 1995. This is precisely what changed in 1996. Up until and including 2004 the annual growth rate of labour productivity in the US was 2.1 per cent, while it fell to 0.9 per cent and 1.5 per cent in the Eurozone and Japan respectively during the same period.

Since this sharp increase in US productivity could not be explained by a decline in employment, two questions arose: How is it possible to explain the sudden rise in the development of productivity and the associated burst of growth in the United States? And why is there no sign of a similar development in the Eurozone and Japan? The prevailing opinion with regard to the first question was that the US had already invested heavily in the information and communications technology sector (IT) in the first half of the 1980s and that the necessary adjustments of the institutional and social environment, in particular with regard to the organisation of work, were already so far advanced by the mid-1990s that the technological change finally bore fruit for the economy as a whole. The four most important determining factors in this respect were: Firstly, the growth of the IT industry induced by high investments; secondly, considerable investments in IT equipment in the other areas of the US economy; thirdly, improvements to the IT infrastructure, including the regulatory environment; and fourthly, the spill-overs of IT producers and IT users from which both the economy and society profited.

In the large countries of the Eurozone (Germany, France and Italy) as well as in Japan, IT industry developed either later or with less dynamism than in the United States and this was exactly the same with regard to the application and diffusion of IT hardware and software. The reasons for this are manifold. With the possible exception of France, none of these countries had a running start in military applications comparable to that of the US. At the beginning of the 1990s the price of IT equipment was significantly higher in Europe and Japan than in the United States. Finally, the application and distribution of new technologies is influenced by the regulatory environment in the same way as the introduction of new innovative products; and not necessarily in a positive way. The fact that regulatory density in Germany, France, Italy and Japan was and still is much higher than in the US was thus another factor which strengthened the international competitiveness of the US in both the short and long term.

The new dynamics of the US economy triggered by the leap in productivity were reflected in the steep increase of private investment, which showed an annual growth rate in excess of 10 per cent in 1996, 1997 and 1998. It was further reflected in the fall in unemployment from 7.5 per cent in 1992 to 4 per cent in 2000: This was the lowest level since the early 1970s. Economic growth, which had only averaged 2.8 per cent in the eight years from 1985 to 1992, rose to an average of 3.8 per cent in the following eight years. The New York Stock Exchange went through the roof: The Dow Jones index increased by roughly 320 per cent between November 1994 and January 2000. The Nasdaq, which reflected the performance of the stocks and shares of so-called "New Economy" companies, was 335 per cent higher in March 2000 than in July 1995. Both indices seemed to have lost all relation to the real economy.

Many things suggested that this loss of reality applied not only to the stock exchange. There is scarcely any other explanation as to why people in some circles seriously claimed not only that the end of history but also, with the New Economy, that the end of economic cycles had been reached. Technological progress, innovations in the

*New York. After Venice in the 15th and 16th centuries, Antwerp and Genoa in the 17th, Amsterdam in the 18th and London in the 19th, New York became the centre of the world economy in the 20th century. Where will the centre of the world economy be in the 21st century?*

financial system and the globalisation of production and distribution structures would, together with the enhanced quality of interventions in economic policy, turn economic cycles into slight ripples on the otherwise calm surface of the water. This is highly reminiscent of the euphoria that greeted the effects of the fine-tuning approach in macro-economic policies in the early 1970s and it must have been a huge shock to those who believed in endless growth when the bubble of the "dotcom boom" burst in the autumn of 2000.

## Changing Economic Conditions
## and Financial Crises
## at the End of the 20th Century

Stock exchange speculators obviously not only work on a short time-scale, but, like many politicians, often also have a short memory. Otherwise they would have realised that every speculative bubble has to have its sudden, and often brutal, end. The initial situation is always characterised by a high degree of liquidity in the economy, low interest rates and easily obtainable credit and therefore profitable, usually short term investment options offering speculative profits. The first investors to discover these assets promising high returns and helping the market to surge ahead can normally be sure of their profits. But when after a certain period of time — following the so-called herd instinct — a large number of investors participate in this lottery and irrational optimism and exuberance spread more and more, forces inherent to the upturn process are created which subsequently lead to its sudden crash. Key factors in this respect are the decoupling of share prices and prices in general from longer term real economic values and the expansion of speculative credit, which accelerates the downward spiral as soon as the peak of the boom has passed.

Even though the process of economic growth and the collapse of speculative bubble this time also followed the above described basic pattern, developments at the end of the 20th century were characterised by a number of new determinants, which decisively affected the scope of the process and the potential depth of the crisis. These new factors, which were also at the root of the speed with which share prices or prices in general rose and fell, included: Firstly, the application of modern information and communications technologies; secondly, deregulation in the financial sector; thirdly, the liberalisation of short term international capital movements; and fourthly, financial instruments which become ever more complex, in particular the rapidly growing trade in derivatives described as "financial weapons of mass destruction" by stock exchange guru Warren Buffett in 2003.

The increasing application of information and communications technologies since the beginning of the 1980s, as well as the Internet after 1991, ensured that any information on price fluctuations and their background spread around the globe within a fraction of a second. Among the unambiguously positive effects of this development were: Increased market transparency, the potential reduction of asymmetric information levels as well as the possibility of carrying out both national and international financial transactions electronically without any loss of time. After all, each of these factors contributed to making things work better and contributed in particular to the increased efficiency of the national and international capital markets. There is, however, no doubt that the increased dynamics and the speed of response of the financial markets due to the application of new technologies can also contribute to increased volatility and uncontrollable cumulative effects.

This relates, on the one hand, to the effects of the normal herd instinct and the fact that central banks have less time to respond in the event of a crisis. On the other, this applies to the problematic macroeconomic implications of computer-aided purchasing and sales programmes. They may not have actually triggered the chain reactions on Wall Street and subsequently on stock exchanges around Asia and Europe, but they certainly intensified them immensely. The so-called "Black Monday" on 19 October 1987 saw losses of roughly 500 billion dollars on the New York Stock Exchange alone. The crash would probably have continued and dragged down the real economy as well if the Federal Reserve Board had not effectively prevented it by immediately injecting liquidity into the marketplace through the purchase of government bonds as well as several reductions of the interest rate.

The deregulation of the financial sector and the liberalisation of the national financial markets, promoted in the 1980s predominantly in the United States and Great Britain, are further developments which, on the one hand, increase the potential for the efficiency of the financial and capital market and, on the other hand, the risk of financial crises. In theory increased freedom for financial institutions brings various advantages with it. It means improved opportunities for financial investors to invest their money where the largest profit can be expected in the context of a wider range of investment options, with adequate risk spreading. Entrepreneurs who require financing usually have a more varied range of offers in a less regulated market, allowing them to define the best loan deal not only according to interest rates but also an extended range of terms and conditions.

The practice, however, also implies a number of risks which should not be overlooked. The following are at the fore: Firstly, that the obligations and responsibilities of the relevant regulatory authorities are not sufficiently adapted to the changed market conditions; secondly, that the deregulation of financial institutions enables access to new businesses whose risk cannot be assessed; and thirdly, that the prospect of state aid in the case of a crisis increases the level of recklessness. Probably the most striking example in this respect is the crisis of the American savings and mortgage banks which led to the insolvency and closure of more than 1,000 institutions between 1986 and 1995. Apart from the consequences of the second oil crisis and the volatility of interest rates, which had already weakened the sector since the end of the 1970s, the combination of mismanagement, corruption, poor bank supervision and political failure during this period resulted in a total loss of 153 billion US dollars, of which American taxpayers ended up paying no less than 124 billion. Furthermore, since the bank crisis was one of the main reasons for a global economic recession in 1991/92, the rest of the world also had to pay its fair share.

Deregulation efforts in the 1980s were, however, not limited to certain national capital markets but—wherever possible—also extended to international financial markets at the instigation of the International Monetary Fund and the US government. The magic word was liberalisation of international payment transactions—and not sim-

*New York Stock Exchange. Today's world financial centre has been the starting point for three far-reaching global economic and financial crises during the past 150 years: 1857, 1929 and 2008.*

ply with regard to foreign direct investment and other longer term foreign commitments, but also in terms of short term capital transactions. The underlying idea was that the exploitation of marginal exchange and interest rate differences would lead worldwide to the optimum utilisation of scarce financial resources, meaning that short term international financial flows could contribute to the global market equilibrium. There is no doubt that this is largely true for industrialised nations with a highly developed banking system. Nevertheless, the question arises here whether international financial transactions amounting to roughly 1.5 billion US dollars each year, a figure approximately thirty times higher than that for global trade, can, under certain conditions, also have destabilising and even negative systemic effects. Massive currency speculations with regard to the devaluation of the British pound in September 1992 and the revaluation of the Japanese yen in 2003 are just two examples amongst many.

Since the demand for complete capital market liberalisation had in the meantime also been directed at the newly industrialising economies, it rapidly led to disaster in those countries which accepted it — namely the Four Asian Tigers and later, as a sort of chain reaction, in Russia and Latin America. The classic example of this is the Asian financial crisis of 1997/98. The turbulence started in Thailand which, despite increasing economic difficulties, tried in vain to use central bank interventions to maintain the parity of its national currency, the Baht, against the US dollar. There were at least three reasons why the Bank of Thailand — just like the central banks of several other Asian Tigers which attempted to support their currencies via interest rate rises and exchange market interventions — had scarcely any chance of success with this action.

On the one hand, the continuous upward revaluation of the US dollar since around 1993 had had a negative effect on the international competitiveness of Thailand's export economy, as it also did in the case of the Asian Tigers which had pegged their currency to the dollar. On the other, at the same time there was a slump in the global demand for computer chips, which meant a considerable loss in export income not

378

only for Thailand but also for Taiwan and Korea. In addition to this, China — after a currency devaluation — appeared as a new and strong competitor in many traditional export markets of emerging Southeast Asian countries. All this resulted in a growing balance of payment deficit for the previously so successful Asian Tigers. Moreover, a particularly high level of nervousness could be sensed in Southeast Asian financial markets. This was caused among other things by many foreign banks and other investors — primarily from Germany and Japan — not hedging their short term financial investments as they believed that, with the dollar peg, there was no currency risk.

After speculation had won its wager with the Thai Baht the stock exchange in Bangkok collapsed and the financial crisis spread to the real economy, the crisis then first erupted also in Malaysia and the Philippines and then in Indonesia and, shortly after, in Korea. Even though Hong Kong was supported by China its stock exchange had to accept losses of more than 60 per cent in just one year, like those of other Asian Tigers countries. Tokyo and Frankfurt each sustained a loss of 38 per cent during the same period and the Dow Jones index fell by 19 per cent. Let us leave to one side the question of the appropriateness of the assistance of the International Monetary Fund and in particular the conditions under which credit was granted, based on the so-called Washington Consensus. Even if there is much to be said in favour of the argument that at least the austerity policy prescribed by the IMF was excessive, there is no clear evidence that the alternative route adopted by Malaysia would have produced better results for the economy as a whole.

It is, however, undisputed that Korea as well as Thailand and Malaysia committed a serious error of policy in maintaining restrictions on foreign direct investment and long term capital imports and liberalising short term capital flows before establishing the necessary institutional arrangements. They should not simply have bowed to the demands of the IMF and the US government in this respect. In terms of economic policy the correct sequence of actions would have been initially to free long-term capital flows, then to strengthen the banking system, the regulatory environment and banking supervision, before finally liberalising short term capital flows.

The stock exchanges in the United States and Europe were to recover quickly from the losses caused by the Asian financial crisis. The decisive factors for this were on the one hand, that the collapse of stock markets in industrial nations — apart from Japan — did not have a noticeable effect on the real economy and, on the other hand, that the capital withdrawn from Asia and other regions affected by the crisis was now looking for investment options in North America and Western Europe. This further boosted the so-called dotcom boom. Japan did not profit from this development. On the one hand, it had still not recovered from the shock of the upward revaluation of the yen following the Plaza and Louvre accords in the second half of the 1980s. On the other, it was still suffering from the crash of the Tokyo Stock Exchange and the bursting of the property bubble in 1990 and 1991. Since the Asian financial crisis, including stagnation in Japan, led to falling prices for raw materials, including for crude oil — which caused the crisis to spread to Russia — the risk of inflation was reduced. This prompted the central banks to keep the interest rate low at first.

As a result and in spite of the transition towards a more restrictive monetary policy since the middle of 1999, a new speculative bubble developed. Professional speculators and trusting investors invested billions of US dollars in companies which had not yielded a single profit and which, when viewed realistically, were extremely unlikely to do so. This bubble burst in 2000. The terrorist attacks on the United States in September 2001 further intensified the crisis on the world's stock markets but first and foremost aggravated its effects on the real economy. Further negative impact was created by heightened tensions in the Middle East conflict, continued economic instability in emerging countries in Asia and Latin America, the invasion of Afghanistan by US troops and the exposure of high-level corruption in a number of important American companies. It was above all thanks to the Federal Reserve Board, which slashed its discount rate from 6.5 to 2 per cent between August 2000 and May 2001, the emergency liquidity injected into the markets by the American, European and Japanese central banks in the immediate aftermath of the terrorist attacks as well as the decidedly strong impulses in financial policy in the United States that the world witnessed a relatively short recession instead of the next global economic crisis.

## *The Sub-Prime Crisis*
## *as a National and International Systemic Crisis*
## *of the Banking and Financial System*

The fact that, in a sense, the seeds for the next crisis had already been sown is, at least with hindsight, confirmed by the following three developments. Firstly, the expansive fiscal policy of the U.S. government led to a renewed ballooning of federal budget deficits — after the U.S. government had actually in the 1990s recorded a budget surplus for the first time for many years. The result was not only an increase in capital imports but also a deterioration of the starting point for a counter-cyclical fiscal policy in case of a crisis. Secondly, financial investors increasingly turned towards the property market following poor results on the stock markets, thus further fuelling the already looming boom in this sector. Consistently low interest rates were an additional incentive in this respect. Thirdly and lastly, from today's point of view and against the background that there was no general burst of inflation apart from a strong increase in property prices, the Federal Reserve Board probably hesitated too long in adopting the restrictive monetary policy that was once again necessary. It must, however, be added that the first increase of the key interest rate by the Federal Reserve Board in August 2004 had no effect on long term interest rates and therefore, with an inverse interest rate structure, did not initially help to slow down the property market.

But all these things — as well as the existing global economic imbalances — were basically only amplification factors. They were not the decisive reasons for the sub-prime crisis, the financial and economic crisis which hit the global economy in 2007 and 2008. It is also not possible to blame this economic crisis solely on the inappropriate behaviour of profit-seeking financial investors and bank managers, although their exaggerated pursuit of yield may have contributed to dubious risk management in individual cases. And the deeper causes for the crisis can certainly not be found in the market economy system or globalisation, as many politicians would have the population believe. Just as with the global economic crisis of the 1930s and the Asian financial crisis, the causes of this crisis are a complex and simultaneously disastrous combination of the in the main rational conduct of key market players and policy errors, this time primarily relating to the national and international regulatory framework of the banking and financial system. Nevertheless, it can also not be denied that internationally integrated financial, goods and service markets can fuel the flames of any financial or economic crisis, whatever its cause, intensifying and accelerating its advance around the world. This particularly applies when the crisis has its origin in a predominant national economy like the United States.

Yet if one poses the questions why the sub-prime boom occurred at all and what the political, economic and social reasons were which allowed it to spiral completely out of control, the following aspects must in particular be emphasised, irrespective of the international dimension: Firstly, the unusually low equity ratio of American investment banks; secondly, the fact that in the US, the liability for mortgage loans is limited to the collateral object and does not include other assets of the lender; thirdly, the increase of the originally common lending limit of 80 per cent to 100 per cent and above in the light of continuously rising property prices; fourthly, quite apart from their lax credit assessment procedures, caused by their profit seeking, the banks came under increasing political pressure to grant mortgages to borrowers whose ability ever to pay back their loans was questionable from the very start; fifthly, the availability of refined techniques, namely the securitisation of dubious loans, by means of which individual banks could legally transfer unacceptable risks to third parties; and sixthly, the systematic overvaluation of the new financial instruments by the rating agencies.

The 1975 regulation stating that the equity ratio of American investment banks had to be 8.3 per cent was simply abolished by the US Securities and Exchange Commission (SEC) in April 2004. The justification for this was that the business partners of these institutions were first and foremost other banks and institutional investors that were able to assess the investment risks of their activities themselves. As a result, the equity ratio of the large investment banks, e.g. Morgan Stanley, Bear Stearns, Lehman Brothers, Goldman Sachs and Merrill Lynch, was only between 3.2 and 4.6 per cent in 2006. This low equity ratio enabled the banks to extend their business volume by 22 to 33 times more than their share capital by expanding their exposure to capital markets. On the one hand, this allowed a return on equity of 25.7 to 40.7 per cent before tax and led, on the other, to profits going to shareholders while any losses had to be borne by creditors and, in the case of an existential crisis, by the tax payers through government rescue packages. It is clear that such an asymmetric distribution of possible profits and losses provides the bank management with an incentive to take extremely high risks. The fact that the bank managers and traders participated in the profits themselves is almost secondary, as in this environment a bank which pursues a conservative strategy becomes a natural target for takeover.

A second asymmetry with regard to making profits and preventing losses that was no less important was caused by the incentive patterns in which the US property buyers operated. Since the liability of the mortgage holder in the United States is, in contrast to Germany and other Continental European countries, limited to the collateral property, regular income and all other assets are excluded from the security and, therefore, not at risk. As long as property prices keep rising a mortgage holder can therefore only win; and house prices in the US did indeed rise by 190 per cent between 1996 and 2004, in other words by an average of 11.2 per cent each year during this period. Financially speaking, the buyer of an overpriced house had nothing to lose, at least with a 100 per cent mortgage, if there were a sudden property market crisis. All he had to do was hand his house keys in at the bank and the mortgage was in practice repaid. Therefore, even at the end, when property prices were clearly excessive, there were constant incentives which resulted in unrestrained speculation.

Another factor which additionally fuelled this process was the Community Reinvestment Act passed in 1977, an initiative of the US government on urban redevelopment and the prevention of the development of slum areas. This Act was revised and re-enforced in 1995 in view of the growing neglect of urban residential districts. The new programme was characterised by policy stipulations which virtually forced banks to grant mortgages with a lending limit of 100 per cent without carrying out credit assessments. These loans, which for political reasons had a strong ethnic orientation and were initially also called Ninja loans (no income, no job, no assets), formed an essential part of the later sub-prime credits. At the same time, this area of mortgages, which were socio-politically motivated by politicians, represents the real social problem today. This group of mortgage holders in particular were to a large extent those borrowers whose inexperience was shamelessly exploited by unscrupulous brokers. And it is exactly this segment of the population which did not buy a property primarily as a speculative investment but in order to fulfil the dream of owning their own home. The problems of this group of house owners could certainly not be resolved by just handing the keys over to the bank.

Yet even these loans proved to be a lucrative business for the banks, as they made a profit from the mortgages in the form of commissions and fees and transferred the risk as so-called mortgage-backed securities (MBS) to their business partners, thus profiting once again. As long as the buyers were American financial institutions, the first buyers, at least, did not usually have illusions about the credit standing of the acquired papers. These institutions normally pooled and structured various MBS papers of various credit standings, thus creating so-called security backed securities (SBS). Quite often papers from other, usually dubious credit risks — for example car financing loans,

384

commercial mortgages or credit card debts — were added and the next generation of papers, subsequently marketed as collateral backed obligations (CBOS), was created. In the end, nobody really had an overview of which risks were hidden how or where, especially as securitisation supposedly went into six generations and more.

It would be going too far to examine here all the details of these transactions. It would require studying the instrument of credit default swaps (CDS), the technique of structuring within the various papers according to different credit standing levels and many other complex constructions. It would also require analysing the influence of the accounting policies of the IFRS, which probably intensified the crisis, being based on current market values and not on the lowest value principle. What is decisive, though, is that despite all the manoeuvres and tricks the risks remained somewhere in the system and that moreover even banks and financial institutions — in the United States and particularly in Europe — often did not have the faintest idea about the junk bonds in which they had invested their assets and those of their clients — unless they had deliberately neglected the risks in favour of quick and easy profit. Aside from the apparently attractive interest rates this is probably the only explanation why a significantly larger proportion of toxic papers remained in the banking system than in the case of the dotcom crisis. Finally, it cannot be denied that the rating agencies' misjudgement of the risks associated with the new financial instruments may well have also played a vital role. Aside from the issue of true independency of these agencies, the fees of which were paid by the banks, the most surprising fact in this context is that quite a few of the toxic papers were accorded a rating which was higher than that of most of their component parts.

When the rational behaviour of an infinite number of individuals and companies leads to private and socio-politically unacceptable results in the existing framework of a market economy, one is drawn to the conclusion that there is a crisis in the system. In other words, the national and international regulatory environment and possibly also the responsible supervisory and control authorities do not meet requirements. In any case the development of the financial sector cannot be called normal when within a single year 83 banks fail or have to be partly or completely nationalised. This is additionally underlined by the consequences of this development for the economy as a whole, which were in the end responsible for turning an expanding financial crisis into a global economic one.

## From a Financial Crisis to a Global Economic Crisis

Three causal mechanisms are primarily responsible for the fact that the problematic development in the banking and financial sector hit the real economy with full force. The first aspect is the expansion of global economic imbalances. Even at the beginning of the 1980s the American savings rate was still roughly 10 per cent; after which it fell constantly until it was almost zero in 2005. Since it is most likely that wealthy Americans still saved a part of their income, this means that the ordinary citizen lived far beyond his means and used credit to finance his consumption. The basis for this was, on the one hand, increasing property prices, which helped to increase credit limits. According to estimates available, consumers spent an extra 8 cents for every dollar of apparent capital gains per household. Another incentive for consumption was mortgages, which could be acquired for up to 125 per cent of the value of the property. They enabled the purchase of not only the house but also of new furniture or a car, which were usually not included in the collateral security.

When private households no longer save, the state permanently records a budget deficit and companies wish to finance at least a part of their investments on the capital market, the only option left to close the financial gap is capital import. And America's capital account deficit has indeed reached unparalleled dimensions in recent years, averaging 5 per cent of the gross domestic product. The main creditors were China, Japan and Germany. China and Japan financed the United States primarily by purchasing government bonds, while German credit institutions also invested their excess liquidity to no small degree in sub-prime securities and related credit default swaps. This backfired drastically when the American property market crashed.

The fall in house prices began in June 2006 and accelerated so quickly during the next two and a half years that there was an average drop in prices of 28 per cent and a loss in value of more than 7 billion dollars by the end of 2007. This resulted in excessive indebtedness of millions of homeowners, drastic losses due to mortgage defaults and therefore also in considerable losses in the case of securities based directly or indirectly on mortgages. Inasmuch as these papers or the mortgages were still in the hands of the banks and balanced at the original market value, this led to a substantial need for write-offs and significant losses in equity. The consequence was, on the one hand, a clear under-capitalisation of many credit institutions and, on the other, increased mistrust within the banking sector resulting in a complete standstill in trading between banks in August 2008 and an extreme reluctance to grant credit to the private economy.

However, the real economy did not simply collapse because of the credit crunch, which spread quickly around the globe due to the international nature of the financial sector. A further factor was the interaction of multiplier and accelerator effects which continually intensified the recession and spread the economic crisis from the US around the whole world. The property crisis resulted in a dramatic decline in building contracts and also in a clear weakening of private consumption due to homeowners' financial loss of assets. The reduced demand of households then hit the consumer goods industry and subsequently also, on top of the credit crunch, private investment. All this together led to a rise in unemployment and a further decline in private consumption. The downward spiral was additionally fuelled by the fall of Lehman Brothers on 15 September 2008, the nationalisation of the world's largest insurance company AIG two days later and the subsequent collapse of stock markets around the world.

387

If one bears in mind that the US economy still represents approximately 25 per cent of the gross world product, it is self-evident that, with a relatively short time lag, the American demand for imports slowed down and the crisis seized the real economy in Europe and Asia, not only because of the international interdependencies of financial sectors but also because of the demand shortfall for goods and services on the world market. Emerging countries in Asia, in particular China, were the hardest hit by the American demand shortfall. Among the industrial nations the global crisis had the worst effect on those countries which, like Germany and Japan, have their comparative advantages in capital goods export. In addition, globalisation-intensive sectors, such as international shipping, shipbuilding and international air services, as well as structurally weak sectors, such as the automotive industry, suffered particularly heavy losses.

It may seem astonishing that the 2008 economic and financial crisis was not the crisis which had been feared for many years, given increasing global economic imbalances. The crisis was not in fact triggered by a lack of confidence in the US currency but by the bursting of a speculative bubble within the United States that, because of the high economic and particularly financial interdependencies of a globalised world, carried the other regions along with it. Aside from the systemic dimension of the crisis with respect to the US economy, attention must also be drawn to systemic aspects of this crisis at international level. These mainly originated in the lasting inadequacies concerning international cooperation with regard to an effective international order for the global financial system.

The sub-prime crisis has at least shown that the equity requirements of the banks and other financial institutes as well as the risk monitoring of banking supervision systems based on the so-called Basel II regulations were still insufficient, that there were still too many opportunities in the financial sector to hide risks in balance sheets or to not specify them at all and that the risks inherent in financial innovations must be made more transparent. Moreover it has become clear during this crisis that rating agencies not only failed in their methods but also that their assessments were by no means free of conflicts of interests.

The short term priority of national and international economic policy was, without doubt, to guide the world economy back onto a path of appropriate economic growth. On this front considerable fiscal stimulus and accommodating monetary policies succeeded in bringing both advanced and emerging countries out of the recession as early as 2009. But even in 2011 the recovery is still hesitant. First it was held back because households, financial institutions, other companies and eventually governments had to repair their balance sheets. Later it remained hesitant as unemployment levels stayed stubbornly high and economic policy stimulus measures were successively withdrawn. And still in autumn 2011 it seems that the downside risks are higher than the upside risks. The former include renewed weakness in the housing markets, in particular in the United Sates and the United Kingdom, an unsettled fiscal situation in the US and Japan and a still unresolved sovereign debt crisis in the periphery countries and also Italy in the Eurozone.

Although the Eurozone debt crisis seems to have changed priorities on the international policy agenda the second challenge resulting from the 2008 economic and financial crisis, namely far reaching regulatory reforms for national and international financial markets, will play an important part in determining whether the next upturn, if it finally becomes self-sustaining and more dynamic, will be of shorter or longer duration. Of course at national level several countries have already strengthened regulatory and super-visory frameworks for the financial sector. And also at international level, the new Basel III agreement, setting higher equity ratios and tougher liquidity standards, is on its way. But it will take until 2013 for the first measures to be implemented and until 2019 for all provisions to be in force. Compared with many time horizons and the speed of reaction in financial markets this is an eternity. Indeed, it appears that the sovereign debt crisis and its implications for the banking system in the Eurozone provide some clear indications that even the strengthened regulations of Basel III and in particular the valuation of sovereign bonds in the balance sheets of the financial institutions may already require a further revision now.

# CHAPTER 10

# Hamburg Metropolitan Region: Vibrant Economic Centre in the North of Europe

H amburg is the economic and cultural centre of the largest metropolitan region in the north of Europe with 5 million inhabitants. The city boasts one of the three largest ports in Europe and is the world's third largest civil aviation industry location. Other leading economic sectors based in the Hamburg Metropolitan Region include logistics, maritime technology, media and IT, as well as life sciences and medical technology. Hamburg is the global centre of container shipping and ship financing. Furthermore, the city has for many years been an up-and-coming centre for national and international trade fairs and congresses.

The Hamburg Metropolitan Region has 27 universities, colleges and technical colleges with roughly 100,000 enrolled students. 85,000 of them study in Hamburg itself and about 10,000 are from overseas. Besides the university and higher education sector, there are approximately 250 research institutes in the region, some of which are internationally renowned, such as the Deutsches Elektronen-Synchrotron (DESY) or the Bernhard Nocht Institute for Tropical Medicine. Other fields of research in which Hamburg's institutes or scientists have made

*The Hamburg Ballet is one of Hamburg's most important cultural ambassa-dors with several tours each year, bringing artistic director John Neumeier's choreographies to all parts of the world. The photo above is a scene from Neu-meier's ballet "Seasons – The Colors of Time".*

fundamental breakthroughs are optics, nanotechnology, composites, climate research, oceanography and meteorology.

Despite its economic importance and dynamic and the fact that it is the largest industrial and port city in Germany, Hamburg is still a favoured place to live and a popular destination for tourists from around the world. Hamburg is the metropolis on the waterfront, boasting more bridges than Venice or Amsterdam, and is seen as one of the most attractive European destinations for cruise ships. Hamburg is a centre for shoppers and a cultural metropolis. The city not only features a wide range of theatres, museums and concerts; it is also one of Europe's top centres for musicals and the ballet company of the Hamburg State Opera is world class. The citizens of Hamburg and even the tourists enjoy the many large public parks and inviting footpaths along the Rivers Alster and Elbe. Hamburg has been award-ed the title European Green Capital 2011 by the European Union.

# From the Concept of a Transborder Axis
## to a Model for the Economic Development
### of the Lower Elbe Region

Hamburg's relationship with its neighbours was initially characterised by fierce competition before increasingly moving towards cooperation. The development of common interests, which initially focused on the safety of shipping on the River Elbe and the expansion of the ports, represented the forefront of this process of change. The Köhlbrand treaties of 1866 and 1909, the Hamburgisch-Preußische Landesplanungsausschuss (The Hamburg-Prussian Regional Planning Committee), established in 1928, as well as the treaty between Hamburg and Prussia, signed one year later, on the formation of a port association that included Hamburg, Altona and Harburg, were important steps in this development. The Greater Hamburg Act of 1937, which incorporated the competitor Prussian ports and Wandsbek, would have provided an opportunity for truly effective, large-scale and longer term regional planning. World War II, however, quickly put an end to any ambitions of this kind.

It was only after the end of the 1950s, when the city's population had exceeded the 1.8 million mark anticipated in the 1950 Development Plan, that questions about the city's relationship to its neighbours were addressed with more urgency. On the one hand, economic relations between Hamburg and the hinterland intensified, and, on the other, the settlement process shifted increasingly to outlying communities. This latter development marked the start of a new long term trend which was particularly promoted by the desire to own a home and by the increasing individual mobility made possible by the car. The rise in the residential density in Hamburg's suburbs, as well as the development of large estates such as Osdorfer-Born or Steilshoop, failed to halt the growing commuter movement. As this process primarily related to the northern hinterland, a joint planning council was established between Hamburg and Schleswig-Holstein in 1955.

A corresponding joint institution for Hamburg and Lower Saxony followed in 1957.

The next urban planning scheme for Hamburg, the 1960 Development Plan, showed the first signs of taking into account changes in the shape of regional politics. The same applies to the bilateral promotion funds, established in 1960 and 1962 between Hamburg and Schleswig-Holstein and between Hamburg and Lower Saxony respectively. Through these funds Hamburg was involved in the financing of certain local infrastructure projects in the neighbouring federal states. However, the real break-through in common regional planning was achieved with the "Entwicklungsmodell für Hamburg und sein Umland" (Development Model for Hamburg and its Hinterland), developed in full cooperation with Schleswig-Holstein and Lower Saxony and presented to the Hamburg Parliament by the then Mayor, Herbert Weichmann, on 2 July 1969. The special features of this model were the explicit, only slightly modified application of the axis concept, developed by Fritz Schumacher 50 years earlier, the definition of Hamburg's city centre as a hub surrounded by central sites with various functions and graded relevance, and the emphasis on an orientation towards the south for future urban development, which could also be found in Schumacher's plans.

As the development model with its axis end-points in Wedel, Elmshorn, Kaltenkirchen, Bad Oldesloe, Schwarzenbek, Geesthacht, Lüneburg, Buchholz and Stade covered an area far beyond Hamburg's borders it could never acquire legal force. However, as a long term framework which at first had no obligations with regard to deadlines or financing, it did excellent service for many years. It determined the main traffic axes, as well as the ring and tangential connections — including an outer northwestern ring from Bad Oldesloe via Kaltenkirchen and Elmshorn and with a permanent Elbe crossing to Stade; it defined the guidelines for possible future developments in housing, workplaces, education, shopping facilities and leisure centres, as well as other community supply systems; and it was used as the decisive policy guideline for cooperation in regional planning across local borders.

394

Apart from confirming the reserve areas for port expansion, already agreed upon in 1960/61 with the explicit aim of improving the competitiveness of the port, the 1969 development model was essentially a regional planning framework for the city region with the goal of creating an attractive urban environment for the population within a radius of 40 kilometres of Hamburg's city centre. The question of the national and international competitiveness of the economic region, and in particular the securing of economic growth, employment and wealth, would, however, have required a different approach. Besides the ideas about a desirable future traffic infrastructure and the specification of possible commercial and business areas, it would have not only been important to pay greater attention to the economic dimensions but also, and in particular, to have taken the economic region instead of the city region as the starting point of these reflections.

Such a concept was presented in 1970 by the then Senator of Economics and Transport of Hamburg, Helmuth Kern, with the "Modell für die wirtschaftliche Entwicklung der Region Unterelbe" (Model for the Economic Development of the Lower Elbe Region). With explicit reference to economic developments in other regions of the Federal Republic — as for example the Rhine-Main region or the regions around Munich and Stuttgart — it was clearly pointed out that economic competition with regard to economic power and wealth not only occurs between specific individual locations but increasingly between regions with higher economic integration, where state, regional, district and other borders play only a minor role, if any.

A region that does not wish to fall behind its competitors needs a strategic vision in terms of economic and location policy which goes beyond these borders. It must develop common concepts for the economic potential of the region and component parts of the region and use them as the basis for setting functional priorities as well as main focuses of promotional activity that have been accepted by everyone. It must guarantee infrastructural planning over and above regional borders, and, whenever necessary, provide joint finance for major projects.

In the economic development model for the Lower Elbe as well as in the urban development plan of 1969, the geographical demarcation of the relevant region related to Hamburg, Schleswig-Holstein and Lower Saxony, but not to Bremen. The end points of the development axes of the new model were, however, extended from Itzehoe to Brunsbüttel, from Kaltenkirchen to Neumünster, from Bad Oldesloe to Bad Segeberg and Lübeck, from Geesthacht to Lauenburg and from Stade to Cuxhaven. With a population of 3.5 million people, this region had more inhabitants than the Rhine-Main region (2.8 million) or the Stuttgart region (2.7 million). It was anticipated that more than four million inhabitants would be living in the North German economic region with Hamburg as its central location by the end of the century. Apart from the inclusion of Lübeck, the 1970 model for the economic development of the Lower Elbe region can with hindsight be viewed as the initial conceptualisation and analytical basis for subsequent preparatory work on the realisation of the Hamburg Metropolitan Region.

## A Northern German State
### versus Institutionalised Cooperation

The fact that it took more than 20 years from the presentation of the model for the economic development of the Lower Elbe region until the Senate of the Free and Hanseatic City of Hamburg and the federal governments of Lower Saxony and Schleswig-Holstein finally decided on 22 November 1991 to intensify their cooperation in the metropolitan region on a trilateral basis and set it on a new, long term foundation, can only astonish someone who has not dealt with the post-war discussion about the territorial reorganisation of the area to be covered by the Federal Republic of Germany.

As early as 1946 the British occupying forces put forward proposals to create larger political and economic units in North Germany and to establish a northern state that would include Schleswig-Hol-

*The Köhlbrand Bridge, inaugurated in 1974, is the second longest road bridge in Germany and with a clear height of 53 metres the highest bridge in Hamburg. It is mainly used for port traffic and carries roughly 30,000 vehicles each day. Because of its bold architecture, it was awarded the title of "the most beautiful bridge in Europe" at the European Steel Construction Award in 1975.*

stein, Hamburg, Lower Saxony and Bremen. This plan was vehemently rejected by today's two city states, and in particular by Hamburg. The reorganisation of the states in the north of the future Federal Republic of Germany was again put up for discussion in 1947. This time it was not the occupying forces but the then Minister President of Schleswig-Holstein who in light of the structural weaknesses of his state had developed the idea of creating a new state called Lower Elbe, which was to include Schleswig-Holstein, Hamburg and northern areas of Lower Saxony. Once again, Hamburg—more than Lower Saxony or Bremen, which was not directly involved—considered this proposal to be wholly unacceptable.

Since the reorganisation of federal territory—with the aim of economic effectiveness—was, according to Article 29 of the West German Basic Law (Grundgesetz), a constitutional issue even after the foundation of the Federal Republic of Germany, it is not surprising that new options were continually being developed by both politicians and economists. Apart from the formation of the federal state of Baden-Württemberg in 1951 and the incorporation of the Saarland in 1957, all these initiatives were without political consequences. Between 1965 and 1972 alone, various minister presidents—including those from Schleswig-Holstein and Lower Saxony—presented six different proposals for the creation of a northern German state that would be viable in terms of population, economic and financial power and wealth. This was complemented in November 1972 by the very thorough and competent report of the so-called Ernst Commission, appointed by the Federal Minister of the Interior, which by contrast envisaged a northern or northeastern state (comparable with the economic region Lower Elbe) and a northwestern state (Bremen and the rest of Lower Saxony).

When this approach also failed—in North Germany due chiefly to fierce resistance by the state governments of Hamburg and Bremen—the German government postponed the reorganisation of federal territory and did not even put it back on the agenda at the time of German reunification. It clearly took a number of negative experiences in the 1970s and 80s to convince at least Hamburg to change its basic political attitude toward the need for intensified and effective cooperation with its neighbours. Significant circumstances contributing to this were the structural crises in traditional economic sectors, such as shipbuilding or the oil industry, the increasing weakening of the city due to migration to the surrounding hinterland, as well as the long term rising budget deficits, which had already forced Hamburg's Senate to announce rigorous austerity measures in 1975. To this was added the realisation that the Lower Elbe region, whose national product per capita was in 1966 still approximately 29 per cent above the Federal average and 8 per cent above that of Bavaria and Baden-Württemberg, was increasingly losing ground to the urban agglomerations in the south and south-west of Germany.

Not only the growing north-south divide within Germany, but also Hamburg's clearly inferior dynamics with regard to population development and economic growth compared to certain foreign economic regions, were in complete contrast to the city's claim to being, as in the historical past, one of the leading, internationally networked economic centres with global significance. It was not about competing with established world-class cities, such as London, Paris, New York or Tokyo. The decisive factor was that Hamburg should be in a position to hold its own in the international competition between locations, as well as in cooperation with second-order economic regions, such as Rotterdam, Barcelona, Milan and the Öresund region in Europe, Toronto and Chicago in North America, and Osaka in Japan.

One aspect in this respect is that a certain critical mass, roughly 3.5 to 4 million inhabitants, is of significance. Another and possibly even more important point is that a metropolitan region is characterised by specific functions relevant to growth, innovation and networking which, usually bundled via their core city, have an internally integrative effect and an external effect that is in equal measure polarising and attractive. Examples of this are decision and control centres of political and economic power, nodes of national and international transport and information systems, clusters of various future-oriented, usually knowledge-intensive activities in the industrial and service sectors, as well as an internationally recognised research base linked to a competitive education system. There is no doubt that these functional categories provide the scope for numerous individual articulations. Nonetheless, a region that wishes to play a successful role in the international competition between locations within an increasingly globalised economy must develop a strategic approach aimed at these criteria.

Furthermore, it is important that such a development strategy — no matter how flexible with regard to a changing economic, technological and social environment — should provide a reliable longer term investment framework for the economy that reaches well beyond a single legislative period. The same applies to the longer term stability of investment data gathered according to economic policy criteria within a framework of consensual cooperation between different, politically autonomous federal states and regional administrative bodies. When considering the policies of the three North German federal governments from this point of view, doubts definitely arise about whether everyone involved in this process was always sufficiently aware of the significance of these requirements. Repeated arguments about energy policy and the deepening of the Lower Elbe can serve as examples.

The 1970 model for the economic development of the Lower Elbe region emphasised positive interactions between the centre and the hinterland in regional development. This means: The stronger the position of the centre, the more beneficial the expected radiation towards the hinterland. And vice versa: The strengthening of the hinterland has a positive effect on the centre. That this is not about creating homogenous spaces but about intensifying the economic and social exchange between the main centre, the various sub-centres and their periphery from the point of view of a functional division of labour is clearly shown in the regional development concepts for the Hamburg Metropolitan Region presented earlier. A first version of this concept was published in 1994; revised editions, including territorial expansion up to Cuxhaven and Brunsbüttel at the instigation of a number of administrative districts in Lower Saxony, were issued in 1996, 2000 and 2005. A new strategic framework for action for 2011 to 2013 was adopted in 2010.

A special amendment to the earlier regional development concepts was the model "Metropole Hamburg – Wachsende Stadt" (Metropolis Hamburg – Growing City) presented by the former Hamburg Mayor Ole von Beust in 2002. Three aspects deserve special attention in this context: *Firstly*, this model, as its title indicates, focuses more on the requirements of the core city than the regional development plans. *Secondly*, the challenges for location policy in the context of internationalisation and globalisation are taken more into account than in the regional development concepts. And *thirdly*, the fact that this amendment was necessary from Hamburg's point of view indicates a further decisive aspect: That consensual cooperation for the development and implementation of an effective strategy in the face of European and global competition between the metropolitan regions is only the second best solution compared to a northern state. This is a fact which cannot be hidden by the successes of the constantly intensified cooperation that began over 15 years ago.

Let us examine just two arguments — among many others — why a northern state is to be preferred to trilateral cooperation with regard to the strategic orientation of regional, cross-border location and development policy for the Hamburg Metropolitan Region. Firstly, it is illusory to assume that substantial differences in goals and conflicts of interest between the partners are in principle excluded when important regional decisions are made. All three federal governments are obliged to act on behalf of their own electorates, and in the case of the two non-city states this obligation relates to the entire federal state and not just to the areas which are part of the Hamburg Metropolitan Region. Cooperation, which in the context of fundamental conflicts of interest in practice means conflict minimisation, can only in exceptional cases achieve ideal solutions for the metropolitan region. Secondly, the economic rule of economies of scale also applies to state administration. Assuming that optimally effective regional administration starts with a unit of approximately five million inhabitants, a northern state and the administrative reforms made possible thereby would not only result in improved decision-making processes, but at the same time contribute to maximising the budgetary efficiency of the participating regional administrative bodies.

## Hamburg Metropolitan Region: Vision and Political Objectives

From early 2012 onwards the Hamburg Metropolitan Region will cover the urban area of the city of Hamburg as well as seven administrative districts in Schleswig-Holstein; eight administrative districts in Lower Saxony and two administrative districts of Mecklenburg-Western Pomerania, as well as the cities of Neumünster and Lübeck.

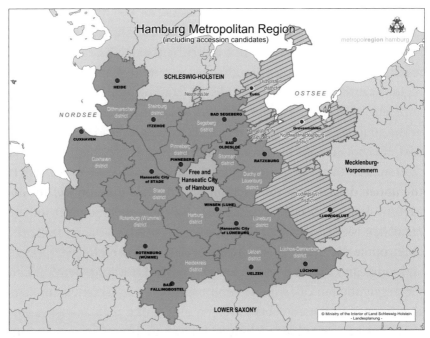

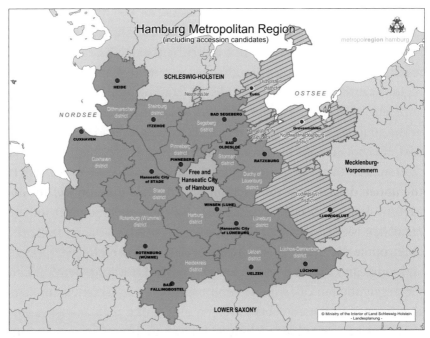

After an enlargement in 2012 the Metropolitan Region Hamburg will have more than 5 million inhabitants of which nearly 1.8 million live in city of Hamburg, 1.7 million in Schleswig-Holstein, 1.2 million in Lower Saxony and more than 300,000 in Mecklenburg-Western Pomerania.

Boasting an area of 26,115 square kilometres and 5.2 million inhabitants, the Hamburg Metropolitan Region will be only second to Berlin-Brandenburg in terms of territory, and amongst the eleven German metropolitan regions it comes fifth behind the Ruhr region, the Dresden/Leipzig region, Berlin-Brandenburg, Frankfurt/Rhine-Main and Stuttgart in terms of population. As far as its gross domestic product per economically active individual is concerned, the Hamburg Metropolitan Region, which recorded roughly 67,000 Euros in 2009, is only outclassed by the Munich Metropolitan Region. Since 2004 Hamburg and its metropolitan region have been in the fast lane as regards economic growth and the development of productivity. When also taking into account as a criterion the internationally networked economy of the metropolitan region, especially in the sectors

402

of port and logistics, shipping and aviation, as well as biotechnology and media, the Hamburg region must belong to the four or five German metropolitan regions which can be said to have not only national but also international, or at least European, importance. The other regions are those around Berlin, Munich, Frankfurt and Stuttgart.

If one wishes to describe and assess the economic and social development of the Hamburg Metropolitan Region in the most recent past, it is not enough simply to present a list of statistical data without reference to the predefined political objectives. The basis for this is the updated version of the "Regionales Entwicklungskonzept für die Metropolregion Hamburg" (Regional Development Concept for the Hamburg Metropolitan Region) of 2000, as well as the 2002 model "Metropole Hamburg – Wachsende Stadt" (Metropolis Hamburg – Growing City) and its revised version of 2003. Both concepts are based on largely the same premises: Firstly, that within the context of a further intensification of globalisation national and international competition between locations will increasingly take place between regions with concentrated and integrated service and production capacities; secondly, that the transition from an industrial society to a globally networked information and knowledge society will further boost structural change and the related pressure on the economy and society to adapt; and thirdly, that it is a question of focusing all the region's efforts in order successfully to face the new challenges.

It is moreover true for the Hamburg Metropolitan Region that the underlying conditions of economic development have changed fundamentally since German reunification in 1989, the opening up of Central and Eastern Europe in the 1990s and the eastern enlargement of the European Union in 2004. As a large European economic centre, Hamburg is no longer located only on the trans-European transport route from Scandinavia to Southern and Western Europe: Today it is — as it was earlier in its history — a major European port, a trade hub between Western Europe and overseas on the one hand, and Central, Eastern and South-Eastern Europe, including Russia, on the other. An advantageous geographical location, an efficient port, combined with the respective knowledge-intensive business services, in particular logistics, as well as a wide range of nationally and internationally competitive companies in other sectors, are, however, only a few of the ingredients for success in the international competition between locations.

There must also be an economic and social policy strategy that is oriented towards the future and actively aims to shape the medium and longer term political and administrative framework for foreseeable economic and social developments. Such a strategy must help to increase the economic power and wealth of the region. It must create a climate and regulatory environment that stimulate the economy and foster structural change, investment and innovation. It must adapt the infrastructure in the broadest sense of the term to future requirements. It must make the city and the region attractive as a dynamic, creative and inviting location for existing as well as future companies and for people who are looking for a new job and/or wish to move.

The Regional Development Concept of 2000 and the model "Metropole Hamburg – Wachsende Stadt", each on its own and understood as a complementary unit, can be seen in this light as a first step in the right direction. However, they must be assessed very differently with regard to their contributions to the formation of a political identity and their power to motivate, with regard to their specific objectives, and with regard to the extent to which they have so far been turned into reality. Particularly the Hamburg model succeeded in creating a spirit of optimism that not only encompassed large parts of the city but, together with the real dynamic that it created, also went further and led to a positive knock-on effect for the region and far beyond. The fact that a large part of the relevant population now identifies itself with the Hamburg Metropolitan Region is a further positive step forward in the development. This clearly shows that the concept of the Hamburg Metropolitan Region no longer merely represents a vision of the political and economic elites but is also felt as a positive reality and a desirable future by large parts of the population.

404

Apart from the objective of further increasing Hamburg's population, the main goals of the Hamburg model and the Regional Development Concept had much in common. Both concepts focused on promoting the growth of the economy and of employment, an adequate expansion of the infrastructure, the appropriate provision of residential and commercial areas, the nationally and internationally efficient promotion of the location, family support, as well as nature conservation and environmental protection. With regard to embedding these objectives in the concept of sustainable development, here defined as a development which meets the requirements of today's generation without endangering the opportunities of future generations, the Hamburg model used the term "smart growth". In respect to the Regional Development Concept, which puts greater explicit emphasis on the needs of environmental protection and sustainable development than the Hamburg model, it seems important to quote at least the following sentence from the official document: "Sustainability requires a dynamic economy in order to ensure prosperity, employment and social stability."

### Competence Clusters
### as dynamic Priority Sectors:
### Potential Gains and Risks

Even if all cities have their own special characteristics, there are certain strategies in economic policy which are of general importance, irrespective of the geographic location, specific economic features relating to function or structure, or the cultural or general atmosphere. Such an approach is the promotion of dynamic activity clusters. In terms of a region, this is a critical mass of large and small companies which have vertical and/or horizontal business relations with each other within the framework of a specific value creation chain and simultaneously profit jointly from a certain physical and institutional infrastructure, including education and research institutions.

As long as a cluster follows a dynamic trend of development and adapts innovatively and flexibly to the permanently changing economic, technological and social environment, or actively shapes the trend in the relevant sector, it offers considerable advantages for the companies and also for the region. Companies benefit from the larger number and wider range of qualified labour, from the concentration of sector-specific services and supply companies, from the prospect of economies of scale, from the reduction of transaction costs, from the availability of a cluster-specific infrastructure, from the greater attention of the political and administrative decision makers, as well as from technology and knowledge transfer. The exchange of knowledge and experience takes place between the companies as well as between business and research, and includes the exchange of "tacit knowledge" and interactive learning. The important thing is that this promotes, in particular, competencies that are primarily created via personal contact, are linked to the locality and can thus scarcely be separated from the cluster.

As a general rule, the advantages of successful clusters for the region are that they send out strong growth impulses for the city and the hinterland — and do so even when the clusters as such do not represent the majority of the working population. As long as clusters maintain their inherent dynamics they increase the potential for innovation and simultaneously lead to a higher rate of new company formations. Moreover, clusters are often characterised by above average productivity increases, so that other economic sectors also benefit from the income effects due to higher wages. Quite often clusters also raise the networking potential with other innovative and dynamic growth regions and can therefore contribute to successful integration into the international network of the beneficiaries of globalisation.

Numerous examples from the economic history of Hamburg prove that the development of clusters is not just a modern-day phenomenon and that clusters do not have an eternal life. The rise and fall of the brewing industry and related trades at the time of the Hanseatic League, the development of the textile industry in the 17th century as well as the development of the sugar business up to the 19th century, but also the post-war boom and decline of the shipyards and some of their supplier industries in the recent past, are striking examples of this phenomenon. During their ascent clusters are characterised by dynamic interaction and creative innovations. The stage of maturity can be longer or shorter, depending on whether the cluster is able to constantly renew itself by means of positive structural adjustment. The decline is usually heralded when the cluster adopts a defensive character.

Yet clusters can, under certain circumstances, also create severe problems of economic policy and this in particular when their development was considered as highly successful over a longer period of time. A good example for this situation is when the cluster policy has forced a region to become one-sided in its area of specialisation. On the one hand, economic monocultures can, depending on the sectoral focus, considerably increase the sensitivity of the regional economy to business cycles and international financial and economic crises. On the other, in the case of a sector-specific structural crisis the difficult question soon arises when and how a policy of government subsidies should be reversed. Experience — including that in the shipyard crisis in Hamburg, but not just there — shows clearly that the preservation of structures that are no longer competitive is politically more attractive than rapid adjustment — even if all the parties involved basically realise that delayed adjustment is economically the most expensive type of adjustment.

Having said this, the question arises how the development of clusters and the policy towards them in the Hamburg Metropolitan Region should be assessed. As the Hamburg Senat continues to support an active cluster policy also at present the general policy concept "Metropole Hamburg – Wachsende Stadt" from 2002 and revised in 2003 still offers a good starting point for this discussion. The economic policy model is "promotion of competence clusters with international significance". A positive point to emphasise is that direct intervention in the market process is fundamentally rejected. The primary

408

goal is the strategic development of already existing structures and potentials by means of the qualification and promotion of young people, cluster-relevant research and development, and the promotion of networks and common marketing, as well as establishing and expanding a cluster-specific infrastructure.

The port industry and logistics, East Asia trade, in particular with China, the aviation industry as well as the media landscape, including IT, have proven to be well-established economic structures with a long tradition in Hamburg that are still demonstrating their national and international competitiveness and at the same time a future potential that is far from exhausted. Two further sectors named by the Senate which relate to growing markets in the 21st century while at the same time being less subject to economic cycles and to crises than traditional areas of activity are the fields of life sciences and renewable energies. Furthermore, the Senate has decided to promote two new and promising horizontal key technologies, namely optical technologies and nanotechnology, within the framework of its cluster policy. Another cluster initiative, called Maritime Economy North Germany, comprising shipbuilding and the shipyard supply industries in Hamburg, Schleswig-Holstein and Lower Saxony is in the early stages of development. It is, however, not yet possible to say whether it will turn out to be an innovative and forward-looking or a defensive venture.


## Positive Structural Adjustment:
### Port Industry – Logistics – China

The economically most important cluster in the Hamburg Metropolitan Region includes port industry and logistics, with a special sub-cluster that relates to the economic relationship between Hamburg and China. The three predominant trends that have characterised port development in recent decades were the continued decline of the shipbuilding industry, the success story of the container and the related industrialisation of maritime transport, as well as the integration and digitisation of the transport chain. Structural changes in the shipbuilding industry were primarily triggered by changes in the competitive landscape of the world's shipbuilding markets, and in the port industry and logistics by technological and organisational progress. The decisive catalyst here was the deepening and widening of the international division of labour, even though it is unclear, particularly as regards the remarkable development in container transport, whether falling transportation costs resulted in the expansion of trade or the increased demand for shipping triggered the unrivalled productivity leap of transportation.

Although Hamburg can still be seen as a universal port with the transhipment of general cargo as well as bulk goods, the decision of the Senate and Parliament in 1967 to place special emphasis in the future on the expansion of the efficient container terminals was fully justified by the subsequent development of this new method of transportation. After a mere 41,000 TEU (twenty-foot standard containers) in 1968, almost 70,000 TEU were already being handled in 1970, which, however, only corresponded to approximately five per cent of the total general cargo transhipment at that time. The figure of one million TEU was exceeded in 1985. By 1995 almost three million TEU were handled, totalling more than 80 per cent of the general cargo transhipment. Ten years later the figure had reached more than eight million TEU, and finally in 2007 the so far all-time record level of 9.9 million TEU, still unbroken in 2011, was achieved. This meant that Hamburg ranked ninth in the world and second in Europe behind Rotterdam, which achieved 10.8 million TEU.

It makes sense that such a dynamic development required an appropriate policy on the part of the Senate. The two key decisions in this respect were, on the one hand, the Harbour Development Act of January 1982, and, on the other, the establishment of the Hamburg Port Authority. Through the Harbour Development Act, which succeeded the Harbour Extension Act of 1961, the territory of the port was extended from 6,300 to 7,500 hectares. Since only parts of the total area will be required in the near future, this can be seen as a proactive territorial provision. The assumption here is that with increasing globalisation there will be a meteoric rise in maritime transport in the future, too, and indeed many things suggest that the 2008 financial and economic crisis and its aftershocks, just like the economic slump in the first half of the 1980s, will have no significant effect on this historical trend.

The establishment of the Hamburg Port Authority (HPA) in 2005 detached all port-related responsibilities from a variety of Hamburg authorities and transferred them to a central institution. The responsibilities of the HPA cover all issues of port strategy and port planning, the modernisation and enhancement of the efficiency of the infrastructure on both water and land, including the harbour railway and roads, the safety of shipping and the maintenance of the harbour waters as well as estate and property management. Apart from the centralisation of responsibilities, the most important element in establishing the HPA may have lain in the fact that the HPA, as an institution of public law, can finance port-related investments directly via the capital market — after prior approval from the tax authority. The importance of this aspect is especially underlined by current estimates for the relevant financial requirements, which for the period up to 2015 amount to 2.9 billion Euros.

The availability of appropriate berth and terminal capacities is, however, only one factor determining a port's competitiveness. Another factor is the further transformation of the port from a place of goods transhipment, which, because of the interruption of the transport flow, lives from reloading, storing and partially also further processing, into an integrated logistics centre where containers are forwarded quickly, promptly and securely thanks to increasingly automated processes. The latter applies to the entire transportation chain from the source of the cargo, wherever that may be in the world, right up to the final recipient. It is clear that such a comprehensive logistical solution can only be achieved in a satisfactory manner via an IT network that is fully integrated across all the involved companies. For almost 30 years now such all-encompassing port and logistics information system has been provided by DAKOSY AG. Shareholders and users of this system include freight forwarders, line agents, transhipment companies, carriers, quay companies, shipping companies and even the customs authority. DAKOSY is also networked to the IT system of the harbour railway, guaranteeing ideal coordination of rail transportation with both the harbour railway and Deutsche Bahn.

Even if a third of all the containers which arrive in Hamburg stay in the metropolitan region, the port is still in permanent competition not only with the neighbouring port of Bremen and in the near future also with Wilhelmshaven, but also with Rotterdam and Antwerp. In order to stay ahead of these competitors in the long term, on the one hand efficient transport links to the hinterland are required, and on the other, in view of the increasing size of ships, the guarantee of a sufficient fairway depth and width in the Outer and Lower Elbe. Existing and foreseeable bottlenecks with regard to both problem areas can, however, not be solved by the Senate and the other interested parties in Hamburg alone. The fact that close coordination with the federal government and/or the other federal states is required for all issues of this kind can be a significant disadvantage, at least when competing with ports situated at the mouth of the Rhine.

The natural hinterland of Hamburg's port is, besides the German interior, the Scandinavian countries and the entire Baltic region, as well as Eastern and South-Eastern Europe, including Austria and Switzerland. Deliveries to the northern catchment area, which accepts, just like the metropolitan region, roughly one third of the containers arriving in Hamburg, primarily take place via feeder ships and only partially via the rail network. Problems with feeder traffic could arise in the medium term due to the restriction of the Kiel Canal to ships with 1,500 TEU. If the canal is not expanded to enable the passage of ships with 2,500 TEU, Hamburg may well lose its location-related competitive advantage in Baltic Sea traffic to Rotterdam. Since the fundamental decisions concerning this issue have obviously been made and even the financial backing seems to be secure, it is important to commence work without delay. In this respect, too, it is important that new opportunities for rail traffic are opened by the planned Fehmarn Belt crossing.

Access to the eastern and south-eastern hinterland is provided mainly via rail links and only to a smaller extent via inland navigation vessels. Similarly, unmistakable problems relating to the handling of this third part of Hamburg's container transhipment have been evident for years. Rail links are operating at the limit of their capacity. Inland navigation has to be directed via the Elbe Lateral Canal. Improvements to the shipping conditions on the Upper Elbe, first and foremost concerning all-year-round navigation with a minimum water depth of 1.6 metres, as specified by the "Bundesverkehrswegeplan" (German Federal Transport Infrastructure Plan) of 1992, are still waiting to be implemented. The ecological concerns raised against the realisation of this measure appear to be short-sighted. It is not just that the deepening of the channel would hardly affect the natural landscape of the Elbe: If only an additional 25,000 containers could be transported on inland navigation vessels, it would result in 15,000 less heavy goods vehicles on the roads.

In the short term, the deepening and widening of the fairway in the Lower and Outer Elbe is more urgent than solutions to the various problems of links to the hinterland. For many years the maximum permissible width of ships in the Panama Canal was the standard benchmark for growth in the size of container ships. These third and fourth generation so-called Panamax ships with a cargo capacity of 3,000 to 5,000 TEU were up to 295 metres long, had a maximum width of 32.5 metres and a draught of 13.5 metres. The 1976 Harbour Plan envisaged adjustments to the Elbe fairway to accommodate ships of this size. This plan was implemented roughly 20 years later. This latest fairway deepening was actually not completed until 1999; i.e. more than five years after the next generation of container ships with a capacity of roughly 6,000 TEU and a draught of up to 14.5 metres had entered service. A capacity of 8,000 TEU and a draught of 14.5 metres have been standard practice since 1997.

Only ships with a draught of up to 12.5 metres can currently call at Hamburg's port irrespective of the tide. Fully laden container ships of the third and fourth generation can only reach Hamburg when the tide allows it within a time window of a good hour. Ships of the fifth and sixth generation can only visit Hamburg when they are not fully laden. Departure from the port with a draught of 14.5 metres is practically impossible even on the flood wave, due to the early reverse tide. In the highly capital-intensive industrialised maritime transport sector, this situation is economically unviable for shipowners, terminal operators and clients who usually work according to the just-in-time principle. There is absolutely no doubt that the decision about a prompt further deepening and widening of the Elbe fairway revolves around the question whether Hamburg wishes to remain a world-class port in the future or not.

It goes without saying that risks should not be taken with regard to the safety of the dykes and that justified environmental concerns must be taken into account. At the same time, economic realities should not be forgotten either: *Firstly*, that roughly 163,000 jobs in the Hamburg Metropolitan Region are directly or indirectly dependent upon the port, of which almost 60,000 people do not actually live in Hamburg but in the area around, in Lower Saxony and Schleswig-Holstein; *secondly*, that approximately 70 per cent of port-related jobs are associated with container transhipment; *thirdly*, that more than 50 per cent of the containers handled in Hamburg's port are involved in trade with Asia, predominantly with China, Singapore, Japan and South Korea; and *fourthly*, that it is generally the Europe-Asia route on which fifth and sixth generation container ships with a capacity of up to 13,000 TEU and a draught of 14.5 metres and more are increasingly being used. The next generation of container ships will accentuate these problems.

The trend to increasingly larger ships has not been hit by the 2008 economic crisis, which has resulted in a severe slump in global trade and a dramatic fall in freight rates. On the contrary, it has been further intensified. The success of the container has always been linked

More than 200 years of Hamburg
maritime shipping tradition

**The Aug. Bolten shipping company**

At home on the seven seas

to the fact that container transportation is eight times more productive than traditional general cargo shipping. With the transition from 8,000 to 12,000 TEU ships, a further gain in productivity of between 20 and 25 per cent can be recorded. This is a clear indication of which type of ship will be the standard in the future — a ship which already requires the Elbe fairway to be deeper than 14.5 metres. If the currently planned deepening and widening of the Elbe fairway is further delayed and Hamburg misses out on this opportunity, the consequences will be felt far beyond the port industry.

As far as German foreign trade is concerned, Hamburg represents the hub for the dynamically developing economic relationships with Asia and, in particular, with China which, including Hong Kong, had no less than a 35 per cent share in Hamburg's container traffic in 2010. More than 700 Hamburg-based companies are actively involved in trade with China. Hamburg is the gateway to Europe for many Asians. Of the approximately 4,000 branch offices of foreign companies in Hamburg, roughly 650 are the European and/or German headquarters of Asian companies. 400 of them come from China alone. Japan is represented with roughly 100 companies. It is scarcely credible that these companies will still prefer Hamburg as a location if the city's port becomes a "secondary port", which, in terms of Asian trade, is only supplied via feeder ships from Rotterdam and Antwerp.

Another question is what will become of the other elements that are currently an integral part of the port and logistics cluster as well as the China cluster under such conditions. This applies, on the one hand, to certain flagship events, such as the top-level economic conference "China meets Europe", which has been organised bi-annually by the Hamburg Chamber of Commerce since 2004. On the other, Hamburg's previous successes in establishing and promoting logistics-related educational and research institutions could also be put into question. Besides institutions specialised in initial and further training the main players in academic education would also be affected: The Technical University of Hamburg-Harburg and the associated newly established Fraunhofer Center for Maritime Logistics and Services, the Kühne Logistics University and the Hamburg School of Business Administration, as well as the Northern Business School, the University of Hamburg, the Helmut Schmidt University and the Hamburg University of Applied Sciences. The relevant areas of education and research in this respect are logistics and logistics management, operation and supply chain management, as well as shipping and ship financing.

The additional fact that the International Tribunal for the Law of the Sea and the International Logistics Court of Arbitration are also based in Hamburg should be mentioned for the sake of completeness.

## Hamburg Metropolitan Region:
### *The World's Third Largest Hub for the Aviation Industry*

The port, shipping and foreign trade, indeed, even the press and publishing industries have played a huge role in the way Hamburg has been seen around the world for centuries. However, it is much less well known that aviation has been a major feature of Hamburg for more than 100 years. On 5 March 1910 Graf Ferdinand von Zeppelin held a rousing speech, convincing the merchants of Hamburg that aviation would be the long-distance means of travel in the future. Just one year later the Hamburger Luftschiffhallen GmbH was founded in Fuhlsbüttel; today's Hamburg Airport is therefore the oldest German commercial airport still in operation. In 1919 regular flights to Berlin commenced; and significantly it was a shipyard, namely Blohm & Voss, which started constructing seaplanes in Hamburg-Finkenwerder in 1933. During the Second World War the flying boat BV 138, then the world's largest plane, was built there. Today the Hamburg Metropolitan Region is the world's third largest civil aviation hub after Seattle and Toulouse.

The key players in the aviation cluster in the Hamburg Metropolitan Region are Airbus, Lufthansa Technik and Hamburg Airport. They are joined by approximately 300 predominantly medium and small-sized companies which function as suppliers and service providers. The total number of employees in this sector amounted to almost 40,000 in 2010, of which roughly 17,000 worked for Airbus, 7,500 for Lufthansa Technik, almost 6,000 directly and indirectly for Hamburg Airport, and about 9,000 for the remaining approximately 300 aviation-related companies. These figures do not include people employed in aviation-specific activities at Hamburg's various training and research facilities or the almost 7,000 employees of Airbus in Bremen, Nordenham and Varel, which, by contrast with Stade and Buxtehude, belong to the North German aviation cluster but not to the Hamburg Metropolitan Region.

In Hamburg-Finkenwerder Airbus operates a fully integrated aircraft plant whose areas of competence range from development and production to delivery. Apart from a smaller assembly facility in Tianjin/China Airbus Hamburg is the central location for the assembly and delivery of all single-aisle aircraft of the Airbus fleet, including the Airbus A318, A319, A320 and A321. The Senate also saw many heated discussions before creating the conditions for the extension of the runway at the Airbus plant, thus ensuring Hamburg's participation in the construction of the Airbus A380, currently the world's largest commercial airliner. Today the Hamburg facility is responsible for the structural and equipment assembly of all front and rear fuselage sections. Moreover, the complete interior fitting out, paintwork and final acceptance as well as delivery to customers in Europe and the Middle East are carried out in Hamburg.

One special focus for all types of Airbus is the Hamburg facility's competence in the development of cabins and cabin systems. The special value of this specialisation in terms of economic policy lies in its positive employment effect. On the one hand, cabin systems are one of the most work-intensive stages of aircraft production and, on the other hand, each cabin is usually redesigned three times during a plane's life cycle.

With its 28 operating subsidiaries and affiliates in Europe, America and Asia Lufthansa Technik is world leader when it comes to the

*The Airbus 380, currently the world's largest civilian passenger airliner. The bow section, the front and rear body parts as well as the rudder assembly come from Germany; the central body section and the cockpit are manufactured in France; Great Britain delivers the wings and Spain the elevator assembly. Final assembly takes place in Toulouse. Cabin furnishing and external painting are subsequently carried out in Hamburg. Airbus has two delivery centres: Toulouse for customers from North and South America as well as Asia and Africa; and Hamburg for customers from Europe and the Middle East.*

maintenance, repair and overhaul of commercial airliners, including their engines and components. Logistics is another key area, especially in terms of the fast and worldwide provision of spare parts for aircraft. In the corresponding circles Lufthansa Technik is moreover recognised and valued worldwide for turning normal commercial airliners into luxury business and private jets, the range extending from the small Airbus family A318 Elite and A319 ACJ to the Boeing 777 and the A380. In close association with its support of maintenance optimisation for more than 300 airlines and its development of functional and/or luxurious VIP jets Lufthansa Technik also maintains its own development centre for cabin components.

Apart from its strategic role in the national and international air transport links of the metropolitan region Hamburg Airport, which served 13 million passengers in 2010, is active in the worldwide marketing of its competence in the areas of airport management, environmental protection and the conceptual design of future airports. The range of services offered by the suppliers and service providers of Hamburg's aviation cluster goes far beyond just cabin technology and interior fitting. The Stade Airbus plant specialises in the processing of carbon-fibre reinforced plastics and supplies the rudder assemblies for all Airbus aircraft. Other companies manufacture products and coating systems for surface protection or are active in the field of measuring and control technology. The multitude of special components and equipment elements supplied by third parties is almost beyond imagination.

Companies in the service sector are also concerned with engineering services in design, construction, technical documentation and IT consultancy as well as with logistics. For example, a subsidiary of the world's third largest logistics provider, Kühne & Nagel, situated approximately 12 kilometres away from the Hamburg Airbus plant operates a fully automated logistics centre to ensure the just-in-time supply of almost 50,000 parts to the production facility. For certain components, e.g. doors, even the pre-assembly of accessories is carried out at this centre. In order to optimise the production process the entire logistics of Airbus, including that at other German and European locations, has been outsourced, making the logistics supplier an integral part of the supply chain.

All the activities of the three large and also the various small companies of the cluster are supported and accompanied by a wide range of cooperation in the areas of application-oriented research and development as well as initial and further training. As with the port and logistics cluster, the key players are once again the Technical University of Hamburg-Harburg, the Hamburg University of Applied Sciences and the Helmut Schmidt University. They are joined by the Technical Centre in Hamburg-Finkenwerder, which is specialised in aircraft construction, the Hamburg Centre of Aviation Training (HCAT), through which the aviation cluster of the Hamburg Metropolitan

Region also underlines its claim to be a centre for initial and further training as well as qualification in professions relevant to aviation construction, and finally the Centre for Applied Aviation Research (ZAL), founded in June 2009. The main focus of research and training includes, amongst other things, materials technology, optimisation of structural components, aerodynamics, flight control, safety technology, cabin systems, fuel cell technology and systems engineering.

In 2000 the Hamburg Parliament passed an Aeronautics Research Programme that granted subsidies totalling 18 million Euros to 42 research projects until the end of 2005. This programme was continued between 2006 and 2010, providing subsidies worth 26.9 million Euros. In 2008 Hamburg's aviation industry was chosen by the Federal Ministry for Research as one of the five most important German economic clusters out of an original group of 38.

This means that within this programme, running until 2013, Hamburg's aviation cluster is carrying out three flagship projects and more than 20 research and technology projects totalling 80 million Euros, of which 40 million Euros will be funded by the German Federal Government. With the exception of the research and development sector, the aviation industry is also supported by the Senate of the Free and Hanseatic City of Hamburg in respect to the qualification of employees, international cooperation and cluster management.

The momentum of cluster and government funding, not only for the provision of commercial areas and an adequate infrastructure, but first and foremost also in the areas of training and qualification, as well as research and development, should help the North German aviation cluster to remain a technology- and innovation-intensive growth engine for the Hamburg Metropolitan Region as globalisation progresses. However, it should also be remembered that the aviation sector is particularly susceptible to economic changes and crises. Worldwide epidemics, terrorist attacks on aircraft, economic slumps as well as financial and economic crises will always lead to considerable turbulence in this sector.

## Creative Industries: Media – IT – Design

Hamburg has also always been a popular location for the press and publishing industry. In 1830 Hamburg was considered the city with the most newspapers in Germany. After the Second World War it was the British occupying forces that turned Hamburg into the press capital of the Western Zones and later the Federal Republic of Germany. Since this sector is geared towards urban centrality and the density of active information networks it is not surprising that the media industry as well as the currently closely related IT and design sectors now represent a further important competence cluster in the Hamburg Metropolitan Region.

The advertising industry, including public relations, publishing and printing houses, radio and television, as well as the film, music and culture industry, all belong to the media sector. Of the more than 25,000 companies employing almost 66,000 people in this sector, about 15,000 operate in the field of advertising and PR. However, the longer term competitiveness of the location is not decided by the critical mass but primarily by the quality of the services on offer. The fact that Hamburg's advertising industry passes this test, too, is proven by its numerous national and international awards. Hamburg-based agencies are award winners at the Cannes Lions International Advertising Festival on an almost regular basis — a competition whose top award in the advertising industry is comparable with the "Golden Palm" of the Cannes film festival.

Even though a number of national daily newspapers have relocated to Berlin, Hamburg is still considered as the German press centre. Besides some local daily newspapers with a relatively high circulation, 50 per cent of the German mass circulation press is still published in Hamburg; this includes 80 per cent of all German TV guides. The stars of Hamburg's press include what is probably the most up-market weekly newspaper, *Die Zeit*, the critical news magazine *Der Spiegel* and the magazine *Der Stern*, which is renowned amongst other things for its informative photo articles. The economics magazines *Capital* and *ManagerMagazin* are also published in Hamburg. However, these newspapers and magazines are not necessarily those amongst Hamburg's magazine and newspaper production with the highest circulation. Nonetheless, nine out of the ten German magazines with the highest circulation come from Hamburg.

In addition to the large periodicals publishing houses the Hamburg Metropolitan Region is also home to many acclaimed book publishers, here too maintaining an old tradition. In the 19th century there were a number of courageous publishers in Hamburg who were not afraid to publish the first editions of books dealing with the social and political issues of the day, some of which are still relevant today. Heinrich Heine, whose main publisher had been Julius Campe since 1827, and Karl Marx, whose first volume of *Capital* was published by Meißner in 1867, are prominent examples. Today there are approximately 100 book publishers in Hamburg. Some of them, for example Rowohlt, have established a reputation far beyond Germany's borders.

Besides the approximately 2,000 companies in the publishing industry, the roughly 650 companies in the printing business and the various firms in the film industry, as well as the radio and television sector that represent the traditional areas of Hamburg's creative industries, an extremely dynamic IT market with around 9,500 companies has become established in Hamburg in recent years. One of the most important reasons for this is the increasing fusion of technology and contents. In 2000, that is to say, before the dotcom crisis, *Time Magazine* called Hamburg "Germany's Hottest City for Digital Media". At that time nobody could have imagined that just two years later Hamburg would be making headlines as the bankruptcy capital of the new economy. Today Hamburg is once again one of the booming European regions of the application-oriented IT industry.

The four strongest sections of this industry are the multimedia area with 2,800 companies, data processing services with roughly 2,300 companies, software consultancy and development with approximately 2,000 companies, as well as hardware consultancy with 1,500 companies. The production of equipment and components as well as the telecommunication sector represent just four per cent of all IT companies in Hamburg. However, in contrast to the other segments of this industry, which are characterised by a prevailing small business structure, a number of large companies with several thousand employees are active here. These include the European headquarters of Sharp and Olympus and the German headquarters of Panasonic and Philips.

While the multimedia service providers and a number of extremely successful commercial and informative websites, for example *Spiegel Online*, have turned Hamburg into an Internet hotspot, the city is now well on the way to becoming known as a national and international "game city". A total of 150 companies with roughly 2,200 employees produce products for the computer games market, which ranges from online and mobile games to console and PC games. Although the computer games industry only became established in Hamburg after the dotcom crisis, several of the most popular computer games in Germany come from Hamburg today, despite the still relatively long production times.

The decisive factor for this successful development is, amongst other things, state funding for the enhancement of the industry's basic conditions. This includes, on the one hand, the "Initiative Gamecity: Hamburg", a public-private partnership which represents the largest regional network of the digital game industry in Germany. On the other hand, Hamburg supports this new growth sector by means of prototype funding for business start-ups as well as the dedicated property "Gamecity: Port", supported by public-private finance, which provides new gaming sector businesses with small offices at reasonable terms and conditions for a maximum of three years. Neither should one underestimate the significance of this increasingly important professional environment for the gaming sector. The more complex games become, the more important it is to have continuous contact, to exchange experience and ideas, as well as to cooperate with other sectors of the media and IT cluster.

It is often forgotten that design also belongs to this cluster. Design is everywhere — from product design for toothbrushes, drills, kitchen furniture and computer keyboards, to communications design for annual reports, election posters, holiday brochures and PR brochures. Product and communication design often go hand in hand. This is particularly the case when it is not only a question of a product being practical, stylish and affordable, but when its purchase and use is associated with certain social or political values. Examples of this are, on the one hand, luxury goods, such as extravagant fashion items or expensive cars which are intended to raise the self-esteem and image of their owner. On the other, this also applies to goods and services that express a specific lifestyle, for example a commitment to environmental protection.

There are currently more than 2,000 design companies and freelance designers in Hamburg, of which, according to their own figures, roughly 75 per cent are active in communications design and 25 per cent in product design. There are numerous reasons why Hamburg has increasingly become not only a media and IT hotspot over the past ten years but has also made a mark for itself as a competence centre for design. Firstly, design has become ever more important for the sales of goods and the transmission of ideas in recent years; secondly, there is a high concentration of consumer goods industries in the Hamburg Metropolitan Region for which design, apart from advertising, plays a vital role both for the products themselves and for their packaging; thirdly, beside traditional photo and graphic design, Internet design has gradually become more and more important not only for the economy in general, but first and foremost also for the media sector; and fourthly, the mutually complementary relations between media, IT and design have in general become increasingly intertwined in recent years.

Hamburg offers a broad selection of opportunities for training and further education in all three sectors. Just as with the port and logistics cluster and the aviation cluster, Hamburg has at its disposal a wide range of specialised schools and research institutions. The field of media management is, for example, covered by the Hamburg School of Business Administration, the Hamburg Media School as well as the Hans Bredow Institute. Journalists are trained at the Akademie für Publizistik, the Henri Nannen School and the Hamburg Media School. The Miami Ad School offers special courses in advertising. The specialist area of the Animation School is the field of digital video contents. To this must be added a range of lectures related to media, IT and design at the University of Hamburg, the Technical University of Hamburg-Harburg and the Hamburg University of Applied Sciences.

Given the increasing cross-sector demand for networking—between producers and users as well as between economy, science and administration—the initiative Hamburg@work was founded in 1997. With more than 2,500 members from more than 650 companies, this public-private partnership is today the largest national network of the media, telecommunications and IT industry.

The three principal lines of action of Hamburg@work include: *Firstly* the media city Hamburg which combines all support activities for the media and advertising industry; *secondly* the eCommerce City-Hamburg which promotes Hamburg as a leading location of the national and international online business; and *thirdly* gamecity Hamburg which through the "Gamecity Port" and other initiatives enhances the dynamic development of the digital game industry in the city.

### Competence Clusters in New Growth Sectors: Life Sciences and Medical Technology as Well as Renewable Energies

In contrast with the traditional sectors, where the comparative advantages of Hamburg are self-evident, coverage of the new sectors must focus on very particular fields of activity that are specific to Hamburg and demonstrate internationally recognised excellence here, rather than attempting to cover every aspect of them. Only then will it be possible to turn these clusters into an unmistakeable feature of Hamburg's location profile by which the city and its hinterland can clearly differentiate themselves from all other locations which, following a certain trend, have also recognised the fields of life science, renewable energies, as well as nanotechnology and optics as promising sectors.

In the fields of life sciences, medical technology and pharmacy Hamburg can look back on a long tradition just as it can in the traditional sectors. C.H.F. Müller was established in 1865 and became the first company to produce technical X-ray tubes just a few weeks after the discovery of X-rays in 1895. The Hamburg plant has been part of the Philips Group since 1927 and is considered one of the most state-of-the-art production sites for X-ray tubes and equipment in the world today. A further example is Beiersdorf, whose founders developed and patented the world's first adhesive bandage in 1882. Today Beiersdorf, which is still based in Hamburg, is one of the world's leaders in the pharmaceutical and cosmetics industry and the "Hansaplast" brand is the market leader in more than 20 countries.

It would go too far to list the wide range of biotechnology, medical technology and pharmaceutical companies which — although highly regarded around the world and in Europe — call the Hamburg Metropolitan Region their home. In the processing industry alone, meaning without pharmaceutical trade and healthcare, this sector includes roughly 500 companies. Moreover, Hamburg boasts a number of internationally renowned research institutions in the field of life sciences. Most of them are located at the University of Hamburg, with the University Medical Centre Eppendorf and the Heinrich Pette Institute for Experimental Virology and Immunology leading the way. Life sciences-oriented research is also carried out at the Technical University of Hamburg-Harburg and at the Hamburg University for Applied Sciences. Furthermore, outside the university environment, Hamburg's life science scene encompasses the Bernhard Nocht Institute for Tropical Medicine and numerous special activities of DESY (Deutsches Elektronen-Synchrotron). In addition to these primarily government-financed research centres Hamburg is also the home of

Germany's largest private clinical research organisation, Askelpios pro-research.

The majority of these companies and research institutions have existed for many years. It is therefore astonishing that cooperation between the individual companies and the exchange between economy and research only took place selectively and more or less accidentally for many decades. The economic structure, which is predominantly based on small businesses, may be one of the reasons for this; the traditionally invisible barrier between economy and independent science another. Additionally, it is not unusual in real life that a latent potential for development is not fully used when it is based solely on the local decision-making process that determines market activity. This was exactly the situation in which a state initiative was able to promote the overall networking of the various fields of activity and help to build links between potential cooperation partners by instituting a cluster.

The North German Life Science Agency Norgenta was thus founded in 2003; not, however—as originally planned—as an institution of the Hamburg Metropolitan Region, but as a project and service company of the federal states of Hamburg and Schleswig-Holstein in order to coordinate the increasing life science activities in North Germany. Norgenta's tasks include enhancing the region as a location by creating networks between companies already established in the region, recruiting and promoting new companies and research institutions as well as initiating and subsequently supporting strategic, innovative projects in medicine, medical technology, biotechnology and pharmacy.

Beyond that Norgenta plays a leading role in the international positioning of the North German life science cluster. One example of this is Norgenta's representation of the interests of the region in the ScanBalt meta-network. The biggest and most visible international success to date in which Norgenta played a decisive part is probably the establishment of the "European ScreeningPort" in Hamburg. This is a European centre for modern drug research which provides the link between academic research and the pharmaceutical industry by providing the reliable and cost-effective identification of new drugs in standardised development processes and therefore advancing their further development for tomorrow's medicines. There is no doubt that the ScreeningPort will also play an effective role in firmly establishing the North German life science cluster in the international marketplace.

The future will show if and to what extent this will also be possible in the area of renewable energies. The preconditions are very favourable. There is little doubt that the demand for renewable energies and for the installations required for their generation — considerably. According to Bloomberg in 2010 alone world investment in renewable energies amounted to more than 200 billion dollars, and the trend is rising. The worldwide installed capacity for wind energy, for instance, is forecast to increase from 100 GW in 2010 to 850 GW by 2020. German equipment producers will particularly benefit from the decision that the government is committed to raising the share of renewable energies in electricity production to about 35 % by 2020. Beyond this, a strong home market is normally the best platform for successful exports.

In the Hamburg Metropolitan Region, as well as in the rest of Schleswig-Holstein, the production of energy generation installations focuses primarily on the areas wind and biomass, but also in particular in Hamburg on hydrogen which is an important energy carrier and means of energy storage. Furthermore, there are quite a number of companies active in project development and the planning of installations, as well as their certification. A further relevant service sector is financing, which is in part being directed specifically towards "green projects". A total of approximately 400 companies belong to the renewable energy sector in Hamburg and Schleswig-Holstein, of which, however, only 100 are actually based in Hamburg. This industry also provides employment for roughly 9,000 people in Schleswig-Holstein and approximately 2,000 people in Hamburg.

These figures do not include employment in the relevant research infrastructure.

# Big Wheels Turning

## Vision Hamburg – Responsible Growth

Hamburg is feeling the winds of change: The metropolitan region has championed wind energy since the early nineties. The unique concentration of wind energy enterprises and facilities in Hamburg is truly electrifying. Many renowned companies have based their headquarters or distribution centers in the city on the Elbe River. Hamburg also is home to the world's leading institutions for the certification of wind power plants.

www.hamburg-economy.de

Hamburg

Research on renewable energies is carried out in Hamburg at the Hochschule für Angewandte Wissenschaften, the Technical University Hamburg-Harburg and the Helmut Schmidt University and in the wider Metropolitan Region in universities and institutes in Lüneburg, Stade, Buxtehude and Lüchow-Dannenberg. Regarding the four latter locations it is interesting to note that they are situated in Lower Saxony. Research in Schleswig-Holstein is concentrated in Kiel, Flensburg and Lübeck.

Apart from the special case of hydrogen and also fuel cells, neither Schleswig-Holstein nor Hamburg has limited itself to any particular specialisation in the broad spectrum of renewable energies. This is in principle to be welcomed, since here it is indeed a question above all of entrepreneurial decisions. Nonetheless it seems as if Schleswig-Holstein has found its regional strength in the areas of biomass and wind energy, while Hamburg appears apart from hydrogen to be specialising in the areas of solar energy and services geared towards renewable energies, such as planning, maintenance and financing. This means that the sector-specific value added chains as well as the relevance of research are very rarely limited to just one of the federal states. Since the corresponding cluster management is still in the development phase in both federal states, one might well ask whether a solution supported by both, Hamburg and Schleswig-Holstein, similar to the one for life sciences, would not be the better arrangement here, too. In the light of recent and ongoing developments at the international level, in particular in the United States, China and India, one might even be in favour of a North German cluster including Lower Saxony and Bremen instead of a bilateral one.

## The Targeted Promotion
## of Horizontal Key Technologies: Optics
## and Nanotechnologies

The clusters for key horizontal technologies optics and nanotechnology, also initiated by Hamburg, are completely different to the traditional clusters, where the policy is based on promoting competitiveness and innovation in existing economic structures by indirect funding and networking. The decisive goal here is to prevent Hamburg losing ground to its national and international competitors in terms of research, development and application. This relates to both efficient technology transfer to existing economic sectors as well as the expansion of the development potential of completely new activities. After all there can be no doubt that a location where these two technologies are not mastered and widely used will fall behind in global competitiveness — and not just in the high-tech sector but also in many traditional areas.

Optical technologies have always been applied to generate and utilise light. Other traditional applications included spectacles, binoculars, sextants, cameras and video equipment. Today modern optical technologies in the form of DVD players and flat screen TVs are used in almost every household. With regard to their commercial and industrial application optical technologies are found in measurement technology, medical technology, information and communications technology as well as production engineering. Examples of industrial applications which are either common or are currently being further developed in Hamburg include laser-guided machine tools, printing technology and image processing communications systems, laser-based welding equipment for shipbuilding and vehicle construction, as well as laser-generated structures in aircraft construction.

Already 2007 more than 500 laser systems had been installed in more than 100 companies in Hamburg and surrounding areas. Many of these companies — both in Hamburg and nationwide — are medium-sized companies. This offers Hamburg a great opportunity as the investments required to catch up with competitors, for instance in the south of Germany, are not as high as in the traditional capital-intensive industries. It is, however, remarkable that the percentage of employees in this sector with a university degree is 21 per cent compared to an average of just 8 per cent in the processing industry. The corresponding figures for the costs for research and development are 9.7 per cent and 5 per cent. Both highlight the vital need for appropriate training and research activities.

The current training and research institutions in the Hamburg Metropolitan Region include the Institute of Applied Physics and the Institute of Laser Physics at the University of Hamburg, the Institute of Laser and System Technologies at the Technical University of Hamburg-Harburg, DESY as well as GKSS in Geesthacht. In addition, the Laser Zentrum Nord founded in 2009 as a link between science and industry is now providing particularly the small and medium-sized businesses in the metropolitan region with access to the results of the latest research in laser technology. In 2012 a Centre for Free Electron Laser Science, which is currently being established for 50 million Euros immediately adjacent to the DESY campus, will open up further important research options, especially in the field of X-ray lasers. An operational approach to cooperation between business and science across several federal states can be seen in the Hamburg-based competence network HansePhotonik e.V., which not only includes Schleswig-Holstein and parts of Lower Saxony, but also Bremen.

The second key horizontal technology which is specifically promoted in Hamburg is nanotechnology. In principle, this is an umbrella term for a wide range of quite varied technologies which, however, all have one thing in common; that is, they refer to structures and processes on the nanoscale. With regard to the structures, this means at least one dimension must be smaller than 100 nanometres: One nanometre being defined as one billionth of a metre. With regard to the technology, it is about producing modules of this size in a targeted manner and/or manipulating them with respect to their properties.

The potential application range of nanotechnology is almost unlimited. The building industry, the chemical and pharmaceutical industry, shipbuilding and automotive construction, the aeronautical and aerospace industry, measurement and sensor technology, the energy industry, the environmental protection industry, medical technology and healthcare, even the food industry—all these sectors will profit from nanotechnology applications in the medium and long term. Nanotechnology is already part of everyday life with regard to many products. Its most advanced application is surface functionalisation and finishing. But nanotechnology has also already found its way into the electronics and cosmetics industry as well as the development of new materials.

For example, conventional paints can become insensitive to light, UV resistant and scratch-proof by adding nanoparticles. Carbon nanotubes, which are roughly 10,000 times thinner than a human hair, ensure that plastics are more stable in shape, stronger and electrically conductive. The application of nanocoatings to windows and other smooth surfaces can not only enhance their antireflective properties, but can also produce a kind of self-cleaning action on the surface due to the water and grease resistant effects. Nanoparticles are added to skin creams, deodorants and sunscreens to boost their effect and skin compatibility. In the food and pharmaceutical industry nanotechnology can be used to seal nutrients and agents; and in medicine their application can improve diagnoses and therapies.

In Hamburg nanostructure research started nearly 20 years ago at the University of Hamburg. In the meantime Hamburg has a wide range of scientific institutes and other institutions which have completely or partially specialised in research and the practical development of nanotechnology applications. Besides the research activities of the University of Hamburg, particularly at the Hamburg Institute for Applied Science, to which the special research area "nanomagnetism" of the German Research Association was assigned in 2005, the Technical University of Hamburg-Harburg has been dealing with questions of material research, especially in the field of nanocomposites, since 1993. Further key institutions in Hamburg's nanoscience and technology scene are DESY, the Center for Applied Nanotechnology (CAN) founded in 2005, and the Interdisciplinary Nanoscience Centre of the University of Hamburg (INCH) founded around the same time.

The fields of activity at INCH include: Firstly, research on the synthesis and self-organisation of nanoscale materials; secondly, the further development of nanoanalytical methods; thirdly, controlled nanomanipulation for the targeted development of artificial structures with specific properties; and fourthly, nano-bioorganisation, i.e. the application of nanotechnology methods in biotechnology and medical technology. CAN is a public-private partnership whose members include, amongst others, well-known industrial companies and it has the Hamburger Sparkasse as its financial partner. Besides contract research the main role of this institution is technology transfer from research to application, with the current focus on medical technology, pharmacy and cosmetics.

Even if nanotechnology has also been chosen as one of the principal areas for promoting research and development in several other German federal states it seems essential that Hamburg, as with the optical technologies, continues to demonstrate international excellence in this sunrise technology and that the Senate funds activities in this area appropriately. It is, however, equally crucial—and this applies to both key technologies—that the state's involvement, apart from applying these technologies in the public sector, is limited to indirect funding through research, facilitating technology transfer and establishing the basic framework conditions. The identification of potentially profitable products and their pursuit on the market must remain an entrepreneurial task.

## The Necessity of an efficient Infrastructure

Even if Hamburg with its 18 state or state-recognised universities has not yet succeeded in joining the circle of Germany's elite universities clear progress has been made in recent years. This relates, on the one hand, to performance-oriented structural reforms, capacity restructuring and the bundling of sub-critical small units, as well as new approaches towards a stronger profile by defining fields of research emphasis, especially in the traditional state university sector. On the other hand, this relates to the successful development of private universities, for example the Bucerius Law School, the Hamburg School of Business Administration and the Kühne Logistics University.

Another development which is important for the city's future is that Hamburg now also pays greater attention to engineering and technology-oriented training and research. Even though the significance of these fields of study for the national and international competition between locations had been recognised for quite some time the city's merchants, who were more interested in international trade, appeared to be oblivious to this fact. The three institutions which constituted the exceptions were: *Firstly*, the Hamburgische Schiffbau-Versuchsanstalt, established in 1913; *secondly*, the GKSS Research Centre Geesthacht, founded in 1956 as the Gesellschaft für Kernenergieverwertung in Schiffbau und Schifffahrt; and *thirdly*, Deutsche Elektronen-Synchrotron (DESY), established in 1964 and almost exclusively committed to basic research in the natural sciences.

It was not until the mid-1970s — with the establishment of the present-day Helmut Schmidt University, at which, amongst other things, the fields of electrical engineering and mechanical engineering are represented — that the traditional neglect of technical-scientific disciplines slowly came to an end. Lastly research commenced at the Technical University of Hamburg-Harburg in 1980. The HafenCity University of Architecture and Metropolitan Development, newly founded in 2006, is also involved in drawing together different areas of ex-

436

pertise and a further orientation towards engineering sciences. So the process of catching up has already started. And it is particularly rapid in the fields of research relevant to clusters. But a comparison of Hamburg with the other leading technology locations in Germany and Europe shows that this task is still far from being completed.

Another key economic area of the infrastructure in which there is acute pressure, despite concepts and plans having been extensively discussed for quite some time, is the transport system. This not only relates to adapting the fairway of the Upper and Outer Elbe and the all-year-round navigation of the Upper Elbe. Apart from the repeatedly occurring bottlenecks experienced by inner-city traffic and local and regional public transport, this refers primarily to the strategic road network as well as to southbound rail services. On the one hand, Hamburg still requires an eastern bypass, which is supposed to be achieved by extending the A21 motorway and including the B404. This measure would provide relief to congested sections of the A1 and A7 motorways and thereby create additional capacity for the still dynamically increasing northbound port traffic. Furthermore, this connection is required to cope with the increasing amount of traffic resulting from the construction of the Fehmarn Belt crossing. On the other hand, the westward continuation of the A20 motorway from Mecklenburg-Western Pomerania via Geschendorf up to the A7 motorway and its subsequent extension as a western bypass of Hamburg with a privately financed toll crossing of the River Elbe between Glückstadt and Stade is still awaited.

By contrast, clear progress is currently being made with the realisation of the so-called Hafenquerspange (port link road), which promises to enhance west-east traffic through the port while creating a direct connection between the A1 and A7 motorways. Another important requirement that cannot be delayed and would ensure an improved connection of the port to the hinterland is the construction of the much cited Y route of Deutsche Bahn. By altering the route of passenger traffic the existing line between Hamburg and Hanover is to be used exclusively for freight traffic, ensuring that these two means of transportation do not permanently hinder one another on an already congested route.

All these measures would, by the way, not only be beneficial for commercial transport. The time it takes passengers to travel from Hamburg to Hanover by rail could be cut by 20 minutes. Fewer traffic jams on the motorways are also beneficial for car traffic and mean reduced environmental pollution. However, it is not enough if only Hamburg is convinced of the economic and social advantages of the various infrastructure investments mentioned here. As soon as these measures involve a federal waterway, for example the River Elbe, or a federal motorway the involvement of the federal government in Berlin is necessary. Apart from the Hafenquerspange, which will only run through Hamburg territory, all the other projects require constructive cooperation with Schleswig-Holstein and/or Lower Saxony. In certain cases even the European Commission is involved. Concerning the deepening and widening of the Outer and Lower Elbe fair way the commission has a say with respect to the environmental implications. As regards the Y route of Deutsche Bahn and the Fehmarn Belt crossing, both projects have now been included into the so-called Trans-European Networks with the consequence that Brussels would normally participate to 30% in their constructions costs.

### Urban Modernisation

Dynamic economic growth and higher employment, to which education and research, investments in the transport system as well as many other types of infrastructure investments make their contribution, are definitely also a determinant and often even a prerequisite for quality of life. It is in the nature of things that this becomes even clearer with flagship urban projects. And if there is currently one project that puts all other European ones in the shade, it is definitely the construction of the HafenCity Hamburg. Located just a ten minute walk from the city hall, the transformation of an old, 157 hectare port

*In most parts of the world a harbour city is associated with industry and dirt, and sometimes even with drugs and violence. The Hamburg HarbourCtiy is the complete opposite. It is clean and green, and it is a favourite quarter to live and work.*

quarter into an integrated residential and business district will increase the size of the inner city by 40 per cent.

This inner city modernisation project is unique not only in Europe, but also worldwide with regard to its size and as an urban planning and architectural concept. The plans envisage the creation of living space for 12,000 people and workplaces for 45,000 people, providing an intensive mix of uses. There will also be a wide variety of other attractions: Shops, restaurants, coffee shops and bars; a cruise terminal, a marina and a tall ships harbour; nurseries, schools, a Science Centre and the HafenCity University; art galleries, the Design Port and a maritime museum, attractive pedestrian zones, a 10.5 kilometre long quayside promenade as well as many public parks with a clear view of the water; and, last but not least, the new landmark of Hamburg, towards which all ships calling at the inner port, just like the cruise ships, must head: The Elbphilharmonie, an architectural high-

439

*Bird's eye view of Hamburg in 1981.*

light with the ambition of becoming one of the world's best concert halls.

The total cost of this project will be in order of 9 billion Euros, of which nearly 80%, namely 7 billion Euros have been raised from private investors. Many leading companies, for example Germanische Lloyd, Kühne & Nagel, SAP, the Spiegel Group or Unilever, have already taken the decision to relocate their headquarters or their Hamburg offices to the HafenCity. And since environmental aspects also played a major role in the conceptual design of this new city quarter even Greenpeace has chosen to set up its new German headquarters here. The centre of the HafenCity will be the Überseequartier (Overseas District), which is connected to the cruise line terminal via the 400 metre long pedestrianised Überseeboulevard (Overseas Boulevard). Once the HafenCity has been completed roughly 80,000 visitors are expected to descend on the promenade every day.

The Elbphilharmonie will be the most expensive individual project and its costs have gradually increased to roughly 450 million Euros from the 150 million Euros originally planned in 2003. But even if one might expect the responsible planners in an old Hanseatic city to be able to do their sums better, it is not the fact that the costs have risen but the amount by which they have risen that is surprising. Sydney and Rio de Janeiro suffered similar experiences in 1973 and 2008 respectively. Oslo, whose opera house was also completed in 2008, estimated the budget at more than 500 million Euros from the start. The fact that completion of the Elbphilharmonie will take about three years longer than planned cannot be seen as a typical Hamburg trait. However, if there is one typical Hamburg trait with regard to the financing of this prestige object, it is without doubt the traditionally generous financial support provided by the city's businesses and citizens, who between them have donated almost 80 million Euros towards the project.

But the new HafenCity is not the only urban modernisation project which has been tackled recently in Hamburg and should provide lasting improvement in the quality of life in the city in the next five to ten years. Another venture relates to the southbound crossing of the River Elbe and includes the regions of Veddel, Wilhelmsburg and the inner harbour of Harburg. In contrast to the HafenCity this project, for which the Hamburg Senate has initially provided 120 million Euros for infrastructure investments, may be less spectacular but it is more complex from the point of view of its socio-political aspects and in terms of urban planning.

The plan is to make an area of the city more attractive and better to live in; a district with comparatively wide social divisions that is facing the problems of poverty, immigration and integration, divided up by a multitude of congested main roads, and where politicians, economists and the local inhabitants have very different views of the required measures. It is to be hoped that the International Building Exhibition Hamburg 2013 and the International Garden Show, which takes place at the same time, will not only provide new incentives but also help to create a consensus and, in specific areas, even contribute to practical solutions.

## Hamburg: The 2008 Global Financial and Economic Crisis

There is no doubt that the three large operational clusters, port and logistics, aviation, and media and IT, as well as the new clusters health economy, life sciences, medical technology and renewable energies, will all belong to the growth sectors of the future. The economic significance of the three traditional clusters is, amongst other things, expressed by the fact that they provide jobs for roughly 300,000 people, in other words almost 30 per cent of the working population, in Hamburg. In contrast to the new cluster initiatives all the three are, however, also easily affected by cyclical downturns and other financial and economic crises.

Thus the number of sea-going vessels calling at Port of Hamburg fell from 12,217 in 2007 to 9,843 in 2010. After a decrease from 140.4 million tonnes in 2007 to 110.4 million tonnes in 2009 the transhipment of cargoes recovered slightly to 121.1 million tonnes in 2010. Container traffic fell from 9.9 million TEU in 2007 to 7.0 million TEU in 2009 and increased again to 7.9 million TEU in 2010. A development which may be of concern for Hamburg is the fact that both Rotterdam and Antwerp suffered much less from the shipping crisis. Furthermore both surpassed their pro-crisis record levels already in 2010. There were several possible reasons for this: Firstly, more than 20 per cent of all the containers handled in Hamburg in 2007 were for Russian customers and a large percentage was also for the Ukrainian and Polish markets. Since the 2008 economic and financial crisis resulted in a more severe slump in economic activity in these countries than in the mainly German hinterland of Rotterdam and Antwerp, there is no doubt that this also affected container handling. A second reason was that, following considerably decreased fuel prices, feeder traffic throughout the Baltic region could also be operated cost-effectively from the Benelux countries.

Another reason why Hamburg has slipped from second to third place in container handling in Europe could be the limited accessibility of the port. Since the crisis has led to an increased utilisation of fifth and sixth generation container ships, especially for trade with Asia, and these cannot call at Hamburg when fully laden, it is very likely that the decline in Hamburg's container handling may also have something to do with a loss of competitiveness due to the delayed deepening and widening of the fairway of the River Elbe. This would definitely be the more threatening development for Hamburg in the long term, as it is not always possible to regain traffic lost once new routes have been established. More broadly it underlines the fact that important infrastructural investments lose nothing of their urgency, particularly in times of crisis, or even when facing an expected slump in tax revenues as in 2009.

Apart from these explanations for the crisis-related decline of Hamburg's container handling activities in 2009, the question also arises whether there are any other reasons for the loss of Hamburg's competitiveness compared with other North Sea ports. A possible element could be the somewhat thoughtless Hamburg port policy. Harbour fees had always been relatively high and despite this were raised by a further 4 per cent in March 2009, in the middle of the economic crisis. Only the future will tell whether the negative psychological effect caused by this increase can be undone by the incentive-based reduction of fees concluded in December 2009.

Another fact is that no shipping company apart from Hapag-Lloyd has yet had the opportunity to have a share in a container terminal in Hamburg and thus have its own berths, the so-called "dedicated terminals". It is not unlikely that this too played a role for Mærsk when choosing Bremerhaven as its hub and for COSCO when recently relocating its European headquarters from Hamburg to Rotterdam. In a major crisis it could seem only normal that shipping companies utilise the capacities of their own terminals elsewhere first before allowing their ships to sail all the way to Hamburg, where higher port fees are charged.

As long as there were capacity shortages at the container terminals the strict refusal of "dedicated terminals" may have been justified, since a terminal dedicated to a particular shipping company can limit overall capacity if the berths cannot be made available to other shipping companies when they are empty. But this is a short term argument. For Hamburg to retain large container services in the longer term, a decision needs to be taken whether to show more flexibility regarding the issue of "dedicated terminals" when constructing the fifth terminal on Steinwerder.

Hamburg's ship operators have suffered from the reduced freight movements and the fall in freight rates, which was no less than 80 per cent for container traffic between the beginning of January 2008 and the end of June 2009. These losses could not be recovered even by lowering the cruising speed from 20 to 15 knots, a common practice that increases the number of ships being used while reducing fuel consumption by up to 50 per cent. At the peak of the crisis about 12 per cent of the roughly 4,800 container ships worldwide were without freight. Even major shipping companies were struggling to survive. This applied, in particular, to those that could neither be supported by financially strong parent companies or large sovereign wealth funds, as is the case with a few leading shipping companies from Japan, China, Singapore or Denmark.

Furthermore, it must be remembered that 75 per cent of worldwide time-charter contracts for container ships had been concluded in Hamburg in recent years, that 35 per cent of all the world's container ships had been financed in Hamburg, and that approximately 25 per cent of the global container ship fleet were managed by companies based in and around Hamburg. It does not require much imagination to picture the implications of the 2008 economic and financial crisis for the port industry and shipping in Hamburg, as well as for the almost 60 Hamburg-based financial institutions involved in ship financing.

The lack of freight and low freight rates meant first of all that the large shipping lines were not extending current charter contracts or, if possible, were even terminating them prematurely. Subsequently the charter companies, some of which own more than 100 ships in Hamburg, could only decide whether to sign new contracts at reduced freight rates or to lay up their vessels. In both cases this could result in the charter companies no longer being able to bear the financial costs. This was followed by a domino effect throughout the financial and investment sector. The problems of HSH-Nordbank, which were, however, further compounded by financial investments in toxic papers are a striking example of the problems facing ship financers.

But this was not where the chain reaction ended. There were apparently more than 1,500 container ships still under construction or at least on the order books of the large shipyards, predominantly in South Korea, Japan and China. Even if only a proportion of these new capacities entered the market, a considerable delay could be expected before the crisis in container shipping abated, even if the global economy and international trade started to recover. Many of the things recently occurred in the container shipping industry were similar to the tanker crisis of the mid-1970s when several Hamburg registered super tankers, built by HDW in Kiel and partially state funded, sailed straight from the shipyard to the Geltinger Bay, where they were immediately laid up. Economists refer to this trend of excessive production and capacity expansion as a "pork cycle" — a phenomenon that is, as can be clearly seen, not only restricted to the investment behaviour of pig breeders.

Another industry in Hamburg which has been affected by the shipping crisis was the maritime industry, including the sectors of ship and boat building, shipbuilding suppliers, marine technology and a number of maritime service providers. After the shipyard crisis of the mid-1970s and subsequent cuts in non-competitive capacities the construction of merchant ships was basically only carried out by the J. J. Sietas shipyard, founded in 1635. The company showed great foresight by devoting its main attention to heavy lift vessels, chemical tankers and other special-purpose ships besides medium-sized container ships. However, even this company would not have survived the current crisis without massive financial backing and further far reaching restructuring.

New constructions at Blohm & Voss were almost entirely limited to naval ships, offshore equipment and luxury mega-yachts, though it will most probably discontinue its civil shipbuilding in the not too distant future. The company has still operated successfully in the repair sector, profiting not only from its extended floating dock capacities but, in particular, also from the availability of the "Elbe 17" dry dock, which is still one of the largest in Europe, measuring 351 metres in length. Super tankers and large heavy lift vessels, which can no longer call at Hamburg when fully laden due to their draught, are still frequent visitors when they require repairs or other work below the waterline. Large cruise liners, such as the Queen Mary 2, which have started arriving in Hamburg in increasing numbers also use this dock on a regular basis.

Another important branch of industry in this context is represented by the various suppliers to the shipyard industries. The competitiveness of this mainly medium-sized sector, which has seen increased specialisation in the high-tech sector and engineering services, is, amongst other things, also underlined by the fact that more than half of the industry's turnover relates to exports. Even German shipowners who had their vessels built in the Far East still provided special support for the industry. What the current shipbuilding crisis, which is increasingly also hitting the Asian shipyards, will mean for the currently roughly 6,000 employees in this area is uncertain, at least in the short term. In the longer term, the Far East shipyards will probably not be able to survive without high-tech supplies from Germany.

Air traffic is also particularly susceptible to crisis. This has become very apparent in recent years after the 9/11 terrorist attacks on the United States and during the outbreak of so-called bird flu. The number of passengers and the amount of air freight have also dropped worldwide as a result of the 2008 financial and economic crisis. As was also the case with container shipping, the slump in demand in this industry only set in after a certain delay. However, since April 2008 the number of passengers on international flights has fallen annually by 5 per cent and the amount of air freight, which is predominantly transported as additional cargo on normal regular services, by 19 per cent. In addition the greatest losses in passenger travel have been recorded in the premium segment, which is particularly profitable for airlines, and nobody currently knows whether the passengers who switched to economy class will ever return to their business or first class seats.

The consequence is that international airlines have struggled with huge losses. According to estimates by the international air transport organisation IATA, the annual loss of the global aviation industry was 9.4 billion dollar in 2009 and still 2.8 billion dollars in 2010. Many large airlines have also reduced their capacities by not renewing expiring leasing contracts for aircraft. It is therefore not surprising that international airlines as well as leading aircraft leasing companies have postponed all or some of their expansion plans; the consequence of this for Boeing, Embrayer and Bombardier, but also for Airbus, has been the risk that many contracts regarding aircraft deliveries will have to be renegotiated or completely cancelled. After a strong recovery of international air transport already in 2010 the situation in the aviation industry improved, however, much more rapidly than it has in the container shipping sector and shipyards.

Considering that the third largest Hamburg cluster, namely media and IT, is — at least in large sub-areas — highly susceptible to cyclical fluctuations and crises due to its dependency on advertising revenues, it is actually surprising that the 2009 real gross domestic product in Hamburg was only down 2.1 per cent compared to 2008, while the figures for Germany as a whole were minus 3.4 per cent. The unemployment rate reached the 8.6 per cent mark in Hamburg in 2009; but even this figure is significantly better than that for the other two city states, Berlin and Bremen. And considering that approximately 200,000 working people commute to Hamburg each day from the hinterland, one is entitled to ask the question whether the unemployment rate of just 7.8 per cent in Schleswig-Holstein is really that much better.

## *Challenges*
## *for Economic Policy*

There are numerous reasons for the comparatively favourable economic developments in Hamburg, which, in terms of economic growth and employment, have distinguished Hamburg positively from many other parts of Germany even during the 2008 economic and financial crisis. The following five aspects are especially important within this context: *Firstly*, in addition to the large clusters Hamburg still enjoys an extremely diversified economic structure; *secondly*, the credit and insurance industry has been able to hold its ground relatively well through the difficulties caused by ship financing and the sub-prime crisis; *thirdly*, turnover in the wholesale and retail sector only recorded a moderate decline by the end of 2008; *fourthly*, Airbus has not

*The Elbphilharmonie, Hamburg's new landmark, which, together with the HafenCity, marks the city's transition to the 21st century.*

experienced tangible production constraints, despite the aviation crisis; and *fifthly*, Hamburg's economy probably has a predominantly medium-sized structure.

The diversity of the economic structure in the metropolitan region is, amongst other things, underlined by the number of employees who cannot be allocated to the official competence clusters. For example, roughly 30,000 people work for the 151 credit institutions and financial service providers and a further 40,000 for the more than 150 insurance companies. 35,000 people are employed in the food industry. The chemical industry boasts 13,000 employees in Hamburg and 16,000 in the surrounding areas. The largest private employers in Hamburg after Airbus and Lufthansa, including Lufthansa Technik, are the Asklepios Kliniken Hamburg GmbH and the Hamburger Sparkasse, which — founded in 1827 — is the oldest and largest independent savings bank in Germany. Furthermore, Hamburg is the seat of a number of so-called "hidden champions", that is to say companies which, on the one hand, do not belong to one of the five clusters, but, on the other, are still European or global leaders in their respective sectors.

Examples of this are: In the primary industry Aurubis, known as Norddeutsche Affinerie until the end of March 2009, the largest copper producer in Europe and the world's largest copper recycler; in mechanical engineering Hauni, the founding company of the Körber Group, which has been the global market and technology leader in the international tobacco industry for many years; in the international brand market Beiersdorf, a world leader in skincare and certain other pharmacy products; in the luxury goods sector Montblanc, founded in 1906 and officially entered as Simplo Filler Pen Co. in Hamburg's commercial register two years later, and still one of the leading international manufacturers of writing instruments and life style accessories; in retail trade the Otto Group, which is not only the international market leader in the mail-order business, but also in digital shopping; and finally in the service sector Hamburg Messe and Congress, which not only organises a full range of major international exhibitions and congresses in the field of the leading industrial clusters in Hamburg but far beyond, including in the areas of sport and lifestyle.

The great diversity of Hamburg's economic structure and the fact that a number of highly innovative companies which do not belong to the official competence clusters have risen to become international industry leaders clearly demonstrates that the increased attention paid to the promotion of the clusters by the city's political and administrative decision-makers must not lead to this policy being followed at the cost of the other industries and companies located in the region. The top priority of regional and location policy remains to ensure a general economic and social climate that promotes entrepreneurial activity and encourages investment and innovation, as well as creation.

Throughout the process of adapting the framework of economic, social and environmental policies to whatever higher political objectives it is essential to make sure that the corresponding measures do not have a long term negative impact on the proper functioning of the markets, on the flexible adjustment of economic structures or on entrepreneurial initiative. Going further, it is necessary in the longer term to create reliable planning perspectives for regional and urban development policies. On the one hand, this means the far-sighted management of land usage with regard to the provision of commercial and residential areas, clear statements on the future perspectives for local taxation policy and a clear set of binding guidelines for regional or urban environmental protection policies. On the other hand, it is important to provide the economy and, beyond that, the population with practical details about the infrastructural measures that can be expected in the medium term.

Companies making decisions about their location and investments, as well as people who live and work in the metropolitan region or who wish to move there, must be offered a view of how the region is expected to develop. This refers to the necessary investments for securing the competitiveness of the port and the energy supply, as well as long-distance transport links and plans for the local transport system. Other important location factors are the strategic decisions expected relating to the education and training systems and the further expansion of higher education and the research infrastructure. The same applies to the policy areas of housing, healthcare provision and public safety, as well as culture, entertainment and sport.

There is no question that these orientations already apply to the closed model of a national economy. However, they gain greater significance in a globalised world where competition between locations is at international, not just at national level. Capital is mobile. Qualified workers often are, too. But also economic activities — particularly in service sectors, such as sea transport — can often easily be relocated from one place to another. In order to be among the winners in a globalised society it is essential to also consider international interdependencies and feedback effects when formulating regional and location policies.

Even under conditions of sustained and high non-inflationary economic growth and a largely satisfactory employment situation, it is not usually easy to set out the priorities for action or to consider the various measures in the face of limited resources. In the current situation of moderate economic growth, high uncertainty and even the prospect of a possible recession, the decisions regarding an appropriate strategy for regional and location policy become infinitely more difficult. As public debt, at present in Hamburg about 25 billion Euros, leaves no room for a further budget deficit, the question arises which criteria should be given priority in adjusting public spending to the expected tax revenues.

First of all a distinction must be made between operating expenditure and capital expenditure. In terms of operating expenditure, cuts suggest themselves where savings also make a contribution to reducing any overregulation or bureaucracy. Furthermore, a planned rise in operating expenditure should be temporarily abandoned wherever it does not lead to irreversible damage. In terms of capital expenditure, a distinction must be made between those expenses which in-

453

crease the growth and employment potential of the location in the future and those which primarily improve the quality of life without short or medium term growth and employment-relevant effects. The first group includes the majority of expenses for science and research, the long-distance road and rail infrastructure, as well as the deepening and widening of the fairway of the Lower and Outer Elbe. Expenses for the second group can either be deferred or, if, politically possible, definitely cut.

The new Hamburg Senate which took office in March 2011 is fully aware of this and has made budget consolidation one of the highest policy priorities. Assuming that according to the historical trend tax revenues increase at an annual rate of 2 per cent, it has been decided that until 2020 public expenditures should not rise by more than one per cent. Furthermore, the Senate has taken the decision that this policy of reducing the structural budget deficit would definitively exclude once-off measures such as the sale of public property—an approach which was frequently used in the past. In addition, there are two further challenges with respect to the ongoing budget consolidation process: The first is improving the quality of the budget by shifting resources from public consumption towards public investment. The second is to take into account the depreciation of public infrastructure and other traditional off-budget items such as longer term financial commitments, for instance in form of pensions. It would be highly desirable therefore to re-enforce the application of the system of double-entry bookkeeping which not only records annual revenues and expenses, but also changes in the value of public assets.

One problem facing Hamburg is that it does not have the capacity to make independent decisions on many of the regional planning and infrastructure measures which will determine the competitiveness of the location in the future. The constructive cooperation of the administrative districts of the metropolitan region, the state governments of Schleswig-Holstein and/or Lower Saxony and, in certain cases, also the German federal government is often required. Particularly in this

*Called by about 120 cruise ships with 300,000 passengers in 2011, Hamburg is one of the most favoured cruising destinations in Northern Europe. Yet the city had to wait for nearly 40 years to see its name again taken all over the world by a cruise ship. A new "Hamburg", will take up service in May 2012. The ship with a length of 144 meters and 198 cabins for 400 passengers, will serve the premium segment of the market and cruise the Baltic, the North Sea and the Mediterranean Sea as well as during the European winter the Caribbean, South America and the Antarctic.*

time of crisis it is important to realise the importance of Hamburg as an economic and cultural hub across the entire region and far beyond. If Hamburg were to get left behind in the international competition between locations this would also be a major setback for Northern Lower Saxony and Southern Schleswig-Holstein. But in Hamburg, too, it should not be forgotten that in the globalised world of today a small city state would have far fewer chances in the international competition between locations if it did not have a thriving hinterland. It is vital, therefore, that all the parties involved put aside their own special interests and instead focus on the longer term future of the entire region when making the decisions that are facing them. This is the only way to demonstrate convincingly that institutionalised cooperation across federal states is equal in value to a politically integrated northern state.

# PART VI

# Globalisation
# and Global Governance
# in the 21st Century

# CHAPTER 11

# From US Hegemony
# towards a
# Multipolar Power Structure

The process of globalisation has always been characterised by shifts in political and economic power centres. After the centre of gravity had left the Mediterranean basin with first Athens and Rome and then Venice in the lead, the Portuguese and the Spanish dominated a major part of the world economy and its centre moved initially to Antwerp and later to Genoa. This was followed by the rise of Amsterdam in the 17th and the first half of the 18th century. In the 19th century Great Britain was the geopolitical and economic powerhouse and London became the centre of the world economy. Finally, in the second half of the 20th century and until now, it is the United States who represent the most powerful country and New York is the world's uncontested economic and financial capital.

Shifts in geopolitical and economic power configurations have in most cases been associated with turbulent times. Frequently they occurred in connection with economic and financial crises. But also the loss of military superiority and/or international economic competitiveness of the world leader played a prominent role. Today the world is faced once again with many of the particular patterns which marked the beginning of a power shift in the past. Not only that the world economy has still not fully recovered from the 2008 economic and financial crisis. The military capabilities of the United States are overstressed; the US fiscal position is becoming increasingly difficult and both US domestic and foreign debt is at record levels.

Of course this does not mean that the United States will be replaced soon by a new global leader. But there are many indications and arguments for an evolution towards a multipolar power structure in which — more than Japan and Europe in the second half of the 20th century — the newly emerging economies such as China, India and perhaps Russia and Brazil will exercise growing influence. Whether this development, too, implies turbulent times ahead depends on many circumstances.

One important dimension is the future economic development of the major players — in particular the United States, China, the European Union, India and Japan. Another is that multipolar power structures are less predictable in terms of international policy preferences than a hegemonistic situation. There is not only the permanent tension between cooperation and conflict, but at the same time the prospect of ever changing coalitions. In a world of growing complexity and interdependence this may further contribute to increasing uncertainty.

### United States:
### The End of Global Hegemony?

The second half of the 20th century was the golden age of the United States. It was the most powerful country in geopolitical, economic and military terms. It counterbalanced Soviet hegemonic ambitions and served as military policeman in peace-keeping world-wide. It shaped the post-WWII international economic order both to the benefit of the free world and to the advantage of itself. And it could do so because it represented over long periods the world's most competitive economy as well as the leading country in science, technology and finance. When the Soviet Union imploded in 1989 the United States was finally left the only superpower on the global geopolitical and economic scene.

This does not mean, however, that the US has been spared the experience of any major crisis. It suffered a deep recession after the end of the Korean War. It lost its elected President through murder in 1963. It was hit as many others by the first and second oil shock. It lost the Vietnam War and failed to maintain the Bretton Woods System. It experienced double digit inflation in the 1980s. It managed the crisis of the savings and loan banks in the late 1980s and early 1990s as well as the dot.com crisis in the year 2000. And even the terrorist attacks against the Twin Towers in New York and the Pentagon in Washington in September 2001 did not break, but united the country in mourning and finally once again motivated it. Crisis situations were perceived as a challenge and each time the United States recovered—quite often for some observers much more rapidly than expected.

Whether this will happen once again after the Great Recession which followed the financial crisis of 2008 is still an open question. There are at least four arguments which in their combination could render the path to sustained non-inflationary economic growth and higher employment and the solution of some other current problems such as overcoming bottlenecks in the infrastructure more difficult. A *first* and perhaps most worrying fact with potential highly adverse implications in the longer run is the budget deficit of around 10 % of GDP and a public debt in the order of 13,500 billion dollars which corresponds to about 93 % of GDP in 2010. A *second* problematic aspect is that, in contrast to likewise highly indebted Japan, most of the public deficit—and as a consequence of the public debt—is financed abroad, mostly by China and Japan, thus perpetuating the US current account deficit. Both these facts reduce the US government's ability to act freely at domestic as well as at international level.

*Thirdly*, not only the public sector, but private households, too, have lived for a long period above their means and have accumulated

461

a debt burden in the order of 92 % of GDP. Most dramatic is the situation of mortgaged home owners, of whom in the first quarter of 2010 still 24 % were left with negative equity. Not only that this reduces locational mobility on the labour market, it represents a time bomb should interest rates rise, households in trouble be forced to sell and house prices further fall. *Fourthly*, neither the jobs lost over several decades through progressive de-industrialisation nor those lost as a result of the 2008 economic and financial crisis in an over-extended banking sector will be re-created soon. As a consequence unemployment could remain much higher in the near future than was normal in the past. Already today long term unemployment is higher than ever since the 1930s and hidden unemployment and more generally poverty are also estimated to be on a sharp rise.

Nevertheless, one should not forget that American society has a long tradition in cultivating optimism and self-confidence and on that basis in positively responding to even the most demanding challenges. This could, despite all present difficulties, serve as a point of departure for a first promising best case scenario. Here, the recovery from the Great Recession is further strengthening and the US President, either the present or the next, would be able to negotiate a bi-partisan compromise on balancing the budget over the next ten years and reduce public debt to about 70 % of GDP. This would still be twice as high as the pre-crisis level, but would surely represent a better outcome than foreseeable based on present policies. The talk about a "bankrupt" nation would find an end. Financial markets and investors would regain confidence in the US economy and the outlook for sustained non-inflationary growth and higher employment would be further improved.

If the recovery underway were sufficiently robust, a considerable part of the consolidation could be contributed from the termination of fiscal stimulus, the winding up of financial rescue measures and from automatic stabilisers. Improving the efficiency of government and the reform of entitlement programmes such as pension and public health care would be a second source of expenditure reductions.

But this would still not be enough. Additional savings would be needed and possible candidates for budget cuts would certainly include military expenditure which together with homeland security is about 80 % higher today than it was in the heydays of the Cold War. And, of course, government revenues would have to be increased, too. Some of this is automatic and due to rising incomes. Another part would be achieved through a combination of an elimination of tax breaks, an increase of the upper marginal rate and a broadening of the base of the income tax and the introduction of a value added tax.

As the whole range of possible measures, if vigorously implemented, may result in bringing about higher government revenues and expenditure savings as required to achieve the initial budget deficit and public debt reduction objectives, there may be even scope to use some of the potential "surplus" to improve the structure of the budget by shifting resources from consumption to investment. The areas where public investment could have the highest return would probably include education, infrastructure and innovation. Affordable housing for low income earners, environment protection and development aid, the latter to counterbalance certain geopolitical ambitions of the Chinese, could be other promising fields.

From a purely economic and fiscal perspective this optimistic comeback scenario leading to sustained economic growth, higher employment, a balanced budget, reduced public debt and the regaining of a certain room for manoeuvre in making political decisions would clearly be an achievable option. What makes it an "Alice in Wonderland" scenario is the present-day political climate in the United States. The US Constitution was conceived as an institutional framework with a built-in obligation and necessity for compromise. If the culture of an informed debate and compromise is superseded by irreconcilable ideological conflict, the carefully balanced-out relations between the US President, the Senate and the House of Representatives can easily end up in a complete blockage of important political decisions. Looking at the political scene in the US today, this seems in fact to describe the prevalent situation in the US budget deficit and public debt discussion and not only there. Yet even after the 2012 presidential elections an end to this deadlock cannot unfortunately be guaranteed.

As a consequence, one has to review at least two other scenarios: A first one where the political blockage in Washington results in non-action or too little action leading either to inflationary growth or to stagflation; and a second, where in action or too little action undermines confidence in the US economy and produces a double dip with the associated recession and deflation. Both these developments, in particular with regard to their medium and longer term implications, would be highly undesirable—not only for the American people or the world economy but also in a geopolitical perspective. Even under the conditions of the optimistic come-back scenario there is little doubt that the role of the United States would be less dominant in an increasingly multipolar world. Under the alternative scenarios this tendency would be further strengthened and with shrinking economic and military capabilities the US would face even more difficult trade-offs between domestic and foreign policy objectives.

At least at a quick glance it could seem that the scenario characterised by inflationary growth or stagflation might be preferable to that of a double dip recession. An apparent advantage could be seen in the fact that inflation would contribute to reducing the real value of the over-extended public and private debt. But there are many caveats. *Firstly*, the domestic costs of inflation can be very high, in particular when the process gets out of control and finally ends up in a crash resulting in a recession; *secondly*, inflation is associated with regressive distributional effects, hitting the poor people and the middle class more than the rich. Increasing taxes, heightened administrative efficiency and a selective reduction of public services would therefore be by far the better option.

*Thirdly*, as mentioned before, most of the American public debt is financed abroad. As inflation would undermine confidence in the US dollar, except for extremely high interest, the US would have growing difficulties financing its deficits and refinancing its debts. Worse and in fact most probable, foreign creditors would tend to liquidate their dollar assets. In addition to the initial impact of inflation, a number of second round effects would then drive the exchange rate of the US dollar even further down and could easily lead to a severe crisis on international financial markets. Clearly, if no determined counteraction is taken the talk of the bankrupt nation and the prospect of US sovereign default could in fact become a possible reality. As this situation would be highly undesirable for all parties and especially for the United States there is still all hope that US policy makers will wake up. One risk is that they still do too little too late, the other is that the consolidation policies overshoot and the recovery stalls. The latter result would be part of the second of the unfavourable scenarios.

Either in the light of a possible downgrading of US creditworthiness or after recognising the dangers involved in the inflationary avenue US policy makers could embark on a panic-driven effort towards budget and debt consolidation. The package finally agreed upon may by and large, although not necessarily in its composition, correspond to what would in principle be needed in order to move the US economy towards the trajectory of the optimistic scenario. But one of the underlying conditions for success in this favourable scenario is a robust recovery from the Great Recession. As long as this precondition is not fulfilled restrictive fiscal policies aiming at the long term sustainability of public finances are not without major economic risks.

In particular if a double dip is looming on the horizon, policy makers need to act more carefully. A gradual elimination of fiscal stimulus and financial rescue measures as well as the operation of automatic stabilisers will still be possible. The same applies for improving the efficiency of the public sector. Should the Fed have in the meanwhile adopted a more restrictive monetary policy stance, there may be also some scope for another round of quantitative easing. With regard to desirable tax increases, the choice must fall on those where the negative impact on private consumption and investment is the smallest. A shift from public consumption to public investment would under all circumstances be helpful in a longer term perspective. And even expenditure cuts could still be envisaged, but primarily with respect to those government outlays which reduce demand abroad and not on domestic markets.

Should recovery be weak, still no time can be lost in achieving consolidation of the budget and public debt by around 2020. Not only could this eventually provide the US government with the necessary fiscal room for manoeuvre to respond to unexpected contingencies. It would also be crucial to deal with the economic and fiscal implications of ageing populations which extend far into the second half of the century. Even if the retirement age were raised from 65 to 67 years, the combination of large cohorts of post-WWII baby boomers leaving active work, a further increasing life expectancy and growing health care outlays per recipient will impose huge expenditure increases on the US pension and health care entitlement systems. At the same time it is expected that the labour force and hence the social security contributor population will grow only slowly. As a consequence even if present-day fiscal consolidation demands are met by and large, this does not at all mean that the future of the US budget would not any longer be a concern.

Overall, the prospects for the United States are not rosy. The most favourable scenario has no chance of becoming reality as long as ideological conflicts supersede the formerly well-established culture of an informed debate and compromise. The inflationary trajectory is not sustainable if the US goes it alone. Should a major part of the world join it in an attempt to reduce their debt, too, it may work for a few years as it did in the early 1980s. But the crash is preconditioned. Furthermore, when playing with inflation and associated exchange rate adjustments the United States has to be wary with regard to the role of the dollar as the world's dominant reserve currency. In the 1980s there was no potential alternative. Today there is the Euro, and in five to ten years there will be the Chinese RMB too.

Successful budget and public debt consolidation under conditions of a weak recovery would require as much mutual agreement and bi-partisan compromise as in the favourable scenario. As a consequence, it appears that the United States is at present very much in a deadlock.

*Just short-term frustration or the precursor of a social explosion? 1 % of the US population owns more than 40 % of the national wealth, 5 % about 60 %. The top 20 % earn 50 % of the national income. 46 million US citizens live below the official poverty line. 50 million have no health insurance.*

One only can hope that the next presidential elections will result in a clear political majority. But even then limited economic capabilities together with overstretched military resources may imply that the international role of the United States, even though it remains the most influential superpower, will increasingly shrink. Leaving aside sovereign default and a melt down of international financial markets, the worst case would be that the United States does not achieve the necessary long term sustainability of its public finances and remains for a long time a lame duck. The second worse case could be that, faced with the difficult trade-offs between domestic and foreign policy priorities, the US would become inward-looking despite a further globalising world.

# China:
## The Rise of a New Superpower

China's progress during the economic reform era that began in 1978 is one of the great success stories of the second half of the 20th century. Within less than three decades China has transformed itself from a dormant, introspective giant into a dynamic powerhouse of major significance for the world economy. With a GDP of 5.88 trillion US dollars in 2010 it has become the world's second largest economy — not only in terms of purchasing power parities but also at market exchange rates. China has the world's second largest manufacturing sector and ranks number one in the export of goods. Lastly, about 350 million Chinese attain income levels equal or above the OECD average. This is a remarkable accomplishment by any standards. It is the fruit of a strategy to embark on far-reaching economic liberalisation and to integrate China into the world economy.

In the longer term, sustaining high rates of economic growth will require a vigorous pursuit of the reform process. Most important in this context is a shift in emphasis and approach. Past policies, in particular in the 1980s and 1990s, were primarily based on the liberalisation of specific markets and on the development of individual segments of the economy. As the scope for market forces to operate has progressively increased the administrative distinctions among the various segments of the economy have come to have less and less economic meaning. This is particularly true where the problems of individual areas and the policies needed to solve them have become intrinsically interdependent.

Despite all economic progress and more attention being paid to social cohesion in recent years, considerable effort will need to go into integrating the domestic economy and maintaining an appropriate balance between the powers and resources of the centre and the provinces. Nearly 50 % of the population lives far away from the prosperous urban centres and per capita income differences are enor-

468

mous at about 10,000 dollars in Shanghai and Beijing and less than 1,000 dollars for the majority of the people. These are the extremes. According to more sophisticated OECD estimates, which take into account internal migration and domestic price differentials, overall inequality between the rural and urban population remains in the order of 1 to 2 or 3. This means that inequality in China is lower than in South Africa, Brazil, India and Russia but still at the level of the United States and much higher than in Japan or the core EU countries except the United Kingdom.

Looking ahead there seems to be a general consensus that economic expansion in China over the next one or two decades and its share in the world economy will increase further—albeit with a progressive decline of economic growth rates. This is due to the fact that the catch-up process with the advanced countries will increasingly be completed and that advances in proximity to the technological frontier are always more difficult. Nevertheless the future is always uncertain and there is no single pre-determined route for China's continued rise to economic pre-eminence.

The most critical factors on the domestic front will be the handling of the economic reform process on the one hand and the management of the problems of social cohesion on the other. Economic reforms need to be vigorously pursued concerning the monetary policy framework, the further opening of financial markets and the lowering of product and labour market barriers. In the social policy realm the main challenges are improving country-wide education levels, unifying social safety nets and pushing ahead with health care and pension reforms. But the external environment will also play an important part in shaping the future path of the Chinese economy. Depending on the interplay of these factors, overall outcomes would differ significantly.

An optimistic scenario could be constructed based both on an ongoing strengthening market orientation of the Chinese economy as the authorities press ahead with economic and social reforms and on a favourable external economic and political environment. Growth rates for output would continue along the current long term trajectory with a slight decline towards 9 % p.a. in the earlier period and 7 later. The rates of growth of Chinese exports may remain several percentage points higher. These rates would be sustained for quite some time, supported by high levels of domestic saving and investment — including foreign direct investment — as well as by an international economy that is able and willing to absorb the flood of mainly labour-intensive manufactures. This continued high export growth would be possible because China itself, after making further progress in market liberalisation, is importing not only raw materials but also goods and services at an appropriate order of magnitude.

In this scenario significant amounts of domestic and foreign funds are allocated to the expansion and efficient operation of transport and energy infrastructures and for environmental improvements. Moreover, low trade barriers coupled with foreign investment and equity participation serve to stimulate competition on domestic markets. Strong growth helps to accommodate much of the surplus rural labour moving to industrial and urban areas. As the growth process spills over into the less developed provinces, the widening of regional disparities within the country not only slows but is effectively reversed. Comprehensive social policy reforms at the expense of the central government would reduce public sector saving. Micro-economic reforms, in particular product and labour market reforms and other regulatory changes, are managed successfully.

Monetary and fiscal policies as well as a prudent adjustment of the exchange rate ensure avoiding overheating and volatile fluctuations in macro-economic performance. This is the configuration which would allow China to overtake the United States as the world's largest economy, first in terms of purchasing power parities and soon thereafter at market exchange rates, too. But being the largest economy does not necessarily mean being the technology leader and even less so being the richest in terms of per capita income and national wealth. With a per capita income at roughly 20 % of the OECD average China still has a very long way to go.

470

There are three major assumptions underlying this overall positive scenario. *Firstly* that the international environment will remain favourable to China's export-led growth strategy. *Secondly* is that the Chinese government implements an ambitious reform agenda and in particular succeeds in addressing the issue of increasing inequalities regarding both regional and urban-rural disparities. And a *third*, not explicitly mentioned condition, is that China's economy does not run into major environmental and resource constraints. Any of these challenges alone could have major negative impacts on the continuation of the dynamic growth performance but they could also act together and worsen the situation further. Most importantly if growth slows economic and social reforms would be much harder to pursue and the ultimate and extreme consequence could be a vicious circle of stagflation, delayed reforms and social unrest.

The first of the less optimistic scenarios is based on a less favourable external environment. In this context China's labour-intensive export drive could run into three major problems. *Firstly*, the United States economy would not be able to come to grips with its enormous public and private debt. In that case slow economic growth together with high unemployment and increasing protectionist sentiment would considerably reduce the capacity of the US economy to absorb high and rising levels of imports from China. *Secondly*, other OECD countries, in particular those who do not hold such a strong competitive position on the international market for capital equipment goods as Japan and Germany, could react with hostility to the assault on their remaining light manufacturing, textile, clothing, footwear and other affected, frequently labour-intensive industries. That China is moving fast towards world leadership in such areas as new energy technologies and electric cars may even be a concern for Japan and Germany. *Thirdly*, the newly industrialising and developing economies, in particular in the Asian region, may react negatively to the penetration of their domestic markets and to the competition on their export markets from rival Chinese products. Thus export rates could fall below growth rates depressing output, aggravating adjustment pressures and creating internal political, economic and social tensions which would slow the reform process.

As a consequence domestic problems begin to pile up. Chinese export industries would lose their dynamics and could even suffer from over-investment. If a major shift to sustained domestic demand has not yet occurred, expansion in economic activity would be insufficient resulting in rising unemployment, in particular among the 140 million migrant workers. To the extent that the establishment of effective social security and health care systems has been delayed when dynamic growth performance would have made this still easy, further necessary reforms of state-owned enterprises and agriculture could grind to a halt, too. Partly related to this reforms in public finances and the banking system may also stall. Should inflationary pressures start building up again the result could be a phase of stop-and-go macroeconomic policies that in addition would undermine confidence in the business climate. In terms of regional development the depressive effects of slower export expansion are magnified in the less developed provinces. With sharply falling living standards social discontent increases and the liberalisation process suffers a further setback.

A second less optimistic scenario could be built on the assumption of a favourable external environment but more thorny problems associated with the internal development of the Chinese economy. Major political and social difficulties could arise for at least three reasons: *Firstly*, because of rising unemployment as the dynamic coastal regions may not any longer be able to absorb the migrant labour arriving from the rural areas. In such a case social unrest would be a real possibility and the bureaucracy will have to react. *Secondly*, with exports growing at brisk pace, mainly to the benefit of the rapidly industrialising coastal areas, regional as well as urban-rural disparities in the level of development and prosperity may continue to grow apace. As a result political and social cohesion could become an even more urgent problem than it is already now. *Thirdly*, should the reform process not be implemented as necessary, freed up prices and supply bottlenecks could feed inflationary pressures and make macro-

472

economic management much more difficult and this, too, could result in bureaucratic and interventionist policies including price controls gaining ground.

Apart from drawbacks in economic evolution and potential social unrest directly or indirectly related to this, there are a number of other domestic issues which could challenge the further pursuit of the to date successful development strategy — even when the external environment remains favourable and income distribution issues are not at the root of major social problems. Most prominent in this context are environmental constraints and in particular widespread water shortages. This could be the basis of a second variant of the less optimistic scenario due to internal conflicts.

China's exploitable water resources per capita are among the lowest in the world. According to one source over 400 of 660 cities experience water shortages, 90 % of the aquifers have various degrees of contamination and over-pumping of ground water in the North China Plain amounts according to certain estimates to some 4 billion m³ per year. Alongside energy, water is one of the greatest concerns of the Chinese government and a broad range of measures to reduce water consumption have either already been taken or are under serious discussion. Saving water, changes in agricultural practices, price reforms and desalination are the obvious choices. The most spectacular investment project in this context is a gigantic infrastructure project which after its completion in 2050 is expected to address regional water imbalances and allow the transfer of 45 billion m³ per year from the north to the south of the country. But this is four decades from now and much can happen in the meantime.

In a sense environmental and water supply problems, in particular due to their uneven distributional effects both at regional and group-specific level, tend to generate the same kind of social tensions as high unemployment and unsustainable inequalities in living conditions. Also in this context social protest or even unrest cannot be excluded and it is clear that the authorities will intervene to maintain order. There is no doubt that China's government bureaucracy is clearly reluctant to let go the levers of power, much like bureaucracies elsewhere in the world. That reluctance has often been overcome during the reform period by the willingness of the political leadership to override these interests, even if this meant at least on the surface a diminution in the power of the Party itself. In political or social crisis situations, as described in the three less optimistic scenarios, when the political leadership could feel more insecure, it can certainly not be excluded that the interests of the Party and the bureaucracy could merge again because the leadership sees the levers of bureaucratic control as essential to keeping political control over parts of the population.

The scenarios serve to illustrate a range of crucial issues for China's future. Perhaps most importantly, they raise questions concerning the sustainability of China's economic growth and the role that would be played by the international trading system, by a further successful reform process and by policies which ensure that economic progress is sustainable in the longer term both under social and environmental aspects. In addition they show clearly that a shift from external to domestic demand through a reduction of domestic savings and prudent currency appreciation would not only be beneficial for the world economy as a whole, but also for China. On the one hand it would reduce China's export dependence and on the other it would reduce the danger of protectionist reactions by China's main trading partners. And there is no doubt that the optimistic scenario would be the most desirable future both for China and for the world economy as a whole.

### The European Union: An Economic Giant with little Geopolitical Clout

No single European country, neither Germany nor France nor the United Kingdom, has the size and economic weight to represent on its own a major player in world geopolitical and economic affairs in the 21st century. The only potential relevant power is the European

Union. With a total population of around 500 million, a total GDP of 14.7 trillion US dollars and a common currency for at present 17 of its 27 member states, the EU's population is much smaller than that of China or India but larger than that of the United States. In terms of GDP the EU is slightly ahead of the US and reaches nearly three times that of China or Japan. Yet to exercise decisive influence in world politics the size of the population and the economy are only two of the necessary conditions. Others include military strength, a clear international agenda and the political power to pursue it. Overall concerning the three latter dimensions — despite much progress otherwise — today's European Union is fairly weak.

The European Union is a confederation of individual nation states and not a federal state. Nevertheless there are many policy domains in which member states have transferred all or major parts of their sovereignty to a common EU executive body, the European Commission. This includes such areas as international trade and agriculture, competition and subsidies, consumer protection and the environment as well as economic, social and territorial cohesion. The most important fields so far de facto kept outside any effective European competence are foreign affairs and security policy. Recent illustrations of this lack of a common European approach are the engagement of France and the United Kingdom in the civil war in Libya without effective EU consultation and the fact that Germany voted with China and Russia and not on the side of its traditional Western allies in a related UN Security Council decision.

Yet, despite of this and some other deficiencies European integration, in particular in general economic and fiscal policies, is one of the greatest success stories since the end of the Second World War. In a step-by-step process over more than 60 years most of Europe, with the notable exception of Norway and Switzerland has today been united in a single continent-wide market allowing the free circulation of goods, services, capital and people, combined with a customs union with a common tariff for all goods entering the territory. The EU is the world's number one exporter and importer and the largest trad-

475

ing partner of the United States, China, India and Russia. Apart from the integrated market, the second most important achievement is the European Monetary Union with a common currency, the Euro. With the exception of the United Kingdom and Denmark, all EU countries are committed to joining the Euro as soon as they meet the convergence criteria. Already today the Eurozone represents three quarters of EU GDP. After only ten years in existence, the new currency is the world's second most important reserve currency after the US dollar, and its share in international transactions and central bank reserves is continually rising.

As there is little medium term prospect that the European Union will evolve towards a federal state, if ever, the role of the European Union in the world and in particular in the global economy will very much be determined by the progress of necessary institutional reforms, by the EU's economic and social strength and by the future of the Euro. In a positive scenario, apart from better balancing widening and deepening in the integration process, both member governments and the European Commission would learn their lessons from the 2008 economic and financial crisis and the subsequent sovereign debt crisis especially in Greece, Ireland, Portugal and Spain.

On the macro-economic front, and in particular in the Eurozone, member governments in cooperation with the Commission would effectively strengthen the Stability and Growth Pact through more binding debt and public deficit criteria, including semi-automatic sanctions. They would broaden and deepen ex-ante supervision of budget policies — and this not only with respect to the central government's budget but also taking into account subnational budgets and social security. They would create a sufficiently powerful permanent crisis resolution mechanism with tough conditionality. And they would not contest the independence of the European Central Bank.

At micro-economic level governments and the Commission, each in their respective areas of responsibility, would further streamline regulations with the aim of enhancing competition on markets for products and services. They would improve the quality of public expenditure by shifting resources from consumption and support of non-competitive industries towards future-oriented investment. They would heavily invest in education and training and reduce excessive rigidities on the labour market. More generally, they would make all efforts to provide an overall economic and social climate which is conducive to entrepreneurship, innovation and risk-taking. The result would be a quantum leap in growth potential and in economic performance in the long run.

Unfortunately, even if there were broad consensus on the need for such a reform agenda policy makers are faced with some major difficulties regarding its implementation. Particularly important in this context are three kinds of asymmetries: *Firstly*, most of the benefits of policy reforms, in particular of supply side policies, materialise only after a certain time lag. But the costs of the adjustment process are felt in many instances immediately. *Secondly*, although these policies are very effective in raising macro-economic productivity, creating new jobs and combating inflation, their benefits are normally spread thinly all over the economy. In contrast, the related burdens are in many cases sartorially and/or regionally concentrated and clearly visible. *Thirdly*, jobs not created have no vote; jobs lost or in danger can be decisive with regard to the outcome of the next elections. As a result political opposition to reform policies builds up quite easily whereas support is often almost silent. The consequence is obvious. When the economy performs well, reforms are seldom considered as being urgent or even necessary, and when the economy is in the middle of a crisis, they may not go far enough or even not happen, because the time is not convenient. These observations could be the basis for a second scenario for the European Union which is less positive.

In this scenario it is assumed that Eurozone members succeed in implementing the macro-reform package including a strong commitment by France and Germany that, in contrast to the past, they would now adhere to the rules, too. The coordination of economic and in particular fiscal policy is much improved. The European Central Bank

477

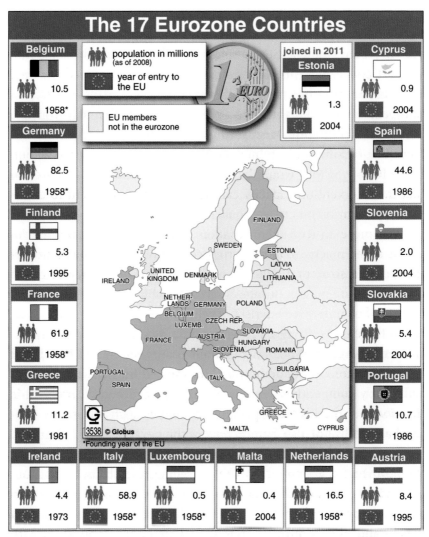

## The 17 Eurozone Countries

**Belgium**
10.5
1958*

population in millions (as of 2008)

year of entry to the EU

EU members not in the eurozone

**joined in 2011**
**Estonia**
1.3
2004

**Cyprus**
0.9
2004

**Germany**
82.5
1958*

**Spain**
44.6
1986

**Finland**
5.3
1995

FINLAND
SWEDEN
ESTONIA
LATVIA
LITHUANIA
IRELAND
UNITED KINGDOM
DENMARK
NETHER-LANDS
GERMANY
POLAND
BELGIUM
LUXEMB.
CZECH REP.
FRANCE
AUSTRIA
SLOVAKIA
HUNGARY
SLOVENIA
ROMANIA
PORTUGAL
ITALY
BULGARIA
SPAIN
GREECE
MALTA
CYPRUS

**Slovenia**
2.0
2004

**France**
61.9
1958*

**Slovakia**
5.4
2004

**Greece**
11.2
1981

G 3538 © Globus
*Founding year of the EU

**Portugal**
10.7
1986

| Ireland | Italy | Luxembourg | Malta | Netherlands | Austria |
|---------|-------|------------|-------|-------------|---------|
| 4.4 | 58.9 | 0.5 | 0.4 | 16.5 | 8.4 |
| 1973 | 1958* | 1958* | 2004 | 1958* | 1995 |

*The Eurozone was established on 1 January 1999 and included at the beginning eleven member countries of the European Union. Today there are 17 countries officially participating, and beyond that six smaller European states are using the Euro as their sole currency, too. The Eurozone is managed by the European Central Bank and the Euro Group composed normally by the finance ministers, in exceptional cases by the Heads of State of the Eurozone member countries.*

would act as the guardian of the stability of the Euro. It would re-focus on monetary policies and renounce buying treasury bonds from over-indebted countries. Euro bonds would definitely be ruled out. Support concerning problems with excessive sovereign debt would come in the form of time-limited guarantees, not loans first from a European Financial Stability Facility (EFSF) and after 2013 from the European Stabilisation Mechanism (SEM). The core capital of both these institutions — 440 billion Euros for the EFSF and 780 billion Euros for the SEM — would be leveraged to several trillion Euros so that the intervention capacity can be considered sufficient to counteract speculation on international financial markets.

Even more difficult than the successful conclusion of the reform efforts at the macro-economic front could be the implementation of the required structural adjustment. This applies in particular to the countries at the periphery, but also to Italy, which suffer from a severe decline of competitiveness vis-à-vis the core economies. A first issue is that there is no effective provision in the Eurozone context that increases in wages and non-wage-labour costs need overall be aligned to the evolution of productivity and for those countries which are not sufficiently competitive, remain clearly below. A second problem is that some of the least competitive economies such as Greece, Portugal and Italy, but also France, have a comparatively high degree of employment protection and anti-competitive market regulations. Furthermore higher economic growth would in principle facilitate structural adjustment policies. But it is exactly the group of countries with the most urgent reform requirements that suffer most from budget deficits and/or debt burdens, thus having no room to manoeuvre with regard to growth promoting fiscal stimulus. As a consequence, they cannot on their own grow out of the crisis, but have to shrink out of it.

This second scenario demonstrates clearly the complexity, the difficulties and potential time frames which are associated with the indispensable convergence process called for in the European Monetary Union, where currency depreciation as a policy instrument is no longer available. In order to bring public debt down to 60 % of

GDP by 2030 Greece, Portugal, Ireland and Spain, but probably also Italy, would have to maintain a significant primary budget surplus of between 7 and 3 % for the next 20 years. According to the same source: Assuming 2 % inflation it would take these countries about five years of zero growth in unit labour costs to return to their comparative 1990 level of competitiveness. And even this may not be sufficient as the EU core countries will in the meantime improve their competitiveness, too.

Considering the potential political fall-out of this second scenario in particular in the periphery countries, there is every reason to look at a third option. Some observers believe that the initial design faults of the European Monetary Union, which came to the forefront through the 2008 economic and financial crisis, would now get the ball rolling to close the books on the Euro dream. But these doomsday prophets may by far underestimate the political determination of present European leaders, especially the German Chancellor and the French President, to do everything to not be associated in future history books with the collapse of the Euro, one of the two greatest achievements in six decades of European integration. And, of course, also in economic terms, giving up on the Euro would result in an extremely costly policy error in both the short and the long term perspective.

The third and at present most realistic scenario therefore implies that, in addition to the structural adjustment efforts by the periphery countries themselves, the core countries would further help these countries to deal with the debt dynamics. If needed, this assistance will not only be provided by means of special loans and lowering the cost of borrowing through the EFSF or the ESM, but also through a once-for-all reduction of the initial burden of the debt. In particular for Greece such debt restructuring, both in form of depreciation of the principal and possibly through an extension of the repayment periods, is finally, but rather late under discussion. The proposal adopted by European leaders on 27 October 2011 would see private investors take a 50 % cut in the face value of their Greek bonds, which would

480

reduce the public debt of the country from 160 % to 120 % in 2020. The counterpart of this deal, which also includes another loan of 100 billion Euros between now and 2014, are very tough obligations with respect to both long term fiscal discipline after debt stabilisation and the most rigorous approach to wage restraint, privatisation of state-owned enterprises, regulatory reform and structural adjustment — and all this to the maximum degree and at the highest speed which is politically feasible and socially acceptable. Even under these conditions consolidation may take a decade or more.

Whatever the future holds in store, there is every prospect that with growing, partly policy-enforced convergence of member countries and with the European Monetary Union strengthened, the European Union will remain a strong player at least in world economic affairs. Even in 2010 the overall budget deficit of the Eurozone was at 6 % of GDP and total public debt at 84 %. The budget deficit of the United States was at 11 % of GDP and public debt over 90 %. And there is very little doubt that American public debt will rise more sharply in the foreseeable future than that of the Eurozone. Together with comparative inflationary expectations, the final result could in fact be a promising future for the Euro and not at all the end of a dream. Or to put it a different way: In the kingdom of the blind… — the US dollar being potentially weak and the Chinese RMB not yet ready — the one-eyed man is king.

## India: The next Economic Giant on the Horizon

Independent since 1947 and under the political leadership of Nehru until 1964, India chose international isolation and adopted a Soviet-style economic planning system. The official economic policy objective was self-sufficiency. But the result over a period of nearly four decades was the so called "Hindu rate of growth" of about 3.5 %. A new market-oriented economic policy approach, first experimented with in the 1970s and then forcefully implemented since the early 1990s, prepared the ground for a remarkable success story. After achieving an initial economic growth rate of 5.5 % in the first period a second shift to a higher growth trajectory occurred in 1995, resulting in real GDP growth of 7.3 %. p.a. Around 2003/2004 India experienced a third jump in the trend growth rate of real GDP to above 8.5 %. Forty million jobs were created between 2006 and 2010. Today and in PPP, the country represents the fourth largest economy in the world after the United States, China and Japan, leaving Germany just behind.

Nevertheless, as in the other countries dealt with so far, also in India there is a whole range of unfinished business. Although expenditure for key infrastructure investment has risen sharply, physical bottlenecks and low quality of services still impact negatively on macro-economic productivity. Notwithstanding that each child aged between 6 and 14 years has the right to compulsory and free education and 20 million previously out-of-school children are now enjoying formal education, due to a relatively poor education quality and low levels of graduation human capital formation is still insufficient to sustain the high growth trajectory in the long term. Further reforms are badly needed in labour, product and financial markets. There are still considerable barriers to trade and foreign direct investment which, together with administrative red tape, restrict competition, impede investment and reduce productivity growth. Finally, social policies need to be improved to reach the poor and combat extreme inequalities more generally. According to recent World Bank estimates 37 % of India's population, representing 420 million or one third of the world's poor, are living below the poverty line.

There is no doubt that the design and implementation of reform policies is much more difficult in a democracy and especially under conditions of a multi-party coalition and competitive populism than under an authoritarian regime. Both pushing them through and making them a success is, as a rule, not possible without negotiation, compromises and broad social acceptance. As regards the future of economic and social development in India, aside from the availability of

*Looking at the modern office buildings of Mumbai, the Indian economic capital with its high concentration of financial institutions and industry, one has difficulties to imagine that 50 % of the inhabitants of this city are still dwelling in slums and that one third of the world's poor are living in India.*

resources and the political will of the government it will be exactly this dimension which heavily co-determine whether the country will pursue a scenario of continuity, a scenario of further accelerated growth or a scenario where the economy swings back to a more moderate growth path with a return to slow human and social development.

The continuation scenario would assume that economic growth remains relatively high for some time, but still below its maximum potential. It would be characterised by a reform policy approach which supports present trends and otherwise primarily operates at the margin. Thus policy attention would be heavily focused on the development of major cities and such states which are prospering anyway, on the dynamic evolution of upper-knowledge intensive industries such as ICT, bio-tec, pharma and related services. And reforms predominantly progress where either short term, clearly visible gains or easy consensus can be achieved.

483

The government remains hesitant, however, in implementing most of the necessary fundamental reforms. It refrains from addressing major inefficiencies in state-owned enterprises. It delays the improvement of the education system. It backs off from a profound overhaul of the extremely restrictive labour market regulations. As a consequence, despite low wage levels private manufacturing tends to remain overly capital-intensive and as employment creation does not match the growth of the working age population unemployment will be further rising. At the same time very little is effectively done for poverty alleviation. This is mainly an issue for speeches in parliament and on red letter days. And with respect to the subsidies paid for food, electricity and petroleum, the government will still have to pay four rupees to get one effectively transferred to the poor. The other three get lost in administration or through corruption.

According to this scenario, India would not overcome the present dual economy and society. Delhi, Mumbai, Bangalore and a few other urban agglomerations would evolve as 21st century cities with impressive skylines, modern transport and communication infrastructures and a rising number of households with an income comparable to the OECD average and above. These parts of the country would fully participate in the globalisation process. In contrast, most of the rural areas, and this concerns in particular the states dependent primarily on agriculture, would remain underdeveloped and apart from television and a few telephone lines be basically cut off from the outside world.

There is little doubt that such drifting apart is not sustainable. On the one hand, it would result in further increasing migration from the rural areas to the cities and contribute to ever growing slums, implying an increasing potential for social unrest, crime and the spread of diseases. On the other, the tensions between the rich and the poor states could lead to a real test of national political structures. This could be the moment when the political leadership would shift its attention to the real problems of the country and turn to an inclusive development strategy corresponding to the second scenario. In principle, they should have done so since long. But sometimes democratic systems—and this, of course, not only in India—need a certain level of crisis before more fundamental reforms are seen as the only viable option.

Had the economic and social development strategy corresponding to the optimistic scenario been implemented from the outset, there is little doubt that the Indian economy would have—after 1978, the early 1990s and 2003—in all probability made a fourth time jump to a permanent higher growth trajectory—maybe from 8.5 to 10%—much earlier. In this scenario the government would embark on a comprehensive, strategic reform programme. The priority areas would include human development through improved education and health care, labour market reform, infrastructure, rural development, enhancing competition on product, services and capital markets, tackling inefficiencies in state-owned enterprises, upgrading fiscal policy by improving the quality and effectiveness of spending and broadening the tax base, alleviating poverty and last but not the least improving governance by streamlining the administration and fighting corruption.

Comparing India with other emerging economies such as China and Brazil, both literacy rates and government spending for education are still much lower. Insufficient government outlays are partly compensated for higher private spending. The result is, however, that differences in educational attainments across social background and gender are widening. Furthermore, in India the average time children spend at school is ten years, in other emerging countries it is thirteen. Overall higher enrolment and longer school attendance are just two aspects of improving education. They need to be complimented by higher quality in teaching and better school management. Here, too, India has a lot to do to catch up with other emerging countries. Most importantly the reform of the education system is not only, and for India perhaps not even primarily, an issue of cultural accomplishment, it is the most effective vehicle for economic and social integration—pre-supposing that there are sufficient jobs available.

Exactly this point illustrates why the Indian government has to carry out not just one reform at any given time, but needs to make progress on several fronts in parallel. India's labour market regulations are more restrictive than those of China and Brazil and even more than those of all OECD countries but two. As a consequence, even though manufacturing employment has risen in recent years, less than 5 % occurred in companies which could exploit at the same time low labour costs and economies of scale and on this basis successfully compete on international markets. A consolidation of the 46 central and 200 state labour laws together with a reduction of the stringency of labour protection would make a major contribution to the expansion of smaller enterprises, to overall job creation, to the movement of labour out of agriculture to more productive uses and to alleviate poverty. It would also raise macro-economic productivity and lift potential economic growth.

This is not the place to discuss all necessary reforms and how they interact in detail. Doing this would also require a discussion of the interplay between rural development and infrastructure, in particular water management, of the relationship between economic performance, competition and further liberalisation of markets, and of the interaction of nearly all the reforms with inequality and poverty. There is no doubt that, in principle, many in the Indian political leadership are well aware of what would be required to initiate another positive step change in the country's economic and social development. But the future is not predetermined. On the one hand, domestic political dynamics in a democracy do not necessarily guarantee that the longer-term and general good for a country always keeps the upper hand over the short-term and frequently partial interests. On the other, there is no certainty either that the international environment will remain favourable.

A third scenario is therefore that India gets stuck with only moderate economic growth and even more gradual human and social development. At domestic level, this would imply that the Indian political leadership would not succeed in working out or effectively implementing a coherent strategy in response to the complex political, economic, social and environmental challenges facing the coun-

486

try over the coming three decades or so. Infrastructure bottlenecks could represent an increasingly important obstacle to high economic growth, in particular in industry. Too few improvements in the education system could lead to a lack of skilled labour, rising unemployment and increasing frustration of the youth. Too little progress in rural development could result in growing migration from the underdeveloped states to the cities and slow down poverty alleviation both at the country side and in the urban areas. Further rising inequality combined with entrenched corruption could evolve into a political and social time bomb with a huge explosive potential. And of course, should there be an accumulation of several such problems; India could also have increasing difficulties to remain a winner in the international competition for foreign direct investment which would accentuate the down-turn.

But even if domestic policies are by and large adequate and successful, India could run into problems in case of a major deterioration of the dynamics of the global economy. It is true that both India and China managed the 2008 economic and financial crisis quite well, but this was so far a short-term event, and a general recourse to protectionism could be prevented. Yet, the longer-term implications of this crisis, in particular in the United States and Europe, have still not yet been absorbed. Should, as a consequence, world economic growth slow in the longer-run, there is little prospect for the Indian economy not to be hurt.

## Japan:
### An Economic Powerhouse in the Doldrums

The rapid reconstruction of Germany after the Second World War was considered world-wide as an economic miracle, but the economic success story of Japan was by far more exciting. In terms of GDP, Japan surpassed Great Britain in 1967, France in 1968 and even Germany already in 1969. Since then and for the next 40 years Japan stood out as the second largest economy. Only the United States with three times the population was economically more important. The world was fascinated. Herman Kahn, one of the most prominent futurists of the time, stated in a publication on Japanese development prospects that "it would not be surprising if the 21st century turned out to be the Japanese century". And he was not alone. Still in 1979 Ezra F. Vogel, a distinguished Harvard academic, published a book entitled "Japan as Number One: Lessons for America" and his basic thesis was that the Americans could learn from the Japanese how to manage the transformation towards the post-industrial society. And certainly, extrapolating the 35 year long past trends, nobody could imagine what would happen to the Japanese economy and society in the next 35 years.

Over the 1960s and 1970s Japan still benefitted from a demographic dividend, with many young people entering the labour force. Only very few observers were aware in the early 1980s that there could be a severe problem with population ageing. As all other OECD countries, Japan had suffered from two oil shocks and several economic cycles in the 1970s and 1980s and always recovered well. There was some concern about rising property prices, but only until it was too late; hardly anyone in Japan or elsewhere could imagine the dramatic economic consequences the implosion of the real estate bubble in 1990 could imply for the Japanese economy in the long term.

In fact, from 1973 until 1990 Japan also remained by far the most dynamic industrial country. Average real economic growth rates were at 4.1% p.a. compared to 3.1% for the United States and 2.4% for Germany. A frequent worry was over-heating and inflation, not depression and deflation. But exactly this was the new Japanese reality for the next decade and beyond. With the notable exceptions of 1991, 1996 and 2010 economic growth never recovered to a level above 3%. The average rate over the 20 years from 1991 to 2010 was no more than 0.9%. Unemployment rose to levels never seen before. Over the same period inflation remained at 0.4%, with a total of 8 years in the negative. And all this happened despite continuous and ambitious monetary easing by the Bank of Japan and expansionary fiscal policies, resulting by 2011 in general government gross financial liabilities of more than 200 % of GDP. That Japan was, in addition, hit in 1995 by an earthquake in the Kobe area and in 2011 by a major catastrophe in form of the combination of an earthquake, a tsunami and a nuclear accident associated with enormous human suffering have made and still make things worse, but they are not the root of the underlying problems, the solution of which will determine the country's longer term future.

The three fundamental challenges to which Japan has to respond with urgency if it wishes to overcome the nearly two decades' long economic stagnation, are the economic and social implications of the ageing population, the consolidation of public finances where the room for further expansionary policies is anyway exhausted and a breakthrough towards better macro-economic performance on the basis of higher productivity growth. All three tasks are demanding. They require vigorous action, in particular in domestic structural policy reforms and more international openness both in economic and social terms. This is not to say that Japan has not already made considerable progress in many of the relevant fields, but the necessary reforms frequently came fairly late and probably did not go far enough. Furthermore, in a rapidly changing world reforms which met the requirements of yesterday in most cases do not meet those of tomorrow. Reform policy is a permanent effort and policies which were well designed to respond to the necessities of the past more often than not turn out to be inappropriate for solving the problems of the future.

The scenarios for the long term economic and social development of Japan resulting from these challenges are quite obvious. The most favourable option assumes that the Japanese government, most other relevant political, economic and social actors and in particular also the electorate wake up and support in a common endeavour a huge and comprehensive reform programme. The worst scenario would be just discussing the problems, but not decide to do something uncomfortable and perhaps even unpalatable. This would be inevitably the road towards decline. And decline is so easy. It is powered by inertia; it does not require courageous actions; it just happens. In between these extremes is the usual third way. This approach, however, is frequently paved with bad compromises, full of potholes and if not very carefully designed and managed, always fraught with the danger of an involuntarily slippage into the worst case scenario.

As concerns demographic developments, low birth rates and zero immigration will in all probability result in a shrinking population with an officially estimated decrease from a peak of 127 million around 2005 to no more than 95 million in 2050. High life expectation together with the former trends will accelerate an ageing population. The share of elderly persons over 65 which was at 11.6 % in 1989 and 20 % in 2006 is projected to rise to around 25 % in 2030 and to nearly 40 % in 2050. The three most critical developments in this context are a shrinking working-age population, an increasing dependency rate and in all probability a decrease in overall savings.

After having reached a peak of 87 million in 1995, the population aged 15 to 65 is expected to fall to a mere 52 million in 2050. As a consequence, only if Japan succeeds in offsetting the decline in the labour force by increasing overall labour productivity by an average of about 1 % annually over the whole period, would the GDP not shrink. Compared to productivity levels of other OECD countries and to long term past trends in Japan, this is not impossible: Even long term stagnation of GDP would already require vigorous efforts in structural reform. Achieving positive GDP growth beyond that would be still more demanding. Sparking innovation; enhancing competition, including in network sectors; reducing producer support to agriculture; raising the efficiency of the financial sector; and lowering restrictions on foreign direct investment are illustrations of such measures.

Another part of the strategy would be slowing down the decline of the labour force. In principle there are three possibilities. *Firstly*, compared to other OECD countries female labour force participation rates are still extremely low in Japan. But to raise them would mean changing the habit that mothers stop working after their first child is born. This would require more and better facilities for childcare, measures to ensure that women have fewer difficulties combining work with family responsibilities, and perhaps also some efforts to provide women with more equal rights in the working world. *Secondly*, immigration into Japan is zero and the share of permanent foreign residents in the country is between 1 and 2 %. Even if Japan does definitively not want the high numbers of immigrants finding new homes in North America or Europe, there might perhaps be some room at least for university trained, highly qualified middle class people who would contribute to innovation and increasing productivity. And *thirdly*, as in other counties with ageing populations, there is the option of raising the retirement age.

The latter measure could also help to improve the fiscal position, which is the second major challenge facing Japan over the next decade or more. Among all OECD countries Japan has the highest ratio of public debt over GDP—even higher than Greece, the problem child of the Eurozone. Nevertheless, Japan compares favourably to Greece, because its public debt is financed on the basis of domestic savings. The difficulty for Japan is that after 18 consecutive years of budget deficits the country's public debt level is rapidly approaching a point where it becomes unsustainable: *Firstly*, because of the debt dynamics involving a growing share of interest payment in the public budget; *secondly*, because of the prospect of rising interest rates; and *thirdly*, because the ageing population which, even if the retirement age is adjusted, will not only lead to sharply increasing health costs, but in all probability also to a decrease of domestic savings.

Under the assumption that interest rates remain at no more than 1.5 % above nominal growth, Japan would need a permanent surplus of 3 % over GDP in the primary budget balance just to stabilise the public debt ratio. In order to achieve consolidation the respective surplus would have to exceed this rate for many years. These are much higher rates than presently planned by the government. Taking into account the budgetary implications of the reconstruction costs after the 2011 major catastrophe, which are estimated at about 1% of GDP over at least six years, budget cuts alone will never be sufficient. Raising the retirement age could relieve some of the spending pressure of an ageing population. But revenue increases, too, in particular through higher consumption taxes, would be unavoidable.

Budget consolidation would be easier if economic growth could be speeded up, all the more as both restrictive fiscal policies and an ageing population would have a potential negative impact on the dynamics of domestic demand. But then the long term productivity growth trend of about 1% annually would not be enough by far either. On the one hand, domestic structural reforms would need to be even more vigorous and on the other, the opening to the outside world in terms of trade, foreign direct investment, technology transfer and immigration might be even more profound and radical. And, of course, under all circumstances it would be important for the success of any longer term adjustment strategy aimed at reducing Japan's present vulnerabilities that the international environment remains favourable. One can hope for this, but it is not at all certain.

There is no doubt that the challenges Japan faces over the next two decades or so are daunting. The Japanese, however, have always shown unusual solidarity in times of crisis. They could do so once again even though the deterioration of the country's economic situation is more or less creeping and the point of an immediate threat has not yet been reached. Delayed adjustment is the most expensive adjustment and much delay can be seen already. Only a strong Japan can be an influential and powerful player in world economic affairs, and if this is the ambition of the Japanese government and the Japanese people, there is very little choice. The first best scenario may be politically unrealistic. But whatever form the knife edge walk out of the present severe difficulties may take, any third way must definitively be on the safe side and sufficiently far away from the edge. The alternative would be the road to decline.

# CHAPTER 12

# The Future of Global Governance

Since the end of the Second World War, it has been primarily the United States which shaped the international economic order. It engaged the Europeans and Japanese in building up and strengthening the multilateral system of free trade, foreign direct investment and technology transfer. It pushed for the free convertibility of currencies and the liberalisation of international capital flows. It succeeded in convincing an increasing number of countries of the advantages of a market economy, economic openness and active participation in the on-going globalisation process.

The gains in efficiency and wealth were, however, not only to the benefit of the participating countries and the world economy as a whole; an important dimension in the process was also that the ever increasing international economic interdependence also supported the domestic and foreign policy interests of the United States. The importance of this latter aspect became obvious in particular whenever certain world economic developments faced the US government with major trade-offs between its domestic and the international interests. Among many others, one illustrative example is the run-up to the collapse of the Bretton Woods System at the end of the 1960s. Here a choice had to be made between a restrictive monetary and fiscal policy stance which would have met the needs of the international monetary system or the opposite which was, in fact, realised as only this was in line with domestic policy priorities.

Looking at other such self-serving decisions, which nearly all occurred when the United States experienced a phase of relative weakness, it appears that political, economic and military strength is a precondition for any major power to exercise international influence, to provide a systemic orientation in global economic affairs and to be able and willing to bear the side costs of global leadership. At present, the United States is once again in a comparatively weak position. The recovery after the economic and financial crisis of 2008 is still fragile; unemployment is at record levels; military capacity is about to be overstrained; and perhaps worst of all, as the budget deficit is at 10 % and public debt approaching 100 % of GDP, both are severely affecting the freedom of the US government to make and implement cost-intensive decisions.

At the same time there are other developments on the world political and economic scene which may be changing the game plan of the future dramatically. When Europe and Japan in the 1950s and 1960s and several generations of newly industrialising countries in later years achieved their economic take-off, they never contested American dominance, and it was by and large commonly shared political, economic and social values which made American leadership relatively easy. With the emergence of China and India in particular and the rise of Brazil, Russia, South Africa and a number of other developing countries more generally, the hegemonic position of the United States will definitively be in long term decline. This does not mean that the US will not remain for quite some time the most powerful, one of the richest and the technologically most advanced country, but the other players will increasingly insist on co-determining world political and economic affairs and, with some probability, not necessarily on the basis of a set of commonly shared fundamental values.

A second aspect which makes the world of the future different from the past is the increasingly higher degree of global interdependence. Apart from the threat of nuclear war and nuclear proliferation,

494

the possible destruction of the ozone layer and the problem of generalised poverty in certain parts of the world, most international issues arising in the second half of the 20th century, even if they had global reach, could in principle be resolved by international co-operation within the triad of North America, Europe and Japan and a few other like-minded countries. To the extent that other players were involved such as the OPEC group, negotiations were normally straightforward. Today in contrast, the world is faced with a growing number of truly global issues and many of them are extremely complex and interconnected. Climate change, longer term energy, food, water and cyber security as well as international migration are a few illustrative examples. Such global challenges require global responses and an international governance architecture which does not represent the emerging political and economic power structures of the 21st century appears increasingly inappropriate.

A third important dimension affecting global governance is the increasing number and the growing weight of non-government actors. On the one hand, these include multinational corporations and transnational business organisations which may either request government action and support it or undermine it—both at domestic and at international level. On the other hand, there are ever more powerful NGOs, networks of experts, civil society groups and faith-based organisations which are highly effective in articulating special issues, reframing the policy agenda and mobilising the public. The most effective vehicle in the latter context is the Internet. In many cases such actors are valuable partners of government efforts. But sometimes such groups, in particular if they focus on just one issue area, thereby ignoring interconnectedness and the general interest, and/or if they fuel emotions and fear on irrational grounds, can make appropriate policy design much more difficult.

Global governance is the process of decision-making, based on the interplay of the various relevant actors, with regard to global or international issues which transcend a considerable number of states, economies, societies, cultures and national histories. Already in the past and even in the second half of the 20th century, when leadership in the context of globalisation was no longer forced on the various other players—or at least if so, by soft power and not through military action—, there have nearly always been open or disguised tensions; on the one hand between efficiency and legitimacy and on the other between the adherence to a rule-based system and the temptation of the more powerful to take exception whenever the rules played against major domestic interests.

A multipolar power configuration characterised by diverging interest profiles and differences in fundamental values will not necessarily resolve these problems, but may under certain conditions even amplify them. As at the same time the number and complexity of global issues and their interconnectedness are reaching new heights both in quantitative and in qualitative terms, global governance is at a critical crossroad. Among the many options three stand out as possible prototypes: *Firstly*, managed globalisation, primarily based on international co-operation; *secondly*, muddling through where insufficient reform of the international governance system and adhocracy prevails; and *thirdly*, power play, in particular by and among the most forceful.

### *Managed Globalisation:* <br> *The Conflict* <br> *between Efficiency and Legitimacy*

Overall there is no doubt that the post-WWII multilateral global governance system with the United Nations, the IMF, the OECD, the World Bank, the Bank for International Settlements and a number of other international organisations within or outside the UN framework served the world very well. Most outstanding were the contributions of the UN Security Council in preserving peace at least at world level, of the IMF in terms of macro-economic surveillance, of the OECD concerning the general economic policy dialogue among member countries and the focus on structural policies, of the GATT/WTO with regard to the development of a rule-based multilateral trading system and of the World Bank as concerns support of developing countries. This does not imply that each of these organisations could not have performed better in particular cases and circumstances. But the overall balance remains positive.

Nevertheless, the conflict between efficiency and legitimacy was a permanent feature of the system. As regards legitimacy the United Nations Organisation with its broad membership was certainly the most appropriate forum but apart from the Security Council, which is even now highly restricted, the UN was surely not the most efficient body. But even the overall more effective organisations with restricted membership, such as the OECD, or those with non-equal voting rights, such as the IMF, were increasingly by-passed by smaller informal groupings of leading countries such as the G5 created after the first oil crisis, becoming G6 respectively G7 in the mid-1970s and G8 after 1998. Finally, the economic and financial crisis of 2008 has clearly demonstrated that world economic issues can no longer be effectively dealt with in a format which excludes the emerging economies such as China, India, Brazil and a few others. The forming of a G20 is therefore the most recent innovation in global governance. But this group also does not escape the usual shortcomings, and it may incorporate even all of them: It is still too small to be legitimate and it may already be too big to be efficient.

In terms of political realism an all-inclusive coordinated management of the globalised world, based on multilateral co-operation among a vast majority of UN member countries, appears therefore practically excluded. Even within the G20 some members will be more equal than most of the others and the two candidates standing out at present are the United States and China. India will still need some time to join the first league. The extent to which the European Union at least at a later stage and Japan could be serious partners will primarily depend on the question of whether they get their internal problems resolved.

Assuming economic stabilisation of the Eurozone, Europe would have the overall potential, but only if the EU moved to a higher degree of political integration, spoke with one voice and acted accordingly—including in such areas as foreign affairs and security policy. Japan, the smallest potential actor in this context, will only have sufficient weight if it succeeds in overcoming its longer term economic problems. Two further countries which may exercise more influence than the rest of the G20 group could be Russia and Brazil. But Russia compared to its ambitions may still be too weak for quite some time, whereas Brazil is still too much inward-looking. At least at present it seems unlikely that it would take international initiatives of its own, but of course whenever in its interests it would support the position of China or other emerging countries.

The old global power configuration with the United States in the lead and Japan, Germany, the United Kingdom, France and in trade matters the EU as the most powerful partners worked fairly well until the late 1990s. On the surface there would not be any reason why the new combination of major powers with the United States and China more equal than the others and possibly India, the EU, Japan as well as Russia and Brazil playing a greater role should not be able to manage the world economy at least equally successfully. Nevertheless, there are three issues which deserve attention.

*Firstly*, the old power configuration was based on a group of countries which shared common fundamental values. This is not guaranteed in the new configuration. *Secondly*, the interests of the old group of leading countries were more homogeneous and the results of their actions overall more predictable. As regards the new group, the world may be faced with ever shifting coalitions among the G20 members. And *thirdly*, even if the cooperation among G20 members should turn out to be by and large effective, there still remains the more general problem that such informal groups as the G20 — and the G7/8 before — need an institutional capacity for common analysis, multilateral negotiation and implementation of the decisions agreed upon.

498

*The G20 is the first significant incarnation of a global governance architecture for the 21st century. The member countries represent 90 % of GDP, more than 80 % of world trade and two thirds of the world population. The G20 was established in 1999 as a group of finance ministers and central bank governors. Since the 2008 financial and economic crisis regular meetings are also held at heads of state level.*

This points to the urgent need for a reform of the existing major international organisations or if this is not possible to the in principle less desirable alternative to create new ones. As a rule reform must take into account *firstly*, the new political and economic realities in terms of representation; *secondly*, the new issues to be included in an up-dated mandate and/or programme of work; *thirdly*, as appropriate, an adjustment of procedures; and *fourthly*, as a consequence necessary organisational changes. There is not enough space here to deal with the particular reform imperatives concerning the relevant international organisations in detail. A few of the more general issues pertinent and illustrative in this context will be discussed in relation to the next scenario.

At this stage it appears important to spell out why even in a G20 configuration effective international cooperation within the institutional framework of international organisations is of paramount importance. The G7/8 process has already clearly demonstrated that meetings of heads of states, supported by national "sherpas", cannot deliver the kind of public good which is essential to the success of international cooperation and global governance in terms of effectiveness, credibility and accountability in the long run. Not only that such gatherings — even at G20 level — still lack legitimacy; the results of these kinds of meetings are primarily non-binding political declarations about desirable orientations as seen by the participants. What is still needed in addition is enhanced inclusiveness and the overcoming of the capacity deficit of the informal groups.

There is little doubt that even a dedicated secretariat in support of such groups can hardly provide the necessary forum and platform for dialogue and negotiations to elaborate the desired and necessary international rules, codes of conduct or multilateral surveillance activities. As a consequence, any kind of operational managed globalisation in the multipolar world of the 21st century may require *firstly* an effective steering group, the G20, perhaps principally led for the next decade or so by the United States and China; *secondly* a reformed or partly renewed framework of multilateral organisations with an experienced permanent and independent international secretariat; and *thirdly* a close and trusted relationship between the steering group and the formal multilateral structures. This does not mean that the many other informal groupings would cease to exist. But most of them, including the non-government actors, would focus on particular issues or interests and feed their work directly or indirectly into the mainstream global coordination and cooperation process.

In fact, to a certain extent this kind of cooperative process between the G20 and the existing international organisations is already now on the way to materialising. For example: The G20 called on the IMF to enhance global and country-specific economic and financial surveillance with a focus on systemic risks and vulnerabilities and continue its activities to further improve the global capacity to cope with shocks of a systemic nature. They invited the Bank for International Settlements (BIS), in particular the BCBS and the FSB, to further advance work on a new financial regulatory framework and both the BIS and the World Bank together to collaborate on regulatory reform pertaining specifically to emerging economies and developing countries. They asked the OECD to cooperate with the FSB and others to enhance consumer protection in the financial sector and again the OECD together with the International Energy Agency and the World Bank to analyse in more detail oil market and oil price developments. Furthermore, the IMF and the World Bank were asked to develop targeted initiatives to financially support developing countries in need and contribute to ensuring food security. Last but not least, the G20 is initiating and pushing forward reforms of international organisations, most visibly so far at the IMF and the BIS.

Looking ahead to the future, the G20 may, however, increasingly be faced with conflicting requirements. On the one hand, the group may be most effective if it continues to focus on economic, financial and development affairs. On the other, the range of issues requiring efficient leadership in the global governance framework of the 21st century is much broader, as is the capacity of the whole patchwork of international organisations. Still very close to the present concerns of the G20 — beyond the institutions already mentioned above — are the FAO, ILO and some other specialised UN bodies such as UNIDO, UNDP or UNEP. But the need for efficiency and in particular coherence of work and policy approaches goes much further. International health issues which are dealt with at WHO or nuclear safety which falls under the responsibility of IAIA are just two examples.

It is true that the G20 has already expanded its agenda since the 2008 meeting in Pittsburgh which almost exclusively focused on "a framework for strong, sustainable and balanced growth". But even with the setting up of further working groups there will be limits. One way to overcome the inherent capacity deficit and continued action as an informal global governance group could be designating a certain number of important issue areas permanent agenda items, others reviewed regularly every three years or so and a third type be placed on the agenda whenever there is need either due to a looming global crisis or when international cooperation in a certain field is in a deadlock and needs some new impetus and orientation. Setting and agreeing on the agenda will not be easy. And as previously in the old configuration, there remains the challenge that all stakeholders, large and small, need to trust the system, commit to collective action, play by the rules and not opt out whenever they find this more convenient.

## *Muddling Through: The Difficulties of Reforming the Global Governance Architecture*

Any such vision of managed globalisation, even as a scenario of future global governance structures and processes, will surely invite violent protest. "Vertical multilateralism" may still belong to the most polite expressions which such a model could provoke. And, of course, there is hardly any question about the democratic deficit, the continued lack of legitimacy and the fact that the leading countries would always try to look after their own interests and policy priorities first. No government is elected or otherwise instated with the aim of realising world welfare at the cost of its own people, a behaviour pattern that has very much been reinforced by the fact that growing international interdependence has over time resulted in increasingly strong interrelationships between domestic and international issues.

Developments in international trade and investment policy are a good illustration of this. In the early years of GATT negotiations, trade liberalisation was primarily a matter of discussion among technocrats who tried to equalise the overall benefits from liberalisation among participating countries. Already in the 1970s domestic interest groups raised their voice more forcefully and turned trade negotiations from a more technical to a political process. Since the street protests against the OECD Multilateral Agreement on Investment in

1998 and the protest movements around the 1999 WTO Ministerial Meeting in Seattle, politically and ideologically motivated mass activism of anti-globalisation groups is a recurrent concomitant of major international conferences or meetings. G8 and G20 meetings are no exception.

As neither anarchy nor a return to a fragmented, nation-based world economy appears to be an attractive alternative, there appears in fact no other option than accepting global leadership by the G20 and even inside this group some major players being more equal than others in order to ensure efficiency. The persistent lack of legitimacy would partly be compensated for through the close interrelationship and cooperation of this group with existing international organisations with an independent professional secretariat and broader membership. But there are limits. An important precondition for effective and constructive cooperation with the existing international organisation is an adequate reform of these institutions. This requirement may be the Achilles heel of the optimistic scenario, called "Managed Globalisation".

Leaving aside cooperation between central banks in the framework of the BIS, a cursory glance at the IMF, the World Bank, the OECD and the WTO would suggest the following: The IMF is probably most advanced in the reform process. From 2012 onwards the ten largest shareholders will be the ten systemically most important countries in the world economy. Membership and voting rights on the Executive Board will be aligned accordingly. And in particular in the light of the 2008 economic and financial crisis, the mandate of the IMF has been widened and strengthened. With the recently decided capital increase its intervention capacity will also be enhanced. Partly due to the kind of issues on the agenda, but partly perhaps also because of its most suitable, already existing internal structure, most of the missions entrusted by the G20 to one of the existing international organisations in the past three years have been handed over to the IMF.

To a certain extent the debate on the reform of the World Bank focuses on the same or similar themes as that on the IMF. This is primarily true with regard to governance issues such as participation, representation, voting rights and the leadership selection process. But this covers only part of the critical discussion. Other important issues are ambiguities with respect to the accountability of the shareholders and the management, and perhaps most importantly and partly related to this, key weaknesses in strategy formulation. According to a recent assessment by a High Level Commission on the Modernisation of the World Bank Group Governance, "the institution currently lacks effective mechanisms to formulate a clear strategy that can be used to set priorities, balance trade-offs, and align operations and resources with strategic goals," and "Mission creep is endemic, weakening accountability for results and increasing the risk that resources will be misallocated or spread too thin, undermining the institution's effectiveness". This dimension of the reform may be harder than just further transferring voting rights from industrialised countries to emerging economies and developing countries.

As regards the OECD, the organisation has always flexibly adjusted its work programme and helped its member governments to identify, analyse, evaluate and respond to the strategic challenges of a rapidly changing world economy. The OECD has also extended its membership, but this does not include the new major players China, India, Brazil and Russia. Even if working relationships with these countries have been intensified in recent years, the effectiveness of international cooperation and surveillance on the basis of shared views on economic developments and policy and in particular peer pressure is not the same. Another difficult issue is that to be effective at global level the organisation may have to adjust at least part of its internal structures to the G20 configuration. To gain the agreement the many small European member countries to such a move may be politically very difficult, if not impossible. Nevertheless, if it does not happen the OECD could easily lose influence at global level.

The WTO, in contrast, appears to already be in a major crisis now. From a formal point of view the broad membership with equal voting rights would provide this organisation with the highest degree of legitimacy. Furthermore, the organisation has succeeded over time in broadening its activities into quite a few areas initially excluded from its mandate. Trade in agriculture and trade in services on the one hand and behind-the-border issues such as TRIMs and TRIPs are the most pertinent examples. There is also no doubt that the WTO's internal procedures have become more democratic and transparent than those of the GATT. As before, the WTO serves as the guardian of the present multilateral trading system and its trade policy review work is highly appreciated. But with the Doha Round completely in deadlock and many longstanding bilateral issues unsettled, questions arise not only about its efficiency, but even about its relevance.

There is no doubt that a rule-based approach combined with an effective dispute settlement mechanism would be an ideal solution to many international issues. In particular it would protect the interests of smaller countries, at least as long as the major players adhere to the rules. As to the present reality with regard to the WTO, it appears, however, that there is "greater disengagement from the US and the EU (and of domestic constituencies within them), greater dissatisfaction from the BICs (China, India, Brazil) and their reluctance to make concessions and greater discontent from the LDCs that complain about marginalisation".

Looking at the whole patchwork of relevant international organisations and in particular at the prospect of effective and timely reforms of the IMF, the World Bank, the OECD and the WTO it is extremely doubtful that their structures and processes will be adapted to the geopolitical and economic realities of the 21st century as forcefully and rapidly as desirable. The IMF could perhaps be an exception.

All the prospects thus exist for an evolution that could be considered as a second scenario, called "Muddling Through" where vertical multilateralism would be combined with selective multilateralism. This means whenever a problem corresponds to the capabilities and power patterns of the existing multilateral structures and processes, there is a good chance that the analytical work and the relevant negotiations would be performed in one or a combination of the present

*The "Chateau de la Muette", the OECD headquarters in Paris, is since more than 50 years a brand name for independent expert economic and social analysis and policy advice. It is here where high-level government officials regularly discuss policy approaches and exchange their experiences across the whole range of macro-economic, structural, social, environmental, trade and development policies.*

international organisations. Otherwise there would be either specific arrangements, postponement of action or power play by the large countries.

Specific arrangements may lead to acceptable results if they involve the relevant players, large and small, in a particular policy area and focus on very concrete issues. To the extent that the problems to be resolved are of a regional nature, this format may work because the relevance of potential actors is *inter alia* defined by geography. In the case of more global issues there will nearly always be a heated debate concerning which countries are relevant. The struggle at the latter front can easily result in the setting up a so-called "Royal Commission" characterised by analysis and dialogue but never resulting in binding decisions and actions. Sometimes, in particular when certain more powerful countries feel that an issue is not yet ripe for decision or action, such an outcome may in fact be part of a hidden agenda.

Indirect and direct postponement of action is frequently the most favoured solution should the interests of the most powerful players be too divergent. The danger of this approach is that certain undesirable developments become irreversible and/or that the options for action are increasingly narrowed down. More often than not this is the one-way road to a situation where policy makers tend to justify their too late and then precipitate, frequently ill-advised ad-hoc decisions with the argument that they had no alternative, whereas the truth is that they no longer had an alternative. Climate change may be the most serious global issue where such a process is now under way despite all pressure from expert panels and civil society groups. But there are many others, and most of them are increasingly interconnected.

Again and again the international community may therefore be faced with urgent complex challenges and crisis-driven issues. Most of these will require both a global and effective governance authority which sets the agenda, the priorities and the direction, and ongoing efforts within the established international cooperation frameworks. Issue-specific special, frequently temporary arrangements and even more so ad-hocery are as a matter of principle always second best solutions. But even this format of international cooperation would certainly still be better than the third possible scenario, in which the large countries are pursuing their national interests regardless of the common global good. Perhaps the threat of such a development could at least in the longer term provide the necessary incentives to seriously push for the reform of the existing international organisations, even if it means, in particular for smaller countries, losing a certain degree of status and apparently existing influence.

## Power Play:
## Ultima Ratio or Permanent Temptation?

There may be two reasons why power play by the large countries, both in general and among themselves, cannot be discounted as a potential reality. One is increasing frustration with regard to the effectiveness of the established institutional framework of international cooperation. The other is that the major players become or remain inward-looking. As a consequence, they would take new initiatives on global or broader international issues only when necessary in order to satisfy pressing domestic interests.

The United States, although it will remain the most powerful country also in the new more multipolar power configuration, will in all probability be increasingly constrained in its international ambitions by persisting concerns about economic growth, high unemployment and above all a further worsening fiscal position. This reduces the capacity and willingness of the country to assume global responsibilities and pay for the side costs of a global leader. At least in a medium term perspective it seems that the US needs to come to grips with a number of domestic issues first, before it can be expected to again take care of the common good at global level. But this does not exclude targeted power play even of a unilateral nature wherever major US interests are at stake.

Europe and Japan, the two other major economic power houses of the old world order, will on all probability remain weak on the geopolitical scene. They may be able to protect themselves if it comes to power play, but they may hardly wish to take any initiatives in this sense themselves. Japan is in an ambiguous and difficult position. Geographically and culturally it belongs to the East, and in terms of its political and economic system it has associated itself with the West. With the burden of a rapidly ageing population and unresolved fiscal problems, as the smallest of the economic powers of the past it may increasingly be forced to take sides. This would be particularly rele-

*Structural change including through international trade always results in generating winners and losers. Yet, theory and experience demonstrate that defensive and protectionist policies are rarely to the benefit of the potential losers, even if the foreign competition is considered to be unfair. The only promising longer-term option is flexible adjustment to the new economic, social and technological circumstances.*

vant if the controversy is between the United States and China. Japan's strength in the scenario of power play may be that it would always be courted as a heavyweight ally.

With the debt problems of some periphery countries of the Eurozone still unsettled, the European Union, both member governments and the European institutions, will focus its attention primarily on economic and financial stabilisation and — alongside emergency measures — on the urgent task of reforming internal economic and fiscal policy architecture. But even independently of these immediate challenges and — with the exception of international trade and monetary policies — the EU's voice at global level will not correspond to the size of the population, to the total GDP or the military force of its member countries combined as long as there is not a higher degree of integration, including in particular foreign affairs and defence policies. As Japan, also Europe may therefore always be a much sought-after ally, but perhaps with a focus on the leading member countries, as the EU as a whole may be less predictable and under certain circumstances even less reliable.

The real countervailing power to the United States in geopolitics will be China which since very recently is the second largest national economy of the world. The country has been a member of APEC since 1991 and of the WTO since 2001. It is levelling up its influence in the IMF and the World Bank—most forcefully since the 2008 economic and financial crisis. And more importantly still, China has a permanent seat on the UN Security Council and is member of the G20. In many respects China has therefore accepted the existing post-WWII political and economic world order inherited from the times of US hegemony—including the more recent innovations such as the G20. But it would be wrong to conclude from this that China has equally accepted the same degree of US leadership as Europe and Japan have done before. Not only will China co-determine the rules of the game in the future, it will also insist that its own foreign policy principles be respected.

One of the most critical leitmotifs in this context is the traditional, centuries old Chinese policy doctrine which today is also part of the UN Charter, namely the principle of non-interference in the internal affairs of another sovereign country. For China itself this has two dimensions: On the one hand, China is opposed to the meddling of Western countries in issues regarding Tibet, Taiwan and human rights violations on Chinese territory. On the other, China feels free to engage in business, for instance for oil and gas as well as mineral and agricultural raw materials, with whatever brutal dictator is happy to accept its money. There are no moral constraints such as the Western countries and Japan tend to impose on themselves.

Yet, with reference to the UN Charter, China finds much support for its particular interpretation of the non-interference principle elsewhere and not only by the favoured despots whose power to oppress and exploit their own people is thereby strengthened. Russia, for instance, shares this extensive interpretation of non-intervention by

*The IMF, a specialised UN agency headquartered in Washington D.C., supports global economic growth and stability. The principal activities include macro-economic surveillance, fostering international monetary cooperation and providing policy advice and resources for countries in balance of payments difficulties.*

pointing out that the problems in Chechnya, even if they come close to ethnic cleansing, are an internal matter. But also for Brazil and most of the ASEAN countries unconditional support of this policy principle is a sensitive matter since they consider every attempt to force Western values and principles on a developing country as neo-colonialism.

Alongside China India is the second rising political and economic power which can be expected to take major influence on the future evolution of global and broader international economic affairs. In the medium term the country's political forces are still very much absorbed by internal economic and social development issues and security problems, in particular on the border with Pakistan. But with a population more numerous than China's in a few years and an economic growth potential that promises higher rates of increase than those expected for China in the longer term future, India has all the prospects of becoming the third largest player on the world's political and economic scene after China and the United States.

Nonetheless, in contrast to the US in the second half of the 20th century and in a sense similar to China even today, it is still not clear what role India wants to play in shaping the new international political and economic order for the 21st century. One interesting option could be that India serves as an effective broker whenever major conflict between the United States and China looms in the power play world. But there are many areas in this kind of world where India also has to take care of its own national interests first.

One obvious example where the domestic interests of the Big Five, namely the US, China, the EU, India and Japan, could easily clash, is the struggle for scarce energy resources and other raw materials. Already today China's aggressive resource-oriented investment strategy not only in Asia, but also in Africa and Latin America is regarded by some observers with increasing concern. A second worry, partly apparent up already today, is export restrictions, in particular for critical metals and rare earths. Still other possibilities for growing uneasiness include techno-nationalism and cyber conflicts. But it is not only the potential tensions between the major powers which make power play an undesirable future. The certain losers would in the final instance be the smaller countries and with them the world economy as a whole.

Alongside any speculation on what might happen under conditions of power play it is equally important to reflect on what might not happen if the major powers decide their actions primarily on the basis of their primarily short term domestic policy priorities. The debate on climate change is an illustrative example of what may happen in a power play world when the interests of the US, China, India, the EU, Russia, Brazil, Japan and other G20 members are too far apart. Bind-

512

ing decisions and related actions are postponed. At the very moment, however, when all or at least the decisive majority of the world's leading countries accepts the urgency of co-operative joint action, it may be very or even perhaps too late. Overall world development, the fight against poverty at international level, humanitarian assistance to the citizens of failed states—all these may be issue areas which easily move down in the priority ranking for action when they are not supported by the international community at large.

Fortunately, the pure forms of the three scenarios of global governance will in all probability never be the mirror image of the reality of the future. The scenario called "Managed Globalisation" may be too ambitious and optimistic, although it may even be heavily criticised by some quarters and not be considered as at all desirable. The power play scenario may in certain areas have the advantage of high effectiveness, but definitively implies two significant drawbacks. On the one hand, it could derail from co-operation of the most powerful into a power struggle based more or less on the rules of the jungle. On the other hand, it would not necessarily lead to the common good. The solution of real global issues could be postponed; the interests of the smaller countries would no longer be protected and the needs of the weaker parts of the world population might be ignored.

Finally, the scenario of muddling through is not ideal either. It combines vertical multilateralism with selective multilateralism and implies that whenever the major powers get frustrated because of lack of effectiveness of inclusive international co-operation, the recourse would be to power play. As there is no workable and overall acceptable concept for the replacement of the present institutional framework for international co-operation, the only way forward appears, therefore, muddling through combined with a forceful reform effort with regard to the existing international organisations—a reform that ensures that effectiveness and legitimacy are well balanced.

Most of the ideas and a broad variety of models to respond to this challenge are, in fact, already available. What is apparently still lacking in many cases is the sense of urgency and the political will. But as in other areas of domestic and international policies, defensive approaches which try to preserve the out-dated structures of the past are definitively doomed to fail. There is no way to resist the necessary adjustment of global governance structures and processes to the new geopolitical, economic and social realities of the 21st century. The only choice the international community has is whether the transition is well designed and pro-active or crisis-driven and, as a consequence, with more unpredictable outcomes.

*Next page: Hamburg in the late evening with the "Blue Goals" of Hamburg-based light artist Michael Batz during the FIFA World Cup 2006.*

# Bibliography

Abelshauser, Werner. *Deutsche Wirtschaftsgeschichte seit 1945*, Munich 2004

Acharya. "New Threats to India's Growth", in: *Financial Times*, 2011

Ahrens, Gerhard. *Krisenmanagement 1857: Staat und Kaufmannschaft in Hamburg während der ersten Weltwirtschaftskrise*, Hamburg 1986

Ambrosius, Gerold / Petzina, Dietmar / Plumpe, Werner (ed.). *Moderne Wirtschaftsgeschichte*, 2nd Ed., Munich 2006

Ambrosius, Gerold. "Von der Kriegswirtschaft zur Kriegswirtschaft 1914–1945", in: North, Michael (ed.). *Deutsche Wirtschaftsgeschichte: Ein Jahrtausend im Überblick*, op. cit. pp. 287 ff.

Arbeitskreis Volkswirtschaftliche Gesamtrechnungen der Länder. "Bruttoinlandsprodukt – preisbereinigt verkettet – 1991 bis 2008", www.vgrdl.de/Arbeitskreis_VGR/tbls/tab02.as

Arnal, Elena / Förster, Michael. "Growth, Employment and Inequality in Brazil, China, India and South Africa: An overview", in: OECD. *Tackling Inequalities in Brazil, China, India and South Africa: The Role of Labour Market and Social Policies*, Paris 201

Attali, Jacques. *Une brève histoire de l'avenir*, Paris 2006

Attali, Jacques. *La crise, et après?*, Paris 2008

Attali, Jacques. *Tous ruinés dans dix ans?*, Paris 2010

Baasch, Ernst. *Hamburgs Seeschiffahrt und Waarenhandel vom Ende des 16. bis zur Mitte des 17. Jahrhunderts*, Hamburg 1893

Baasch, Ernst. *Hamburgs Handel und Verkehr im 19. Jahrhundert*, Hamburg 1901

Bahnsen, Uwe. *Die Weichmanns in Hamburg: Ein Glücksfall für Deutschland*, Hamburg 2001

Baschet, Jérôme. "Pourquoi Christophe Colomb est parti en Amérique", in: *L'Histoire*, no 296, March 2005, pp. 36 ff.

Beine, Christine. "Fahrrinnenanpassung: Der Wert der Tiefe", in: *Hamburger Wirtschaft*, no 7, 2009 2nd Ed., Paris 2006

Berlin-Institut für Bevölkerung und Entwicklung (Hg). *Talente, Technologie und Toleranz – wo Deutschland Zukunft hat*, Berlin 2007

Bernanke, Ben S. "Challenges for State and Local Governments", *Board of the Federal Reserve System*, Speech at the 2011 Annual Awards Dinner of the Citizens Budget Commission, New York 2011

Beust, Ole von. "Halbzeit in Hamburg – Handeln im Bund: Eine Bestandsaufnahme", lecture in: Der Übersee-Club e.V., Hamburg, on September 22nd, 2003

Beyfuss, Jörg. *Weltwirtschaftliche Perspektiven der Ölkrise*, Cologne 1974

Bezbakh, Pierre. *Histoire de l'économie: des origines à la mondialisation*, Paris 2005

Bing, Wolf. "Hamburgs Bierbrauerei vom 14. bis zum 18. Jahrhundert", in: *Zeitschrift für Hamburgische Geschichte* no 14, 1909, pp. 209 ff.

boerse.de. "Die Asienkrise 1997/1998", www.wissen.boerse.de/Wissen/Boersengeschichte/Die Asienkrise_19971998/2e2086c#start_content

boerse.de. "Die_Hamburg-Krise (1799)", www.wissen.boerse.de/Wissen/Boersengeschichte/Die Hamburg-Krise(1799)/19e197c#start_content

boerse.de. "Die Weltwirtschaftskrise 1857", Teil I: "USA", www.wissen.boerse. de/Wissen/Boersengeschichte/Die_Weltwirtschaftskrise_1857_(Teil_1_US/202242b#start_content; Teil II: "Europa", www.wissen.boerse.de/Wissen/Boersengeschichte/Die Weltwirtschaftskrise_1857_(Teil_2_Eu/2081417#start_content

Borchard, Knut. *Wachstum, Krisen, Handlungsspielräume der Wirtschaftspolitik*, Göttingen 1982

Borchardt, Knut. *Globalisierung in historischer Perspektive*, Munich 2001

Bordo, Michael D. "Some Historical Evidence 1870 – 1933 on the Impact and International Transmission of Financial Crises", Working Paper No. 1806, New Bureau of Economic Research, Cambridge, MA, 1985

Boyer, Regis. *Les Vikings*, Paris 2002 und 2004

Bracker, Jörgen / Henn, Volker / Postel, Rainer (ed.). *Die Hanse: Lebenswirklichkeit und Mythos*, Lübeck 2006

Bracker, Jörgen. "Hamburg – Der Weg zur Hansestadt", in: Bracker, Jörgen / Henn, Volker / Postel, Rainer (Ed.). *Die Hanse: Lebenswirklichkeit und Mythos*, op. cit. pp. 331 ff.

Braudel, Fernand. *Civilisation matérielle, économie et capitalisme*, Volume I: *Les structures du quotidien*, volume II: *Les jeux de l'échange*, volume III: *Le temps du monde*, Paris 1979

Braudel, Fernand. *Les Mémoires de la Méditerranée*, Paris 1998

Braunberger, Gerald / Fehr, Benedikt. *Crash: Finanzkrisen gestern und heute*, Frankfurt/Main 2008

Brenken, Anne / Kluyver, Urs. *Schönes Hamburg*, Hamburg 2002

Briquel-Chatonnet, Françoise / Gubel, Éric. *Les Phéniciens: Aux origines du Liban*, Paris 1998

Brody, Richard G. / Miller Mary J. / Rolleri, Michael J. "Outsourcing Income Tax Returns to India: Legal, Ethical and Professional Issues", in: *The CPA Journal*, www.nysscpa.org/printversions/cpaj/2004/1204/p12.htm

Brondel, Georges. *Europe a 50 ans*, Bourg-en-Bresse 2003

Brunner, Karl (ed.). *The Great Depression Revisited*, 2nd Ed., Boston / The Hague / London 1982

Buchheim, Christoph. *Einführung in die Wirtschaftsgeschichte*, Munich 1997

Bundesagentur für Arbeit. Statistiken: "Arbeitsmarkt in Deutschland", www.statistik.arbeitsagentur.de

Bundesministerium für Bildung und Wissenschaft. "Optische Technologien: Wirtschaftliche Bedeutung für Deutschland", Bonn / Berlin 2007

Bundesministerium für Wirtschaft und Technologie. "Kompetenznetze Deutschland – Überblick: Netzwerk- und Clusteraktivitäten der Bundesländer", Berlin 2008

Bürklin, Wilhelm. *Die vier kleinen Tiger*, Munich 1993

Büsch, Johann Georg. *Geschichtliche Beurtheilung der großen Handelsverwirrung im Jahre 1799*, Hamburg 1858

Carl Robert Eckelmann AG (ed.). "1865 – 1990: Zum 125-jährigen Jubiläum", Hamburg 1990

Carroué, Laurent. *Géographie de la mondialisation*, 2nd Ed., Paris 2005

Carstensen, Peter Harry. "Schleswig-Holstein und Hamburg: Gemeinsam wirtschaften, gemeinsam wachsen", lecture in: Der Übersee-Club e. V., Hamburg, on June 17th, 2008

Central Intelligence Agency. "The World Factbook", Washington 2011

Claussen, Georg W. "Industrie – Eckpfeiler der Hamburger Wirtschaft", in: Handelskammer Hamburg (co-ed.). "Freie und Hansestadt Hamburg: Monographien deutscher Wirtschaftsgebiete", op. cit. pp. 54 ff.

Coldstream, J. Nicolas. "Les Phéniciens dans la mer Egée", in: "Les Phéniciens à la conquête de la Méditerranée", *Dossiers Histoire et Archéologie*, no 132, November 1988, pp. 44f ff.

Cordes, Peter / Kuckarts, Michael. *Hamburgs Industrie im Wandel – 100 Jahre Industriekommission der Handelskammer Hamburg*, Hamburg 2000

Cotterell, Arthur (ed.). *Classical Civilizations*, London / New York / Victoria / Toronto / Auckland 1993

Curry, Timothy / Shibut, Lynn. "The Costs of the Savings and Loan Crisis: Truth and Consequences", in: *FDIC Banking Review*, vol. 15, no. 2, December 2000, pp. 26 ff.

Dahrendorf, Ralf. "Die neue Gesellschaft: Soziale Strukturwandlungen der Nachkriegszeit", in: Richter, Hans Werner. *Bestandsaufnahme*, op. cit. pp. 203 ff.

Dannemann, Günter / Luft, Stefan. *Die Zukunft der Stadtstaaten*, Bremen / Boston 2005

Deininger, Jürgen. "Oikumene und orbis terrae: Globales Denken und Globalisierung in der antiken Welt", in: Hopf, Klaus J. / Kantzenbach, Erhard / Straubhaar, Thomas (ed.). *Herausforderungen der Globalisierung*, op. cit. pp. 57 ff.

Diamond, Jared. *Collapse: How Societies Choose to Fail or Succeed*, London / New York / Toronto 2005

Diehl, Markus / Nunnenkamp, Peter. *Lehren aus der Asienkrise: Wirtschaftspolitische Reaktionen und fortbestehende Reformdefizite*, Kiel 2001

Dollinger, Philippe. *Die Hanse*, Stuttgart 1998

Dohnanyi, Klaus von. "Unternehmen Hamburg", lecture in: Der Übersee-Club e.V., Hamburg, on November 29th, 1983

Dougherty, Sean M. / Herd, Richard / Chalaux, Thomas. "What is Holding Back Productivity Growth in India? Recent Microevidence", in: *OECD Journal of Economic Studies*, Vol. 2009, Paris 2009

Draguhn, Werner (Hg.). *Asiens Schwellenländer: Dritte Weltwirtschaftsregion?*, Hamburg 1991

Dubrau, Charlotte. "Airbus-Werk in Stade feiert 50-jähriges Bestehen", in: *Welt Online* on August 17th, 2009

Düdden, Dietmar. "Hamburg – Gewinner der Globalisierung", in: Hüls, Rainer (ed.). *Hamburg auf dem Weg zur Weltstadt*, op. cit. pp. 27 ff.

Elmeskov, Jørgen. "The General Economic Background to the Crisis", Paper presented to the G20 Workshop on the Causes of the Crisis: Key Lessons, Mumbai 2009

Engel, Sandra / Tode, Sven. *Hafen – Stadt – Hamburg*, Hamburg 2007

Ess, Hans van. "Der Wandel der Republik Korea vom Entwicklungsland zum Industriestaat – ein Modell?", in: Opitz, Peter J. *Auf den Spuren der Tiger*, op. cit. pp. 103ff.

European Commission / Eurostat. "The EU in the World: A Statistical Portrait", Luxembourg 2010

Exenberger, Andreas / Cian, Carmen. *Der weite Horizont: Globalisierung durch Kaufleute*, Innsbruck / Vienna / Bozen 2006

Farrell, Diana / Greenberg, Ezra. "The Economic Impact of an Ageing Japan", in: *McKinsey Quarterly*, 2005

Financial Stability Forum. "Report of the Financial Stability Forum on Enhancing Market and Institutional Resilience", Basel 2008

Försterling, Manfred. *Die Hamburgische Bank von 1923 Aktiengesellschaft*, Hamburg 1965

Foundation for the Future. "Global Transitions and Asia 2060: Climate, Political-Economy and Identity", *Bellevue*, WA 2010

Frankel, Jeffrey. "Globalisation of the Economy", in: Nye, Joseph S. / Donahue, John D. (ed.). *Governance in a Globalizing World*, op. cit. pp. 45 ff.

Frantz, Ulrich. *25 Jahre Welthandelspolitik*, Berlin 1975

Freie und Hansestadt Hamburg, Staatliche Pressestelle. "Leitbild: Metropole Hamburg – Wachsende Stadt", Hamburg 2002

Freie und Hansestadt Hamburg / Handelskammer Hamburg / Industrieverband Hamburg e. V. "Masterplan Industrie", Hamburg 2007

Freiwald, Eckhard. *Hamburgs Achsenmodell – Landesplanung am Beispiel Hamburg*, Hamburg 2007

Freytag, C. T. *Die Entwicklung des Hamburger Warenhandels von der Entstehung des Deutschen Reiches bis zum Ende des 19. Jahrhunderts (1871–1900)*, Berlin 1906

Freytag, Michael. "Stadtgestalt als Identitätsmerkmal", in: Hüls, Rainer (ed.). *Hamburg auf dem Weg zur Weltstadt*, op. cit. pp. 41 ff.

Friedman, Thomas. *The World is Flat: A Brief History of the Globalized World in the 21st Century*, London / New York / Toronto 2005

Furceri, Davide / Mourougane, Annabelle. "Financial Crisis: Past Lessons and Policy Implications", OECD Working Paper, Paris 2009

G20. "The Seoul Summit Document", Seoul 2010

Gälli, Anton. "Taiwan – Schwierige Selbständigkeit einer chinesischen Provinz", in: Opitz, Peter J. *Auf den Spuren der Tiger*, op. cit. pp. 129 ff.

Gelberg, Birgit. *Auswanderung nach Übersee*, Hamburg 1973

Gemeinsame Landesplanung Hamburg / Niedersachsen / Schleswig-Holstein (ed.). "Regionales Entwicklungskonzept 2000: Leitbild und Handlungsrahmen", Hamburg, Hanover, Kiel 2000

Giersch, Herbert. *Die offene Gesellschaft und ihre Wirtschaft*, Hamburg 2006

Gómez Bellard, Carlos. "Les Phéniciens au Levant et en Catalogne", in: "Les

Phéniciens à la conquête de la Méditerranée", *Dossiers Histoire et Archéologie*, no 132, November 1988

Government of Japan, Economic Planning Agency. "Economic and Social Development Plan 1967–1971", Tokyo 1967

Greenspan, Alan. *The Age of Turbulence: Adventures in a New World*, New York 2007

Grobecker, Kurt. *Kurt Eckelmann goes ashore: The history of the Eurokai Group*, Hamburg 1991

Groppe, Hans-Hermann / Wöst, Ursula (ed.). *Über Hamburg in die Welt: Von den Auswandererhallen zur Ballinstadt*, Hamburg 2007

Hamburger Sparkasse (ed.). "Hamburg: Von Altona bis Zollenspieker", Hamburg 2002

Hammel-Kiesow, Rolf. *Die Hanse*, Munich 2004

Handelskammer Hamburg. "Branchenportrait: Luftfahrtstandort Hamburg", Hamburg (n.d.)

Handelskammer Hamburg / Behörde für Wirtschaft und Verkehr Hamburg (ed.). "Hamburg als Industrieplatz", Hamburg 1952

Handelskammer Hamburg. "Jahresberichte", Hamburg 1952 bis 1971

Handelskammer Hamburg (co-ed.). "Freie und Hansestadt Hamburg: Monographien deutscher Wirtschaftsgebiete", Oldenburg 1985

Handelskammer Hamburg. "Branchenportrait: Maritime Industrie – Ein traditionsreicher Hamburger Wirtschaftszweig im Wandel", Hamburg 2006

Handelskammer Hamburg. "Eckpunkte für eine Clusterpolitik in Hamburg – Cluster richtig auswählen und entwickeln", Hamburg 2006

Handelskammer Hamburg / IHK Schleswig-Holstein. "Clusterpolitik in Hamburg und Schleswig-Holstein", Hamburg / Lübeck 2009

Handelskammer Hamburg. Hamburg 2030 – Ein Projekt der Handelskammer Hamburg, Hamburg 2010

Hauser, Heinz (ed.). *Protectionism and Structural Adjustment*, Grüsch 1986

Hedstrom, Margaret / King, John Leslie. "Epistemic Infrastructure in the Rise of the Knowledge Economy", in: Kahin, Brian / Foray, Dominique (ed.). *Advancing Knowledge and the Knowledge Economy*, op. cit. pp. 3 ff.

Heim, Michael. *Die Ursachen der Weltwirtschaftskrise: Analyse der ökonomischen Eskalation, 1929–1933*, St. Katharinen 2007

Heiniger, Yvonne / Straubhaar, Thomas, et al. *Ökonomik der Reform: Wege zu mehr Wachstum in Deutschland*, Zurich 2004

Helmsmuseum. "Der Domplatz und der 'Mythos Hammaburg' ", www.helmsmuseum.de/index.php/17907

Helmsmuseum. "Neue Ergebnisse vom Hamburger Domplatz", www.helmsmuseum.de/index.php/17906

Henning, Friedrich-Wilhelm. *Die Industrialisierung in Deutschland 1800 bis 1914*, Paderborn 1973

Hering, Rainer. "Bildung in Hamburg", in: Pelc, Ortwin. *Hamburg: Die Stadt im 20. Jahrhundert*, op. cit. pp. 64 ff.

Herzig, Arno (Hg.). *Das alte Hamburg*, Berlin / Hamburg 1989

Hesse, Friederike / Mildner, Stormy. "Der Internationale Währungsfonds und die Entwicklung der internationalen Finanzbeziehungen von 1945 bis 2000", www.weltpolitik.net

Heymann, Eric. „Containerschifffahrt: Wendemanöver gelungen", in: *Deutsche Bank Research* (ed.), Frankfurt am Main 2011

High-Level Commission on Modernisation of World Bank Group Governance. "Repowering the World Bank for the 21st Century", Washington 2009

Hoffmann, Erich. "Lübeck und die Erschließung des Ostseeraums", in: Bracker, Jörgen / Henn, Volker / Postel, Rainer (ed.). *Die Hanse: Lebenswirklichkeit und Mythos*, op. cit. pp. 34 ff.

Hoffmann, Erich. "Konflikte mit auswärtigen Mächten", in: Bracker, Jörgen / Henn, Volker / Postel, Rainer (ed.). *Die Hanse: Lebenswirklichkeit und Mythos*, op. cit. pp. 835 ff.

Holst, Sanford. *Phoenicians: Lebanon's Epic Heritage*, Los Angeles 2005

Holst, Sanford. "The Phoenician Experience", www.phoenician.org

Hopf, Klaus J. / Kantzenbach, Erhard / Straubhaar, Thomas (ed.). *Herausforderungen der Globalisierung*, Göttingen 2003

Hüls, Rainer (ed.). *Hamburg auf dem Weg zur Weltstadt*, Hamburg 2006

Huret, Jules. *De Hambourg aux Marchés de Pologne*, Paris 1900

IMF. "IMF Board Approves Far-Reaching Governance Reform", in: *IMF Survey online*, 5 November 2010

Initiative Zukunft Elbe. *Die Elbe: Lebensader der Region*, Hamburg 2006

Initiativkreis Europäische Metropolregionen in Deutschland. *Europäische* "Metropolregionen in Deutschland: Ansatz – Akteure – Aktivitäten", Stuttgart 2006

Institut du Monde Arabe. "La Méditerranée des Phéniciens", offprint *L'Express*, Paris 2007

Institute for Alternative Futures / Robert Wood Johnson Foundation. "Vulnerability, Scenarios on Vulnerability in the United States", Palo Alto, CA 2011

"Internet World Stats", www.internetworldstats.com/stats.htm and www.internetworlddtats.com/list2.htm

IW-Consult (in co-operation with the Initiative Neue Soziale Marktwirtschaft and the *Wirtschaftswoche*). "Bundesländer im Vergleich: Wer wirtschaftet am besten? Sechstes Bundesländerranking", Cologne 2008

IW-Consult (pp *Wirtschaftswoche* and Initiative Neue Soziale Marktwirtschaft): "Deutsche Großstädte im Vergleich. Untersuchung für das Jahr 2007 und den Zeitraum von 2002 bis 2007. Fünfter Großstadtvergleich", Cologne 2008

Jaacks, Gisela (ed.). *Hamburgs Geschichte: Mythos und Wirklichkeit*, Hamburg 2008

Jakubec, Ivan. *Schlupflöcher im "Eisernen Vorhang": tschechoslowakisch-deutsche Verkehrspolitik im Kalten Krieg. Die Eisenbahn und Elbschifffahrt 1945 – 1989*, Stuttgart 2006

Jantzen, Günther. "Handelsgeschichtliche Betrachtungen", in: Lehe, Erich von / Ramm, Heinz / Kausche, Dietrich. *Chronik der Freien und Hansestadt Hamburg*, op. cit. pp. 477 ff.

Jenks, Stuart. "Von den archaischen Grundlagen bis zur Schwelle der Moderne", in: North, Michael (ed.). *Deutsche Wirtschaftsgeschichte: Ein Jahrtausend im Überblick*, op. cit.pp 15 ff.

Jesse, Wilhelm. "Der wendische Münzverein", *Quellen und Darstellungen zur hansischen Geschichte* N. F. vol. 6, Lübeck 1928

Jochmann, Werner (ed.). *Hamburg: Geschichte der Stadt und ihrer Bewohner*, vol. II: *Vom Kaiserreich bis zur Gegenwart*, Hamburg 1986 (vol. I see Loose, Hans-Dieter)

Kahin, Brian / Foray, Dominique (ed.). *Advancing Knowledge and the Knowledge Society*, Cambridge, Mass. / London 2006

Kern, Helmuth. "Gegenwarts- und Zukunftsaufgaben der Hamburger Wirtschaftspolitik", speech to the Bürgerschaft on April 10th 1967, reprint in: *Schriftenreihe der Behörde für Wirtschaft und Verkehr der Freien und Hansestadt Hamburg*, No 3, Juli 1967

Kern, Helmuth. "Ein Modell für die wirtschaftliche Entwicklung der Region Unterelbe", in: *Schriftenreihe der Behörde für Wirtschaft und Verkehr der Freien und Hansestadt Hamburg*, No 9, (without year, probably 1970)

Keynes, John Maynard. "The Reparation Police of Germany", lecture in: Der Übersee-Club e.V., Hamburg, on August 25th,1922

Keynes, John Maynard. "Prospects of Sterling and the Gold-Standard", lecture in: Der Übersee-Club e.V., Hamburg, on January 10th, 1932

Kiesewetter, Hubert. *Industrielle Revolution in Deutschland*, Stuttgart 2004

Kindleberger, Charles P. *The World in Depression 1929 – 1939*, London 1973, reprint 1977

Kindleberger, Charles P. "The World Economic Slowdown since the 1970s", Seminar Paper No. 229, Institute for International Economic Studies, Stockholm 1982

Kindleberger, Charles P. *World Economic Primacy 1500 – 1990*, New York / Oxford 1996

Kirchberg, Dennis. *Der Aufstieg der Tigerstaaten im 20. Jahrhundert: Eine historische Analyse*, Saarbrücken 2007

Kissinger, Henry. *On China*, New York 2011

Klein, Bernhard. *Histoire romaine: De la légende d'Énée à la dislocation de l'Empire*, Paris 2005

Klemm, Günther. "Die Freie und Hansestadt Hamburg und Norddeutschland: Mehr als nur Kooperation?", in: Dannemann, Günter / Luft, Stefan. *Die Zukunft der Stadtstaaten*, op. cit. pp. 162 ff.

Kleßmann, Eckart. *Geschichte der Stadt Hamburg*, Hamburg 1981

Kloberg, Erik. *Werftensterben in Hamburg: Der Niedergang des Schiffbaus 1970 – 1988 und die Politik des Senats*, Hamburg 1990

Kludas, Arnold / Maass, Dieter / Sabisch, Susanne. *Hafen Hamburg. Die Geschichte des Hamburger Freihafens von den Anfängen bis zur Gegenwart*, Hamburg 1988

Knauer, Martin / Tode, Sven (Hg.). *Der Krieg vor den Toren; Hamburg im Dreißigjährigen Krieg 1618 – 1648*, Hamburg 2000

Kock, Karin. *International Trade Policy and the Gatt 1947 – 1967*, Stockholm 1969

Köhnemann, Jörg. "Giants of the future: 366 metres long, 48 metres wide, with space for more than 13.000 containers", in: *BILD Port Magazine*, October 2007

Kopitzsch, Franklin / Tilgner, Daniel (ed.). *Hamburg Lexikon*, Hamburg 1998

Krawehl, Otto-Ernst. *Hamburgs Schiffs- und Warenverkehr mit England und den englischen Kolonien 1814 – 1860*, Cologne / Vienna 1977

Kresse, Walter. *Materialien zur Entwicklungsgeschichte der Hamburger Handelsflotte 1765 – 1823*, Hamburg 1966

Kresse, Walter. *Die Fahrtgebiete der Hamburger Handelsflotte 1824 – 1888*, Hamburg 1972

Krieger, Martin. *Geschichte Hamburgs*, Munich 2006

Krüger Ulf. "Musikstadt Hamburg", in: Pelc, Ortwin. *Hamburg – Die Stadt im 20. Jahrhundert*, op. cit. pp. 134 ff.

Kuckarts, Peter. *Hamburgs Industrie im Wandel – 100 Jahre Industriekommission der Handelskammer Hamburg*, Hamburg 2000

Kunz, A. "Historische Verkehrsstatistik von Deutschland (Seeschiffahrt)", DFG-Forschungsprojekt, Project of Research of DFG, www.hgisg-ekompendium. ieg-mainz.de

Kynge, James. *China*, Hamburg 2006

Lahaine, Ludwig / Schmidt, Rud. *Hamburg, das deutsche Tor zur Welt. 1000 Jahre hamburgische Geschichte*, Hamburg 1936

Lamy, Pascal. "Globalistion and Global Governance", in: *The Globalist*, November 7th, 2006

Laucht, Hans. *Hafenprojekt Scharhörn: Eine Planung im Spiegel der Zeit (1948 bis 1980)*, Aumühle (without year)

Lehe, Erich von / Ramm, Heinz / Kausche, Dietrich (ed.). *Chronik der Freien und Hansestadt Hamburg*, Cologne 1967

Lenkungsausschuss der Gemeinsamen Landesplanung in der Metropolregion Hamburg (ed.). "Metropolregion Hamburg: Ziele, Strategien, Handlungsfelder, Projekte", Hamburg (without year)

Lenkungsgruppe der Gemeinsamen Landesplanung in der Metropolregion Hamburg: "REK – Regionales Entwicklungskonzept für die Metropolregion Hamburg: Leitbild und Orientierungsrahmen", Hamburg / Hanover / Kiel 1994

Lenkungsgruppe der Gemeinsamen Landesplanung in der Metropolregion Hamburg: "REK – Regionales Entwicklungskonzept für die Metropolregion Hamburg: Handlungsrahmen", Hamburg / Hanover / Kiel 1996

Lesourne, Jacques. *Les Mille Sentiers de l'avenir*, Paris 1981

Lesourne, Jacques. *Les Crises et le XXIe siècle*, Paris 2009

Llewellyn, John / Westaway, Peter. "Europe will work", see Nr. 36

Llewellyn, John. "Lessons from the Financial Crisis", unpublished manuscript, January 2009

Loose, Hans-Dieter (ed.). *Hamburg: Geschichte der Stadt und ihrer Bewohner*, vol. I: *Von den Anfängen bis zur Reichsgründung, Hamburg 1982* (vol. II see Jochmann, Werner)

Maass, Dieter. *Der Ausbau des Hamburger Hafens 1840 bis 1910*, Hamburg 1990

Maaß, Stephan. "Bund erhebt Hamburger Luftfahrtindustrie zum Spitzencluster", in: *Welt Online* on September 3rd, 2009

Maddison, Angus. *The World Economy*, Vol. I: *A Millenial Perspective*, vol. II: *Historical Statistics*, Paris 2006

Maddison, Angus. *Contours of the World Economy, 1 – 2003 AD. Essays in Macro-Economic History*, Oxford 2007

Maizière, Thomas de. "Die provokante Frage: Lässt Globalisierung Politik noch zu?", lecture in: Der Übersee-Club e.V., Hamburg, on September 10th 2008

Mennier, Sophie. "Is the WTO still relevant?", Paper prepared for the Workshop on "Global Trade Ethics and the Politics of WTO Reform", Princeton University, 18 February 2009

Meyer, Jens. "Hamburg braucht größeren Nord-Ostsee-Kanal", Interview in: *Hamburger Abendblatt* on February 23th, 2009

Michalski, Wolfgang. *Infrastruktur im Engpaß*, Hamburg 1966

Michalski, Wolfgang. "Die volkswirtschaftliche Problematik der Luftverunreinigung, dargestellt am Beispiel der Bundesrepublik Deutschland", in: *Hamburger Jahrbuch für Wirtschafts- und Gesellschaftspolitik*, 11th year, 1966, pp. 124 ff.

Michalski, Wolfgang. *Die volkswirtschaftliche Problematik der Gewässerverunreinigung, dargestellt am Beispiel der Bundesrepublik Deutschland*, Tübingen 1967

Michalski, Wolfgang / Stodieck, Helmut, et al. *Perspektiven der wirtschaftlichen Entwicklung in Japan*, Stuttgart 1972

Michalski, Wolfgang. *Export Trade and Economic Growth: Conclusions Drawn from the Federal Republic of Germany's Post-War Development*, Hamburg 1972

Michalski, Wolfgang. "Costs and Benefits of Protection", in: Hauser, Heinz (ed.). *Protectionism and Structural Adjustment*, op. cit. pp. 25 ff.

Michalski, Wolfgang. "Neue Herausforderungen an die Industrieländer durch die Globalisierung der Märkte", in: Klaus-Heinrich Standtke (ed.). *Internationale Zusammenarbeit im größeren Europa*, Internationale Akademie Schloss Baruth, Berlin 1997, pp. 25 ff.

Michalski, Wolfgang. "Globalisation versus Regionalism", in: Austrian Ministry of Economic Affairs (ed.). "Future Competitiveness of Europe", Vienna 1998, pp. 15 ff.

Michalski, Wolfgang. "Governance in the 21st Century: Power in the Global Knowledge Economy and Society", in: *Foresight, The Journal of Future Studies, Strategic Thinking and Policy*, vol. 2, no. 5 October 2000, pp. 471 ff.

Michalski, Wolfgang. "Economic Development Prospects of China and the Implications for the World Economy", Centre regional d'investissement, Marrakesh, 2004

Michalski, Wolfgang. "Responding to the Challenges of the 21st Century Transitions", in: Kuklinski, Antoni / Pawlowski, Krzysztof (ed.). *Futurology – The Challenges of the XXI Century*, Nowy Sacz 2008

Michalski, Wolfgang. "The Future of Gobalisation", Paper prepared for the Sasakawa Peace Foundation, July 2011 (Parts of this paper have been used, albeit considerably revised, for chapters 11 and 12 of this publication).

Mildner, Stormy. "Multilaterale Handelsliberalisierung nach 1945", www.welt-politik.net

Mildner, Stormy. "Internationale Handelsbeziehungen in der Zwischenkriegszeit", www.weltpolitik.net

Mineralölwirtschaftsverband / AEV. "Geschäftsberichte", Hamburg 1968, 1970, 1975

Moltmann, Günter. "Hamburgs Öffnung nach Übersee im späten 18. und 19. Jahrhundert", in: Herzig, Arno. *Das alte Hamburg*, pp. 51 ff.

Mommsen, Wolfgang J. (ed.). *Das Zeitalter des Imperialismus*, Fischer Weltgeschichte vol. 28, Frankfurt/Main 1969

Mossé, Claude (Hg.). *Une Histoire du Monde Antique*, Paris 2005

Nariai, Osamu. "Exploring the Japanese Economy", Tokyo 2005

Narlikar, Amrita / Kumar, Rajiv. "From Pax Americana to Pax Mosaica: Bargaining over the New Economic Order", Paper prepared for the Sasakawa Peace Foundation, May 2011

National Bureau of Economic Research. "US Business Cycle Expansions and Contractions", Washington 2008, www.nber.org

Niemeyer, Hans Georg. "Zur Einführung: Frühformen der Globalisierung im Mittelmeer", in: Hopf, Klaus J. / Kantzenbach, Erhard / Straubhaar, Thomas (ed.). *Herausforderungen der Globalisierung*, op. cit. pp. 47 ff.

No author. "Hamburg – Das Schiffbauzentrum Westdeutschlands", in: Handelskammer Hamburg (co-ed.). *Hamburg als Industrieplatz*, op. cit. pp. 44 ff.

Nomura Global Economics. "Europe will work", Tokyo 2011

Norel, Philippe. *L'Histoire économique globale*, Paris 2009

North, Michael (ed.). *Deutsche Wirtschaftsgeschichte: Ein Jahrtausend im Überblick*, 2nd Ed., München 2005

North, Michael. "Von der atlantischen Handelsexpansion bis zu den Agrarreformen (1450–1815)", in: North, Michael. *Deutsche Wirtschaftsgeschichte: Ein Jahrtausend im Überblick*, op. cit. pp. 112 ff.

North, Michael. "Der wendische Münzverein", in: Bracker, Jörgen / Henn, Volker / Postel, Rainer (ed.). *Die Hanse: Lebenswirklichkeit und Mythos*, op. cit. pp. 754 ff.

Nye, Joseph S. / Donahue, John D. (ed.). *Governance in a Globalizing World*, Washington / Cambridge, MA, 2000

Nye, Joseph S. "The Future of Europe", www.project-syndicate.org, 2010

OECD. "Policy perspectives for international trade and economic relations", Paris 1972

OECD. "Towards Full Employment and Price Stability", Paris 1977

OECD. "Interfutures: Facing the Future – Mastering the Probable and Managing the Inpredictable", Paris 1979

OECD. "Technical Change and Economic Policy", Paris 1980

OECD. "Positive Adjustment Policies: Managing Structural Change", Paris 1985

OECD. "Costs and Benefits of Protection", Paris 1985

OECD. "Structural Adjustment and Economic Performance", Paris 1987

OECD. "Historical Statistics 1960 – 1997", Paris 1999

OECD. "Economic Survey: United States", Paris 2001

OECD. "Economic Survey: China", Paris 2005

OECD. "Economic Survey: Brazil", Paris 2006

OECD. "Economic Survey: Russian Federation", Paris 2006

OECD. "Competitive Cities in the Global Economy", Paris 2006

OECD. "Economic Survey: India", Paris 2007

OECD. "Globalisation and Emerging Economies: Brazil, Russia, India, Indonesia, China and South Africa", Paris 2008

OECD. "Clusters, Innovation and Entrepreneurship", Paris 2009

OECD. "Economic Outlook" no. 88, Paris 2010, and no. 89, Paris 2011.

OECD. „Economic Surveys: United States", Paris 2010

OECD. "Economic Surveys: China", Paris 2010

OECD. "Growth and Sustainability in Brazil, China, India, Indonesia and South Africa", Paris 2010

OECD. "Economic Policy Reforms: Going for Growth", Paris 2011

OECD. "Economic Surveys: Japan", Paris 2011

Opitz, Peter J. *Auf den Spuren der Tiger: Entwicklungsprozesse in der asiatisch-pazifischen Region*, Munich 1997

Osterhammel, Jürgen / Petersson, Niels. *Geschichte der Globalisierung*, Munich 2005

Osterhammel, Jürgen. *Kolonialismus: Geschichte – Formen – Folgen*, Munich 2006

Parker, A. J. "Trade within the Empire and beyond the Frontiers", in: Wacher, John. *The Roman World*, op. cit. pp. 635 ff.

Parker, Jeoffrey (Hg.). *The Times Compact History of the World*, London 2006

Peiner, Wolfgang. "Metropole Hamburg – Wachsende Stadt", lecture in: Der Übersee-Club e. V., Hamburg, on April 2nd 2003

Peiner, Wolfgang. *Handeln für Hamburg*, Hamburg 2011

Pelc, Ortwin. *Hamburg: Die Stadt im 20. Jahrhundert*, Hamburg 2002

Petersson, Astrid. *Zuckersiedergewerbe und Zuckerhandel in Hamburg im Zeitraum von 1814 bis 1834*, Stuttgart 1998

Pfaff, William. "The Future of the United States as a Great Power", 15th Morgenthau Memorial Lecture on Ethics and Foreign Policy, Carnegie Council on Ethics and International Affairs, New York 1996

Plumpe, Werner, unter Mitarbeit von Eva J. Dubisch. *Wirtschaftskrisen*, 2nd Ed., Munich 2011

Prager, Hans G.. *Reederei F. Laeisz. Von den Großseglern zur Containerfahrt*, 4. revised Ed. Hamburg 2004

Prange, Carsten. *Auf zur Reise durch Hamburgs Geschichte*, Hamburg 1990

Prange, Carsten. "Der Schiffbau und seine Organisation", in: Bracker, Jörgen / Henn, Volker / Postel, Rainer (ed.). *Die Hanse: Lebenswirklichkeit und Mythos*, op. cit. pp. 691 ff.

Prange, Carsten. "Hamburger Gewerbemühlen", in: Bracker, Jörgen / Henn, Volker / Postel, Rainer (ed.). *Die Hanse: Lebenswirklichkeit und Mythos*, op. cit. pp. 696 ff.

Preuß, Olaf. *Eine Kiste erobert die Welt*, 2nd extended Ed., Hamburg 2007

Reckendrees, Alfred. "Die bundesdeutsche Massenkonsumgesellschaft: Einführende Bemerkungen", in: *Jahrbuch für Wirtschaftsgeschichte*, 2007/2, pp. 17 ff.

Reckendrees, Alfred. "Konsummuster im Wandel. Haushaltsbudgets und privater Verbrauch in der Bundesrepublik 1952 – 98", in: *Jahrbuch für Wirtschaftsgeschichte*, 2007/2, pp. 29 ff.

Reich, Robert B. *Aftershock*, New York 2010

Reinhard, Wolfgang. *Kleine Geschichte des Kolonialismus*, Stuttgart 1996

Richtberg, Walter. "Medienplatz Hamburg", in: Handelskammer Hamburg (coed.). "Freie und Hansestadt Hamburg: Monographien deutscher Wirtschaftsgebiete", op. cit. pp. 230 ff.

Richter, Hans Werner. *Bestandsaufnahme. Eine deutsche Bilanz 1962*, Munich / Vienna / Basel 1962

Rothschild, Kurt W. / Schmahl, Hans-Jürgen. *Beschleunigter Geldwertschwund. Ursachen und Konsequenzen*, Hamburg 1973

Rovan, Joseph. *Geschichte der Deutschen: Von ihren Ursprüngen bis heute*, Munich / Vienna 1995

Sachverständigenrat zur Begutachtung der gesamtwirtschaftlichen Lage. "Währung, Geld, Wettbewerb: Entscheidungen für morgen", Stuttgart / Mainz 1971

Sachverständigenrat zur Begutachtung der gesamtwirtschaftlichen Lage. "Vollbeschäftigung für morgen", Stuttgart / Mainz 1974

Sachverständigenrat zur Begutachtung der gesamtwirtschaftlichen Lage. "Im Standortwettbewerb", Stuttgart 1995

Sartre, Maurice. "Rome: L'empire modèle", in: *L'Histoire*, no 270, November 2002, pp. 44 ff

Schiller, Karl. "Hamburg – Standort der Industrie", in: Handelskammer Hamburg (co-ed.). "Hamburg als Industrieplatz", op. cit. pp. 9 ff.

Schmahl, Hans-Jürgen. "Stagflation in der Bundesrepublik", in: Rothschild, Kurt W. / Schmahl, Hans-Jürgen. *Beschleunigter Geldwertschwund. Ursachen und Konsequenzen*, op. cit. pp. 13 ff.

Scholtissek, Stephan. *Multipolare Welt*, Hamburg 2008

Schramm, Percy E. *Hamburg – ein Sonderfall in der Geschichte Deutschlands*, Hamburg 1966

Schröter, Harm G. "Von der Teilung zur Wiedervereinigung 1945 – 2004", in: North, Michael. *Deutsche Wirtschaftsgeschichte*, op. cit. pp. 356 ff.

Schukys, Sven. "Die Einwirkungen des Dreißigjährigen Krieges auf den Fernhandel Hamburgs", in: Knauer, Martin / Tode, Sven (ed.). *Der Krieg vor den Toren: Hamburg im Dreißigjährigen Krieg 1618 – 1648*, op. cit pp. 213 ff.

Schütt, Ernst Christian. *Die Chronik Hamburgs*, Dortmund 1991

Seiler, Otto J. *Aug. Bolten – Wm. Miller's Nachfolger*, Hamburg 2001

Senat der Freien und Hansestadt Hamburg – Staatliche Pressestelle (ed.). *Entwicklungsmodell – Hamburg und Umland*, Hamburg 1969

Sillem, Martin. "Hamburg – Eine vitale Verbindung", in: Hüls, Rainer (ed.). *Hamburg auf dem Weg zur Weltstadt*, op. cit. pp. 119 ff.

Sinn, Hans-Werner. *Ist Deutschland noch zu retten?*, 3rd Ed., Berlin 2005

Sinn, Hans-Werner. *Kasino-Kapitalismus*, Berlin 2009

Sinn, Hans-Werner. "How to rescue the euro: Ten commandments", in: *VOX*, October 3rd, 2011

Stadt Hamburg. "Von der Hammaburg bis zur Hafen-City", www.fhh.hamburg.de

Statistisches Amt für Hamburg und Schleswig-Holstein (ed.). "Monitor Wachsende Stadt 2005, 2006, 2007", Hamburg 2005, 2006, 2007; in addition: "Anhang zum Bericht 2007", Hamburg 2007

Statistisches Bundesamt. Länderkurzberichte: "Singapur", Wiesbaden 1967 und 1977

Stenzel, Georg. "Hamburgs industrielle Entwicklung", in: Handelskammer Hamburg (co-ed.). "Hamburg als Industrieplatz", op. cit. pp. 22 ff.

Stiglitz, Joseph E. *Globalization and Its Discontents*, London 2002

Stiglitz, Joseph E. / Charlton, Andrew. *Fair Trade*, Hamburg 2006

Stolze, Dieter. "Das Wirtschaftswunder – Glanz der Zahlen und Statistiken", in: Richter, Hans Werner. *Bestandsaufnahme. Eine deutsche Bilanz 1962*, op. cit. pp. 264 ff.

Straubhaar, Thomas. "Boomtown Hamburg: viel Grund zu Optimismus", in: Hüls, Rainer (ed.). *Hamburg auf dem Weg zur Weltstadt*, op. cit. pp. 127ff.

Stücker, Britta. "Konsum auf Kredit in der Bundesrepublik", in: *Jahrbuch für Wirtschaftsgeschichte*, 2007/2, pp. 63 ff.

Stürmer, Michael. *Welt ohne Weltordnung*, Hamburg 2006

Sywottek, Arnold. "Der Wiederaufbau des zerstörten Hamburgs", in: Schütt, Ernst Christian. *Die Chronik Hamburgs*, op. cit. pp. 495 ff.

Sznycer, Maurice. "Les Phéniciens et la mer", in: "Les Phéniciens à la conquête de la Méditerranée", in: *Dossiers Histoire et Archéologie*, no 132, November 1988, pp. 8 ff.

Tharoor, Shashi. *India: From Midnight to the Millennium and Beyond*, 2nd Ed. New York 2006

The Economist. "The Future of Europe: Staring into the Abyss", London 2010

The Economist. "The future of Japan: The Japan Syndrome", London 2010

Tietmeyer, Hans. Lecture at the conference "60 Jahre Soziale Marktwirtschaft", Berlin, June 12th 2008

Tilly, Richard. *Globalisierung aus historischer Sicht und das Lernen aus der Geschichte*, Cologne 1999

Totzke, Thorsten. "Blohm & Voss", www.lostliners.de

Trautfetter, Gerald. "Was Städte sexy macht", in: *Der Spiegel*, no 34, 2007

Trinh, Tamara. "China & India: Der Aufstieg der Mittelschicht – Facts and Figures", Deutsche Bank Research, Berlin 2006

Uchatius, Wolfgang. "Alles ist weg", in: *Die Zeit*, no 42 October 11th, 2007

Verband deutscher Schiffswerften e.V. "Deutscher Schiffbau", annual reports of several years 1960 until 1972

Verband deutscher Schiffbauindustrien e.V. "Deutscher Schiffbau", annual reports, 1974 and 1975

Verg, Erik. *Das Abenteuer, das Hamburg heißt*, Hamburg 2003

Verg, Erik. "Wachstum ist nicht alles – Großstadt im Umbruch", in: Schütt, Ernst Christian (ed.). *Die Chronik Hamburgs*, op. cit. pp. 579 ff.

Virmani, Arvind / Malhotra, Rajeev. "Shaping the Indian Miracle: Acceleration towards high growth", in: OECD. "Growth and Sustainability in Brazil, China, India, Indonesia and South Africa", Paris 2010

534

Volkmann, Rainer. "Überlegungen zur Clusterförderung", in: Hüls, Rainer (ed.). *Hamburg auf dem Weg zur Weltstadt*, op. cit. pp. 135 ff.

Wacher, John (ed.). *The Roman World*, London 2001

Walter Rolf. *Geschichte der Weltwirtschaft: Eine Einführung*, Cologne / Weimar / Vienna 2006

Wang, Aileen / Wheatley, Alan / Keiko, Ujikane. "China's $ 5.88tn GDP Overtakes Japan with US in Sights for 2025", in: *The Independent*, 2011

Warnock, Francis E. "How Dangerous Is U.S. Government Debt?", in: "Capital Flows Quarterly", Council on Foreign Relations, New York / Washington 2010

Weber, Curt. "Rohöle aus Venezuela und dem Mittleren Osten", in: Handelskammer Hamburg (co-ed.). "Hamburg als Industrieplatz", op. cit. pp. 68 ff.

Weber, Klaus. *Deutsche Kaufleute im Atlantikhandel 1630 – 1830*, Munich 2004

Weber, Steven. "The End of the Business Cycle?", in. *Foreign Affairs*, vol. 76, no. 4, July / August 1997, pp. 375 ff.

Weichmann, Herbert. "Für Hamburgs Zukunft", Speech to the Bürgerschaft on July 7th 1969, reprint in: Senat der Freien und Hansestadt Hamburg – Staatliche Pressestelle (ed.). *Entwicklungsmodell – Hamburg und Umland*, Hamburg 1969

Welck, Karin von. "Kultur als Zugpferd der städtischen Entwicklung", in: Hüls, Rainer (ed.). *Hamburg auf dem Weg zur Weltstadt*, op. cit. pp. 163 ff.

Wendt, Kurt. "Hamburger Werft-Poker", in: *Die Zeit*, no 09, 25. 2. 1966

Wendt, Reinhard. *Vom Kolonialismus zur Globalisierung: Europa und die Welt seit 1500*, Paderborn / Munich / Vienna / Zurich 2007

White, Thomas H. "United States Early Radio History", www.earlyradiohistory.us

Wiechmann, Ralf. *Edelmetalldepots der Wikingerzeit in Schleswig-Holstein: Vom "Ringbrecher" zur Münzwirtschaft*, Neumünster 1996

Wiechmann, Ralf. "Arabische Münzfunde des 8. bis 11. Jahrhunderts im Ostseeraum", in: Hübner, U. / Kamlah, J. / Reinfandt, L. (ed.). *Die Seidenstraße: Handel und Kulturaustausch in einem eurasischen Wegenetz*, Hamburg 2001, pp. 169 ff.

Wiechmann, Ralf. "Haithabu und sein Hinterland – ein lokaler numismatischer Raum? Münzen und Münzfunde aus Haithabu (bis zum Jahr 2002)", in: *Berichte über die Ausgrabungen in Haithabu 36: Das archäologische Fundmaterial VIII*, Neumünster 2007, pp. 182 ff.

Wiechmann, Ralf. "Ansgar, Störtebeker und die Hanse. Geschichtsbilder und Geschichtsmythen", in: Jaacks, Gisela (ed.). *Hamburgs Geschichte: Mythos und Wirklichkeit*, op. cit. pp. 62ff.

Wiechmann, Ralf. "baugabrot ok harka gri pir – Ringbruchstücke und Schild-trümmer: Silberschätze als Ausweis des wikingerzeitlichen Handels", in: Historisches Museum der Pfalz (ed.). *Die Wikinger*, Speyer / München 2008, pp. 164 ff.

Wiemer, Rolf. "Industrie und Gewerbe in Hamburg", in: Lehe, Erich von / Ramm, Heinz / Kausche, Dietrich. *Chronik der Freien und Hansestadt Hamburg*, op. cit. pp. 549 ff.

Wiese, Eberhard von. *Hamburg. Menschen – Schicksale*, 2nd Ed., Berlin / Frankfurt/Main 1967

World Bank. "World Development Indicators Database, Country Files: Brazil, China, India, Russian Federation", Washington 2009

World Economic Forum. "China and the World: Scenarios to 2025", Cologne / Geneva 2005

World Economic Forum. "India and the World: Scenarios to 2025", Cologne / Geneva 2005

Woronoff, Jon. *Wirtschaftswunder in Fernost: Japan, Taiwan, Korea, Singapur, Hongkong*, Heidelberg 1986

WTO. "International Trade Statistics 2008", Geneva 2008

WTO. "Trade Profils 2008", Geneva 2008

Zachcial, Manfred. "Wandel im Welthandel", Interview in: *Initiative Zukunft Elbe: Die Elbe: Lebensader der Region*, op. cit. pp. 6 ff.

Ziegler, Dieter. "Das Zeitalter der Industrialisierung", in: North, Michael (ed.). *Deutsche Wirtschaftsgeschichte: Ein Jahrtausend im Überblick*, op. cit. pp. 197 ff.

Zunkel, Julia. *Rüstungsgeschäfte im Dreißigjährigen Krieg: Unternehmerkräfte, Militärgüter und Marktstrategien im Handel zwischen Genua, Amsterdam und Hamburg*, Berlin 1997

The Free Encyclopaedia Wikipedia has occasionally been consulted for the search of facts and sources. Yet, all relevant information has bee verified on the basis of other sources.

# Quotation Credits

p. 71 Quoted from Bracker, Jörgen / Henn, Volker / Postel, Rainer (Ed.).
*Die Hanse, Lebenswirklichkeit und Mythos,* loc. cit., p. 335

p. 117 Quoted from Braudel, Fernand.
*Civilisation matérielle, économie et capitalisme,* Volume III:
*Le temps du monde,* loc. cit., p. 279

p. 172 Quoted from Henning, Friedrich-Wilhelm.
*Die Industrialisierung in Deutschland 1800 bis 1914,*
loc. cit., p. 106

p. 175 Quoted from Rovan, Joseph.
*Geschichte der Deutschen: Von ihren Ursprüngen bis heute,*
loc. cit., p. 499

p. 201 Quoted from Ahrens, Gerhard.
*Krisenmanagement 1857: Staat und Kaufmannschaft in Hamburg während
der ersten Weltwirtschaftskrise,* loc. cit., p. 25

p. 201 Quoted from Ahrens, Gerhard.
*Krisenmanagement 1857: Staat und Kaufmannschaft in Hamburg während
der ersten Weltwirtschaftskrise,* loc. cit., p. 11

p. 202 Quoted from Verg, Erik.
*Das Abenteuer, das Hamburg heißt,* loc. cit., p. 130;
also in Kleßmann, Eckart. *Geschichte der Stadt Hamburg,* loc. cit., p. 528

p. 218 Quoted from Ahrens, Gerhard.
*Krisenmanagement 1857: Staat und Kaufmannschaft in Hamburg während
der ersten Weltwirtschaftskrise,* loc. cit., p. 93

p. 218 Quoted from Verg, Erik. *Das Abenteuer, das Hamburg heißt,*
loc. cit., p. 130; also in Kleßmann, Eckart. *Geschichte der Stadt Hamburg,*
loc. cit., p. 529

p. 288 Försterling, Manfred.
*Die hamburgische Bank von 1923 Aktiengesellschaft*, loc. cit., p. 21

p. 288 Försterling, Manfred.
*Die hamburgische Bank von 1923 Aktiengesellschaft*, loc. cit., p. 31

p. 310 Quoted from Claussen, Georg W.
*Industrie – Eckpfeiler der Hamburger Wirtschaft,*
in: *Handelskammer Hamburg* (Co-Ed.). *Freie und Hansestadt Hamburg:*
*Monographien deutscher Wirtschaftsgebiete*, loc. cit., p. 54

p. 405 *Gemeinsame Landesplanung Hamburg / Niedersachsen /*
*Schleswig-Holstein* (Ed.). *Regionales Entwicklungskonzept 2000:*
*Leitbild und Handlungsrahmen*, loc. cit., p. 7

p. 423 Quoted from *Always-On, Magazin der digitalen Wirtschaft,*
November 2008, p. 11

p. 504 High-Level Commission on Modernisation
of World Bank Group Governance. *Repowering the World Bank*
*for the 21st Century*, op. cit., pp. x and 3 f.

p. 506 Narlikar, Amrita / Kumar, Rajiv.
*From Pax Americana to Pax Mosaica: Bargaining over*
*the New Economic Order*, op. cit., pp. 8 f.

# Illustration Credits

akg images: pp. 39, 94, 99, 118, 377

Archiv Murmann Verlag: pp. 8–9, 32, 40–41, 48, 71, 83, 85, 125, 144, 163, 169, 177, 196, 206–207, 210, 280, 313, 355, 509

Badekow, Holger: p. 392

Batz, Michael / Zapf, Michael: pp. 397, 516–517

bpk: p. 212

Beer, Karl-Theo: p. 81

Chronik Verlag: pp. 216, 292

Corbis: pp. 467 (Julie Dermansky), 483 (Frederic Soltan / Sygma), 511 (Martin H. Simon)

de Champeaux, Dominique: pp. 269

Denkmalschutzamt Hamburg Bildarchiv: pp. 219 (Wutcke, Paul), 304 (Beutler, Willi)

ELBE & FLUT, Thomas Hampel: p. 439

Federau, Bernt: pp. 440–441

Focke Museum, Bremen: p. 72

Getty Images: pp. 259, 261

Hafen Hamburg Marketing e.V.: Cover picture

Airbus: p. 419

Helle / arturimages: p. 363

Herzog & de Meuron: p. 450

hhla.de / hamburger-fotoarchiv.de: pp. 296–297, 316

Kunadt, Thomas: p. 323

Metropolregion Hamburg: p. 402

# Acknowledgments

Special thanks go to all those who supported me with information, sources and encouragement when writing this book. The numbers unfortunately make it impossible to name everyone who has contributed to this book.

Some of them have read large parts of the manuscript and provided numerous hours of discussion as well as extensive and detailed advice. I am particularly grateful for their commitment.

- Dr Karl-Joachim Dreyer, Chairman of the Supervisory Board, Hamburger Sparkasse AG
- Dr Claus Gossler, Member of the Executive Board, Verein für Hamburgische Geschichte
- Helmuth Kern, Senator for Economic Affairs and Transport (1966–1976), Hamburg
- Jacques Lesourne, Professeur d'économie emeritus, Conservatoire National des Arts et Metiers (CNAM); Membre de l'Académie des Technologies, Paris
- Angus Maddison, Professor of Economics emeritus, University of Groningen
- Dr Ortwin Pelc, Head of Department, Hamburgmuseum – Museum of Hamburg History
- Dr Klaus Rensing, MBA, Zentrums- und Clustermanagement, Asklepios Kliniken Hamburg GmbH
- Axel Schroeder, Managing Partner, MPC Münchmeyer Petersen & Co. GmbH, Hamburg
- Nikolaus W. Schües, Owner F. Laeisz, Hamburg
- Martin Sillem, Director, Donner & Reuschel Aktiengesellschaft, Hamburg
- Dr Barrie Stevens, Deputy Director, Advisory Unit to the Secretary General OECD, Paris
- Gesche Stevens-Westensee, Lecturer for English and History, Bougival

542

- Gunnar Uldall, President of Bundesverband Internationaler Express- und Kurierdienste e.V.; Senator for Economic Affairs and Employment (2001–2008), Hamburg
- Dr Ralf Wiechmann, Head of Department, Hamburgmuseum – Museum for Hamburg History

They have all helped me with advice and criticism in their area of expertise and on the basis of their special experience. Nonetheless, responsibility for anything which may be factually incorrect or could be interpreted differently lies solely with the author of the book.

A special thank goes to the publisher Dr Sven Murmann who picked up on my idea of writing a book about the long term perspective of globalisation and inspired me to give this book a strong Hamburg dimension. Furthermore, I would like thank all the staff at Murmann Verlag, who met the exceptional challenges of this work successfully, for the great efforts.

This book could never have been finished in the time available without the understanding and active support of my wife, Christina Michalski, my daughter, Carolin de Champeaux, and my son, Christoph Michalski, who have always assisted me in their way—either with critical comments or active suggestions when evaluating the sources or proofreading and final editing. I also extend my sincere thanks to them.

# Contents

Introduction

11

544

CHAPTER 6

## Hamburg: The European Continent's Leading Port and Trading Hub

183

PART V
## Globalisation as Race to Prosperity: On the Necessity of Positive Adjustment Policies in a stable Macro-Economic Environment

CHAPTER 9
## Globalisation at the Crossroads?

333

# About the Author

© Asmus Henkel

**Wolfgang Michalski** is an internationally recognised expert in the analysis of longer term economic, social and technological developments and their implications for decision-making. He is Managing Director of WM International — a company providing strategic analysis and policy advice to governments, business and international organisations.

From 1980 until the end of 2001 he was Director of the Advisory Unit to the Secretary-General of the Organisation for Economic Co-operation and Development (OECD). His prime responsibility was to identify and analyse the emerging domestic and international economic policy issues likely to confront member governments in the years to come and help decision makers in government and business to identify and evaluate the strategic challenges of a rapidly changing world economy.

Wolfgang Michalski has been chairman and director of several renowned research institutes. He received his PhD in 1964, qualified for full professorship in 1970 and has held a professorship of economics at the University of Hamburg since 1972. He was awarded a Doctor honoris causa by the Warsaw School of Economics in 2001. His publications include 13 books and over 150 papers in collective volumes and professional journals which have been translated into more than ten languages.

As Hamburg Ambassador, Wolfgang Michalski represents the Free and Hanseatic City of Hamburg in Paris.